# FROM COLOMAN THE LEARNED TO BÉLA III (1095-1196)

## Hungarian Domestic Policies and Their Impact upon Foreign Affairs

by

Z. J . Kosztolnyik

EAST EUROPEAN MONOGRAPHS, BOULDER
DISTRIBUTED BY COLUMBIA UNIVERSITY PRESS
NEW YORK

1987

EAST EUROPEAN MONOGRAPHS, NO. CCXX

*To Our Daughters,*
*Karen and Elizabeth*

# CONTENTS

# List of Abbreviations

| | |
|---|---|
| *ASS* | Acta sanctorum Bollandiana |
| *HZ* | Historische Zeitschrift |
| *HJB* | Historisches Jahrbuch |
| *ITK* | Irodalomtörténeti Közlemények |
| Mansi, *Concilia* | J. D. Mansi (ed), Sacrorum conciliorum collectio |
| Marczali, *Enchiridion* | H. Marczali (ed), Enchiridion fontium historiae Hungarorum |
| *MPG* | J. P. Migne (ed), Patrologiae cursus completus, series graeca |
| *MPL* | J. P. Migne (ed), Patrologiae cursus completus, series latina |
| *MIÖG* | Mitteilungen des Institutes für österreichische Geschichtforschung |
| *MKSZ* | Magyar Könyvszemle |
| *MGHLL* | Monumenta Germaniae historica, Legum collectio |
| *MGH LdL* | Monumenta Germaniae historica, Libelli de lite |
| *MGHSS* | Monumenta Germaniae historica, Scriptores |
| *MPH* | Monumenta Poloniae historica |
| *RHM* | St. L. Endlicher (ed), Rerum Hungaricarum monumenta Arpadiana |
| *SSH* | E. Szentpétery (ed), Scriptores rerum Hungaricarum |
| Szentpétery, *Regesta* | E. Szentpétery (ed), Regesta regum stirpis Arpadianae criticodiplomatica |
| Zádovszky | L. Zádovszky (ed), A szent István, szent László és Kálmán korabeli törvények és zsinati határozatok forrásai |

# PREFACE

In writing this book the author has on various occasions consulted the Hóman-Szekfű Hungarian History, though he has formulated his own points of view, not necessarily always with success, he readily admits. In narrating political and military events; in discussing diplomacy and institutions, the author has turned to the sources. The backbone of the source material is still the *Chronicon pictum*, — in fact, it is the outline of the Chronicle that forms the framework of the book — and he has fused it with data taken from non-Hungarian, that is, German, Frankish, Byzantine, Italian, or even Russian and Polish chronicles. The ordinances laid down in the legislative acts of the Hungarian monarchs also provided basic information, and so did certain items in royal and papal correspondence. The author has attempted to make use of the articles and monographs of recent and earlier historians in the field. The purpose of the book is to bring the events in this interesting century of the Hungarian Middle Ages closer to the reader.

In completing the manuscript the author could not have done without the help and cooperation of his wife and their daughters, Karen and Elizabeth, who not only carefully read the typescript, but helped to prepare the index. All the same, the errors that may inadvertently occur in this work, are the author's alone.

*Texas A &M University*                    *Z. J. Kosztolnyik*

# INTRODUCTION:
## The Three Codes of Law of Ladislas I

Temporibus piissimi regis Ladisclaui omnes nos
regni Pannonici optimates in monte sacro
fecimus conuentus, ... et gentis nostre
expedirentur negocia.

*Decretum II s. Ladislai regis*

In order to be able to survey the results of ecclesiastical
and royal legislation in Hungary during the twelfth century,
it will be necessary to reach back to the three codes of law
of Ladislas I (1077-95) [1]  What may in the chronological
order be the first law book of King Ladislas, may have been
enacted in the early part of his reign, about 1078, though
the composition and contents of its resolutions bear witness
to special Hungarian judicial development that occurred
without any provable outside influence. [2]  The wording
of the articles illustrates the rather primitive — pagan —
social structure that prevailed in the realm. [3]  The crude
wording of the decrees reflects the common raw mentality
of the age, when the legislators, who themselves had natural
intelligence, but did not possess rigorous education, and
lacked experience in the conduct of public affairs, legislated
for and on behalf of the unschooled and ignorant inhabitants of their country. [4]  The product of their legislative
effort: sixteen longer and shorter articles that make six pages
in small print, provides a faithful description of Hungarian
society of the late eleventh century. [5]  It preserved a precious
monument of Hungarian legislation, regardless of the fact
that the earliest known manuscript of these laws dates to
the fifteenth century. [6]

Researchers of the historical sources of the age, and editors
of the collected source material, as, for instance, St. L.
Endlicher and Henrik Marczali, recognize the text of 1078
as the second collection of laws, *Decretum II*, of Ladislas I.
In the chronological order, however, the 1078 laws came
before the enactments of the 1092 synod and (law-day)
assembly of Szabolcs, which researchers acknowledge as

*Decretum I,* the first book of laws of King Ladislas. [7]   This distinction makes sense only in view of the length of the enactments: sixteen in 1078; forty-three in 1092, because the quality and contents of the 1078 laws are not below the quality and essence of the enactments of Szabolcs. At the same time, the material of what has been recognized as *Decretum III,* the third book of laws of Ladislas I, has been dated in a reverse order of chronology of about 1084. [8]

The particular circumstance that the first legislative session by Ladislas I was held at Pannonhalma, "in monte sacro," at the Benedictine abbey established by the first Hungarian monarch, Stephen I (ob. 1038), [9] may only place an emphasis upon the close relationship between the first Hungarian code(s) of law of the reign of Stephen I, [10] and the law books enacted during Ladislas' reign in the last quarter of the same century. At Pannonhalma, the *optimates*: the country's headmen, — bishops and nobles alike, — were the legislators, who in the monastery founded in accordance with the principles laid down by the first Hungarian king, and through the cooperation of the legislative body created by him, enacted legislation. [11]

The text of the laws reveals why it was necessary to place such an emphasis upon legislative continuity dating back to the first Hungarian king. During the years prior to the reign of Ladislas, public conditions in the realm fell incredibly low; his predecessor and older brother, *Géza I* (1074-77), during his short reign failed to obtain the recognition of the Holy See; [12] therefore, for the sake of reestablishing the good reputation of his country, Ladislas held it necessary to gain the approval of Rome. [13] He relied upon the example of his great predecessor, Stephen I, and upon the cooperation of the hierarchy and the nobles, [14] to restore order in the country through legislation. [15] It may be no coincidence that the introduction — actually, article one —, of the, chronologically speaking first, law book used terminology identical with the wording of the prefatory note of Stephen I's book of laws; "et genti nostre expedirentur negocia." [16] The headmen had to take an oath that they would not hide, nor defend, or protect in a church their own relative who had stolen, — or, who had been accused of an act of thievery —, anything over the price of a chicken; such a thief they must hang, and they must confiscate his property. [17] (This latter provision was modified in the Vienna codex to death penalty for the thief's entire family. [18] ) Horrid conditions had to predominate in the country where legislators not only had to take such an oath, but had to confirm it through legislation.

The laws of Ladislas I speak of the monarch as a pious third person; "temporibus piissimi regis Ladislai," — meaning that he was not present at the legislative session. The king may have been away on account of affairs of state, or perhaps warring events prevented him from active participation. [19] It is possible though that Ladislas I wanted to grant freedom of action to his legislators and decided not to interfere with their work. [20] His decision led to the perfect result that every article of the law book expressed support for the monarch, or referred to him —, as if to prove that the king not only acted in the spirit of Stephen I, but, even if indirectly, legislated together with his legislators. In view of the material of this law book, — which dealt with conditions of personal safety and the rights of private property, [21] and called for Draconic measures against thieves, [22] — it was necessary that the law code be enacted with the full approval and cooperation, though without active participation, of the monarch. Let the spiritual and temporal lords, in their capacity of lawmakers, be held responsible, next to the king, for the maintenance of law and order in the country in that they, with the approval and consent of their monarch, do everything possible for the enforcement of their country's laws. [23]

The legislator *optimates* definitely extended their jurisdiction over ecclesiastics, whom they, in case of thievery, punished like lay people, — though they behaved with leniency toward the young cleric (a student; not an ordained priest) accused, and proved guilty, of minor thievery. [24] The spiritual and temporal legislators together protected the country's export of stock meat animals if it took place without royal permission; foreign merchants could purchase horses and oxen only in the presence of the royal law enforcement officer, and only if the merchant obtained specific permission from the court, and limited the number of animals to be purchased to the authorized amount. [25]

Ladislas I's second law book, — second in the order of chronology, but known as *Decretum III*, — may have been enacted in about 1084; [26] it made a reference to Stephen I, whose canonization occurred in 1083. [27] Therefore, it may be difficult to agree with Max Büdinger who said that this law book had been prepared during the days of King Salomon of Hungary, that is, before 1074. [28] Regardless of the fact that the compiler(s) of this code referred to a pagan custom in the second article, the census taking by *Iudex* Karckas (county judge), [29] articles forming the main theme of the book — concerning theft and thievery, — depict the contemporary social scene differently. For instance, were the thief of something of the value of ten denars a free man, *si liber*, they condemn him to death; [30] were the thief's accomplice a free man, they blind him, [31] and sentence him in accordance with the laws of Stephen I. [32] It meant that they not only blinded the free man codefendant of the free man who had become a thief, but gave him an additional sentence according to the first book of Hungarian laws: he had to restore twofold the value of the stolen material. [33] If the codefendant could not restore twofold the stolen values, they sold him into slavery. [34] This decree confirmed the provisions of Stephen I's code of laws that said that a thief, were he a man of free status who has stolen ten denars worth, could, by paying twelfthfold for the stolen goods, redeem himself; and he had to pay an additional fine, the price of an ox. [35] Were the fhief a servant of free status, he restored the value of the stolen articles twofold, and had his nose cut off. [36] Incidentally, the eighth article of *Decretum III* is convincing proof of the fact that it had been compiled in 1084, or shortly thereafter, at the time of Stephen I's canonization.

Undoubtedly, ten denars had to be worth more than the price of a chicken; [37] it may be that they did not consider hanging the thief sufficient punishment for stealing ten denars worth of chattel, or property. In view of this fact, they may have regarded it as just to sell the thief in return; through his act of thievery he lost his rights as a free person; now he would have to do lifelong penance as slave for his theft — his crime against society as a whole. [38]

Of the thirty articles of the law book some concerned

judges; [39] separate decrees dealt with thieves, [40] female thieves, [41] the catchers of thieves, [42] and with slaves who had fled from their masters. [43] The second decree describes contemporary Hungarian society; it mentions the nobles and the non-noble inhabitants of the realm; the upper clergy, the abbots, the royal stewards: *comites* (reeves), and the common free men: *minores* — the free stratum who made up society at this time. [44]

The segment — the census of whose members had been taken by Judge Karckas (Sarchas) — of the free stratum that employed as servants and controlled the *evvrek* (people known by that designation since the days of King Andrew I and Duke Béla [45] ), and other servants, had annually to present them to the monarch on the field (= law) day held on the feast of the Assumption (August 15), to maintain that privilege. [46] If they held the *evvrek* and other servants illegally, they paid a double fine; if they held or controlled them legally (or, had thought that they held them legally), they had to defend their legal privilege before the king. [47]

At the same time, and the same place, members of the *wzbeg* element, too, made their appearance before the monarch; the latter made a decision concerning their social status-quo; most probably, they lived in a temporary enslavement, or in simple servitude in the service of a free man. [48] If someone held, or retained, an *wzbeg* illegally (without proper authorization from the king), he had to present his case to the court for a decision. If an *wzbeg* left his service (servitude) without authorization, they punished him. [49]

Servants who were illegally held (in servitude), and animals that had been stolen, had to be turned in at a royal fort, where they were to be reclaimed by their rightful owner(s). [50] The law regulated judicial behavior; it determined the jurisdiction of the Count Palatine, [51] the royal justices, [52] the county judges, [53] further, that of the reeve of a noble's court. [54] The royal judge, *nuncius regis*, was the king's itinerant justice (an institution contemporary with, and comparable to, the English king's justice-in-the-eyre), who held jurisdiction over the meetings "in civitate:" county-centers of royal administration, of the *centuriones*: hundred men, and ten men: *decuriones* (the latter playing leading roles among the *evvrek* - *ewril*). [55] He held jurisdiction over the

county, — were he to search for thieves; or, were he to be
called upon to restore order of the law [56] (just as his English
counterpart did in the twelfth century [57] ). The jurisdiction
of the royal itinerant justice, *nuncius regis*, ought not be
confused with that of a county judge: *iudex in parochia sua*.[58]
In contrast with the first article of the code, art. 16 stressed
that the king's (itinerant) justice and the county judge were
not the same person, nor did they have the same jurisdiction.[59]

The monarch's itinerant justice, upon his arrival "in
civitate," gathered around him the regional hundred men
and ten men and their subordinates, "cum omnibus sibi
commissis," in order to receive their reports; he also appealed
to the regional nobles and free men for information about
thievery and public disorders. [60] In case of an indictment,
the accused (or, one person from the ten, or hundred) had
to submit — for the ten or the hundred — to an ordeal. Trial
by ordeal was held sufficient to determine guilt or innocence;
were the accused to suffer wounds during the ordeal, they
pronounced him guilty and punished him accordingly. [61]

The king's itinerant justice moved from district to district,
"de uilla in uillam uadat;" he asked the local inhabitants to
inform him about public conditions in their particular region. [62] On account of his mobility, and because of the size
of the territory he had to cover, the itinerant justice represented a higher level of legal procedures, and handled, with
full legal apparatus, court cases a county judge could not,
or dared not pass sentence on. Law protected the person
and judicial activities of the royal justices and county judges. [63]
Law also punished false judges, as well judges who unneces-
sarily prolonged a case in court. The law said that there was
judicial responsibility: one may appeal a sentence handed
down by a county judge. [64]

The person will be invited by a writ with a seal affixed
to it to appear before the judge's court. [65] Interestingly,
certain deeds, as, for example, one's drawing his sword in
public; or, one's attacking someone else's home, were being
viewed and adjudged in a more humane manner. The judge
handed down a sentence after the case had been brought
before his court, to his attention; and he had to formulate
the sentence according to his own judgment. [66] In contrast
with the laws of King Stephen I, who considered security

of human life as the most important responsibility of the court(s) of law, Ladislas I looked upon security of public and private property as more important, as he regarded thievery an occupation unworthy of the inhabitants of his realm. [67]

Ladislas I's collection of laws known as the first book — it contained the resolutions of the Synod of Szabolcs, — was compiled in 1092, toward the end of his reign, [68] as if to bring under one roof the constitutional and legal developments begun by his great predecessor, Stephen I. [69] For instance, it was Ladislas' *Decretum I* (1092) that, for the first time, depicted the constituent parts of the Hungarian legislative assembly simultaneously, though the synod itself may be looked upon as an ecclesiastical and political convention. Here the country's bishops, abbots, and *iobagiones*: temporal lords, held counsel with the monarch; and the decrees they agreed upon were to be approved by the entire population. [70] Of the synod-assembly, the "most Christian" king himself was the president; [71] and it dealt equally with spiritual-ecclesiastical and temporal-political matters; the last two articles concern mainly judicial questions. [72]

The resolutions of the synod-assembly discuss every aspect of church life in Hungary; church organization; "order" of the Mass; ethical and spiritual attitudes of the clerics; observance of Sundays and holidays; declare war on the remains of paganism in the land, and regulate relations between Christians and Jews, Ismaelites and Christians. The peculiar aspect of these resolutions is that several of the forty-three articles are *autochton*: they result from independent thinking, correspond to no known law collection of the times. [73] Nor are the rest of the articles slavish imitations of previous law collections. [74] At the same time, the decrees maintain and confirm the validity of the laws of Stephen I. [75] That is why it is necessary to stress the role of the king's presiding over the synod-assembly; the text of the decrees does not even mention the archbishop of Esztergom, the primate of the realm, by name; he, in fact, remains unknown in the record. [76]

According to the resolutions of Szabolcs (1) every bishop had to visit all monasteries in his diocese regularly; [77] at his arrival at a monastic house, the abbot with his monks

awaited him (the bishop) in front of the building and ex-
changed the kiss of peace with him. [78]

Were the inhabitants of a region to leave their villages
and its church (the people must have been living in tents
still), they had to return there; [79] at any rate, the inhabitants
of such a tent-village constantly on the move made pastoral
work rather difficult for the clergy.

The abbot of a monastery collects the tithe (of income)
from every one of his landholders, and gives it to the
bishop. [80] If someone had promised a gift to the Church,
he had to keep that promise. [81] Were a priest to waste church
income or property (chattel) willfully, he must repay the
damage threefold. [82] Likewise, donation made to a church
cannot be reclaimed by the donor. [83] Ecclesiastical property
cannot be taken away from the Church. [84] Free men living
in the bishopric pay one tenth of their income to the
bishop, [85] whose clerics share from it. [86] The law prescribes
the method of collecting and paying the tithe. [87] It says that a
church building destroyed, or burnt to the ground because
of political turmoil, must be rebuilt. [88] This particular article of legislation points to the days of religious and civil
wars in the country prior to Ladislas' reign, though it revives
an article of similar nature issued by Stephen I. [89] Ecclesiastical buildings in need of repair must be rebuilt by the
bishop. [90]

(2) The provisions of the synod-assembly cover church
organization and the order of holidays of obligation. [91] They
order corporal punishment for the person who fails to attend
Mass on Sundays and holidays; were the church far away,
a representative of the village community has to attend Mass,
with a stick in his hand (used for walking and/or leaning
upon during church service?); three loaves of bread; and
one candle. [92] The article reflects an earlier decree by Stephen
I, [93] and incorporates the resolution of the 1078 Roman
synod. [94] It may also point to the lack of seats, or benches,
in Hungarian churches at this time. [95]

Sundays and holidays are not working days; no business
can be transacted on those days; nor can anyone go hunting. [96] The law says that Ember-days be strictly observed. [97]
Lent begins on Quinquagesima Sunday. [98] The law punishes
pagan customs (still kept), [99] and makes the local village

head and elders responsible for the Christian burial of the inhabitants of the community. [100]

A Jew cannot marry a Christian woman, nor keep a Christian servant maid.[101] Jews have to observe Christian holidays. Were a Jew to break the law, they take away the tool he had been working with.[102] Were an Ismaelite to revert to his old religious ways, they expatriate him. [103]

(3) The law supervises clerical discipline. A new(ly arrived) cleric must have a letter of recommendation on him to prove his identity as an ordained priest.[104] If the local ordinary has accepted the priest among his diocesan clergy, he may not dismiss him without telling him, why? [105] Clerics in transit — presumably missionaries; or clergy travelling to a destination —, are allowed to say Mass in a tent. [106]

The law paid attention to *kalendae*: various religious associations, or conventions, held for the purpose of spreading religious ideas. These confraternities (sodalities) were named *kalendae* after the first days of the months, when members (of the association-confraternity) held their gatherings. The goal of these confraternities (sodalities) was determined by Atto of Vercelli who said that on such occasions clergy and the faithful were to meet together, in order to discuss Christian faith and manner of life, and progress made in the inner lives of the individual members, and to talk about everyday work — that has determined their (social) status in life. During the *kalendae* members also called attention to each other's fault and problems, and tried to solve them. [107] According to the law, were a member to decide to leave the association, he paid ten pounds for conciliation fee to assure his lawful departure from the group.[108] The law book deals with possible disturbances that may occur at these conventions, and provides harsh punishment for clerics who, as members, (may have) abuse(d) their clerical status in the association.[109]

(4) In the field of clerical marriages, the synod-assembly attempts to remain in step with the Gregorian reform ideals amidst then prevalent Hungarian ecclesiastical conditions. For instance, the law recognizes the validity of a priest's first marriage with a virgin;[110] if, however, a priest married for a second time, or married a widow, or mistress for the first time, he had to leave her and do penance in public.[111] In-

teresting is the decree that a priest married to his first wife
may remain married until they (that is, the royal court and
the bishops!) consult with Rome in the matter.[112] Considering the fact that the papal directive on clerical celibacy had
been issued nearly two decades earlier,[113] and during that
time they have canonized King Stephen I, his son, Prince
Emery, and Bishop Gerard of Csanád,[114] it would be
important to find out the reason that caused the court to
delay an inquiry in Rome. The complaint of King Ladislas I
expressed in his letter to the abbot of Montecassino that the
burden of the royal office frequently leads him to make the
wrong (political) decisions; and, because of politics, he cannot make concessions in religious and political affairs,[115] may
provide no sufficient answer, though may lead to a conclusion that in domestic church policy the king did not want,
because he could not afford to surrender his initiative.[116]

After all, in the royal foundation charter issued for the
abbey of Somogyvár in 1091, Ladislas I emphasized the privileges enjoyed by the royal monasteries in the realm, together
with the monarch's privilege to defend, and possibly dispose
of, those monastic communities.[117] The emphasis of royal
privileges is the more interesting because the charter was
signed by and issued in the presence of Cardinal Teuzo, the
papal legate.[118] The only explanation may be that, according to this founding charter, only Frankish monks could in-
habit the abbey; therefore, the Somogyvár monastery remained in close contact with St. Gilles (the mother) monastic community in southern Frankland. In fact, the original
charter has been preserved in the Frankish mother-abbey.[119]

It may well be that Ladislas I, who had a difficult time
dealing with the disorderly conduct of clergymen and nobles
in ecclesiastical matters, was afraid that by granting concessions to Rome he only would undermine his position and
prestige at home, and make it possible for outsiders to intervene in the religious affairs of the country.[120]

It is certainly worth noticing that, int the days of Ladislas
I, both Roman and Byzantine policies have entered and played
roles in questions related to clerical marriages; Byzantine
canon law recognized the validity of a clergyman's marriage,
if he did marry before his ordination.[121] In accordance with
the decrees of the 1090 Synod of Amalfi, held under the

pontificate of Urban II, were a priest to marry his house-keeper, he had to sell her and give the sale-price of the woman to the bishop. [122] Roman influence may be discerned in the article of Szabolcs saying that were a bishop to condone (illegal) clerical marriages (perhaps on account of the shortness of qualified clergymen), he was to be sentenced by all the bishops of the realm and by the king. [123]

(5) The Szabolcs legislative assembly legislated in matters of secular marriages. If someone found out about his wife living in adultery, he could kill her and feel (was) free to marry again; [124] if, however, the murdered wife's relatives regarded the husband's deed too excessive and unjustified, they could bring charges against the man before a secular judge. [125] If a man took his adulterous wife to court, the bishop of the court could give her a canonical sentence. [126] Having performed her penance, she could return to her husband; however, he was not obliged to take her back. If he did not take her back, neither of them could get married again. [127]

The bishop handles court cases dealing with courtesans and witches; [128] death penalty awaits the one who had raped a woman or a virgin. [129] The law books recognize the validity of ordeals, but state that in order to have an ordeal three trustworthy witnesses need to be present at the ordeal. [130]

Legislation held during the reign of Ladislas I supports the king's authority and places emphasis upon the latter's superiority in dealing with religious matters, and with the Roman See. From the letter of Pope Urban II addressed to Coloman the Learned one may draw the conclusion that Rome, in order to avoid greater difficulties, has been lenient with the behavior and decisions made by Ladislas I; but, after Ladislas' death, the papal curia tried hard to change the political initiatives of the new monarch, and, at least in the field of church policy, to neutralize the monarch's authority of intervention. [131]

The new Hungarian policy of the Holy See could only have meant that the consequent behavior and legislative policy of Ladislas I were not effortless. During his reign peace and order have been restored in the realm; and the royal throne had become so strong that it now could afford to let Rome take the initiative in Hungarian religious politics and diplomacy. [132]

NOTES

1. *Chronicon pictum*, cc. 131-41, on King Ladislas I, in E. Szentpétery (ed), *Scriptores rerum Hungaricarum*, 2 vols. (Budapest, 1937-38), cited hereafter as *SSH*, I, 403ff.; C. A. Macartney, *The Medieval Hungarian Historians* (Cambridge, 1953), 133ff.; J. Horváth, *Árpád-kori latinnyelvű irodalmunk stílusproblémái* (Stylistic questions concerning the Latin language literature in the Arpadian age) (Budapest, 1954), 255ff.; J. Pintér, *Magyar irodalomtörténet* (Synthesis of Hungarian literature) 8 vols. (Budapest, 1930-41), I, 341ff.; T. Klaniczay, *A magyar irodalom története 1600-ig* (History of Hungarian literature until 1600) (Budapest, 1964), 60ff.; C. Horváth, *A régi magyar irodalom története* (History of early Hungarian literature) (Budapest, 1899), 27, 32f.; Ladislas' *Vita*, *SSH*, II, 515ff.; G. Érszegi (ed), *Árpád-kori legendák és Intelmek* (Legends and admonitions of the Arpadian age) (Budapest, 1983), 95ff. B. Hóman — Gy. Szekfű, *Magyar történet* (Hungarian history), 5 vols.; 6th ed. (Budapest, 1939), I, 285ff.; B. Hóman, *Geschichte des ungarischen Mittelalters*, 2 vols. (Berlin, 1940-43), I, 290ff. L. Mezey, *Athleta patriae: tanulmányok Szent László történetéhez* (Studies in the history of St. Ladislas) (Budapest, 1980), 19ff., and my review of it in *Catholic Historical Review*, 68 (1982), 130f.; Gy. Székely *et al* (eds), *Magyarország története: előzmények és magyar történet 1242-ig* (History of Hungary: origin and Hungarian history to 1242), 2 vols. (Budapest, 1984), II, 898ff.; my book, *Five Eleventh Century Hungarian Kings: Their Policies and Their Relations with Rome*, East European Monographs no. 79 (New York, 1981), 92ff.

On the name of Ladislas: *laou dosis*, gift to the people, cf. Gy. Moravcsik, "A magyar szókincs görög elemei (Byzantine elements of the Hungarian vocabulary)," *Emlékkönyv Melich János 70 születésnapjára* (Memorial volume to J. Melich' 70th birthday) (Budapest, 1942), 264ff. On Ladislas' canonization, see *SSH*, II, 525, 9-12 (c. 12); *Acta sanctorum*, 60 vols. to October XI (Paris — Rome, 1864-76), Iunii V, 315ff.; G. Pray, *Dissertatio historico critica de s. Ladislao rege Hungariae* (Posonii, 1774), 5ff.; V. Bunyitay, *Szent László király emlékezete* (Essay on King St. Ladislas) (Budapest, 1892), 38; it is still little known. E. Hermann, *A katolikus egyház története Magyarországon 1914-ig* (History of the Catholic Church in Hungary prior to 1914) (Munich, 1973), 92, only mentioned it. For the canonization itself, see Th. Spalatensis *Historia Salonitanorum*, c. 24, in G. H. Pertz (ed), *Monumenta Germaniae historica, Scriptores*, 30 vols. in 32 (Hannover, 1826etc.) cited hereafter as MGHSS, XXIX, 570ff., though it ought to be noted that Béla III (1172-1196) has asked Pope Celestine III (1191-96), and *not* Pope Innocent III (1198-1216), for the canonization. Cf. *ibid.*, XXIX, 575,16, and note 4; therefore, the arguments of J. Horváth in S. V. Kovács (ed), *Memoria saeculorum Hungariae*, vol. I (Budapest, 1974), 158, should be corrected. See my review of this volume in *Austrian History Yearbook*, 12-13 (1976-77), 494ff.

2. See *Decretum II*, in St. L. Endlicher (ed), *Rerum Hungaricarum monumenta Arpadiana*, 2 vols. (Sangalli, 1849), one volume reprint, Leipzig, 1931), cited hereafter as *RHM*, II, 334ff. L. Závodszky (ed), *A szent István, szent László és Kálmán korabeli törvények és zsinatok határozatai* (Sourcebook of the legal enactments and synodical acts of the reigns of St. Stephen, St. Ladislas and Coloman) (Budapest, 1904), 157ff.; St. Katona, *Historia pragmatica Hungariae*, 3 vols. (Buda, 1782etc.), I, 450ff.

3. *Ibid.*

4. "... et quesivimus, qualiter malorum hominum impedirentur studia;" *Decretum II*, a. 1.

5. *RHM*, II, 334-39, esp. aa. 2-4, 10b, 11 and 12.

6. Cf. H. Marczali *et al* (eds), *Enchiridion fontium historiae Hungarorum* (Budapest, 1901), 92.

7. *Ibid.*, 87ff.; *RHM*, II, 325ff.; J. D. Mansi (ed), *Sacrorum conciliorum nova et amplissima collectio*, 31 vols. (Florence-Venice, 1759-98), XX, 758ff.; C. Péterffy (ed), *Sacra concilia ecclesiae Romanae Catholicae in regno Hungariae celebrata*, 2 vols. (Vienna, 1742-43), I, 15ff.; Katona, I, 445f.; I. de Batthyány (ed), *Leges ecclesiasticae regni Hungariae et provinciarum adiacentium*, 3 vols.; rev. ed. (Claudipoli, 1824), I, 433ff.

8. *RHM*, II, 340; Marczali, 96f.; Katona, I, 452f.; I. de Batthyány, "Dissertatio de synodis...," *Leges*, I, 30ff.; G. Adriányi, "Die ungarischen Synoden," *Annuarium historiae conciliorum*, 8 (1976), 541ff.

9. See the founding charter of the abbey of Pannonhalma, anno 1001, in L. Erdélyi (ed), *A pannonhalmi szent Benedekrend története* (History of the Benedictines of Pannonhalma), 12 vols. (Budapest, 1902-07), I, 589f.; or (the abbreviated version), in J. P. Migne (ed), *Patrologiae cursus completus, series latina*, 221 vols. in 224 (Paris, 1844-55), cited hereafter as *MPL*, 151, 1253ff.; *ASS*, Sept. I, 494ff.; Katona, I, 181ff.; my book, 132, note 57.

10. Cf. Hartvic, *Vita s. Stephani regis*, c. 10, *SSH*, II, 415, 1-12; Katona, I, 224ff.; my book, 141, n. 58; for text, *RHM*, II, 310ff.; *MPL*, 151, 1243ff.; Marczali, 67ff.

11. "Omnes nos regni Pannonici optimates...;" *Decretum II*, a. 1, and compare with King Stephen's *Admonitiones*, aa. 4 and 7, *SSH*, II, 619ff.; *MPL*, 151, 1239ff.; Hóman, *Ungarisches Mittelalter*, I, 226ff.; J. Gerics, "Judicium Dei a magyar állam XI századi külkapcsolataiban (Judicium Dei in the foreign policy of the Hungarian state of the eleventh century)," Mezey, *Athleta*, 111ff., esp. 123ff.

12. Cf. my book 84ff., and 185, n. 43.

13. *Ibid.*, 93, and 187f., n. 13 and 14.

14. Cf. Ladislas' *Vita*, a. 1, *SSH*, II, 515,6-11; *Chronicon pictum*, c. 131, *ibid.*, I, 405,13-25. A. Fodor, "László legendák a XV és XVI századi magyarországi breviáriumokban (Ladislas legends in the 15th-16th century Hungarian breviaries)," Mezey, *Athleta*, 57ff., esp. 61f.; for comparison, see *ASS*, Iunii VII, 286f., and 287ff.

15. See the preface of Ladislas' *Decretum I* (1092), *RHM*, II, 326.

16. *Decretum II*, a. 1, *ibid.*, II, 334.

17. Katona, I, 451.

18. "... et omnis familia depereat," *RHM*, II, 335, as opposed to Katona's quote of "omnis facultas eius depereat."

19. See, e.g. *Chronicon pictum*, c. 138, *SSH*, I, 414ff.

20. "Omnes nos regni optimates ... fecimus conuentus;" *RHM*, II, 334, a. 1; P. Lukcsics (ed), *Szent László ismeretlen legendája* (The unknown legend of St. Ladislas) (Budapest, 1930), 31: "sermo I;" *Chronicon pictum*, c. 131.

21. *Decretum II*, aa. 2-5 and 10.

22. *Ibid.*, aa. 1, 10b and 11.

23. *Ibid.*, a. 1.

24. *Ibid.*, a. 11.

25. *Ibid.*, aa. 13-16.

26. *Ibid.*, II, 340ff.; Katona, I, 452; Hóman, *Ungarisches Mittelalter*, I, 291.

27. Cf. Bernoldi Constantiensis *Chronicon*, anno 1083, *MGHSS*, V, 438.; Hartvic, c. 24, *SSH*, II, 434,3-8; my book, 97; Hóman, *Ungarisches Mittelalter*, I, 294, stated it differently: "König Stephan und seine Gefährten wurden eigentlich

vom Volk zu seinen Heiligen geweiht, weil es ihnen das zu befolgende religiose und nationale Ideal gefunden zu haben glaubte." Th. von Bogyay *et al* (eds), *Die hll. Könige* (Graz, 1976), 25ff.; Th. v. Bogyay, *Stephanus Rex* (Vienna-Munich, 1975), 55ff., and my review of it in *Austrian History Yearbook*, 14 (1978), 290ff.

28. M. Büdinger, *Ein Buch ungarischer Geschichte, 1058-1100* (Leipzig, 1866), 86ff., who based his argument on a. 21 (*RHM*, II, 346f.), by saying that it referred to conditions in the realm prior to the reign of Ladislas I; for counterargument, cf. Gy. Pauler, *A magyar nemzet története az árpádházi királyok alatt* (History of the Hungarian nation under the Árpáds), 2 vols. (Budapest, 1893-95), I, 566, and A. Huber "Über die älteste ungarische Verfassung," *Mitteilungen des Institutes für österreichische Geschichtsforschung*, 6 (1885), 385ff.

29. Cf. *Decretum III*, a. 2, *RHM*, II, 342.

30. "... cum omnia substantia pereat;" *ibid.*, a. 8.

31. "... si minus alter ... oculus eruatur;" *ibid.*, a. 8.

32. "... et secundum sancti Stephani regis decreta;" in reference to Stephen's *Leges*, ii:7 (c. 41 in Migne!); this article, together with *Decretum III*, a. 17, may, incidentally, prove that the Decretum III collection has been enacted after the canonization of Stephen I.

33. "De furto liberorum:" ut semel redimat se; *Decretum III*, a. 8.

34. "... venundetur;" *ibid.*; also, *Leges* of Stephen I, ii:7, *RHM*, II, 322 (or, c. 41, *MPL*, 151, 1252bc.).

35. Cf. *Decretum II*, a. 12, *RHM*, II, 338, — ... ut unum bouem persoluat."

36. "... seruus autem ... duplum reddat at nasum amittat;" *ibid.*

37. It was one-third of the price of a three year old ox — cf. L. Erdélyi, *Magyar történelem: művelődés és államtörténet* (Hungarian cultural and constitutional history), 2 vols. (Budapest, 1936-38), I, 91.

38. In the spirit of the laws of King St. Stephen — cf. Stephen I's *Leges*, ii:7.

39. *Decretum III*, aa. 16, also 1, 3, 23-24, 25-26.

40. *Ibid.*, aa. 4, 5, 7, 10-11, 12, 17, 19-20.

41. *Ibid.*, aa. 6-7.

42. *Ibid.*, aa. 9 and 20.

43. *Ibid.*, aa. 5, 13, 21-22.

44. *Ibid.*, a. 2, first paragraph (*RHM*, II, 342; Marczali, *Enchiridion*, 98.)

45. It also reads *ewrek* — cf. *ibid.*

46. *Decretum III*, a. 2, second par.

47. "... uel si qui defendere uoluerit, in praedicta festiuitate uaniat ad curiam et defendat;" *ibid.*, a. 2, second par.

48. Marczali, *Enchiridion*, 98, reads *Wzbech.*

49. *Ibid.*, a. 2 third par. (*RHM*, II, 343, a. 2, third par.). It would be rewarding to compare with Burchkard of Worms, *Decretum*, xv:43, *MPL*, 140, 908ff., saying that work is servitude for sin; or, with the remarks of Ratherius of Verona, *Praeloquiorum libri sex*, i:ll, *MPL*, 136, 172f., saying that "labor vero magis servituti quam libertati videtur conquerere;" also, K. Bosl, "Armut, Arbeit, Emanzipation: zu den Hintergründen der geistigen und literarischen Bewegung vom 11 bis zum 13 Jahrhundert," *Beiträge zur Wirtschafts- und Sozialgeschichte des Mittelalters: Festschrift für Herbert Helbig* (Cologne, 1976), 128ff.; or, F. von Bezold, "Die 'armen' Leute und die deutsche Literatur des Spätmittelalters," *Historische Zeitschrift*, 41 (1879), 1ff.

50. *Decretum III*, a. 13.

51. *Ibid.*, a. 3.

52. *Ibid.*, a. 1.

53. *Ibid.*, a. 16.

54. *Ibid.*, a. 12. "Reges a recte agendo vocati sunt; ideoque recte faciendo regis nomen obtinetur, peccando omittitur;" cf. Ivo of Chartres, *Decretum*, xvi:39, *MPL*, 161, 912cd, and his *Panormia*, viii:59, *ibid.*, 161, 1316c; R. Sprandel, *Ivo von Chartres und seine Stellung in der Kirchengeschichte* (Stuttgart, 1962), 180f.

55. *Decretum III*, a. 1, *RHM*, II, 341.

56. *Ibid.*, a. 1, fifth par.: "nuncius regis de uilla ad uillam uadat siscitando a villanis, ut ubi furem sciunt, monstrent...".

57. Cf. W. Stubbs (ed), *Select Charters of English Constitutional History*, 8th ed., Oxford, 1895, 143, art. 1; B. Lyon, *A Constitutional and Legal History of Medieval England* (New York — London, 1960), 295f.

58. *Decretum III*, a. 16, to the effect that "nemo iudicum extra suam iurisdictionem iudicet." (*RHM*, II, 346)

59. The royal justice "per omnes civitates dirigatur" (a. 1); the county judge "in parochia sua iudicet" (a. 16.).

60. *Ibid.*, a. 1, second par.

61. *Ibid.*, a. 1, fourth par.

62. *Decretum III*, a. 1 fifth par.

63. *Ibid.*, aa. 15, 10 and 23; also, Stephen's *Leges*, ii:9 (c. 43 in Migne).

64. *Decretum III*, aa. 24 and 25.

65. *Ibid.*, aa. 26 and 27.

66. *Ibid.*, a. 28.

67. Cf. Stephen's *Leges*, ii:7, and i:35, with ii:15 (cc. 41, 33 and 49).

68. *Decretum I*, *RHM* II, 325ff.; Mansi, *Concilia*, XX, 758ff.; text preserved in fifteenth century Thuróczy codex, *Clme* 407 of the Hungarian National Museum, ff. 85-88'; and, in sixteenth century Ilosvay codex, *Fol. lat.* 4023, ff. 20'-22, prepared "per manus Stephani de Iloswá, praepositi vicarii ecclesiae Agriensis, a.D. 1544," *ibid.*, f. 138, also at the Museum; it is known from an entry on the inner binding of the codex that Ilosvay was also "lector canonicus" at the episcopal chapter at Várad. For background, see Hóman-Szekfű, I, 303ff.; Hóman, *Ung. Mittelalter*, I 310ff.; C. J. von Hefele, *Conziliengeschichte*, 6 vols.; 2nd rev. ed. (Freiburg i. Br., 1873-90), V, 204ff.; Adriányi, *art. cit.*, 542f.; Büdinger, 86ff. — P. Németh, "Előzetes jelentés a szabolcsi árpádkori megyeszékhely kutatásának első három esztendejéről (Preliminary report on the first three years of excavations at the county seat of Szabolcs in the age of the Arpads)," *Archeológiai Értesítő*, 100 (1973), 167ff., on the earth works of fort Szabolcs.

69. *Decretum I*, preface; F. Helbig, "Fidelis Dei et regis: zur Bedeutungsentwicklung von Glauben und Treue im hohen Mittelalter," *Archiv für Kulturgeschichte*, 33 (1951), 275ff.; background also in S. Hellmann, *Das Mitelalter bis zum Ausgange der Kreuzzüge*, 2nd rev. ed. (Stuttgart, 1924), 228ff.; K. Hampe, *Das Hochmittelalter*, 5th rev. ed. (Cologne-Graz, 1963), 139ff.

70. "... cum uniuersis regni sui pontificibus et abbatibus, nec non cum cunctis optimatibus, cum testimonio tocius cleri et populi;" *RHM*, II, 326.

71. "... synodus habita est presidente christianissimo Ungarorum rege Ladislao;" *ibid.* One may, of course, recall the warning of Isidore of Seville: "principes saeculi nonnumquam intra ecclesiam potestatis adeptae culmina tenent, ut per eamdem potestatem disciplinam ecclesiasticam muniant;" cf. his *Sententiarum*, iii: 51:4, *MPL*, 83, 723b. F. Kampers, "Rex et sacerdos," *Historisches Jahrbuch*, 45 (1925), 495ff.; H. O. Taylor, *The Medieval Mind*, 2 vols., 4th rev. ed. (London, 1925), I, 106.

72. *Decretum I*, aa. 42 and 43, *RHM*, II, 333.

73. As, e.g., *ibid.*, a. 8.

74. As, e.g., *ibid.*, aa. 6 and 27; also, Závodszky, 62f.

75. *RHM*, II, 325ff., preface.

76. *Ibid.*; F. A. Kollar, *De originibus et usu perpetuo potestatis legislatoriae circa sacra Apostolicorum regum Ungariae* (Vienna, 1764), 70; O. B. Gams, *Series episcoporum Ecclesiae Catholicae* (Ratisbon, 1873), 380, provides no answer; Péterffy, I, 14, was contradicted by F. Knauz (ed), *Monumenta ecclesiae Strigoniensis*, 2 vols. (Strigonii, 1873-74), I, 68, by saying that Seraphim was, in 1092, still the chaplain of Ladislas I.

77. *Decretum I*, a. 21. Chalcaedon, anno 451, c. 4, in Mansi, *Consilia*, VII, 374f., and 394bc.

78. *Decretum, I*, a. 36 (Závodszky, a. 35).

79. *Decretum I*, a. 19; about "nomadic" habits, see Otto of Freising, *Gesta Friderici imperatoris*, i:31, *MGHSS*, XX, 368ff.; Gy. Györffy, *István király és műve* (King Stephen I and his work) (Budapest, 1977), 398ff., and my review in *Austrian History Yearbook*, 17-18 (1981-82), 358ff.

80. *Decretum I*, a. 28.

81. *Ibid.*, a. 5.

82. *Ibid.*, a. 6, and compare with the Synod of Mainz, 847, c. 8, and that of Mainz, 888, c. 6, in Mansi, *Concilia*, XIV, 906, and XVIII, 66, respectively. The Hungarian provision is more strict: "tripliciter ecclesiae restituat;" *RHM*, II, 327.

83. *Ibid.*, a. 23.

84. *Ibid.*, a. 24.

85. *Ibid.*, a. 31.

86. *Ibid.*, a. 34.

87. *Ibid.*, a. 41; on the type of coin used: *nummus, ibid.*, a. 43, see B. Hóman, *Magyar pénztörténet* (Hungarian monetary history) (Budapest, 1916), 224, note 1.

88. *RHM*, II, 325ff., aa. 7 and 19.

89. Compare with Stephen's *Leges*, ii:2.

90. *Decretum, I*, a. 8.

91. *Ibid.*, aa. 38-39 (Závodszky and Hefele, aa. 37-38). The substance of Andrew I's *Constitutio ecclesiastica*, anno 1047, an apocryphal decree, cf. *MPL*, 1257f., is confirmed by the *Chronicum pictum*, c. 86, *SSH*, I, 344,1-6, and, among others, by P. Ransanus, *Epithoma rerum Hungarorum*, the last book of his *Annales omnium temporum*, ed. P. Kulcsár (Budapest, 1977), 109 and 112ff., ind. xi and xii; my review in *AHYB*, 17-18 (1981-82), 363ff.

92. *Decretum I*, a. 8.

93. Stephen's *Leges*, i:9 (c. 8).

94. See Concilium Romanum, anno 1078, c. 12, Mansi, *Concilia*, XX, 510 (Závodszky, 66).

95. Batthyány, *Leges*, I, 435, note *d*.

96. *Decretum I*, aa. 12, 15 and 16 (and compare with *MGHCap*. I, 61 and 95, aa. 789 and 802); the weekly market was held on Saturdays, cf. *Chronicon pictum*, c. 94, *SSH*, I, 358,16-17. Also, Stephen, *Leges*, i:8 (c. 7).

97. *Decretum I*, a. 25; compare with Stephen's *Leges*, i:10.

98. *Decretum I*, a. 32: "qui scilicet postquam Ungari carnee dimiserunt, ipsi iterum in secunda et tercia feria coderint, si se nostri consuetudini meliori non consentire dixerint." Gy. Moravcsik, *Hungary and Byzantium* (Amsterdam-Budapest, 1970), 117; K. Holl, "Die Entstehung der vier Fastenzeiten in der griechischen Kirche," *Gesammelte Abhandlungen zur Kirchengeschichte*, vol. II (Tübingen, 1928), 155ff.

99. *Decretum I*, a. 22.

100. *Ibid.*, a. 26.

101. *Ibid.*, a. 10; Synod of Meaux, anno 845, c. 72, Mansi, *Concilia*, XIV, 836c.

102. *Decretum I*, a. 26; Synod of Meaux, 845, c. 73.

103. *Decretum I*, a. 9; on Ismaelites, see A. Bartha, *Hungarian Society in the 9th and 10th Centuries* (Budapest, 1975), 115ff.; my review in *American Historical Review*, 83 (1978), 1243f.

104. That is, "litterae commendaticiae;" *Decretum I*, a. 17; Synod of Meaux, 845, c. 50; Concilium Cabilonense, ii, anno 813, c. 40, Mansi, *Concilia*, XIV, 102.

105. *Decretum I*, a. 18.

106. *Ibid.*, a. 30; *MGHCap.* I, 46, cap. 769, c. 14; Synod of Mainz, anno 888, c. 9, Mansi, *Concilia*, XVIII, 67.

107. See Capitula Attonis Vercellensis, c. 29, *ibid.*, XIX, 250; B. Majláth, "A 'kalandos' társulatok (The *kalendae* confraternities)," *Századok*, 19 (1885), 563ff., spoke of burial associations.

108. *Decretum I*, a. 14; B. Tárkány-Szűcs, *Magyar jogi népszokások* (Hungarian legal customs) (Budapest, 1981), 189f.

109. *Decretum I*, a. 40; Hincmar of Rheims, *Capitula*, c. 15, Mansi, *Concilia*, XV, 478f.

110. *Decretum I*, a. 3; E. Pásztor, "Sulla origini della vita comune del clero in Ungheria," *La vita comune del clero nei secoli XI-XII: atti di settimana di studio, Mendola, 1959* vol. II (Milan, 1962), 71ff.

111. *Decretum I*, a. 1.

112. "Indulgencia ad tempus datur, ... quousque nobis in hoc domini Apostolici paternitas consilietur;" *ibid.*, a. 3/.

113. Cf. C. Mirbt (ed), *Die Publizistik im Zeitalter Gregors VII* (Leipzig, 1894), 266ff.; 326f.; J. Haller, *Das Papsttum: Idee und Wirklichkeit*, 5 vols.; rev. ed. (Stuttgart, 1952-59), II, 415ff.; my book, 193, note 2. On various features of the investiture controversy, see the correspondence of Gregory VII, in E. Caspar (ed), *Das Register Gregors VII, MGH Epp.*, sel. II, 2 vols. (Berlin, 1920-23), i:5, iii:4, also, Sprandel, 24ff.

114. *Supra*, note 27; Katona, I, 467ff.

115. "... quamvis peccator existam, quum cura terrene dignitatis absque gravissimis non potest promoveri criminibus, tamen tue sanctitatis culmen non ignoravi;" cf. E. Szentpétery (ed), *Regesta regum stirpis Arpadianae critico-diplomatica*, 2 vols. (Budapest, 1923-61), I, no. 31; text in V. Fraknói, *Magyarország és a Szentszék* (Hungary and the Holy See), 3 vols. (Budapest, 1901-03), I, 403.

116. The monarch did mention that he had made a request to Rome and expected a positive answer, "perlegatum, quem papa mihi mittet;" *ibid.* J. Deér, "Die Ansprüche der Herrscher des 12 Jahrhunderts auf die apostolische Legation," *Archivum historiae pontificae*, 2 (1964), 153ff.; and, compare with the recently discovered Ladislas legend — cf. L. N. Szelestei, "A Szent László legenda szöveghagyományozódásáról (Ein neuer Fund zur Textüberlieferung der Ladislas Legende)," *MKSz*, 100 (1984), 176ff., esp. 190f., c. 16.

117. See Marczali, *Enchiridion*, 100ff.; G. Fejér (ed), *Codex diplomaticus Hungariae ecclesiasticus et civilis*, 42 vols. in 44 (Budae, 1829-44), cited hereafter as Fejér, *CD*, I, 468f.; Szentpétery, *Regesta*, I, no. 24.

118. "... huius edicti testes est confirmatores sunt: dompnus (sic!) Odilo abbas S. Egidii; dompnus Petrus abbas Sumicensis; Dominus Teuzo cardinalis; dompnus (sic!) Petrus abbas S. Martini,....;" Marczali, *Enchiridion*, 102.

119. There are various versions of the text — see *ibid.*, 100; Szentpétery, *Regesta*,

I, no. 24; Pope Callixtus II did confirm the abbot of Sümeg ( = Sumicensis) in his new position; cf. ep. 193, *MPL*, 193, 198f.

120. "... sicut regale est monasterium, ita omnium bonorum consensu regalis est prohibitio, ne quis mortalium, praeter ipsum regem, super res Ecclesiae iudicare presumat;" Marczali, *Enchiridion*, 101.

121. Cf. Concilium Trullanum, anno 692 (Quinisexta), cc. 3 and 13, Mansi, *Concilia*, XI 942f., and 947bd; the synod had strong anti-Rome tendencies — and it received no recognition from the Roman See; cf. F. X. von Funk — K. Bihlmeyer, *Kirchengeschichte*, 2 vols.; 8th rev. ed. (Paderborn, 1926-30), I, 215f.

122. Cf. Concilium Lefitinum, anno 1090, c. 12, Mansi, *Concilia*, XX, 724a, in reference to *Decretum I*, a. 2.

123. *Ibid.*, a. 4 (Závodszky, 61f.); W. Holtzmann, "Unterhandlungen Urbans II mit Kaiser Alexius II," *Byzantinische Zeitschrift*, 28 (1928), 38ff.

124. He now must reckon with God, "Deo racionem reddat;" *Decretum I*, a. 13; compare with Edictum Rotharii, cap. 212, in K. Fischer-Drew (ed), *The Lombard Laws* (Philadelphia, 1953), 93.

125. "... quod iniuste interfecisset, iudicio discuciatur;" *Decretum I*, a. 13.

126. *Ibid.*, a. 20, *RHM*, II, 329.

127. "... quamdiu ambo vixerint, innupti permaneant;" *ibid.*, Synod of Ingelheim, anno 938, cap. 10, *MGH Const.*, sectio II, I, 15.

128. *Decretum I*, a. 35.

129. *Ibid.*, a. 33.

130. *Ibid.*, a. 29 (Závodszky and Hefele, a. 28).

131. "Reminiscat tunc strenuitas tua religiosi principis Stephani, qui generis tui primus a sancta Romana Ecclesia fidei religionem suscepit;" *MPL*, 151, 481b, dated July 27, 1096. R. Ignácz, "Szent László (Ladislas the Saint)," *Vigilia*, 48 (1983), 687ff.

132. Cf. L. Duchesne (ed), *Liber pontificalis*, 3 vols. (Paris, 1886etc. repr. Paris, 1955-57), II, 373,4-7; Mansi, *Concilia*, XX, 1211f.; *RHM*, II, 375; according to U. R. Blumenthal, *The Early Councils of Pope Paschal II, 1100-1110* (Toronto, 1978), 38, there is no sufficient evidence for the synod of Guastalla.

# I

# The Early Years of Coloman the Learned in the Record of the Chronicles

Qui ab Hungaris Cunues Calman appellatur,
eo quod libros habebat, in quibus horas
canonicas ut episcopus absolvebat.

*Chronicon pictum*, c. 152

It is customary to separate, in terms of origin, the medieval Hungarian chronicles into two chronicle families, that of the *Chronicon Budense*, printed in 1473, and of the *Chronicon pictum*.[1] They may have had a common ancestor.[2] The compilers of the twelfth century Hungarian historical material here being dealt with, can also be identified as two chroniclers. One of them is the anonymous Historian-of-Stephen-III (the king reigned from 1162 to 1172), but formerly known as the Chronicler-of-Géza-II (reigned from 1141 to 1162),[3] who knew some theology. His description of the scene where Boris the pretender (and illegitimate son of King Coloman) kneeled down before, in order to request the protection of, Louis VII, king of the Franks passing through Hungary during the second crusade,[4] — and his request being voided by the (religious) argument of the Hungarian king's representative(s) who said that Boris being a bastard could not receive communion, nor could the king of the Franks protect him —, may illustrate, to some extent, the chronicler's theological training.[5]

The chronicler's style and report, however, reveal a strong bias toward Coloman the Learned.[6] The chronicler may have been the author-compiler of *cc.* 142-170, in the A. Domanovszky edition of the *Chronicon pictum*, in a sense that he also rewrote the narrative of events pertinent to the last years of King Ladislas' reign, cc. 140-41.[7] On the other hand, the second author-compiler, whose literary activity is evident from cc. 169-178 and 180 in the same edition of the text, restricted himself to brief annalistic recordings; besides data concerning the reigns and deaths of kings, he provided little further information. [8]

It is in c. 140 of the *Chronicon pictum* that the Historian-of-Stephen-III, or his later interpolator, reports that shortly before his death King Ladislas conducted a military exercise against Bohemia, and took along his brothers Coloman and Géza, the sons of Géza (1074-1077), on this campaign. [9] The chronicler probably meant nephews when he spoke of the brothers of Ladislas, perhaps on the grounds that later Coloman had his real brother Álmos blinded together with Álmos' son, the future Béla II (the Blind, 1131-41). [10] By writing brothers instead of nephews the chronicler revealed his evil disposition toward Coloman because Ladislas, he said, knew about the bloodthirsty nature of Coloman, and that is why he wanted to make him the bishop of Eger. [11]

The chronicler renders no further explanation of his illogical assertion, though he assumes a distinctly hostile attitude toward Coloman. The monarch, he says, had an ugly appearance, was lame on one leg, a hunchback, who had a speech defect, and was cross-eyed. [12] Could all of this be hatred on part of the chronicler who may well have been an Álmos-sympathizer (in politics) in a sense that his Stephen III was the grandson of Béla the Blind himself, and a great-grandson of the blinded Prince Álmos? [13] If, however, an Álmos — sympathizer, he was a secret ally in his country of (German) imperial interests, who did his best to depict the person and policies of Coloman, the opponent of German expansion, in untrue colors. [14]

It ought to be pointed out that King Ladislas had a German woman for a wife, Adelhaid, daughter of Rudolf of Rheinfelden, the German anti-king; [15] in spite of his having married the daughter of Rudolf, the opponent of the German King Henry IV, the latter was more than anxious to establish and cultivate political contacts with him. At least that is what Henry IV had to say (about his relations with Ladislas) in a letter he sent to Prince Álmos in 1091. [16] At the same time, the daughter of Ladislas and Adelhaid, Pyrisk: Piroska (Irene), married John II Comnenus of Byzantium in 1104. [17] The son of John II and Pyrisk was Manuel Comnenus

Byzantine emperor who, on account of his family ties, shall have firm plans on the Hungarian throne during the mid-twelfth century. [18]

On his death bed King Ladislas sent Prelate Marcellus and royal Reeve Peter to bring Coloman back from Poland, as if to make up to his nephew for his unjustifiable behavior toward him. [19] King Ladislas was aware of similar circumstances in the recent past, when he had fled to Kievan soil, and his younger brother Lampert to Polish territory [20] (as earlier, their father, Béla I (1060-63) fled to Poland [21]), for the reason that they wanted to gain foreign aid and moral support for their struggle to prevent further growth of imperial influence in the country. [22]

In 1095, this was not the case, however; rather, Coloman had to flee to Polish territory in his personal interest because he, in opposition to his uncle's politics, wanted to work for the formation of a pro-papal Hungarian policy. [23] The reason for Ladislas' military expedition into Bohemia was to aid the Czech prince Conrad, the son of Ladislas' brother-in-law, Otto, against Svatopluk who "nocte silentio" had occupied the city of Prague, and was formerly enthroned prince of Bohemia by the bishop of Prague. [24] From the sentence of the chronicler that some Czechs gave the new prince of Bohemia an honorable reception the conclusion may be drawn that Svatopluk was not alone in his conspiracy, but moved with serious support behind him to defeat the not very popular Conrad, friend and ally of Ladislas. [25] It may be that Coloman did not quite agree with the Czech policy of his uncle, and was unwilling to accompany him in a military campaign against the new prince of Bohemia, whose political existence had just then been publicly approved by the bishop of Prague. [26]

From the chronicler's other remark that Coloman did not go to Poland all by himself, [27] one may also conclude that Coloman was not alone in his opposition to Ladislas' political ideas, the Czech policy in particular. [28] In other words, King Ladislas was leading a rather unpopular campaign against Bohemia, when, on the Czech border, he fell ill, "gravis informitas eum invasit," [29] and, with the approval of the nobles, dispatched delegates to summon Coloman back from Poland. [30] It is to be feared, though, that, at this point, the

chronicler is telling only half of the truth. He says that King
Ladislas had designated the younger brother of Coloman,
Álmos, as his heir on the Hungarian throne. [31] It is not clear
from the text when Ladislas made such a decision; had he
decided earlier, or right there on his death bed in the Czech
frontier? [32] If Ladislas made his decision while dying, why
was it necessary to recall Coloman? To clear the king's conscience? Or, did he want to persuade Coloman to accept his
decision? The chronicler says that at a time when Coloman
returned home from Polish territory and Ladislas was already
dead, Álmos himself solved the problem of royal succession
by resigning his claim to the throne on the grounds that his
elder brother had the right by primogeniture. [33] The prince
made his own decision. He let Coloman have the crown; but
he retained for himself the title of prince, together with the
princely-one-third of the realm's territory. [34]

It may be that his portion of the *Chronicon pictum* came
down to us in the interpolation of its fourteenth century
compiler. Although Géza I did have two sons, [35] it was Ladislas, Géza I's younger brother — and not one of Géza I's two
sons — who, in 1077, had been elected regent of the
country; [36] in 1060, it was not Salomon, King Andrew I's
(already crowned) son, [37] but Andrew I's younger brother,
Béla I, who had taken over the government of the realm. [38] In
order to retain credibility, the chronicler (compiler) remarked
that since the *Gesta Ladislai* spoke in depth about King
Ladislas, the reader ought to consult it for additional information. [39] The historical fact is, however, that King Coloman
had, both spiritually and intellectually, far outreached his
royal uncle and predecessor; and Coloman's training in sacred
scripture, writings of the church fathers, and canon law, [40]
made him acceptable in and to ecclesiastical circles. Abbot
Odilo of St. Gilles who had visited Hungary during the dedication of the abbey of Somogyvár in 1091; [41] and Pope Urban
II himself praised in the highest terms Coloman's educational background. [42] A contemporary Polish chronicler Martinus
Gallus, referred to him as the most learned monarch of his
age. [43] The Hungarian chroniclers attest to it that King
Coloman did possess books which he read like a bishop;
therefore, they called him the book-lover-king. [44]

It was upon the death of Ladislas that Coloman returned

to Hungary; they crowned him king, and he, now anointed
monarch, legally transferred the "princely one third" of
landholdings to his brother, Álmos. [45] The chronicler (or,
the late interpolator) could not, however, resist not to depict
Coloman in the darkest colors by saying that during his reign
many evil things had befallen the realm. [46]

Simon de Keza, chronicler of the late thirteenth century,
presents a more objective view of events surrounding
Coloman's succession to the throne. He says that upon the
death of Ladislas, Coloman, son of Géza, reigned for eighteen years, whose body was buried at Székesfehérvár. Coloman
was *presul*: prelate of the Church, who had become king,
and was named *qunwes*: book-lover, because books he had
from which he, the bishop, recited his daily office. [47] In view
of the fact that Keza's statement is supported by c. 152 of
the *Chronicon pictum*: "sicut quidam dicunt," they say that
Coloman was the bishop of Várad who, on account of the
deaths of his brothers had, with papal dispensation, become
king, "regnare compellitur," and the Hungarians called him
*Cunues Calman* because books he had from which he recited
his canonical hours, [48] it may be that he was a bishop who
with papal approval was permitted to marry, but did not
neglect the daily recitation of the divine office. [49] His being
a prelate plus the fact that he remained a bishop on the royal
throne were factors that caused the clerical chronicler — the
Historian-of-Stephen-III — to grow jealous of the king, and
gave him, *ipso facto*, "bad press;" reports depicting his reign
have to be treated with caution. [50]

There may have been another reason for the hostility of
the chronicler toward King Coloman. Judged by the letter
of Pope Urban II, the Roman pontiff supported, though indirectly, the succession of Coloman to the throne; as early
as 1096, the pontiff had expressed his joy that in the person
of Coloman the Hungarian people had gained a monarch
well versed in both secular affairs and canon law, and who
was quite able to lead his people on the right path of tran-
quility and peace. [51] His holiness had, in fact, challenged
King Coloman to lift high the colors of the Church, and to
conduct himself in the spirit of St. Stephen, the founder king.
Let Coloman be humble and show respect toward the Roman
See, and not to be disturbed by the venom of the teachings

of the false apostles who penetrated the Church of God. May wrathfulness not keep him away from the true faith. [52]

The words of the pontiff openly aim at the members of the royal opposition who had attacked the relationship between the Hungarian court and the Holy See, and who had criticised the policy of the court by saying that, in their opinion, the monarch had become a liability. The Historian-of-Stephen-III may have belonged to this narrow circle of the king's opposition. [53] On the other hand, there must have belonged to the king's immediate surroundings a group of counsellors (advisors) from the days of Ladislas I, whose members had, on ideological grounds, opposed any relationship or peacemaking with Rome. [54]

Keza summarizes the accomplishments of the reign of King Coloman in one paragraph. He states that the king dispatched an army to Dalmatia, and had the king of Croatia, Peter, assassinated when the latter had challenged the Hungarian invasion (of Croatia). King Peter was defeated, and the place where he had suffered defeat (was killed) is called Patur Gozdia (today). Keza mentions the conquest of the Dalmatian seacoast and reports that the republic of Venice did not take the loss of Dalmatia lightly. For this reason, the Hungarians kept on harrassing Venetian shipping in the Adriatic from Apulia (in southern Italy).[55] The remarks of Keza were almost verbatim repeated in the last paragraph devoted to the reign of King Coloman in the *Chronicon pictum*, though the compiler of the latter provides a detailed description of the military campaign of Coloman in Apulia itself. [56]

The reign of Coloman coincides with the planning, organization and beginnings of the first crusade. The immediate cause of the crusade lay with the disposition of Emperor Alexius Comnenus of Byzantium; the Seljuk Turks had conquered Byzantine territories in Asia Minor, Syria and Palestine, and through the pope the emperor now turned to western Christendom for military aid. [57] Although the chronicler does not state it, on psychological grounds it may be assumed that Alexius did not request military help from the west, but wanted the west to learn what it meant to struggle to death with the brutal Turks. [58] Emperor Alexius, like any other puny person (in body and soul) felt helpless in face

of the danger confronting him, and wanted others to be drawn
into the by then unavoidable hellish war between the Byzantine empire and the Seljuk Turks. [58a]

The idea of the Christian crusade was not news at the
beginning of Coloman's reign. Already Pope Sylvester II had
admonished the faithful that they should seek the reconquest
of the Holy Land from Islam. [59] The Christian rulers of the
times of Sylvester II were in no position to realize such a
serious plan. [59a] In the early eleventh century, the Byzantine
emperor, Basil II, had his share of a struggle with the
Bulgarians; in fact, Stephen I of Hungary also gave a help-
ing hand for the emperor's anti-Bulgarian campaign. [60] The
contemporary non-Hungarian chronicler reported that the
Hungarian monarch behaved in a most humane manner
toward the captured Bulgarian prisoners of war during the
expedition. [61] Pope Gregory VII had actually received an invitation from the Byzantine court to aid it against the Seljuk
Turks who, in 1074, did threaten the existence of the remains
of the once powerful empire. [62] By 1086, the Seljuks took
Jerusalem; they abused and blackmailed the Christian pilgrims visiting the holy places, and the Christian inhabitants
themselves of the city. [63] In the 1070's, the Roman pontiff
was, however, too preoccupied with ecclesiastical politics,
especially the investiture struggle with the German court,
and paid no serious attention to such a Byzantine request. [64]
Military aid from the west for Byzantium had to wait until
the 1090's, when Pope Urban II called upon the Frankish
nobility to fight, for the sake of Christ the Redeemer, against
the Islamic infidel. [65]

Reading the texts of papal speeches and correspondence,
one may not be too far from the truth in saying that the
Roman pontiff by preaching and organizing a crusade had
a good deal more in mind than answering the Byzantine
call for help. [66] In delivering sermons and speeches directed
at the Frankish nobility on Frankish soil, Urban II wanted
also to lessen the burden of the king of the Franks, Philip
I, upon whom his nobles had placed firm as rock restric-
tions; [67] the pope attempted to ease the pressure on the
monarch by making the nobles go on a crusade and leave,
for a long period of time (or permanently), their land, and,
in accordance with feudal custom, to place their families,

chattel, etc., under the guardianship of the king, their feudal overlord. (The papal sermon did not come down to posterity in the original; the chroniclers recorded it out of memory.) [68] At the same time, he had hoped that the successful completion of the crusade organized under his leadership would, in the sphere of continental interstate policies, restore papal prestige badly damaged during the (previous phase of the) investiture controversy with the empire during the 1070's and 1080's.[69]

The crusade requested by the Byzantine emperor(s) turned out quite differently from the expectations of the Byzantine imperial court. As soon as the poorly equipped and undisciplined armies of the west made their appearance under the walls of Byzantium, Emperor Alexius was not only terrified by the prospect of having those troops marauding the vicinity of his city, but suddenly realized that he might have had lost the initiative of the movement. [70] Although at the Council of Piacenza, 1094, the assembled churchmen had carefully listened to his ambassadors who informed them about the danger that has been threatening Byzantium, and the council promised mercenaries to Alexius, [71] the Council of Clermont, 1095, had already met without the Byzantine delegates; in such a manner had Pope Urban II let it be known that he preached a crusade which impelled not individuals but armies; a crusade that would remain under papal leadership, — its being a western movement, independent of any Byzantine influence. [72]

It was in the spring of 1096 that the first crusading armies lacking leadership, planning and discipline, began to move; those forces behaved in a most uncivilized manner toward the regional population. [73] Among the early crusaders who reached the western Hungarian border was Walter the Penniless (Sansavoir), [74] whose troops, incidentally, were gathered together through the preaching of Peter the Hermit — the hermit who earlier had carried the letters of the Byzantine emperor to the pope and to other leaders of the west, requesting their aid for the Christian cause in Jerusalem. [75] King Coloman had allowed the troops of Walter the Penniless to go through his realm; and the troops actually had a peaceful transit. When the main body of Walter's forces had crossed the Save river, the southern Hungarian frontier,

however, the rear defense units of those forces attacked the
Hungarian border guards, who must have kept their eyes
on those troops from a distance. The border guards defeated
the crusaders, took their booty away (booty acquired in
Hungary?), and placed the captured weapons on the walls
of the border fort of Zimony. [76] It may seem more likely,
however, that exactly the opposite (must have) happened;
it was the border guards, angered and frustrated over the
irregular behavior of the foreigners, who attacked the rear
guard of the crusading force after its main body had actually
crossed the river. The wording of the chronicler, curt as it
is, implies this conclusion. [77] The chronicler spoke of booty
as if to imply that the "crusaders" had not behaved like
crusaders at all in Hungary, and before at least a portion
of them had left the realm's territory, they received their
deserved punishment.

It was at this time that the army of Peter the Hermit
appeared on the western Hungarian border; it comprised
about 40,000 men (?) mostly Germans and Franks. King
Coloman permitted them to pass through his country, but
required from them that (1) they behave themselves during
their sojourn in the country and comit no crimes; and (2) they
pay cash for everything they purchase during their transit in
and through the realm. [78] Shortly thereafter other crusading units arrived on the border, led by two priests, Volkmar
and Gottschalk. These troops were not disciplined at all,
and the king had no choice but to attack and destroy them.
Gottschalk and some of his men were able to flee the
realm. [79] (When the troops of Peter the Hermit reached
the southern Hungarian frontier and saw the weapons that
had been taken away from the rear guard of the previous
crusading forces displayed on the walls of fort Zimony, they
occupied it but quickly withdrew from it when they heard
that the monarch was approaching it with a large army.)
On the other hand, King Coloman had refused entry to the
undisciplined troops of "crusaders" of a certain Count Emerich
without, however, having undertaken defensive measures
against the count and his troops. Whereupon Emerich
besieged Fort Moson (on the western Hungarian border)
where the king had his headquarters; the siege lasted for
several weeks, but the count had lost his nerve to fight and

to attack; he had fled the scene. King Coloman followed
and destroyed the remains of Emerich's forces. The chronicler reports nothing about what may have caused the count
to panic in a critical moment. [80]

The real crusading army led by Gottfried of Bouillon
arrived on the Hungarian border by the end of September
(1096); it comprised some 7,000 infantry and 10,000 cavalry.
King Coloman after some deliberations permitted him to
enter with his troops and pass through Hungary under the
condition that Duke Baldwin, Gottfried's younger brother,
and Baldwin's wife stay, together with some Frankish nobles,
as hostages at the Hungarian court for the duration of the
passage of the crusaders in the country. Gottfried of Bouillon
led his troops under strict order and discipline (and, one
may add, under the steady eyes of the Hungarian troops)
through the realm; after the Franks had crossed the Save
river, Coloman released his noble hostages and provided
them with rich donations. [81]

Upon the departure of the crusading armies Coloman
hurried to Croatia in order to secure for himself the country
occupied by his uncle and predecessor, and to increase his
possession of the as yet unoccupied Croatian territories. In
the spring of 1097, Coloman crossed the Save, defeated King
Peter of Croatia at a hill later named "Peter-Gozd," and
took possession of all Croatia, down to the Adriatic seacoast. [82] He did not disturb the lives of the Croatian people;
honored their laws and customs; nor did he take away their
lands and landholdings. The king only levied a tax on a small
segment of the Croatian population, and exempted twelve
Croatian noble families from any burden of taxes, though
he obliged them to perform instead military services for him.
Each of the noble families (clans) was obligated to provide
the king with ten armed men in time of war. [83]

Prince Álmos controlled one-third of the realm's territory; [84] the king placed the government of Croatia under the
*ban(us)*, royal procurator. He placed the territory south of
the Drave, — except the Serem district, — under the gover-
norship of the ban(us), and divided it into counties. [85] Coloman had not, as yet, occupied the Dalmatian seacoast. The
cities of Dalmatia remained under Venetian rule. [86] The ship-
yards of Venice needed wood from Dalmatia for their ships,

and Dalmatian sailors to man their galleys. King Coloman needed a naval force for the eventual (and planned) conquest of the seacoast; and, for that reason, he began to search for allies against Venice. With the Normans in southern Italy the king had reached an understanding to the effect that they, from their bases in Apulia have frequently harrassed and devastated the Dalmatian seacoast and the inhabitants of the cities. The Normans proved to be the natural allies of Coloman in the Adriatic. [87]

One column of the crusading armies led by Raymond of Toulouse and Adhemar of Puy, the papal legate, headed for the near East. The local inhabitants much harrassed the crusaders who only reached safe haven by entering Byzantine territory at Durazzo. [88] The Hungarian chronicler clearly compared the less humane attitude shown by the population of the Adriatic seacoast with the civilized behavior of the Hungarian monarch shown toward the crusaders passing through his country. [89]

In 1097, after he made permanent arrangement in Croatia, Coloman dispatched an embassy to Duke Roger (Norman) lord of Calabria and Sicily, in order to ask for the hand in marriage of the duke's daughter, Busila. The chronicler says that although Roger was pleased with the request, he asked the Hungarian court to send to him more important individuals as ambassadors, — an understandable attitude in case the Hungarian monarch wanted indeed the alliance with Calabria, and had serious intentions to marry the daughter of the duke. Roger may have feared that Coloman did not take seriously the embassy he had sent; nor had he by sending as ambassadors men of lesser public standing, shown proper respect for the person and political status of the duke. Therefore, Hartvic (Arduin), bishop of Győr and historian: the biographer of Stephen I, [90] and royal Reeve Thomas went to Sicily to formally present Coloman's proposal before the Norman court. It is significant that Roger in turn sent a delegation to Hungary — not to the king, but to Prince Álmos — in order to obtain the approval of Álmos and of the nobles of the marriage plans of their monarch. [90a]

Was this a political ploy on the part of the duke to humiliate the Hungarian ruler because Coloman did at first send two less prominent delegates to represent him in Sicily? Or, did Duke Roger expect more detailed and reliable information about conditions in Hungary from his own delegates than the one he may have received from the ambassadors of the king? Had the Norman court of Sicily harbor any doubts about the marriage plans of the bishop who had become king? Álmos and the Hungarian nobles assured the Normans without delay of their support of the king.[91] As a matter of fact , Roger knew little about conditions in Hungary; who in that realm would have dared to doubt the trustworthiness of the monarch in the twelfth century? It is not in vain that a few decades later Otto of Freising wrote about the Hungarian nobles that they did not dare wisper in their king's presence.[92]

In May, 1097, Roger's daughter Busila accompanied by some three hundred nobles, sailed across the Adriatic, to be met and welcomed on the Hungarian border by Reeve Mercurius and by some five thousand knights who accompanied her to Székesfehérvár. There, out in the open, under tents, the king married Busila in the presence of his people.[93] In late 1098, twin boys, Ladislas and Stephen, were born to the royal couple.[94] As for Venice, the republic was unable to alter the outcome and political development of yesteryear, and offered peace, in fact, a treaty, to the Hungarian court. After some deliberation King Coloman accepted the Venetian proposal, and purposefully left the Dalmatian seacoast in the possession of the republic.[95] It may be that upon the unexpectedly quick conclusion of the political marriage alliance with the Norman court of Sicily, King Coloman hesitated to rely so soon on his father-in-law, asking him to conduct another naval operation against Venice.[96]

Instead of Venice, Coloman now turned his attention in the direction of Kiev.[97] In the spring of 1099, the monarch reached an understanding with Bratislav II of Bohemia in order to parry the danger of an attack in his hinterland while fighting a war on Russian-Kievan soil;[98] then, answering the call for aid from Svatopluk II, grand duke of Kiev, Coloman moved toward Kiev against the princes Vasil and Volodar, the sons of Rastislav. Svatopluk II had broken into the territories of Vasil and Volodar, and suffered a humiliating defeat at the hands of both princes.

The Hungarian monarch had at first besieged fort
Peremyshl (Prsemysl) defended by Volodar and the latter's
Cuman allies. The Cumans had lured the Hungarian troops
into a trap, however; Coloman's forces have been thoroughly
destroyed. Nestor's Russian Chronicle reports that the Hungarian army numbered some 100,000 men, but the *Polovci*:
Cumans of the plains who were crying out like wolfs (before the
attack began), attacked Coloman's forces and killed some
forty thousand of them. Many Hungarian troops drowned
while crossing the San and Viar rivers, though many Cumans
died also. King Coloman was saved only by his nobles who
had surrounded him (in the battle), though two of his bishops
and many nobles died in and after the battle. [99] There is
an entry in the Easter tables of the Pray codex under the year
1099 that Bishop Cupan (Koppány) was killed by the Cumans;
and Bishop Lawrence died in that year. [100] The entry says
nothing about the Kievan expedition of King Coloman, so
it cannot be exactly determined whether Cupan had been
killed in the battle by the Cumans near Kiev, or murdered
by the Polovci-Cumans who had been settled down in Hungary by King Ladislas during the late 1080's. [101] On the other
hand, the chronicler clearly states that Bishops Cupan and
Lawrence (Koppány and Lőrinc) died in the battle near
Kiev. [102] And the king and his immediate staff (followers)
were saved only by their quick flight (*celeriter fugiendo*)
from the field of battle to Hungary. [103]

Interesting is the entry in the *Chronicon pictum*, c. 145,
saying that Lanka, a Ruthenian (Kievan-Russian) princess
and widowed queen (widow of a ruling prince?) had begged
King Coloman on her knees to spare the lives of her people.
But the monarch failed to listen to her pleas, and had, in
fact, kicked her and tossed her away from him. [104] The chronicler here defended the king's behavior by pointing out that
a woman's cry ought not divert a monarch from exercising
what he perceived would be his duty: "non oportet regalem
maiestatem fletu mulieris deterpuri." [105] The Hungarian
chronicler would not, however, hide the discouraging results
of King Coloman's foolish overconfidence displayed in his
Kievan expedition; the monarch had suffered a thorough
defeat, the chronicler says, at the hands of Mirkod, the Cuman
leader. [106]

The same chronicler depicted the defeat of Coloman and of his forces in stark terms; the chronicler hated the king, wanted to hurt his reputation. Undoubtedly, however, the king behaved foolishly and irresponsibly; he moved against Peremyshl without any plans and preparations. His Kievan campaign was very unlike the almost bloodless takeover of Croatia. At Kiev, Coloman had to meet a serious and well organized opposition; he had to fight — and lose — real battles.

In 1102, they crowned Coloman king of Croatia and Dalmatia at Bielograd,[107] and Coloman concluded a treaty with Emperor Alexius Comnenus of Byzantium concerning a military move against, and eventual capture of, Zara, the important and strongly fortified city on the seacoast.[108] In a hard and prolonged siege the king had taken Zara after he had promised the inhabitants of the Latin city that he would assure them full privileges under his administration. The king left a strong garrison behind in Zara, and moved against Trau, which surrendered without a fight. But Spaleto, next on the king's agenda of conquests on the seacoast decided to put up a fight when, according to the annotations of Thomas of Spaleto, the city's known chronicler, Coloman's troops began to devastate the hinterland of the city.[109] Thereupon, the city council of Spaleto accepted the peaceterms of the Hungarian king.

In the agreement Coloman promised that (1) Spaleto was to retain its autonomy under the Hungarian administration; (2) its citizens will be free as before to elect their church (archbishop) and secular leaders. (3) The citizens keep their customs and live under their own laws. (4) They pay no taxes except toll on imports and exports. Two-thirds of the toll goes to the Hungarian court, one-third to the royal reeve of Spaleto. The citizenry shall continue to pay the tithe for the upkeep of the Church. (5) No foreigner (no Hungarian!) may settle down in the city without the permission of the city council. (6) Those who do not like the new administration, may leave at any time. (7) If the king travelled in the direction of Spaleto, he was to take no lodging in the house of a Spaleto citizen.[110]

One has the impression that it was mainly a question of prestige, — that he may further irritate the Venetian republic,

— but no serious political interests that made Coloman to occupy Spaleto. [111] The terms offered by the king to Spaleto assured its citizens better political conditions that the ones they had enjoyed under the rule of Venice. [112] It is to be remembered, of course, that Coloman's charter granted to Spaleto is known only from the confirmed version of the royal charter of liberties given to the city of Trau in 1108, though the annotations of Thomas of Spaleto confirmed the terms of the Spaleto agreement. [113] Interestingly, Coloman's charter for Trau shows some strikingly similar features with the privileges granted by Henry I of England to the City of London. [114] After Spaleto, King Coloman took possession of the island near the coast; finally, the island of Arbe also surrendered to the king. [115]

The entire military operation and diplomatic tact displayed by the king in the Dalmatian cities show Coloman as a thoughtful and serious statesman. On his royal seal, the monarch sits on the throne in his royal robe with the crown on his head; the orb in his left, and the sceptre (or lance) in his right hand: "Colomannvs Dei gratia Vngar(orum) rex." [116] The seal is dated 1109, and it is attached to the charter the king had issued to confirm the privileges of the Byzantine religious women in Veszprém; the charter is the earliest document preserved in the Hungarian royal archives. [117]

The correctness of Coloman's foreign policy may be proven by the then developed political situation south of Hungary. On the grounds that Venice could not, at this time, count upon Byzantine support, the doge laid down his title as prince of Croatia and Dalmatia; and King Coloman, after the death of his Norman wife in 1108, and because of the Hungaro-Byzantine military alliance turned, in 1108, against the Norman Boemund of Sicily, had then broken into Byzantine territory on the Balkans. [118] It is the irony of the situation that Coloman participated in this anti-Norman campaign as the ally of the Byzantine emperor. Byzantine ships transported Hungarian troops across the Adriatic to Apulia, where Hungarian troops occupied the cities of Brundisi and Monopoli. For three months did the Hungarians war in Apulia, when they handed over the occupied area to Venice, and returned home. [119] Could it be that the transfer

of south-Italian (and formerly Byzantine held) territory to
the Venetian republic constituted the price for the back-
transport of Coloman's troops across the sea in Venetian
ships? [120]

In 1111, the king visited the Dalmatian seashore again.
He held an (his national) assembly together with the hierarchy
and nobles of the realm near Zara, where he took the oath
that he will preserve and respect the liberties and politico-
diplomatic integrity of the cities of Dalmatia; he will not
force ecclesiastical leaders upon the cities; he will, in fact,
renounce his right to confirm the bishops and abbots in their
church prebends and positions. The clergy in Dalmatia was
to enjoy the same privileges as the Hungarian clergy. [121] It
may, therefore, come as no surprise that in 1113, upon the
death of Archbishop Crescentius, they elected Manases, bishop
of Zagreb and a friend of King Coloman, as the archbishop
of Dalmatia. [122]


NOTES

1. See SSH, I, 227ff.; facsimile by D. Dercsényi (ed), Chronicon pictum:
Képes Krónika, 2 vols. (Budapest, 1963), vol. I, and its review by Gy. Rónay in
Vigilia, 30 (1965), 44ff.; on its mid-fourteenth century background, cf. D. Dercsényi,
Nagy Lajos kora (The age of Lewis the Great) (Budapest, n.d.), 61ff.; G. Stadtmüller, "Die ungarische Grossmacht des Mittelalters," HJb, 70 (1951), 151ff.;
E. Mályusz, Egyházi társadalom a középkori Magyarországon (Eccl. social structure
in medieval Hungary) (Budapest, 1971), 305ff.; idem, A Thuróczy Krónika és
forrásai (Thuróczy Chronicle and its sources) (Budapest, 1967), 57f. and 61ff.;
Gy. Bónis, A jogtudó értelmiség a Mohács előtti Magyarországon (Judicial Hungarian intelligentsia prior to 1526) (Budapest, 1971), 29ff., on the royal Chapel
and Chancery. Chronicon Budense: Budai Krónika, facsimile edition, with an
introduction by V. Fraknói (Budapest, 1900); a new edition received poor reception (Budapest, 1973); cf. G. Borsa in MKSz, 89 (1973), and ITK, 78 (1974), 263ff.

2. Macartney, 111ff., and 133ff.; J. Horváth, 255ff.; C. Horváth, 26ff.; L. J.
Csóka, A latin nyelvű történeti irodalom kialakulása Magyarországon a XI-XIV
században (Development of Latin language historical literature in Hungary during
the 11th through the 14th centuries) (Budapest, 1967) 513ff., and 527ff.; my article in Church History, 46 (1977), 44ff., appendix.

3. J. Horváth, 270ff., and 280ff.; H. Marczali, Ungarns Geschichtsquellen
im Zeitalter der Árpáden (Berlin, 1882), 68ff.; J. Gerics, Legkorábbi gesta szerkesztéseinknek keletkezésrendjének problémái (Questions concerning the chronology
of the editing of the Hungarian gesta) (Budapest, 1981), 88ff.

4. Chronicon pictum, c. 166.

5. "Cui nuncius ait, quoniam magistri nostri sic interpretantur, ut adulterinam
progeniem ecclesia non communicat;" SSH, I, 459,34-38; W. Plöchl, Geschichte
des Kirchenrechts, vol. II (Vienna, 1955), 431ff.

6. *Chronicon pictum*, c. 143.

7. *SSH*, I, 418ff.; J. Horváth, 277; "were the reader to know more about Ladislas, he should consult the king's *gesta*," wrote the compiler — *SSH*, I, 420,5-9.

8. *SSH*, I, 461ff.; J. Horváth, 279f.; for a different opinion, cf. Hóman-Szekfű, I, 297ff.; for a comparative background, see B. Smalley, *Historians in the Middle Ages* (New York, 1975), 79ff., and A. Gransden, *Historical Writing in England, 550-1307* (Ithaca, NY, 1974), 186ff.

9. *SSH*, I, 419,6-8.

10. *Chronicon pictum*, c. 150.

11. *SSH*, I, 419,8-12, and 421S,2-12.

12. *Chronicon pictum*, c. 143.

13. *Ibid.*, cc. 169 *and* 164.

14. As, e.g., *SSH*, I, 421,17-31.

15. Hóman-Szekfű, I, 326; Hóman, *Ungarisches Mittelalter*, I, 337 — in ref. to Bertholdi *Annales*, anno 1078, *MGHSS*, V, 311, and the *Annales Augustani*, anno 1096, *ibid.*, III, 135. The same source also recorded an earthquake in Hungary in the year 1092: "in provintia Ungarorum una die, VI Kal. Julii, ter terraemotus factus est urbesque submersae sunt;" *ibid.* The date was June 26, 1092. On Berthold, see W. Wattenbach, *Deutschlands Geschichtsschreiber im Mittelalter*, 2 vols.; 6th rev. ed. (Berlin, 1893-94), II, 53ff.

16. Cf. C. Erdmann (ed), *Deutsches Mittelalter: die Briefe Heinrichs IV* (Leipzig, 1937), 32ff., No.23; K. Langosch, *Die Briefe Kaiser Heinrichs IV* (Munster-Cologne, 1954), 66ff.; R. Benson (ed), *Imperial Lives and Letters of the Eleventh Century* (New York-London, 1962), 170f., n. 105, where the editor rendered the wrong translation: Coloman and Álmos were the nephews and not the sons of King Ladislas; "Ladislao autem migrato regnavit post eum filius Geichae regis, Kolomannus." Cf. Simon de Keza, *Gesta Ungarorum*, c. 64, *SSH*, I, 182.

17. *Ibid.*, I, 439,25-28 (*Chron. pict.*, c. 156); Gy. Moravcsik, "Les relations entre la Hongrie et Byzance a l'époque des croisades," *Studia byzantina* (Budapest, 1967), 315. See also, Iohannes Zonaras, *Epitomae historiarum* (ed. Th. Büttner), viii:24 (Bonn, 1897), 748,1-3; or, in J. P. Migne (ed), *Patrologiae cursus completus, series graeca*, 161 vols. in 166 (Paris, 1857-66), cited hereafter as *MPG*, 135, 309f.; also, Iohannes Cinnamus, *Epitomae rerum ab Iohanne et Manuele Comnenis gestarum* (ed. A. Meineke), i:4 (Bonn, 1836), 9,23-10,8; and 31,12-13; or, *MPG*, 133, 317f.

18. Cf. Emperor Manuel's *Novellae constitutiones*, c. xvi, *MPG*, 133, 773f.

19. *SSH*, I, 419,24-29; on Marcellus, see alsó Fejér, *CD*, II, 56.

20. *SSH*, I, 380,7-12.

21. *Ibid.*, I, 355f. (c. 93).

22. *Ibid.*, I, 355f., and 380,10-14 (c. 114).

23. "Ladislaus autem sic ordinavit, ut post eum ipsum Almos regnaret;" *ibid.*, I, 419,30-32. Royal dignity was not a king's birth-right, wrote Manegold of Leutenbach *ad Gebehardum*, in E. Dümmler (ed), *MGH Libelli de lite*, 3 vols. (Hannover, 1891-97), cited hereafter as *LdL*, I, 300f.

24. *SSH*, I, 418,7-20.

25. *Ibid.*, I, 418,20-27; II, 521f. (Ladislas *Vita*, c. 7).

26. "... ab episcopo Pragensi in solio ducali sedit;" *ibid.*, I, 418,19-20.

27. *Ibid.*, I, 419,16-18.

28. Coloman "nocte secessit in Poloniam, audiens quod pater eius et avus Polonie honorifice suscepti essent. ... Rex autem congregato exercitu suo cepit ire contra Bohemos propter iniuriam nepotis sui;" *ibid.*, I, 419,13-16, and 419,18-21.

29. *Ibid.*, I, 419,23-24.

30. "Convocatisque principibus suis ad Colomanum nuncios misit;" *ibid.*, I, 419,24-26, and *Vita s. Ladislai*, c. 7, *ibid.*, II, 522,3-6.

31. "Ladizlaus sic ordinavit, ut post ipsum Almos regnaret;" *SSH*, I, 419,30-32.

32. According to his *Vita*, it had to be on his deathbed: "dum iam regredi cogitaret, egritudine repentina correptus...;" *ibid.*, II, 522,3-4.

33. " ... tamquam cui iure primogeniture videbatur competere;" *ibid.*, I, 420,3-5.

34. *Chron. pict.*, c. 142; *Annales Posonienses*, anno 1098, *ibid.*, I, 126,18-19.

35. "Geysa genuit Colomanum et Almum et filias;" *ibid.*, I, 365,8.

36. "... eum communi consensu ... ad suscipiendum regni gubernaculum concorditer elegerunt;" *ibid.*, I, 403f.

37. *Chron. pict.*, c. 92.

38. *Ibid.*, I, 358,4-6.

39. *Ibid.*, I, 420,5-9.

40. C.f. Letter of Pope Urban II to King Coloman, dated July 27, 1096, *MPL*, 151, 481a.

41. Cf. Marczali, *Enchiridion*, 101, document of 1091; Szentpétery, *Regesta*, I, no.24; Fraknói, I, 29.

42. *MPL*, 151, 481ab.

43. Cf. Martinus Gallus, *Chronicon Polonorum*, ii:29, in *MGHSS* IX, 456.

44. *SSH*, I, 420,34-37, and I, 432f. (c. 152); Haller, II, 430ff., and 612f.

45. "... et duci Almus ducatum plenarie concessit;" *SSH*, I, 420f.

46. *Ibid.*, I, 421,3-5; and I, 420S,25-421S,12.

47. Keza, c. 64, *ibid.*, I, 182f.

48. *Ibid.*, I, 432f. (*Chron. pict.*, c. 152).

49. "... libros habebat, in quibus horas canonicas ut episcopus persolvebat;" *ibid.*, I, 433,1-2. "Reges a recte agendo vocati sunt; ideoque recte faciendo regis nomen obtinetur, peccando omittitur," wrote Ivo of Chartres, *Decretum*, xvi:39, in *MPL*, 161, 912b.; also, Ivo's *Panormia*, viii:59, *ibid.*, 161, 1316c; R. Sprandel, *Ivo von Chartres und seine Stellung in der Kirchengeschichte* (Stuttgart, 1962), 64ff.

50. Cf. Gransden, 170f., on William Rufus; C. W. Bynum, "Did the Twelfth Century Discover the Individual?" *Journal of Ecclesiastical History*, 31 (1980), 1ff.; Gerics, 110ff.

51. *MPL*, 151, 480d-481a; Becker, 167.

52. *MPL*, 151, 481ab; M. Maccarone, "Die Cathedra Petri im Hochmittelalter: vom Symbol des päpstlichen Amtes zum Kultobjekt *Römische Quartalschrift*, 76 (1981), 137ff.

53. Nulla te pseudoapostolorum qui eorum ecclesiam invaserunt, venena corrumpant; nulla perversitas a vera religione seducat; *ibid.*, 151, 481b.

54. "Quid etiam in Heinricum huiusce iniquitatis et praesumptionis auctorem divinae maiestatis iustitia operata sit et operetur," wrote the pontiff to the monarch, "ad tuam existimamus notitiam pervenisse." Cf. *ibid.*, 151, 481c.

55. *SSH*, I, 182f.; I. Kapitánffy, "Magyar-bizánci kapcsolatok Szent László és Kálmán uralkodása idejében (Hungaro-Byzantine relations during the reigns of St. Ladislas and Coloman)," *Acta historica Szegediensis*, 75 (1983), 19ff.

56. *SSH*, I, 432f.; A. A. Vasiliev, *History of the Byzantine Empire* (Madison, Wisc., 1952), 412f.

57. H. E. Mayer, *Geschichte der Kreuzzüge*, 3rd ed. (Stuttgart, 1973), 13ff.; M. W. Baldwin, *Raymond III of Tripolis and the Fall of Jerusalem* (Princeton, 1937), 143.

58. K. Hampe, *Das Hochmittelalter*, 5th ed. (Cologne-Graz, 1963), 139ff.

58a. On Byzantine reaction, see Anna Comnena, *Alexiad*, vi:11 ed. A. Reifferscheid, 2 vols. (Leipzig, 1884), vi:11, or, in *MPG*, 131, 79ff.; Chalandon, 242.

59. It ought to be pointed out that Gerbert wrote the letter before he became pope, and he only requested love and support of Christians living in Islamic areas; cf. T. Havet (ed), *Lettres de Gerbert, 983-997* (Paris, 1889), 22, no. 3: H. Sybel, *Geschichte des ersten Kreuzzuges*, 2nd ed. (Leipzig, 1881), 458f.

59a. C. Erdmann, "Die Aufrufe Gerberts und Sergius IV für das Hl. Land," *Quellen und Forschungen aus italienischen Archiven und Bibliotheken*, 23 (1931-32), 1ff.; A. Gyeysztor, "The Genesis of the Crusades: the encyclica of Sergius IV," *Medievalia et humanistica*, 5 (1948), 3ff. and 6 (1950), 3ff.

60 .Cf. *Fundatio ecclesiae s. Albani Namucensis*, anno 1047, *MGHSS*, XV-2, 963f.; G. Ostrogorsky, *Geschichte des byzantinischen Staates*, 2nd ed. (Munich, 1952), 248f.; my book, 22f.

61. Cf. I. Bekker (ed), J. Scylitzes-G. Cedrenus, *Historiarum compendium* (Bonn, 1839), II, 457ff.

62. Cf. Ph. Jaffé (ed), *Regesta pontificum Romanorum*, 2 vols. (Leipzig, 1885), I, no. 4826 (3587); E. Caspar (ed), *Das Register Gregors VII, MGHEpp. sel.* II, 2 vols. (Berlin, 1920-1923), I, i:49; C. Erdmann, *Die Entstehung des Kreuzzugsgedankens* (Stuttgart, 1935), 149; and, Comnena, *Alexiad*, i:13,2-7.

63. Erdmann, *Entstehung*, 296ff.; W. Holtzmann, "Studien zur Orientenpolitik des Reformpapsttums und zur Entstehung des ersten Kreuzzges," *Historische Vierteljahrschrift*, 22 (1924-25), 167ff.

64. See Bernoldi *Annales*, a. 1075, *MGHSS*, V, 430f.; Bertholdi *Annales*, a. 1078, *ibid.*, V, 308f.; Caspar, *Register*, II, 372, v:14-15; documentation also in M. Doeberl (ed), *Monumenta Germaniae selecta*, vol. III (Munich, 1889), 16ff.; W. Goetz, "Zur Persönlichkeit Gregors VII," *Römische Quartalschrift*, 73 (1978), 193ff.; K. Hampe, *Deutsche Kaisergeschichte in der Zeit der Salier und Staufer*, 12th ed. ed. F. Baethgen (Heidelberg, 1968), 56ff.

65. Cf. H. Hagenmeyer (ed), Fulcher von Chartres, *Gesta Francorum Iherusalem peregrinantium* (Heidelberg, 1913), 130ff.; also, *MPL*, 155, 831f., i:2. On the Council of Clermont, cf. Mansi, *Concilia*, XX, 824ff.; on Fulcher, D. C. Munro, "A Crusader," *Speculum*, 7 (1932), 321ff.

66. Bernoldi *Chronicon*, a. 1095, *MGHSS*, V, 462; P. Charanis, "Byzantium, the West and the Origin of the First Crusade," *Byzantion*, 19 (1949), 17ff.; D. C. Munro, "Did the Emperor Alexios I Ask for Aid at the Council of Piacenza?" *American Historical Review*, 27 (1922), 731ff.

67. A. Fliché, *Le regne de Philippe Ier, roi de France* (Paris, 1912), bk. IV; J. F. Lemarignier, *Le government royal aux premiers temps Capétiens, 987-1108* (Paris, 1965), 141ff.; also, 153; A. Luchaire, *Louis VI le Gros, annales de sa vie et de son regne* (Paris, 1890), 1xvf.

68. As, for example, Baudri of Dol, *Historia Jerosolimitana*, bk. I, *Recueil des historiens des croisades*, 16 vols. (Paris, 1841-1906): *Historiens occidentaux*, 5 vols. (Paris, 1844-95), cited hereafter as *RHC Occ.*, IV, 12ff.; Robert the Monk, *Historia Iherosolimitana*, i:1, *ibid.*, III, 727f.; or, *MPL*, 155, 667ff.; D. C. Munro, "The Speech of Pope Urban II at Clermont," *American Historical Review*, 11 (1906), 231ff.

69. Fulcher, *Gesta*, i:4; William of Malmesbury, *De gestis regum Anglorum*, iv:2, R.S., 2 vols. (London, 1887-89), II, 393ff.

70. Comnena, *Alexiad*, x:5-6; Hampe, *Hochmittelalter*, 151; P. Mass, "Die Musen des Kaisers Alexios I," *Byzantinische Zeitschrift*, 22 (1913), 348ff., esp. quote on 357f.; C. Neumann *Griechische Geschichtsschreiber und Geschichts-*

*quellen im zwölften Jahrhundert* (Leipzig, 188), 28, referred to the *Alexiad* as "a noble document."

71. Bernoldi *Chronicon*, anno 1095, *MGHSS*, V, 461; Hampe, *Hochmittelalter*, 146f.; M. W. Baldwin, "Some Recent Interpretation of Pope Urban's Eastern Policy," *Catholic Historical Review*, 25 (1940), 459ff.

72. Guibert of Nogent, *Historia quae dicitur Gesta Dei per Francos*, ii:4, *RHC Occ.*, IV, 137ff.; *MPL*, 166, 705f.; Fulcher, *Gesta*, i:3; A. C. Krey, "Urban's Crusade: Success or Failure?" *American Historical Review* 53 (1948), 235ff.; A. Fliché, "Urban II et la croisade," *Revue de l'histoire de l'église de France*, 13 (1927), 289ff.; also, B. Leib, *Rome, Kiev et Byzance à la fin du XIme siècle* (Paris, 1924), 180ff.

73. Ekkehardi Uraugensis *Hierosolymita*, in H. Hagenmeyer, *Ekkehard von Aura* (Leipzig, 1888), 122ff.; *MGHSS*, VI, 208.

74. Cf. H. Hagenmeyer (ed), Anonymi *Gesta Francorum et aliorum Hierosolymitanorum* (Heidelberg, 1890), 106ff.; *RHC Occ.*, III, 119ff.; Nogent, *Historia*, ii:8; William of Tyre, *Historia rerum in partibus transmarinis gestarum*, i:18, *MPL*, 201, 237f.; *RHC Occ.*, I.

75. Cf. Nogent, *Historia*, i:7, and the negative view of Meyer, *Kreuzzüge*, 48f.; William of Tyre, i:14.

76. *Chronicon pictum*, c. 143, *SSH*, I, 421f.; Albert of Aix, *Liber Christianae expeditionis pro ereptione, emundatione et restitutione sanctae Hierosolymitanae ecclesiae*, i:7, *MPL*, 166, 392f.; *RHC Occ.*, IV, 265ff.; on Albert of Aachen (=Auensis), see Wattenbach, II, 178ff.

77. "Deinde marchiam illam totam devastabant propter victum, et quicquid rapere poterant, ad castrum portabant;" *SSH*, I, 422,16-20.

78. Albert of Aix, *Liber*, i:7-8; Nogent, *Historia*, ii:8; William of Tyre, *Historia*, i:19; R. Hiestand, "Zum Leben und zur Laufbahn Wilhelms von Tyrus,"*Deutsches Archiv*, 34 (1978),345ff.

79. Albert of Aix, *Liber*, i:25; William of Tyre, *Historia*, i:27.

80 Idem, i:30; Albert of Aix, i:29.

81. Idem, *Liber*, ii:1-7; William of Tyre, *Historia*, ii:1-3.

82. Cf. Thomas Spalatensis *Historia pontificum Spalatensium*, c. 17, *MGHSS*, XXIX, 570ff.; or, in I. G. Schwandtner (ed), *Scriptores rerum Hungaricarum veteres ac genuini*, 3 vols. (Vienna, 1746-48), III, 532ff. Alexius I was afraid of a possible Hungarian attack; cf. Raimundus de Agiles, *Historia Francorum*, c. 3, *MPL*, 155, 295; Keza, c. 64; *Chronicon pictum*, c. 152.

83. See *Vita s. Iohannis Ursini episcopi Traguriensis*, i:4-6, in D. Farlati (ed), *Illyrici sacri*, vols. III-IV (Venice, 1765-1775), IV, 313f.

84. *Chronicon pictum*, c. 142.

85. Spalato, *Historia*, c. 17; the monarch had established Hungarian settlements at the estuary of the Kulpa into the Save - cf. Anonymus, *Gesta Ungarorum*, c. 43, in *SSH*, I, 87f.

86. Spalato, *Historia*, c. 17.

87. *SSH*, I, 433,3-9.

88. Cf. Ekkehardi Uraugensis *Chronica universale*, a. 1096, in *MGHSS*, VI, 212; also, *MPL*, 154, 497ff.; idem, *Hierosolymita*, c. 23, in *MGHSS*, VI, 208. Otto of Freising, *Chronica de duabus civitatibus*, vii:2, *ibid.*, XX, 248.

89. See Robert the Monk (Robertus Remensis), *Historia*, II, 2; on the sojourn of Frankish crusaders and their friendly reception in Hungary; also, Ekkehard, *Chronica*, anno 1101, *MGHSS*, VI, 220; on Ekkehard, cf. Wattenbach, II, 189ff.; further, G. Hahn, *Die abendländische Kirche im Mittelalter* (Freiburg i. Br., 1942), 353ff.; H. Jedin (ed), *Handbuch der Kirchengeschichte*, vol. III-1: *Die mittelal-*

terliche Kirche, vom kirchlichen Frühmittelalter zur Gregorianischen Reform (Freiburg-Vienna, 1973), 506ff.

90. Cf. SSH, II, 401ff.; on Harduin alias Hartvic, see J. Horváth, A magyar irodalmi műveltség kezdetei (Beginnings of Hungarian literary culture), 2nd ed. (Budapest, 1944), 311, and Z. Tóth, A Hartvik legenda kritikájához (An appraisal of Hartvic's Life of King St. Stephen) (Budapest, 1942), 5ff., to argue that Hartvic was not the bishop of Győr, but the abbot of Hersfeld.

90a. Coloman's marriage plans had no anti-Byzantine tendencies; Roger I of Sicily was the archenemy of Bohemund of Antioch; cf. Chalandon, I, 288, and 294f.

91. See Gufredus Malaterra, Historia Sicula ab 887 usque ad 1099, in Muratori, Scriptores, V, 599f., iv:25.

92. Otto of Freising, Gesta Friderici imperatoris, i:31, MGHSS, XX, 369.

93. Ut supra, note 91.

94. Cf. SSH, I, 426,7-10; Ladislas death, ibid., I, 428,10-12.

95. Ibid., I, 183-4-11; Andreas Dandalo, Chronicon Venetum, libri decem, ix:10:11, in Muratori, Scriptores, XII, 259.

96. Cf. Vita Iohannis Ursini, i:6-7, in D. Farlati, Illyrici sacri, IV, 314f.; Coloman's charter, anno 1108, RHM, II, 376f.

97. "Post haec autem rex gloriosus invasit Rusciam;" SSH, I, 423,31-32, and compare with I, 414,28-29; S. H. Cross et al (ed), The Russian Primary Chronicle (Cambridge, Mass. 1953), 187f., anno 1097; A. Hodinka, Az orosz évkönyvek magyar vonatkozásai (Information concerning Hungary in the Russian annals) (Budapest, 1916), 54Aff., anno 1097.

98. Cosmas of Prague, Chronicae Bohemorum libri III, iii:9 (anno 1099), MGHSS, IX, 104; on Cosmas, see Wattenbach, II, 203ff. F. Palacky, Geschichte von Böhmen, vol. I (repr. Prague, 1844), 335ff.

99. Cf. SSH, I, 424,21-32; I, 425,2-3; Cross, Russian Chronicle, a. 1097, 196f., and repeated anno 1099, 198; Hodinka, 75ff., 58Bff., a. 1099; 60Aff., 62Bf., 66A.

100. Cf. Annales Posonienses, anno 1100 (!), SSH, I, 126: "Cupanus episcopus interficitur a Chunis et Laurentius episcopus obiit." P. Radó, Libri liturgici manu scripti bibliothecarum Hungariae (Budapest, 1947), 40, in discussing the Pray codex, ff. 9-9', referred to it as Chronicon Posoniense.

101. SSH, I, 414f.; Zonaras, Epitomae historiarum, xviii:23.

102. SSH, I, 424f.

103. Ibid., I, 425,24-28.

104. Ibid., I, 423f.

105. Ibid., I, 424,10-12.

106. Ibid., I, 425,3-23.

107. Chronicon pictum, c. 146; Marczali, Enchiridion, 126; RHM, II, 376f.

108. Zonaras, Epitomae historiarum, xviii:24; Moravcsik, Bizánci források, 186f.; the campanile of S. Maria church in Zara built by King Coloman in 1105, has the inscription:

> Anno Incar Dni Nri Jhu Cri Mil CV.
> Post victoriam et pacis praemia
> Jadrae introitus a Deo concessa
> Proprio sumptu hanc turrim
> Scae Mariae Ungariae Dalmatiae
> Croatiae construi et erigi
> Jussit rex Colomannus.

Cf. K. Albinioni, Memorie per la storia della Dalmazia, vol. II (Zara, 1809), 13.

109.  Cf. Th. Spalatensis *Historia*, c. xviii.

110.  Szentpétery, *Regesta*, I, n. 41; Marczali, *Enchiridion*, 125ff.

111.  In spite of the fact that earlier, in 1097, he already concluded friendly relations with Michael Vitalis, Doge of Venice — see Szentpétery, *Regesta*, I, nn. 35 and 36; G. Wenczel (ed), *Árpádkori új okmánytár* (A new collection of documents of the Arpadian age), 12 vols. (Pest, 1860-74), *XI, 32f.*

112.  Cf. *Chronicon Venetum* auctore Anonymo, libri V, *MGHSS*, XIV, 73; Dandalo, Chronicon Venetum, ix:9,8, and ix:11,15-17, Muratori, *Scriptores*, XII, 252 and 264f.

113.  Spalatensis *Historia*, c. xviii.

114.  See W. Stubbs (ed), *Select Charters of English Constitutional History* (Oxford, 1895), 107ff.

115.  Dandalo, *Chronicon*, ix:11,16.

116.  Cf. St. Katona, *Historia critica regum Hungariae, stirpis Arpadianae*, 7 1779-82 vols. (Budae, 1778-1801), III, 263.

117.  Cf. Szentpétery, *Regesta*, I, no. 42; Jakubovich-Pais, *ÓMO*, 14ff.

118.  Dandalo, *Chronicon*, ix:10:11, in Muratori, XII, 259; also, *Historia ducum Veneticorum*, cc. 1 and 2, *MGHSS*, XIV, 72ff.; Chalandon, I, 242.

119.  *Chronicon pictum*, c. 152; Keza, c. 64.

120.  Cf. Farlati, IV, 315; Marczali, *Enchiridion*, 125ff.

121.  Szentpétery, *Regesta*, I, no. 45; Wenczel, *Új Okmánytár*, I, 43.

122.  Spalato, *Historia*, c. 18.

# II

# The Investiture Controversy in the Background of King Coloman's First Legislative Assembly

Regni principibus congregatis, tocius senatus
consultu, prefati regis sanctae memoriae Stephani
legalem textum recensuit.

*Decretum Colomanni regis*

The first great confrontation between the Church and the empire ended in 1106 with the death of the German monarch, Henry IV. The problem came to rest for about half a century, but the peace was of short duration.[1] There began a new rivalry for religious and political predominance that had its origins in the previous race, though was not directly connected with it. One has in mind the struggle that ended in 1122, competition between the pope and lay investiture which, in its beginnings, can be traced back to the guidelines laid down by Pope Gregory VII in his *Dictatus papae*.[2] Actually, one can speak of two such confrontations: first, the clash between Gergory VII and Henry IV over the role of *regnum* and *sacerdotium*;[3] and, last, the German policy formulated by Henry V and his advisors concerning lay investiture, — a policy whose viewpoint had some similarity with that of Henry I of England who, at least during the early years of his reign, tolerated no papal interference in appointments to the English hierarchy,[4] — to the effect that the emperor alone designated and invested his bishops in the empire.[5] And yet, by 1106, Henry V had entered, with the consent of his nobles, into an agreement with the papacy on the grounds that in the recent past it was the co-operation of the nobility with the Roman See that had caused public humiliation for his father, the emperor Henry IV.[6] It served the interests of the new German monarch that he was 25, and had participated in the government of the empire since he was 17. He lived in peace with his nobility during the first years of his reign; he tried very hard not to oppose any of them, or members of the hierarchy. [7]

Pope Urban II held church synods regularly in order to assure himself of a reliable ecclesiastical government (both in Rome and at the regional level). He maintained good working relations with religious and political leaders in Rome, northern Italy and in the Frankish kingdom; in fact, the king of the Franks had voluntarily renounced his right to invest churchmen with ring and staff. [8] Thereby the pontiff avoided confrontation with the Frankish monarch, nor had he have any need for negotiating a concordat with that realm. At the same time, however, the Frankish episcopate took its feudal oath of loyalty to Philip I. [9] The situation that high churchmen continued to do homage to temporal rulers disturbed the pope: that may be why the resolutions reached at the synods of Clermont, 1095, [10] — renewed at the synod at Rome in 1099, aimed at loosening relations between churchmen and temporal rulers. [11] Anselm of Canterbury was at any rate a participant of the Roman Synod of 1099, and upon his return to England he refused to ordain English bishops who previously had been invested by the English king, or had performed homage to Henry I. [12]

During the pontificate of Paschal II, the only change that occurred in England was that the king made concessions concerning investitute. The Roman See proposed what it considered to be a provisional solution at first, but the English monarch accepted it as a permanent agreement. This meant that King Henry I had kept his right to nominate English bishops and to have the bishops to do homage to him — before their consecration. On the other hand, he relinquished his prerogative of investing the ecclesiastics with ring and staff. [13] Still, the English example had not influenced the German court; Henry V had no desire to grant any concessions; he had insisted that, instead, it was his imperial privilege to name bishops. The imperial hierarchy and the nobles supported him, with the result that where the English monarch had made concessions to the Church, the German ruler had said no its demands. [14]

It is interesting to note the countermeasures taken by Pope Paschal II in this regard; between 1107 and 1108, he had excommunicated every German bishop who had ignored his admonitions and failed to take a stand on the investiture issue. [15] The pontiff in his dealing with the German bishops made, however, a tactical error by permitting the imperial coronation of the stubborn Henry V. [16] The papal consent meant that Henry V now could go to Italy with an army and, because he was going to attend his own coronation, could take his supporters and nobles with him; and, the pontiff had to face alone the hostile majority of opponents in the City. [17]

In order to remedy the situation the pontiff had worked out a new plan. [18] On the grounds that Henry V invested his churchmen with ring and staff, and handed over to them only the temporal administration of their offices, the pope now had ordered that all ecclesiastics renounce their temporal offices and landholdings held from the emperor. Eventually, the ruler may change his mind and renounce the investiture as useless. The Church can live on the tithe paid conscientiously by the faithful, and the bishops can, therefore, be free of their temporal obligations. [19]

The plan of the pontiff could not be realized. The politico-social order of the day rested upon the idea that the Church had to (and has) fulfill(ed) a secular function. Were the papal plan to succeed (1) the nobles would lose their control of over the Church; [20] (2) the bishops themselves — mostly politicians and military leaders —, would lose influence over public affairs, thereby making themselves defenseless against their secular opposition. [21] (3) The ruler would have to place his constitutional position and political power upon a new foundation. [22]

It is, therefore, understandable that when in St. Peter's basilica they had publicly announced the papal-German agreement signed three days earlier at Sutri, on February 12, 1111, there broke out a well organized tumult in the basilica, during which imperial troops surrounded the pontiff and the cardinals, in order to "protect" them, actually to conduct them out of Rome to the camp of the German king; there the pope and the cardinals accepted the demands of the German court. [23]

Pope Paschal II had agreed to the imperial coronation of Henry V under the condition that lay investiture of the bishop-elect by the king had to take place before the church-

man's ecclesiastical consecration. The affair ended with the
compliance of Henry V with the Holy See, — and with the
simultaneous humiliation of the pontiff. As it was to be forseen, the contemporary Frankish and Roman church re-
formers now turned against the pope. [24] And Paschal II by
revoking under pressure from his reform-group, the conses-
sions he had made to Henry V, had lost for good the respect
and good will of the German court which relied heavily upon
the services of the lay *ministeriales* and the hierarchy. [25] The
only condition that saved the Holy See from complete humiliation was that the German cities held a split opinion in this
matter, and their very shaky territorial cohesion began to fall
apart at this time. The German "south" wanted more political and economic freedom for its cities. [26] It may have been
no coincidence that Agnes, the sister of the emperor, had,
upon the death of her first husband — the margrave of Swabia
—, married Leopold of Austria, as if to establish a good
neighbor policy on the eastern Bavarian frontier, and to build
lasting ties with the court of Bohemia. [27]

In order to strengthen his power base at home, Henry V
needed the support of the duke os Saxony. When the daughter
of Magnus Billing, duke of Saxony, married Henry the Black,
heir of Bavaria, Henry V made Lothair of Supplinburg duke
of Saxony upon Billing's death. Duke Lothair did not, however, tolerate any interference from the court in his regional
affairs and became the sole master of and in Saxon politics,
a position never achieved, or held, by Billing. [28] And yet,
from among the dukes of Saxony, Swabia and Bavaria, only
Frederick of Swabia proved loyal to Henry V; Archbishop
Adalbert of Mainz, the imperial chancellor, was too ambitious a churchman, who constantly intrigued against the
emperor in the political circles of Saxony. [29] After he had
twice been defeated by the Saxon nobles and fled to Mainz,
the citizens of Mainz forced him to make peace with the
archbishop. [30] Perhaps it was his personal humiliation that
had caused Henry V to remain firmly opposed to Rome, and
when he visited the City in 1116, Paschal II could not bring
himself to receive the king, nor to crown him emperor. [31] He
was crowned by the archbishop of Braga who had been excommunicated because of the crowning, — the same archbishop who became anti-pope Gregory VIII in 1118. [32]

During the pontificate of Callixt II the question of investiture began to clear up; Callixt II, in his decree issued at Reims, emphasized the point of view that church buildings and landholdings did not come under lay investiture, thereby to ignore an earlier promise of Henry V that the emperor would surrender lay investiture of church edifices. [33] The pontiff went, in fact, a step further by pronouncing anew the excommunication of both the emperor and his anti-pope. In 1118, the German hierarchy led by Adalbert of Mainz took up position against the emperor, though without the support of the nobles. Among the latter was Henry the Black of Bavaria who stressed the need for working out a relationship with the Holy See. [34] The forceful attitude displayed by the duke and members of the hierarchy had a positive effect: Lampert, archbishop of Ostia (later Pope Honorius II), headed a papal delegation to Worms that on September 23, 1122, concluded a concordat between the court and the Roman See, thus officially ending the excommunication of the emperor. [35]

According to this agreement (1) the German ruler renounced lay investiture with ring and staff; (2) permitted canonical election of bishops (and abbots), and the ordination of churchmen; (3) promised to restore confiscated ecclesiastical property and to assure legal security to all church holdings. On the other hand, (a) the election of German bishops (and abbots) had to occure in the presence of the emperor's personal representative who in a crisis situation could intervene in the election; (b) the ruler had the right to interfere in the secular administration of church affairs, and (c) the bishop-elect had to, before his ordination, take the oath of loyalty to the imperial court. [36] In other words, the monarch may have surrendered lay investiture, but he had kept the administration of ecclesiastical property at his discretion; in fact, he continued to influence the outcome of canonical elections in the Church. [37] (In case of the Worms settlement, there are two documents; one, the imperial deed, preserved in the papal archives; and, two, the papal deed. Both documents represent their own versions of the understanding that had just been reached. The papal deed is very brief and simple — almost a postscriptum note to the effect that its concessions were granted only for the lifetime of Henry

V; upon his death, they ceased to be valid. [38] ) The assembly of high churchmen and nobles gathering at Bamberg in November, 1122, had ratified the concordat; and Pope Callixt II acknowledged its validity during the First Lateran Synod held in March, 1123. [39]

It was this papal-imperial confrontation, followed by a partial papal victory, that had formed the political background of Coloman the Learned's first serious legislative session. His predecessor's to the contrary, and on account of his being a bishop, King Coloman had pursued a policy friendly toward the Roman See, in order to counterbalance, — during the first decade of the twelfth century, — any investiture politics.

Until the Worms Settlement nobody could foresee the outcome of the struggle. The papal plan based upon compromises proved to be too weak at a time when the English island realm and the Frankish king had already clarified their position(s) on the question of investiture in their fields of church policy. From the east, Coloman under no circumstances would embarrass Rome. The laws of Tarcal, more correctly, the enactments resulting from his first legislative assembly, complete: place a roof on, the construction of Hungarian kingship, its institution formulated in accordance with the principles of Roman Christianity, that is, recognizing the spiritual primacy of the Roman pontiff. This is why the king had legislated himself at Tarcal, together with his nobles and the entire Senate, and had, "communi consilio," promulgated the results of that legislation. And that is the reason why, in his first legislative session, he had dealt with church and temporal interests alike. [40]

King Coloman had modified the law codes of Stephen I, and softened somewhat the tone of the legal enactments of Ladislas I. [41] In the beginning of his reign he had held his first legislative assembly at Tarcal near Aszód, attended by his nobles. [42] The decrees agreed upon during this assembly were recorded by a clergyman named Alberic(us), a participant himself, for the personal benefit of Archbishop Seraphim of Esztergom. [43] The remark by Alberic recorded in his transcript, that he did not know Hungarian too well,[44] so his transcript was (may) not (be) very accurate, may imply that discussions in the gathering were held not in Latin, but in Hungarian. [45]

Legislation assured and increased the income and holdings of the Hungarian monarch; for instance, they decided
that ecclesiastical landholdings granted by Stephen I were
to remain in the hands of the Church (churchmen), [46] though
donations given by Stephen I's successors were not to be regarded as permanent donations. [47] Excessive fishery rights
were actually reclaimed by the monarch on the grounds that
such privileges were to benefit only the immediate needs of
a cathedral chapter, or those of a monastic community. [48]

The assembly handled also the problem of land inheritance. Titles of landholdings dating back to the reign of King
Stephen I were to be inherited by the title holder's son, or
his brother, and (or) his direct descendants. Distant relatives of the title holder may not (or, may) inherit, but without proof of a direct descendant, the king may reclaim the
grant (of land, or of office). [49] This restriction concerned
mainly titled land-grants dating back to earlier times; it was
not applicable to purchased land and (eventually) inherited
land. [50]

The assembly recognized and defended the inheritance
of (possessory) rights of the free peasantry; a peasant who
had been forced off his titled landholding was to regain it,
unless he already possessed holdings somewhere else. [51] Evidently, the king and his nobles in the assembly did not tolerate plurality of landholdings, nor the possible use connected with it. If someone usurped someone else's land, he
had to surrender a similar size (amount) of land of his own
to the defendant, in addition to the land he had lawfully
taken, and to pay a fine: ten *pensa(e)*, to the king. [52]

From the text transcribed by Alberic it is evident that
the cultivators and the people who cared for the animals in
those landholdings were slaves and other servile folk. The
escaped servant, or slave, may be retained by the new master
only with the king's permission; were someone to keep an
escaped servant in service without royal warrant, he paid a
fine of fifty *pensa(e)* to the monarch. [53]

A great portion of royal income came from the products
of the land in the castle districts (the area surrounding the
royal fort; it came to be known as the county alias shire), and
from the inhabitants living in the district paying taxes, eight
dénárs a year. (The silver *dénár* formed the part of the golden
*pensa*: forty dénárs made one *pensa*.) [54]

The district folk provided partial service to the king by horse and wagon, and paid only four dénárs in taxes. [55] Those district inhabitants who had redeemed themselves from the burden of slavery, paid a tax for their freedom and for the right to work as free(d) folk. [56] Freemen who stood directly in royal service, paid an eight-dénár tax. [57] The migrant guestworkers: *hospites*, paid no tax, if working and settling down on royal lands and entering the royal military service. [58]

One-third of the collected tax money from the castle districts, together with one-third of toll fees, were received by the reeve of the castle district for his own use, in lieu of payment, — and after taxes and fees were collected. [59] The reeve in turn had to pay by St. Michael's day (September 29) the two-thirds of the collected tax and toll money at the royal residence in Esztergom. If the district reeve had accounted for less money than was his quota he had to remit the double of the original amount. [60] Were the district reeve in his own villages to receive horses and hundred pensa of "smoke-money," he would be obliged to provide, at his own expense, one shielded knight (*vértesvitéz*) for the king's armed forces; were the income of the reeve be about forty pensa, he only provided a shieldless fighting man (warrior) for the king's army. [61]

The assembly legislated for commerce and trade. A merchant who made a profit in his transactions, paid a double toll-fee. [62] To foreigners, and abroad, only oxen may be sold, and only those slaves who had been purchased abroad. [63] That is, the assembly forbade the purchase and sale of Hungarian inhabitants as slaves. It is evident from this particular piece of legislation that even slaves purchased abroad may not be sold so easily in Hungary. [64] Nobody could leave the country without a royal writ signed by the tax-collector of the reeve in the district, and countersigned by the royal tax-collector. Were someone to leave the realm without the king's written permission, he (or, rather, his family) paid a fine of fifty *pensa(e)* to the king. [65] Were the reeve to tolerate, or outright permit, the export of forbidden articles or wares (chattel) from his district, he lost both his office and two-thirds of his personal possessions. Nobody in the realm could afford to ignore the law of the monarch. [66]

The assembly also legislated on Jews and Ismaelites. A

Jew may not possess a Christian slave, and his fields can be cultivated by pagan slaves only. [67] This particular piece of legislation implies that in Hungary at this time there were Jewish landholders (or tenants), and the position of slaves in society was being acknowledged by law. And yet, the position of the Jewish landholder may be questioned. The law says that a Jew may live only at a bishop's residence (residential town), because from this article it is evident that he lived under the jurisdiction of the local bishop. [68] In money matters, were a Jew to borrow money from a Christian, or were a Christian to loan money to a Jew, the transactions had to be performed in front of Christian and Jewish witnesses; and, the amount of the loan may not exceed two or three *pensa(e)*, with the borrower providing security. [69] Were the amount to be borrowed, or loaned, higher than that, the names of the witnesses had to be placed in writing, and the writ properly sealed. [70] In order to prevent theft, any serious amount of purchase and sale had to be recorded. [71]

The Ismaelites could build a church only in a location where the non-Ismaelite portion of the population had moved away. [72] An Ismaelite woman could marry only a Hungarian man, [73] while the Ismaelite guest at a Hungarian house had to be entertained with a pork dish for dinner. [74] Were an Ismaelite to continue in the practice of his (native) Islamic habits, and were someone to report this to the authorities, the person who made the accusation (report) received a share of the (to be) confiscated belongings of the Ismaelite. [75]

The assembly had ordered in the interest of the realm's military defense and security that were an enemy to approach the frontier, the reeve in charge of the area had to provide, with food and horses, two runners to notify the monarch. [76]

The ruler himself may sit in judgment in any court of law. He may attend the circuit of his itinerant justice(s); if he does, he takes two county (district) judges with him to handle the legal problems and complaints of the local inhabitants. [77] The ruler may not, however, be expected to visit each county; he may, therefore, order that every ordinary (diocesan bishop) hold, twice a year, in early May and on the octave day of St. Michael's feast (October 6), a diocesan synod attended by all nobles of the region and the king's county reeve. On these diocesan gatherings held twice a year the reeve is to bring legal problems to public attention, and to take action against any public official who failed in the fulfillment of his duties. [78]

Ordeals may be held at the bishop's residence only, and in the presence of the members of the cathedral chapter. Aside from the episcopal (residence) towns, the cities of Pozsony and Nyitra were designated as places for ordeals to be held at. [79] The person acting as a witness at the ordeal ought to possess at least one plough-share of titled landholding; [80] he ought to go confession before taking the witness stand; were he to bear false testimony against the accused, he lost his titled lands, and they burnt the sign of the cross on his face. [81]

The criminal law code of King Coloman is not as severe as that of Ladislas I. The king's code is strict with thieves, and defines for the first time the legal concept of thief. A thief is the one who steals (has stolen) a four-legged animal; or, articles amounting to the price of such an animal; or, who has taken, without proper payment, clothing worth about twenty dénárs. [82] They blind the convicted thief. [83] And if his wife and sons fifteen years or older had something to do with the theft, they reduce their status to that of slaves. [84] The person who had accused someone of thievery without offering concrete evidence against the accused, will be handled like a thief. [85]

A murderer has to do penance just as a murderer had to do penance in the times of King Stephen I for his crime. In case of murder the bishop will hand down penance, though in certain lighter cases the archdean may pronounce, and the lay (district) judge hand down punishment. [86]

A woman guilty of child murder (abortion?) is sentenced to do penance by the archdean; the bishop (more rarely, the archdean) sentences the woman guilty of adultery, and the man guilty of having stolen a woman (eloping with his wife to be). [87] Woman accused, and found guilty of magic, or of strange behavior, were to be sentenced by the archdean and the county reeve. [88] The king recommended, however, some changes in this regard. He will not recognize witchcraft as a crime on the grounds that witches do not exist. [89] (It ought to be pointed out though that *striga* in the text may denote either a witch, or a monster-feeding-on-human-flesh.[90])

The legislative assembly also dealt with problems of the clergy. The clergyman arriving from abroad must have a letter of recommendation with him to present to the diocesan ordinary. [91] Were a priest be accused of any evil (act), he must clear himself of the charge before the law; if unable to answer charges brought against him, he must leave the country immediately. [92] Only men of good character and conduct may be ordained for the priesthood. [93]

A lay judge may not pronounce a sentence over a clergyman. [94] A lay person may not intervene in ecclesiastical affairs. [95] Everyone, cleric and layman alike, must pay church tax. [96] The royal county reeve will have to pay his tithe out of the one-third he receives from toll fees and taxes paid to the king. [97]

Ember days were to be kept with strict regularity as before. [98] The feast of the Holy Trinity will be celebrated on the octave day of — the Sunday after — Pentecost. [99] Mass can be said only at a consecrated place, though an itinerant cleric — a clergyman in transit — may say Mass on a portable altar, provided it can be set up at a decent location; Mass can be said at any honorable location. [100] A priest should wear clothing different from lay people. [101] The priest may not marry for a second time, nor may he marry a widow, or a woman abandoned by her husband. [102]

In his writ of July 27, 1096, Pope Urban II encouraged King Coloman to follow in the footsteps of his great predecessor, King St. Stephen, and to conduct, in the spirit of the same Stephen, the affairs of the realm, including cooperation between the Church and the royal court. [103] Indeed, the prefatory note to the decrees of legislation prepared by Alberic speaks of the restoration of Stephen I's codes of law, [104] and of the ruler's legislating with the consent of the headmen of the kingdom. [105] It may be worth a while to observe that Coloman's (chronologically speaking) first code of law says nothing about the laws of his uncle, Ladislas I, as if to ignore the legal enactments of his predecessor. This may have happened for a political reason; Coloman may have wanted, in such a manner, to distance himself from the anti-Rome policy initiated by Ladislas toward the end of his reign.

Of the eighty-four articles of the Tarcal assembly fifty-eight are ecclesiastical in nature, as if to lead to the conclusion that the king had, with the approval of his churchmen, taken an active interest in the reorganization of ecclesiastical matters of his country. He has taken the responsibility for the realization of his legal directives. [106] This is why separate articles deal with the relationship of Jews and Christians in the realm, [107] stressing the fact that the royal attention included every inhabitant of the country, — even slaves and servile folk. [108] The monarch would not tolerate the persecution of monster who ate human flesh because such creature did not exist; [109] nor did he permit the sale of Hungarians as slaves abroad. [110]

It is not unimportant that the monarch legislates, — or rewrites — the laws of Stephen I with his Senate's consent, and in the presence of the country's headmen, "regni principibus congregatis; tocius senatus consultu," in order to assure those laws wide publicity. [111]

## NOTES

1. P. Joachimsen, "Der Investiturstreit und die deutsche Verfassung," *Bayerische Blatter für das Gymnasialschulwesen*, 58 (1922), 53ff.; Hampe, *Kaisergeschichte*, 72ff.; idem, *Hochmittelalter*, 157ff.; K. F. Morrison, "Canossa: a Review," *Traditio*, 18 (1962), 121ff.

2. Caspar, *Register*, I, 202ff., ii:55a; S. Kuttner, "Liber canonicus: a Note on the Dictatus papae, c. 17," *Studi Gregoriani*, 2 (1947), 387ff.; Haller, II, 381f.

3. Caspar, *Register*, I, 270ff., iii:10a; Jaffé, I, no. 4978; Otto of Freising, *Gesta Friderici imperatoris*, i:1, *MGHSS*, XX, 352f. On the excommunication and deposition of Henry IV, see Caspar, *Register*, I, 312ff., iv:12, 12a; Jaffé, I, no. 5017; F. Kampers, "Rex et sacerdos," *HJB*, 45 (1925), 495ff.

4. Cf. M. Rule (ed), Eadmer, *Historia novorum in Anglia*, iii (anno 1100), R.S. (London, 1884), 55; M. Manitius, *Geschichte der lateinischen Literatur des Mittelalters*, 3 vols. (Munich, 1911031), III, 581ff.; R. W. Southern, *St. Anselm and His Biographer* (Cambridge, 1963), 298ff. Also, B. Thorpe (ed), Florentini Wigorniensis *Chronicon ex chronicis*, 2 vols. (London, 1848-49), anno 1107; on Worcester, see Gransden, 143ff. Z. N. Brooke, "Lay Investiture and Its Relations to the Conflict of Empire and Papacy," *Proceedings of the British Academy*, 25 (1930), 217ff.

5. Cf. *MGHLL*, sectio IV, const. 1, 100; Hampe, *Kaisergeschichte*, 88ff.

6. Sigebert of Gembloux, *Chronicon*, anno 1107, *MGHSS*, VI, 370; Wattenbach, II, 154ff.; Manitius, III, 332ff. Suger of St. Denis, *Vita Ludovici VI, MGHSS*, XXVI, 50; G. M. v. Knonau, *Jahrbücher des deutschen Reiches unter Heinrich IV und Heinrich V*, vol. VI (repr. Berlin, 1965), 19f.; Sprandel, 116ff.

7. See, e.g. *Annales Paderbornenses*, anno 1110, *MGHSS*, III, 112; Wattenbach, II, 38ff.

8. Bernoldi *Chronicon,* aa. 1089, 1091 and 1095, *MGHSS,* V, 448ff., 450ff., and 461ff., respectively.

9. *Ibid.,* a. 1095; W. Kienast, *Deutschland und Frankreich in der Kaiserzeit,* 3 vols. (Stuttgart, 1974-75), I, 185ff.

10. Cf. Mansi, *Concilia,* XX, 815; F. Duncalf, "The Councils of Piacenza and Clermont," *The First Hundred Years,* ed. M. W. Baldwin, vol. I of K. M. Setton (ed), *A History of the Crusades* 4 vols. (Philadelphia, 1955etc.), 220ff.

11. Mansi, *Concilia,* 963, c. 13.

12. Eadmer, iii cc. 50-59; idem, *Vita Anselmi,* in R. W. Southern, *Life of St. Anselm of Canterbury* (Oxford, 1962), 127, and 137; S. N. Vaugh, "St. Anselm and the English Investiture Controversy Reconsidered," *Journal of Mediaeval History,* 6 (1980), 133ff. Also, B. R. Kemp, "Monastic Possession of Parish Churches in England in the Twelfth Century," *Journal of Ecclesiastical History, 31 (1980),* 195ff.

13. Eadmer, *Historia,* anno 1107; Worcester, *Chronicon,* a. 1107; William of Malmesbury, *De gestis regum Anglorum,* ed. W. Stubbs, R.S., 2 vols. (London, 1887-89), v:394-95 (anno 1101); H. Farmer, "William of Malmesbury," *Journal of Ecclesiastical History,* 13 (1962), 39ff.; the essay by F. Liebermann, "Anselm von Canterbury und Hugo von Lyon," *Historische Aufsätze dem Andenken an G. Waitz gewidmet* (Hannover 1886), 156ff., is still worth reading.

14. See *Ekkehardi Chronicon,* anno 1111, *MGHSS,* VI, 244f., Knonau, VI, 40ff.

15. *Ekkehardi Chronicon,* anno 1107; F. J. Schmale, "Zu den Konzilien Paschals II," *Annuarium historiae conciliorum,* 10 (1978), 279ff.

16. *Ekkehardi Chronicon,* aa. 1110-1111, and compare with the papal account, *MGHLL,* sectio IV, const. 1, 99; U. R. Blumenthal, "Paschal II and the Roman Primacy," *Archivum historiae pontificae,* 16 (1978), 67ff.

17. *MGHLL,* sectio IV, const. 1, 99.

18. *Ibid.,* 1, 83.

19. *Ibid.,* I, 91 and 96.

20. Cf. Bruno of Segni, *Epistolae,* in E. Dümmler (ed), *MGH, Libelli de lite,* 3 vols. (Hannover, 1891-97), cited hereafter as *LdL,* II, 543ff.; U. R. Blumenthal, "Opposition to Pope Paschal II: Some Comments on the Lateran Council of 1112," *Annuarium historiae conciliorum,* 10 (1978), 82ff.

21. *MGHLL,* sectio IV, const. I, 85 and 90; Godfrey of Vendome, *Libellus* I, in *LdL,* 680ff.; Ivo of Chartres, *Epistolae, LdL,* II, 640ff., ep. ad Ioscerannum; Sprandel, 52ff.

22. Placidius on Nonantula, *De honore ecclesiae, LdL,* II, 566ff., c. 73; *MGHLL,* sectio IV, const. I, 100.

23. *Ibid.,* I, 99; Ekkehardi *Chronicon,* a. 1111, *MGHSS,* VI, 244f.

24. Segni, *Ep., LdL,* II, 546ff.

25. Cf. *Disputatio vel defensio Paschalis papae, ibid.,* II, 665.

26. Haller, II, 490ff.; E. Voigt, "Zum Charakter der 'staufischen' Städtepolitik," *Volksmassen: Gestalten der Geschichte; Festschrift Stern* (Berlin, 1962), 19ff.; J. Streisand (ed), *Deutsche Geschichte,* vol. I (Berlin, 1967), 230ff.

27. Hampe, *Kaisergeschichte,* 65 and 105; E. Patzelt, *Österreich bis zum Ausgang der Babenbergerzeit* (Vienna, 1946), 116f.

28. Cf. B. Gebhardt (ed), *Handbuch der deutschen Geschichte,* 4 vols., 8th rev. ed. (Stuttgart, 1954-60), I, 273f.; Hampe, 93; G. Koch, *Auf dem Wege zum Sacrum imperium* (Vienna-Graz, 1972), 61ff.

29. Gebhardt, I, 276f.

30. Ekkehardi *Chronicon,* a. 1106, *MGHSS,* VI, 232ff, esp. the letter, VI,

236f.; Sigebert *Chronicon*, 1106, *ibid.*, VI, 369f.; W. Kienast, *Deutschland und Frankreich in der Kaiserzeit*, 3 vols. (Stuttgart, 197etc.), I, 178ff.

31. Paschal II to Guido of Vienne (afterwards Callixtus II), Mansi, *Concilia*, XXI, 76.

32. Ekkehardi *Chronicon*, a. 1116, *MGHSS*, VI, 250f.; A. Hauck, *Kirchengeschichte Deutschlands*, 5 vols., 5th ed. (Berlin, 1952-55), III, 899ff.

33. Ekkehardi *Chronicon*, a. 1119; Hesso of Strassburg, *Relatio de Concilio Remensi*, *MGHSS*, XII, 422ff.; Wattenbach, II, 195f.

34. *MGHLL*, sectio IV, const. I, 106; Ekkehardi *Chronicon*, a.1121; compare with Geoffrey of Vendome, lib. IV, *LdL*, II, 691; Pope Callixtus II, *Epistolae*, ep. 168, in *MPL*, 163, 1232f.

35. Ekkehardi *Chronicon*, a. 1122, *MGHSS*, VI, 258ff.

36. *MGHLL*, sec. IV, const. I, 107, 108; Jaffé, I,n. 6986; Gebhardt, I, 278f.

37. B. Ladner, *Die Papstbildnisse des Altertums und des Mittelalters* (Vatican City, 1941), 199ff.

38. Gebhardt, I, 278f.

39. *MGHLL*, sectio IV, const. I, 575ff.; Mansi, *Concilia*, XXI, 277ff., esp. 287f.

40. Hóman-Szekfű, I, 347f.; Hóman, *Ungarisches Mittelalter*, I, 363f.; J. Holub, "Quod omnes tangit," *Revue historique de droit francaise et étranger*, 4 (1951), 97ff.; Th. v. Bogyay, *Grundzüge der Geschichte Ungarns*, 4th ed. (Darmstadt, 1981), 6ff.

41. Hóman, *Ungarisches Mittelalter*, I, 310ff., possibly in reference to the preface of the decrees of Tarcal: "... nam quis ambigat ... sancto patre nostro Stephano, uiro quirpe apostolico legem populo nostro datam;" *RHM*, II, 359, though, it should be noted that Alberic made no note of the laws of his predecessor, "regis sanctae memoriae Stephani legalem textum recensuit;" *ibid.*, II, 360. Indirectly, see M. Hellmann, "Die politisch-kirchliche Grundlegung der Osthälfte Europas, Ungarn," in Th, Schieder (ed), *Handbuch der europäischen Geschichte*, vol. I (Stuttgart, 1976), 897ff.

42. The text reads "Concilium Cursollinum," — see *RHM*, II, 359,5-6; Marczali, *Enchiridion*, 104, note 3, — quoted hereafter as Tarcal, *RHM*, II, 358ff. On the royal title, *rex Hungariae*, and the medieval Latin name of the Hungarians, cf. B. Hóman, *Történetírás és forráskritika* (Historiography and critique of sources) (Budapest, 1938), 227f.

43. On Archbishop Seraphim, from 1095 to 1104, cf. Knauz, I, 68. C. Péterffy (ed), *Sacra concilia ecclesiae Romano-Catholicae in regno Hungariae celebrata*, 2 vols. (Vienna, 1742-44), I, 39ff., enumerated, in a chronological oder, (1) Tarcal, alias the Alberic collection; (2) two synods of Esztergom, and order followed by Hefele, V, 322f. On the other hand, Endlicher (*RHM*, II, 351ff.) and Závodszky, 95 and 197ff., maintained a different order of arrangement by speaking of two ecclesiastical and one secular legislative sessions, and a separate Jewish code of laws.

44. "Uerum tamen tu domine, qui in huius populi linguae genere minus me promptum consideras...;" *RHM*, II, 360.

45. "... nec tenuis rei pro foribus stantem intromittit despecta pauperies, ...;" *ibid.*, II, 358; Pintér, I, 202ff.

46. Tarcal, a. 1.

47. *Ibid.*, a. 20 *and* 15.

48. *Ibid.*, aa. 16 *and* 15.

49. "Possessiones quelibet (1) a sancto Stephano datae, humanae successionis quoslibet contingat successores uel heredes. (2) Possessio uero ab aliis regibus data de patre descendat ad filium; qui si defuerint succedat germanus, cuius filii eciam

post mortem illius non exheredentur. (3) Germanus autem predictus si non inueniatur, regi hereditas deputetur;" *ibid.*, II, 362f., a. 20. E. Waldapfel, "Nemesi birtokjogunk kialakulása a középkorban (Formation of the property rights of the nobility in the Middle Ages)," *Századok*, 65 (1931), 131ff. esp. 143ff.

50. Tarcal, aa. 21 and 17. J. Holub, "A vásárolt fekvő jószág jogi természete régi jogunkban (Legal character of purchased real estate in ancient Hungarian law)," in S. Domanovszky (ed), *Károlyi Árpád emlékkönyv* (Memorial volume to Árpád Károlyi) (Budapest, 1933), 246ff.

51. Tarcal, aa. 19 and 15.

52. *Ibid.*, a. 42.

53. *Ibid.*, aa. 39 and 42. Gy. Györffy, "Zur Frage der Herkunft der ungarischen Dienstleute," *Studia Slavica*, 22 (1976), 40ff., and 311ff.

54. Tarcal, a. 45; Gy. Györffy, "Die Entstehung der ungarischen Burgorganisation," *Acta archaeologica*, 28 (Budapest, 1976), 323ff.; idem, *István király*, 491f., commented on the role and position of the *hebdomadarius* in Hungarian society, in accordance with the Bavarian Coda of Laws, i:13, *MGHLL*, III, 269ff., esp. 280,6-9.

55. Tarcal, a. 81. F. Maksay, "Das Agrarsiedlungsystem des mittelalterlichen Ungarns," *Acta historica*, 24 (1978), 83ff.; idem, "Umwandlung der ungarischen Siedlungs- und Agrarstruktur," *Zeitschrift für Agrargeschichte und Agrarsoziologie*, 23 (1975), 154ff., surveyed conditions of the eleventh century through the fourteenth.

56. Tarcal, a. 80; Györffy, *István király*, 507ff.

57. Tarcal, a. 35.

58. *Ibid.*, a. 45; E. Fügedi, "Das mittelalterliche Königtum Ungarn als Gastland," in W. Schlesinger (ed), *Die deutsche Ostsiedlung des Mittelalters als Probleme der europäischen Geschichte* (Sigmaringen, 1975), 471ff.; I. Kniezsa, "Ungarns Völkerschaften im XI Jahrhundert," *Archivum Europae centro-orientalis*, 4 (1938), 241ff.

59. Tarcal, aa. 25 and 78.

60. *Ibid.*, a. 79.

61. *Ibid.*, a. 40.

62. *Ibid.*, a. 33.

63. *Ibid.*, a. 77, and, indirectly, a. 76.

64. "Nemo seruum in genere Hungarorum ... uendat, ... nec ancillam exceptis lingue alterius seruis;" *ibid.*, a. 77.

65. *Ibid.*, a. 82.

66. ".. quod si quis comitum infringeret, aut honore suo priuetur, aut duas rerum suarum partes amittat tercia uero substancia porcio uxoriatque heredibus remaneat;" *ibid.*, aa. 77 and 30.

67. *Ibid.*, aa. 74 and 75; Coloman's *Lex data Iudaeis in suo regno commorantibus*, a. 1, *RHM*, II, 371.

68. "... sed ipsi nusquam, nisi ubi sedes episcopalis est, manere sinantur;" Tarcal, a. 75.

69. Cf. B. Kumorovitz, "Szent László vásár-törvénye és Kálmán király pecsétes kartulája (Merchant laws of King Ladislas and the sealed briefs of Coloman's reign)," *Athleta patriae*, 83ff., in reference to Coloman's Jewish Laws, a. 2, *RHM*, II, 371f. Závodszky, 195f.

70. "... et omnia testium in cartulam scribere;" *ibid.*, a. 3; Kumorovitz, in *Athleta patriae*, 99ff., and note 18.

71. *RHM*, II, 371f., a. 4; B. Blumenkranz, "Jüdische und christliche Konvertiten im jüdisch-christlichen Religionsgespräch des Mittelalters," in P. Wilbert

(ed), *Judentum und im Mittelalter* (Berlin, 1966), 264ff.

72. Tarcal, a. 47.

73. *Ibid.*, a. 48.

74. "... de porcina tantum carne uescantur;" *ibid.*, a. 49.

75. "qui uero eos accusabat, de substantia eorum partem accipiat;" *ibid.*, a. 46; by the mid-twelfth century, Moslem inhabitants in the realm were in the process of becoming Christians. Cf. S. Balic, "Der Islam im mittelalterlichen Ungarn," *Südostforschungen*, 23 (1964), 19ff.

76. Tarcal, a. 36. On the organization of the frontier, see Ladislas, *Decretum* II, aa. 15-16; on the horse in military (county) service, see Györffy, *István király*, 240.

77. "... ubi iudices duos megales (mega ➤ county) cum eo (that is, *cum rege*) comigrent, qui contenciones populi illius discreto examine dirimant;" Tarcal, a. 37.

78. *Ibid.*, a. 2; it may have been such a gathering held anno 1111 that may be referred to in Szentpétery, *Regesta*, I, no. 43.

79. Tarcal, a. 22; on the distinction between "ancestral" and "acquired" property, or holdings, see E. Waldapfel, "Nemesi birtokjogunk kialakulása a középkorban (Development of the rights of landholding in the Middle Ages)," *Századok*, 65 (1931), 131ff., esp. 143ff.; and 259ff. E. Fügedi, "Kirchliche Topographie und Siedlungsgeschichte im Mittelalter in der Slowakei," *Studia Slavica*, 5 (1959), 363ff.

80. Tarcal, a. 26. Hóman, *Pénztörténet*, 491ff.; L. Bendeffy, "Középkori hossz- és területmértékek (Medieval length and surface measures)," in *Fejezetek a magyar mérésügy történetéből* (Chapters from the history of Hungarian weights and measures) (Budapest, 1959), 83ff.; I. Bogdán, *Magyarországi hossz- és földmértékek a XVI század végéig* (Hungarian length and surface measures until the end of the 16th century) (Budapest, 1978), 150ff.

81. Tarcal, a. 83, and compare with Stephen, *Leges*, i:17 and 33. In Tarcal, a. 83, the punishment had been reduced.

82. Tarcal, a. 54.

83. "Fur inuentus in iudicio culpabilis aboculetur;" *ibid.*, a. 53.

84. *Ibid.*, a. 56; J. Holub, "Le role de l'age la droit hongroise du moyen age," *Revue d'histoire de droit francaise et étrangere*, 1 (1922), 78ff.

85. Tarcal, a. 55.

86. *Ibid.*, a. 50, and compare with Stephen, *Leges*, i:14 and 14a (cc. 16 *and* 13 in Migne), *RHM*, II, 310ff.

87. Tarcal, a. 50, second par.; R. Weigand, "Zur mittelalterlichen kirchlichen Ehegerichtsbarkeit: rechtsvergleichende Untersuchungen," *Zeitschrift der Savigny Stiftung für Rechtsgeschichte*, kan. Abt., 67 (1981), 213ff.; A. Szentirmai, "Das Recht des Erzdechanten in Ungarn wahrend des Mittelalters," *ibid.*, 43 (1957), 132ff.

88. Tarcal, a. 58; Pfaff, "Das kirchliche Eherecht am Ende des 12 Jahrhunderts," *Zeitschrift der Savigny Stiftung für Rechtsgeschichte*, kan. Abt., 63 (1977), 557ff.; A. Szentirmai, "Der Einfluss des byzantinischen Kirchenrechts auf die Gesetzgebung Ungarns im 11 - 12 Jahrhundert," *Jahrbuch der österreichischen byzantinischen Gesellschaft*, 10 (1961), 93ff.; E. M. Makowski, "The Conjugal Debt and Medieval Canon Law," *Journal of Medieval History*, 3 (1977), 99ff.

89. Tarcal, a. 57. D. Kurze, "Häresie und Minderheit im Mittelalter," HZ, 229 (1979), 529ff. The king and his synod may have been acting in the spirit of their age; cf. R. C. Dales, "A Medieval View of Human Dignity," *Journal of the History of Ideas*, 38 (1977), 557ff.

90. On "Hexenwahn," see Funk-Bihlmeyer, II, 361; R. Köstler, "Der Anteil des Christentums an den Ordalien," *Zeitschrift der Savigny Stiftung für Rechtsgeschichte*, kan. Abt., 2 (1912), 208ff.; E. Mayer, "Der Ursprung der germanischen Gottesurteile," *Historische Vierteljahrschrift*, 20 (1920-21), 289ff.; G. J. Simons, *The Witchcraft World* (New York, 1974), 59ff.

91. Tarcal, a. 3; S. Mester, "De initiis canonici iuris culturae in Hungaria," *Studi Gregoriani*, 2 (1954), 659ff.; L. Mezey, "Ungarn und Europa im 12 Jahrhundert: Kirche und Kultur swischen Ost und West," *Vorträge und Forschungen*, 12 (1968), 255ff.

92. Tarcal, aa. 3 and 6.

93. *Ibid.*, a. 4, and compare with Ladislas, *Decretum II*, art. 1.

94. Tarcal, a. 6. A. Szentirmai, "Der Ursprung des Archidiakonats in Ungarn," *Österreichisches Archiv für Kirchenrecht*, 7 (1956), 231ff.

95. Tarcal, a. 14.

96. *Ibid.*, a. 25.

97. "Comitibus terciam partem dare decreuimus;" *ibid.*, a. 25; compare with a. 78.

98. *Ibid.*, a. 71, and compare with Stephen, *Leges*, i:10.

99. Tarcal, a. 72.

100. *Ibid.*, a. 68, and, indirectly, a. 69.

101. *Ibid.*, a. 70; compare with Synod of Melfi, can. 13, in Mansi, *Concilia*, XX, 724, and Lateran II, can. 4, *ibid.*, XXI, 527.

102. Tarcal, a. 67. G. Adriányi, "Der Eintritt Ungarns in die christlich-abendländische Volksgemeinschaft," *Ungarn Jahrbuch*, 6 (1974-75), 24ff.; J. P. Ripoche, "La Hongrie entre Byzance et Rome: probleme de choice réligieux," *ibid.*, 6 (1974-75), 9 ff.; Sieben, *loc. cit.*; Schieffer, *art. cit.*

103. Jaffé, *Regesta*, I, no. 5662; *MPL*, 151, 480ff.

104. *RHM*, II, 359,11-14.

105. *Ibid.*, II, 360,5-7.

106. "Iubeas, o praesul, regalium instituta collacionum recolere, uel senatoria regni tocius decreta;" *ibid.*, II, 358,13-14; also, *ibid.*, aa. 9 and 24.

107. *Ibid.*, a. 74; *Lex Iudaeis data*, aa. 1-7.

108. Tarcal, a. 80; Kniezsa, *loc. cit.*

109. Tarcal, a. 57, and compare with *MGH Capitularia*, I, 68f., c. 6; *supra*, note 89; J. B. Russel, *Witchcraft in the Middle Ages* (Ithaca, NY, 1972), 97.

110. Tarcal, a. 77.

111. To the effect that "prefati regis sancti memoriae Stephani lege, textum recensuit." Cf. *RHM*, II, 360,5-7.

# III

# Ecclesiastical Legislation of
# King Coloman
# and Last Years of His Reign

In primis interpellandus est rex.

*I Esztergom*

According to Henrik Marczali, church legislation in Hungary had not been separated from the secular until the reign of King Coloman. Hungarian laws of the eleventh century correspond in this regard to Carolingian capitularies.[1] Development of church life during the peaceful first decade of Coloman's rule made synodical legislation necessary, the first monument of which was the collection of decrees enacted at the (First) Synod of Esztergom.[2] The purpose of this synodical session was to purify spiritual and intellectual life in the realm; it did not deal with dogma, but with ethics, especially with the spiritual life and moral conduct of the clergy.[3]

The date of this synod cannot be exactly determined. Some place it as early as 1089, during Ladislas I's reign;[4] some, in the second decade of the twelfth century.[5] It is evident, however, from its contents that it was held during the first decade of Coloman's reign.[6] In a chronological order, it ought to be placed after the secular legislation of the Tarcal Assembly, whose decrees contained many church-related enactments.[7] Its articles were preserved in a contemporary document, the late twelfth century sacramentary known as the Pray codex.[8] The interesting feature of these enactments is that at the time of their conception royal authority in church affairs was still intact in Hungary. I Esztergom ordered that the monarch take action in church matters; "in primis interpellandus est rex."[9] Only the Second Synod of Esztergom (II Esztergom) paid more attention to papal authority, but it ordered, "ex auctoritate Apostolici," that prayers be said for the King.[10] In view of the fact that Coloman had eventually been pressured to renounce, in favor of Rome, his ecclesiastical prerogatives exercised in the kingdom, I Esztergom must have been held before that renunciation.[11]

It may throw some light upon church conditions in the realm during the twelfth century that the synod still recognized the validity of the priest's first marriage, though it displayed intolerance of married bishops; in fact, it restricted any property acquired by a bishop in favor of the Church.[12] It decreed that an ordained priest may not get married (after ordination to the priesthood).[13] A married priest could become a bishop only with his wife's consent, because (1) the two could not live together as husband and wife, and (2) she could not stay on church precincts.[14] It is significant that the latter synod demanded clerical celibacy; married clergy could not perform church functions and lead married lives. Married clergy had to separate from their wives and pay (child-)support for them.[15]

The synod placed monasteries under a bishop's jurisdiction in a diocese.[16] It made members of the cathedral chapters to converse in Latin.[17] It attempted elimination of remains of paganism with light punishments,[18] and forbade clerics to accept payment for administering the sacraments.[19] The synod forbade a bishop to take serfs (slaves), or freed men for training for the priesthood without their lord's permission (an ordinance that actually says that by this time they had a norm, to provide for the education of candidates to the priesthood, established in the realm).[20] It held strict provisions for the punishment and censure of clergymen who were drunk, thieves, or were regular patrons of the local pub.[21]

This may be why they did not ordain for the priesthood unlearned persons who could not read or write; had such an individual been already ordained, they forced him to continue his clerical education; were the individual unwilling (or, rather, unable) to do that, they suspended him.[22] Uneducated individuals, be they clerics, have always been difficult to discipline. The Hungarian hierarchy had no need for dealing with problems arising from lack of clerical discipline.[23] In connection with this outlook is the synodical decree that says that only certified clerics (that is, priests recognized by the local bishop) were allowed to do parish work. [24]

Therefore, it is understandable that a cleric who could claim no adherence to an ecclesiastical superior (that is, a bishop, or the abbot of a monastery), and who consequently lacked certification, was not permitted to be ordained to the priesthood; nor could a cleric be, on the same ground, accepted by a bishop without a letter of recommendation for a permanent residence in the diocese. [25]

The emancipated slave may be ordained to the priesthood, however. [26] Had he been a slave of the Church, his sons, — sons of the now ordained priest —, also gained emancipation and became free (and faithful) members of the Church. [27]

Within the framework of the beginning crusades many abuses had occurred on account of the legal exempt status of the clergy. One had to prevent such abuses, or at least limit the opportunities that made them possible. That is why the Tarcal assembly had already ordered that foreign clerics arriving in the realm and claiming clerical status, had to possess letters of recommendation, or had to have witnesses who would testify in their behalf. [28]

If a bishop had dispatched one of his clerics to another diocese in an official business, he had to provide him with a sealed letter (of recommendation). [29] When a cleric went to visit another bishopric, he had to have a letter with him. The Synod of Szabolcs had passed such a decree [30] in accordance with church decisions made in the ninth century. [31] The bishops had to keep their eyes upon their clerics; [32] they had to prevent them from making any appeal in a secular court of law in legal matters of secular nature. [33]

Church property was protected by law. [34] The division of the annual church (diocesan) income followed the guidelines laid down by Pope Gelasius in the fourth century. In accordance with those guidelines, the ordinary (= diocesan bishop) received one-forth of the total revenue; his clergy, another one-fourth. The other half of the revenues was used for the upkeep of church buildings in the bishopric, and to provide for the travellers and the poor. [35] In other words, a part of the annual diocesan revenue went directly to the bishop. [36] Were one of the bishop's clerics to become a thief, the bishop, or his deputy: the archdean, was to hand down a decision in the case. [37] Were the cleric to waste ecclesiastical income, or property, he had to repay twofold the wasted amount. [38]

In accordance with the decrees of this synod, a diocese, and parishes in the diocese, had to have planned annual budgets. For example, a new church may not be consecrated without the parish priests' having properly arranged property rights and a reasonable budgeted income. However, an already built church can be consecrated. [39] The abbot of a monastery may take a novice against the security of two furloughs of land; [40] the abbot may not share monastic income (=landholdings) with members of his own family. [41] Clerics pay no tithe, though they contribute one-fourth of their income (for room and board?) to the parish priest. [42]

The abbot of a monastic community may not wear bishop's insignia at church functions; nor may he do parish work. [43] A monk may not make his vows to a bishop, or to an ordained priest. [44] A priest may not perform any work that would be unworthy to his person or to his office, — a decree that may, indeed, present the Hungarian clergy of this age in a bad light. [45]

They fine the individual who made drunk a fellow person at the *kalendae* gatherings held (in the parish) on the first day of the month. [46] Were the individual a priest who (has) made somebody drunk at the *kalendae*, [47] they suspend him and condemn him to forty days of penance; were a priest to make anyone drunk (in public) anywhere, they suspend him, just as they depose a (habitually) drunk clergyman. [48] Were someone to report on a drunk clergyman, they give him monetary reward; were someone to report on a drunk archdean, they pay him the threefold amount of reward money. [49]

Were a noble to force anyone to take a drink (against the person's will), they sentence him to forty days of fast and penance; were the noble to remain a habitual drunk, they excommunicate him. [50]

The synod took strict action against simony. A priest may not sign an agreement, nor may he accept payment for offering Mass. [51] He may not sell his position, nor can he transfer it to somebody else. [52] He may receive no payment for conducting baptisms and funerals. [53] A priest may not, for money, grant dispensation to anyone from keeping a holiday. [54]

Mass: divine service, can be celebrated and holidays observed only in accordance with the established *ordo*; [55] only prayers approved by the synod may be recited in public at divine service; [56] all holidays (of obligation) were to be observed. [57] The parish priest reads out aloud the epistle and the gospel every Sunday and holiday to his flock; in village and small parish churches, he in his sermons explains the Our Father and the Creed to the assembled faithful. [58]

Laymen go to confession and receive Holy Communion three times a year; clerics confess before every major holiday. [59] Were someone to die without having received the sacraments, his (nearest) relative(s) must perform forty days penance. If the person who died without the sacraments had no relatives, the local judge and (village-)elders were to be held responsible for such negligence. [60] In view of the fact that the synod demanded that the bishop build and maintain a house-of-penance at (near) his cathedral, it can be assumed that penitents did their forty day penances at these kinds of spiritual prisons. [61]

The synod was very strict with the cleric who would not attend the diocesan synod; they defrock him. [62] Considering the fact that defrocking: degradation of a cleric to layman status occurs several times in the articles of the synod, the question remains whether they weeded out unfit and uneducated clerics in such a manner from among the ranks of the clergy, or, whether the situation had deteriorated so much that they had to rely upon the strongest measures to enforce church discipline? In the West, they did, already in the ninth century, threaten with excommunication any bishop who was not willing to summon his diocesan synod regularly. [63]

The Hungarian chronicler who, according to János Horváth, had access to information dating to the times of King Coloman, kept silent about contacts between the Hungarian court and the Holy See. [64] Most probably, the chronicler regarded it as normal that the monarch, following in King St. Stephen's footsteps, conducted state affairs according to his own judgement. [65] Such "affairs of state" included filling vacant episcopal (and abbatial) sees in the country. [66] It was Pope Paschal II who had himself complained about this investiture style arrangement of the Hungarian kings in a letter to the bishop of Spaleto; [67] and, in fact, in his communication with the abbot of Fleury in 1102; [68] and yet, in his writ, dated November, 1106, to the archbishop of Kalocsa, the pontiff gave tacit approval of King Coloman's ecclesiastical jurisdiction. [69]

Vilmos Fraknói relied upon these papal letters in an attempt to explain the mission of Cardinal Augustine to Hungary in 1103. [70] Unfortunately, there is no surviving evidence related to the Cardinal's mission, and even George Fejér's *Codex diplomaticus* recorded only the Cardinal's intercession in a quarrel between the Belgrade bishop and a monastery. [71] On the other hand, it may be interesting to note that it could have been at this time that King Coloman had renounced his right of investiture in favor of the Roman See. Undoubtedly, Coloman the bishop who had become king wanted peace with Rome, though it may be assumed that diplomatic considerations, — a rather realistic analysis of the prevalent political conditions —, must have induced King Coloman to undertake these steps, in order to appease the Holy See. [72]

It must not have been easy for a Hungarian king of Árpád's blood to surrender privileges that had been exercised by his predecessors since the days of Stephen I, be he a king who, as a former bishop, had regularly recited his canonical hours. [73]

At the 1106 Synod of Guastalla, King Coloman had indeed renounced his right of investiture (in Hungary). His renounciation of privileges held by his predecessors since the inception of the kingdom seems though to have been made too hurriedly. Following the text of Duchesne's *Liber pontificalis*, and the record of the fourteenth century biographer of Pope Paschal II, it may seem clear that the monarch must have given in to the persuasion of the pontiff. [74] "Iuxta admonitionem vestram dimisimus, et si quod in electionibus huiusmodi minus canonice retractum est, de cetero Deo volente cavebimus." [75]

The biographer's argument may be convincing enough in a sense that Coloman was a bishop, who had obtained papal dispensation to be king. [76] It must have been Coloman's episcopal status, — and, consequently, his spiritual-religious conviction —, that made him seek an understanding with Rome (just as it must have been his position in the Church in England [77] that made Anselm of Canterbury reach a compromise with the Roman See at about the same time. [78]

It ought to be pointed out, on the other hand, that the imperial delegates at Guastalla [79] stood firm in their support of their emperor's claim to *ius regni*, as, indeed, all German bishops named by Henry V were confirmed in their status by the synod. [80] This is quite evident from the papal writ attached to the report by Ekkehard, [81] and from the portion of the papal letter published by Uodalscalcus de Eginine. [82] Therefore, Coloman must have resigned his rights not out of conviction, but because he felt love and loyalty (as a bishop) toward the Roman See.

Henceforth, the Hungarian king could not name, nor invest bishops and abbots, though churchmen said daily prayers for him, [83] **excommunicating everyone who would** dare conspire against the person or office of the king; or, who would be a party to such a conspiracy. [84] They also excommunicate the person who knew about the conspiracy, but failed to report it. [85]

It was after Guastalla, though perhaps only in 1112, that the Second Synod of Esztergom was held. [86] This church gathering dedicated itself to two main problems of the Church in Hungary — clerical celibacy and the steadfastness of marriage. After Guastalla, the question of clerical celibacy was to be handled quickly; according to the decrees of the 1090 Synod of Amalfi and the Roman resolutions of 1099, [87] (1) a bishop could not ordain deacon or priest an individual who was incapable of abstinence. [88] (2) Married clergymen could perform ecclesiastical functions only if they had reached agreements with their wives to interrupt living as married couples. Provisions were made for the support of the wife. [89] (3) Priests living with (or, married to former) concubines had to separate permanently from them, and do penance before readmitted to church services. [90] (4) Priests married for a second time, or married to widows, or to their former housekeepers (servants), were to lose their stallum: church prebens for good. [91]

II Esztergom introduced legislation concerning marriage in some contrast with the provisions of I Esztergom: [92] a marriage could not be dissolved. "Quia scriptum est, quod Deus coniunxit, homo non separet." If a wife fled her husband, she had to return to him. [93] Were the husband to separate from his hated wife, he could do it by becoming a slave; otherwise, the (still free) woman would have to follow him into slavery; if separated, neither of them could marry again.[94] (3) Were a wife be observed (=surprised) in an act of adultery by two witnesses, she would have to do penance before seeking reconciliation with her husband; if they cannot get reconciled with one another, neither of them can marry again. [95] In other words, in cases of adultery, they did not tolerate separation and remarriage. (4) The synod defined anew the marriage rite (as a sacrament), and forbade secret, candestine marriages. [96] (Since 755, in fact, a marriage had to be a public affair. [97]) A marriage must be performed by two sober parties in front of a sober priest. [98] They marry in front of a priest and worthy witnesses, and with the symbol of engagement (ring?), in order to express their intention of marrying each other. [99]

The synod emphasized the proper keeping of all holidays, [100] and stated that no exemptions may be granted from Sunday-rest. [101] It ordered daily prayers for the king, [102] and condemned any conspiracy against him, or the person who knew about such a conspiracy, but failed to report it. [103] The decrees of II Esztergom confirmed the acceptance of celibacy — a major demand of the Cluniac reform movement in the Church in Hungary, and said that they recognized papal authority over that of the king in ecclesiastical matters. [104]

During the reign of Coloman, Jewish laws were also enacted, as if to prove that the monarch was willing to determine the public position of the non-Christian element of society in his country by law. [105] Coloman wished to provide legal protection to that stratum, [106] and to redefine relations between Jews and Christians in the country. [107]

Toward the end of his reign, King Coloman had armed conflicts with his younger brother, Prince Álmos, rather frequently. The prince began to be unruly as early as 1098, although he held by then the princely-one-third of the realm's territory, and his sustenance was provided for (by the king). [108] Álmos slowly turned against his own brother, but the king was able to anticipate his movements. At Várkony, the two armies faced each other on the river Tisza, but the nobles saved the realm from civil war by saying that they would not fight (and die) for neither of them. If it pleased the king, he may have a military showdown with his brother; they, the nobles, shall recognize the winner as their monarch. [109]

Although peace was restored between king and prince, the incident showed Coloman in a dangerously weak situation. It was one thing to avoid civil war; but to speak to the king in the manner the nobles had spoken with Coloman was condemnable. The fact that the nobles did not take action against Álmos (who had opposed his royal brother), and yet, they failed to support the king; and, nobody from among the nobles wished to speak sense to the prince, showed three really weak aspects of Coloman's position.

(1) The king had many enemies in the realm; the opposition must have been unhappy with the king's policies. They did not attack him directly, but would have been happy to see Álmos, or someone else, occupy the throne — instead of Coloman. [110] (2) Prince Álmos must have had a strong party of adherents among the leading stratum of the country's inhabitants; his supporters did not fight for him, but they had accompanied him to camp as if to await the possible outcome of the personal (-political) confrontation between him and King Coloman. [111] (3) It is conceivable that the king had through his legislation shown much strength on the domestic front that may have displeased many of his opponents. [112] Many of the nobles would have preferred to see a less forceful ruler on the throne. The opposition was truly discouraged; they had expected more leniency from a bishop who had become king. Coloman had shown them instead that he was a true Árpád scion, king in name and in deed. [113]

Coloman's benevolent and yet strict behavior may be characterized by the manner in which he handled the domestic crisis of 1105, when Álmos went to the German court to request aid against his own brother, the king. [114] Henry IV displayed, however, no inclination to help the young and irresponsible prince against his brother, a constitutionally elected and crowned monarch; the prince had to leave the court of Henry IV in distress and in a hurry.[115] Álmos was well aware of his public humiliation, — that could, in turn, undermine his position back at home —, and now fled to his brother-in-law, Boleslaw III of Poland. The Polish ruler sympathized with the prince, but wished to clarify the situation between the prince and the king (a decision that speaks well for Boleslaw) by calling for a meeting in his presence of Álmos with Coloman. [116]

The king did not attend the meeting. The chronicler suggested here that he did not go because he feared a (diplomatic) trap (being set up for him); this writer, for one, is of the opinion that he did not go because he, as king, must have found it humiliating to defend his own interests from his brother and before a friendly, still foreign, ruler. An Árpád had no need for such demeaning experience. Álmos, however, made the best of the situation: with Polish forces he broke into Hungarian territory and occupied Abaújvár; thereupon King Colomon, tentatively, agreed to a meeting with Boleslaw III.[117]

Now, it may be that Boleslaw III had certain plans concerning Hungary, but, having perceived strong resistance among Coloman's forces, changed his mind. The meeting took place, where the two rulers made peace (without Álmos), and the two rulers became allies. It was Coloman who agreed to the meeting and signed the alliance agreement in order to neutralize Álmos' position. [118]

It was now Coloman's turn to move against Álmos, whom he had confronted at Fort Abaújvár. The previous scheme had repeated itself: the prince went alone to his brother's camp to beg the king for mercy. Coloman forgave him and the nobles who had sided with Álmos.[119] One ought to note that though the king forgave Álmos, he also punished the prince by taking away from him the princely-one-third of the realm's territory. This punishment was not lessened by the fact that Coloman gave his brother other compensation(s) instead. Álmos was now a publicly humiliated person. [120]

In order to avoid further confrontation (or, abuse by a certain group of individuals among the leading social stratum in the realm that wanted to use him against the king),[121]

Álmos now went on a pilgrimage to the Holy Land. [122] Upon
his return from the Holy Land, the king peacefully received
Álmos; [123] and, because Álmos liked to go hunting, the king
had made arrangements for him. [124] And yet, when Álmos
invited the king to attend the dedication ceremony of the
church and abbey, he had established in honor of St. Margaret
at Dömös, [125] and Coloman had accepted the invitation,
rumor started among the king's followers that his brother
only wanted to murder him during the dedication cere-
monies. [126] The rumor may have been false, as most rumors
are, but only the intercession of the bishops saved the prince
from the wrath of his royal brother. [127]

Álmos vas a good sportsman. He went hunting to the
Bakony woods, when his hawk caught a crow. Observing
the struggle of the two birds, the prince suddenly thought
of his own situation and made the careless remark to his
followers (who, incidentally, were the king's men) that the
crow would surely swear to the hawk not to crow again were
the hawk to save his life. [128] The nobles in the prince's entourage only replied that the hawk should not let the crow
go free because it was a dumb bird. [129] The prince lost his
nerve hearing the reply and fled, perhaps not without reason,
to the German court once more. [130]

Henry V was the new German monarch, [131] who had
plans for and with Álmos against his brother. [132] Henry V
was still angry at Colomon because of the successful Hungarian conquest of Dalmatia and, one may suspect, because
of the daring success of King Coloman's Balkan diplomacy. [133]
Because of it, Henry V led a large army against Coloman
in September, 1108; the archbishop of Cologne, nine bishops,
Duke Welf of Bavaria, Frederick of Swabia, Margrave Leopold of Austria, and Engelsbrecht of Istria, and many others
had accompanied the German monarch on this campaign. [134]
Henry V had even concluded an alliance with Svatopluk of
Bohemia, — consequently, when Henry V besieged Pozsony
on the Hungaro-German border, the Czech duke went on
devastating the Hungarian areas west of the Vág river down
to its estuary near Komárom on the Danube. [135]

Coloman moved into the region east of the Vág — and
north of the Danube —, but was unable to establish contact
with the invading Czech forces; so, he fought off the German

marauders in the Pozsony area instead. The siege of the fort
was prolonged until mid-October, when suddenly Boleslaw
III of Poland had broken into Bohemian territory. [136]

The Polish attack upon Bohemia (evidently, the previous
agreement of Coloman with Boleslaw was working; the Polish
ruler must have appreciated Coloman much, whom the Poles
had regarded as the best educated monarch of his age [137] ),
ended the attack of Svatopluk on Hungarian territories. Henry
V, now left to its own resources, accepted Coloman's peace
offer by the end of October. After he received assurances from
Coloman that Álmos will not be punished, Henry V went
home. [138]

Coloman must have made peace with the Germans so
that he gain a free hand in dealing with the Czechs. It was
his turn to invade Moravia. Svatopluk was, however, prepared for a winter campaign and counterattacked in January,
1109, devastating the border area as far as the town of
Nyitra.[139]

During the last four years of his life Coloman had been
ill frequently. [140] In about 1112, he had his brother Álmos
blinded, [141] so that he may thus assure the throne for his own
son, Stephen.[142] It was very sad that the ill king had also
ordered the blinding of Béla, son of Álmos, and even ordered that Béla be emasculated, — an order the king's reeve
refused to carry out. [143]

Álmos continued to lead a miserable life in Dömös abbey.[144] The king could find no peace of mind. He had terrible headaches that made him unable to think clearly.[145] He
now dispatched reeve Benedict, the son of Both, to the abbey
at Dömös with orders to arrest Álmos, and to take him to
the royal court. The unfortunate prince sought refuge at the
main altar of the abbey church, but the reeve attempted to
drag him out of the sanctuary. In the struggle, his knife
accidentally wounded the prince.[146] Only the monks of the
abbey hurrying to defend the prince prevented his abduc-
tion and certain death.[147] The reeve left hurriedly and in
anger. As he rode through the forest in the Pilis hills, his
horse fell into a ditch. Reeve Benedict broke his neck and
died. [148]

King Coloman had earlier entertained Cardinal Dietrich,
who had previously visited Hungary as a papal legate, and

was now en-route to the German court; [149] and permitted
Cardinal Kuno of Praeneste to pronounce anew the excommunication of Henry V in Hungary. [150] The background of
this excommunication was that Henry V had, in 1110, visited
Rome in order to receive the imperial crown from the hands
of the pope. [151] As a precondition for the imperial coronation, the pontiff wanted to handle the question of investiture in
the empire. Upon the proposal of Henry V, they concluded
the Sutri Agreement, according to which the pope would
renounce the *regalia* (temporal interests), while the German
monarch would make a similar gesture concerning lay investiture (of church benefices). [152]

Henry V knew very well that the German hierarchy would
not approve of surrendering the "regalia." And yet, he made
an appearance at Saint Peter's in Rome in order to be crowned emperor. Thereupon the prelates gathered in St. Peter's
broke out in a noisy uproar, and Pope Paschal II decided
that he could not go through with the imperial coronation.
Thereupon, Henry V had the pontiff arrested, and made
him sign an agreement, in which the German monarch retained the right of lay investiture. [153]

The Cardinals and prelates gathered in Rome began a
strong campaign against the false agreement, signed under
pressure from the German monarch. Cardinal Kuno joined
the opposition, though, at this time, he was visiting Jerusalem.
It was in Jerusalem that he had Henry V excommunicated
and had his excommunication renewed at five different church
synods, — including the one held in Hungary. [154] It may be
that the synod in Hungary was held at Esztergom, [155] at a
time when Lawrence was still archbishop of Esztergom. [156]

King Coloman died on February 3, 1116. [157] He was a
great legislator, who had completed the legislative work of
both kings Stephen I and Ladislas I. [158] He had also established the twelfth bishopric in the realm at Nyitra. [159] He
had fought a good fight for the Christianization of his country. [160] The aim of his foreign policy was to expand the frontier
toward the southwest and the northeast, into Croatia and the
seacoast of Dalmatia, and toward Kiev. [161]

His Russian policy (though, it was correct; it made possible that the Cumans and Petchenegs would not constantly
and at will harrass the territory of the realm), has not been

successful. It led to an at least temporary coalition between Kiev and the Cumans.[162] On the other hand, the conquest of Dalmatia was not only a positive accomplishment,[163] but the realization of essential national — economic goals; it tied the realm into world commerce and assured a wider market for its economic — agricultural products abroad.[164]

The chronicler had rendered the date of Coloman's death incorrectly. Coloman did not reign for twenty-five and a half years, nor did he die in the year 1114.[165] But the chronicler who only hated the learned book-lover king, paid no attention to such minute detail.

## NOTES

1. Cf. Marczali, *Enchiridion*, 111, and compare with the synods of Rheims, 813, can. 8, and of Chalons, 813, can. 4, as recorded in Burckhard of Worms, *Decretum*, ii:62-63, *MPL*, 140, 637ac; on the twelfth century meaning of *ius ecclesiasticum*, cf. Sprandel, 64ff.; on its early context, see A. v. Harnack, *Die Mission und Ausbreitung des Christentums in den ersten drei Jahrhunderten*, 2 vols.; 4th rev. ed. (Leipzig, 1924), I, 496; C. Vogel, "La réforme liturgique suos Pépin le Bref," in Erna Patzelt, *Die karolingische Renaissance*, 2nd ed. (Graz, 1965), 178ff.; and, under Charlemagne, *ibid.*, 214ff. R. McKitterich, *The Frankish Church and the Carolingian Reforms, 789-95* (London, 1977), 52f.

2. For text, cf. *RHM*, II, 349ff.; Marczali, *Enchiridion*, 112f. (selections); quoted hereafter as I Esztergom.

3. "Ut causae clericorum uel ecclesiasticorum rerum canonice finiantur;" *Ibid.*, a. 1.

4. M. Zalán, "A Pray kódex forrásaihoz (On the sources of the Pray codex)," *MKSz*, 1 (1926), 246ff., noted that since Esztergom, a. 26 mentioned "Ordo diuinorum et officiorum" in actual reference to *Micrologus de ecclesiasticis obseruationibus* of Bernald of Constance (ob. ca. 1100; cf. Wattenbach, II, 53ff.), the synod may have been held after 1100; Váczy, *Erste Epoche*, 118f., expressed a similar point of view; on the other hand, Manitius, III, 406, said that it was written "vielleicht im Jahre 1089." Pauler, I, 488, note 320, argued to the contrary by saying that Esztergom, a. 55 (in case of adultery the husband was free to marry again) was more lenient than Szabolcs, a. 20 (in case of adultery the couple, if separated, could not marry again). For the text of the *Micrologus*, cf. *MPL*, 151, 977ff., and I. de Batthyány (ed), *Leges ecclesiasticae regni Hungariae et provinciarum adiacentium*, 3 vols., rev. ed. (Claudipoli, 1824), I, 130ff.; in the Pray codex, ff. v-xxvi', - see Radó, *Libri liturgici*, 36.

5. Péterffy, I, 53, anno 1114; St. Katona, *Historia critica regum Hungariae stirpis Arpadianae*, 7 vols. (Pest-Buda, 1779-81), I, 283, anno 1112; on Katona, see C. Horváth, 696., and Hóman-Szekfű, V, 278.

6. Batthyány, *Leges*, I, 120, recorded it anno 1099.

7. I Esztergom, art. 8, recorded *descriptae festivitates,* already mentioned by Szabolcs (Ladislai *Decretum I*), aa. 37 and 38.

8. Pray codex, ff. i-iii; cf. Radó, *Libri liturgici*, 36; Pintér, I, 263ff.

9. *RHM*, II, 351.

10. Cf. II Esztergom (= *Synodus altera*), art. 1, *ibid.*, II, 373, or Marczali, *Enchiridion*, 117, art. 1. Hóman, *Történetírás*, 191ff., esp. 227f.

11. Cf. L. Duchesne (ed), *Liber pontificalis*, 3 vols. (Paris, 1886etc.; rep. Paris, 1955-57), II, 373,4-7; *RHM*, II 375. N. Roselli (ob. 1362), *Vita Paschalis II papae*, argued that the pontiff had forced Coloman to act; cf. Muratori, *Scriptores*, III-1, 365.

12. I Esztergom, aa. 31 and 33.

13. *Ibid.*, art. 32; G. LeBras (ed), *Histoire du droit et des institutions de l'église en occident*, vol. III (Paris, 1958), 159ff., and 551f.

14. Esztergom, aa. 11 and 33, and compare with Tarcal, a. 67. A. Szentirmai, "Der Einfluss des byzantinischen Kirchenrechts auf die Gesetzgebung Ungarns," *Jahrbuch der Österreichischen Byzantinischen Gesellschaft*, 10 (1961), 76ff.

15. On this, cf. II Esztergom, aa. 8-10, *RHM*, II, 373f.; and compare with Tarcal, a. 65; Burckhard, *Decretum*, ii:108-12, *MPL*, 646ac; A. Szentirmai, "Die Anfange des Rechts der Pfarrei in Ungarn," *Österreichisches Archiv für Kirchenrecht*, 10 (1959), 30ff.

16. Esztergom, a. 37.

17. *Ibid.*, a. 5.

18. *Ibid.*, a. 7.

19. *Ibid.*, a. 43.

20. *Ibid.*, a. 30; Burckhardt, *Decretum*, ii:24, *MPL*, 140, 629ab.

21. Esztergom, aa. 47 and 48; Burckhardt, *Decretum*, xiv:2-6, and 8, *MPL*, 140, 886f.; IV Lateran Synod, 1216, can. 15, Mansi, *Concilia*, XXII, 1003d.

22. Esztergom, a. 6; Council of Toledo, 633, can. 25, Mansi, *Concilia*, X 626f.

23. As if Albericus in his preface to the decrees of Tarcal (*RHM* II, 360,10-13) had been quoting from the writ of Pope Urban II (*MPL*, 151, 481b): "Et ille — that is, King Stephen I, — quidem destructor fuit infidelium, iste, — that is, King Coloman, — rectae conversationis augmentator in iustificatione." On clerical continence, cf. IV Lateran Synod, 1216, can. 15, Mansi, *Concilia*, XXII, 1003d, even forbidding hunting, 1003e.

24. I Esztergom, a. 18, and, compare with Burckhardt, *Decretum*, ii:136-37, 139, in *MPL*, 140, 648cd.

25. I Esztergom, a. 19; H. E. Feine, *Kirchliche Rechtesgeschichte*, 5th ed. (Cologne, 1972), 129f.

26. I Esztergom, a. 30, in ref. to Concilium Bituricense, anno 1031, can. 9, in Mansi, *Concilia*, XIX, 504.

27. I Esztergom, a. 29; B. Schimmelpfennig, "Ex fornicatione nati: Studies on the Position of Priests' Sons from the Twelfth to the Fourteenth Centuries," *Studies in Medieval and Renaissance History*, 12 (1979), 1ff.

28. I Esztergom, a. 21; Burckhardt, *Decretum*, ii:136-37, 139; Tarcal, art. 3.

29. I Esztergom, a. 20.

30. Ladislas' *Decretum I*, aa. 17-18.

31. Cf. Synod of Meaux, 845, c. 50, and Concilium Gabilonense, anno 813, c, 40, in Mansi, *Concilia*, XIV, 830 and 102, respectively.

32. I Esztergom, a. 27; Ladislas' *Decretum I*, a. 21.

33. I Esztergom, a. 25; Stephen's *Leges*, i:4.

34. I Esztergom, a. 42; E. Mályusz, "Die Eigenkirche in Ungarn," *Studien zur Geschichte Osteuropas: Gedenkschrift für H. F. Schmid*, 3 (1966), 76ff.

35. Jaffé, *Regesta*, I, no. 538; Gerhoch of Reichersberg, *Opusculum de aedificatione Dei*, cc. 13-14, *MPL*, 194, 1228.

36. *Ibid.*, 194, 1257f., c. 25; I Esztergom, a. 12; P. Classen,*Gerhoch von Reichers-berg* (Wiesbaden, 1960), 40ff.; W. Neuss, *Das Problem des Mittelalters* (Kolmar im Elsass, n.d.), 22f.; Funk-Bihlmeyer, II, 73f.

37. I Esztergom, a. 57; A. Szentirmai, "Das Recht des Erzdekanten (Archidiakone) in Ungarn wahrend des Mittelalters," *Zeitschrift der Savigny Stiftung für Rechtes-geschichte*, kan. Abt., 43 (1957), 132ff.

38. I Esztergom, a. 14.

39. *Ibid.*, a. 17.

40. *Ibid.*, a.37; G. Constable, *Monastic Titles from Their Origins to the Twelfth Century* (Cambridge, 1964), 43ff.

41. I Esztergom, a. 38.

42. "... que in clero sunt, decime non exigantur, excepta quarta parte parro-chiani presbyteri;" *ibid.*, a. 61.

43. I Esztergom, a. 36; Synod of Poitiers, anno 1100, c. 6, in Mansi, *Concilia*, XX, 1126; P. Hofmeister, *Mitra und Stab der wirklichen Prelaten ohne bischöf-lichen Charakter* (Stuttgart, 1928), 3ff.

44. I Esztergom, a. 39. It is not too clear: "nullus episcopus aut presbyter monachum ordinet;" *ordinet* can mean taking monastic vows — cf. Batthyány, *Leges*, II, 125, note 2, — or, ordination for the priesthood; cf. Péterffy, I, 58f.

45. I Esztergom, a. 58.

46. Ladislas' *Decretum I*, aa. 14 and 36.

47. I Esztergom, a. 47.

48. "Presbyter...deponatur;" *ibid.*

49. *Ibid.*, a. 48a.

50. "Si uero in hoc perseuerauerit, excommunicetur...;" *ibid.*, a. 48b.

51. *Ibid.*, a. 41.

52. *Ibid.*, a. 42.

53. *Ibid.*, a. 43, and compare with Piacenza, anno 1095, can. 13, and the Roman Synod, 1099, can. 12, Mansi, *Concilia*, XX, 806 and 963, respectively.

54. Esztergom, a. 44; I. Karácson, *A XI és XII századbeli magyarországi zsina-tok és azoknak a külföldi zsinatokhoz való viszonya* (Synods held in Hungary during the 11th and 12th centuries, and their relations with synods held abroad) (Győr, 1888), 100. On Karácson, see L. Varga's article in memory of Imre Karácson, in *Vigilia*, 48 (1983), 874ff.

55. Esztergom, a. 26; text of the "Ordo" in Batthyány, *Leges*, II, 130-96, and *MPL*, 151, 977-1022. See *supra*, note 4.

56. Esztergom, a. 46.

57. *Ibid.*, a. 8.

58. *Ibid.*, a. 2. and Szabolcs (Ladislas, *Decretum I*), aa. 11, and 37-38; Stephen's *Leges*, i:9; McKitterick, 80ff.; Funk-Bihlmeyer, II, 164ff.

59. Esztergom, a. 3, and compare with Synod of Tours, 813, can. 50, Mansi, *Concilia*, XIV, 81ff.

60. Esztergom, a. 10; Stephen's *Leges*, i:12.

61. Esztergom, a. 49: "episcopi in unaqueque ciuitate duas domos ad coerce-rendos penitentes faciant;" *RHM*, II, 355.

62. Esztergom, a. 64, and compare with Synod of Mainz, 847, can. 14, Mansi, *Concilia*, XIV, 899ff.

63. cf. Synod of Worms, 868, can. 16, excommunicating bishops who failed to summon diocesan meetings; Mansi, XV, 865ff.

64. Cf. J. Horváth, *Stílusproblémák*, 315ff.

65. Coloman "fuit episcopus Waradiensis, sed quia fratres quos habebat morte

sunt preventi, ideo summo pontifice cum eo dispensante regnare conpellitur;"
*SSH*, I, 432,27-29. Earlier, the chronicler simply said that King Ladislas wanted
Coloman "Agriensem episcopum facere;" *ibid.*, I, 419,11-12. As for the spirit of
St. Stephen, see his *Leges*, i:1-2, *RHM*, II, 311f.; G. Tellenbach, *Libertas: Kirche
und Weltordnung im Zeitalter des Investiturstreites* (Stuttgart, 1936), 15f.; Györffy,
*István király*, 267ff.; my book, 111ff.

66. Esztergom, a. 1; Györffy, *István király*, 177ff.; during the synod. Seraphin(us)
was archbishop of Esztergom (1095-1104); cf. Knauz, I, 68, the same Seraphim
who earlier had signed, as court chaplain, the foundation charter of Somogyvár
abbey in 1091. Cf. Marczali, *Enchiridion*, 101 and 102; later, he became dean,
*decanus*, — see Fejér, *Codex dipl.*, I, 469, — and was sent a legate to the court
of the Polish Boleslav in 1103. Cf. Knauz, I, 71. A gloss added as preface to the
decrees named Lawrence as archbishop of Esztergom; cf. Péterffy, I, 4, — but
not published in *RHM*, — may have been a later addition, cf. Pauler, I, 448, note
320; Gams, 376, mentioned Simon as the ordinary of Pécs in this period, but said
nothing about Esztergom.

67. "Numquid Hungarico principi dictum est: et tu conversus confirma fratres
tuos;" Fejér, *Codex dipl.*, II, 32f.

68. *Ibid.*, II, 13, anno 1102.

69. "... et nullus praeter regem super res ecclesiasticas iudicare praesumat."
Cf. *MPL*, 163, 198f. (dated Nov. 2, 1106). J. Deér, "Der Anspruch der Herrscher
des 12 Jahrhunderts auf die Apostolische Legation," *Archivum Historiae Pontificalis*, 2 (1964), 171ff.

70. Cf. Fraknói, I, 31.

71. Fejér, II, 37f.

72. Based upon the text of the renunciation published by Duchesne: "Denun-
tiamus vobis, Patre venerande, nos legi divine subditos ac secundum eam servire
paratos, ... et investituram episcoporum hactenus a maioribus nostris habitam,
*iuxta admonitionem vestram* (italics mine!) dimisimus, et si quid in electionibus
huiusmodi minus canonice Petro actum est, de cetero Deo volente cavebimus."
Cf. *Liber pontificalis*, II, 373,4-7. The text in *RHM*, II, 375 is based upon Mansi,
*Concilia*, XX, 1211f.

73. "... horas canonicas ut episcopus persolvebat." Cf. *SSH*, I, 433,1-2.

74. "... quam fecit rex Hungariae ad mandatum papae;" cf. E. Martene-U.
Durand (eds), *Thesaurus novus anecdotorum*, 5 vols. (Repr. New York, 1968),
IV, 127f.

75. Cf. N. Roselli (ob. 1362), *Vita Paschalis II papae*, in Muratori, *Scriptores*,
II-1, 365.

76. Coloman was the bishop of Várad — cf. *SSH*, I, 432,27-29, — though King
Ladislas I wanted him to be the ordinary of Eger, cf. *ibid.*, I, 419,11-12.

77. Archbishop Anselm of Canterbury was a reformer in the **Gregorian sense**
in the Church; cf. F. Cantor, *Church, Kingship and Lay Investiture in England,
1089-1135* (Princeton, 1958), 202f. J. A. Green, *The Government of England
Under Henry I* (Cambridge, 1986), 22.

78. A compromise — see F. Barlow, *The English Church, 1066-1154* (London,
1979), 302, contrary to the view held by Hampe, *Hochmittelalter*, 166, reached
without the intervention, but under the influence of Ivo of Chartres: cf. Sprandel,
175. For text, see *Eadmeri Historia novorum in Anglia*, ed. M. Rule. R.S. (London,
1884), 186. Green, 38 and 39, and n. 6.

79. Ekkehardi *Chronicon*, anno 1106, in *MGHSS*, VI, 240,11-26 (and, text B,
*ibid.*, 240,11-24); name also spelled Warstallis (=Wkrstallis), *ibid.*, VI, 244,14,

"oppidum munitissimum Warstal nomine," *ibid.*, VI, 771,12, and note 80. H. Jedin, *Handbuch der Kirchengeschichte*, vol. III-1: *Die mittelalterliche Kirche* (Freiburg-Vienna, 1973), 451, and 453f.

80. Cf. *MGHLL*, IV, const. 1, 562, 565 and 566.

81. *MGHSS*, VI, 240f.

82. Cf. Uodalscalcus de Eginone et Herimanno, *ibid.*, XII, 438,14-37, and, more briefly but concisely drafted in *Translatio sancti Modoaldi*, c. 10 and c. 12, *ibid.*, XII, 295,26-33, and XII, 296,3-18. Brief reference to Guastalla in Donizonis *Vita Mathildis, ibid.*, XII, 401,1109-10.

83. Cf. II Esztergom, art. 1, in *RHM*, II, 373; L. E. Boyle, "The *De regno* and the Two Powers," in J. R. O'Donnell (ed), *Essays in Honor of Anton Charles Pegis* (Toronto, 1974), 237ff.

84. II Esztergom, art. 2, *RHM*, II, 373; Stephen I's *Leges*, ii:17, *ibid.*, II, 310ff. (c. 51 in Migne!), and compare with the Synod of Mainz, 847, can. 5, in Mansi, *Concilia*, XIV, 899f.

85. II Esztergom, a. 3.

86. In view of the contents of II Esztergom, its decrees had to be enacted after the renounciation made by Coloman — cf. G. Wenczel (ed), *Codex diplomaticus Arpadianus continuatus*, 12 vols. (Pest, 1860etc.), I, 43, — perhaps as late as 1112; Péterffy, I, 42ff., implied that some of its decrees simply repeated the resolutions of Tarcal, but II Esztergom, a. 1, may prove that to the contrary. II Esztergom may have been convoked by Archbishop Lawrence, who died in 1116; cf. Knauz, I, 72. The *Constitutio pro clero ecclesiae Arbensis* was signed "per manus venerabilis Laurentii ... in presentia episcoporum, quorum nominae hae sunt...;" *RHM*, II, 378. Judged by the signatures on a document issued in Coloman's reign, Lawrence might previously have been the ordinary of Csanád; cf. Szentpétery, *Regesta*, I, nos. 43 and 46; Fejér, II, 41, and VII, 57.

87. Cf. Council of Amalfi (Melfitanum), a. 1090, can. 12, Mansi, *Concilia*, XX, 721ff.; III Synod of Rome, a. 1099, can. 13, *ibid.*, XX, 961ff.

88. II Esztergom, a. 9.

89. *Ibid.*, a. 10.

90. *Ibid.*, a. 12.

91. *Ibid.*, a. 8.

92. "Si qua mulier a viro suo fugerit, reddatur ei, et quociens fugerit, restituatur ei, quia...;" *ibid.*, a. 4, *RHM*, II, 373, so different from Esztergom, a. 52a: "Si qua mulier a uiro suo fugerit, reddatur marito suo semel et bis; tercia uice, si plebia, sine spe libertatis uenundetur; si nobilis est, sine spe coniugii peniteat." Cf. *ibid.*, II, 355. Also, Stephen, *Leges*, i:30; "abroad," *Liber Papiensis Lotharii*, c. 95, *MGHLL*, sectio IV, const. 1, 557.

93. II Esztergom, a. 4; Esztergom, a. 50; Stephen's Laws, i:33 (Migne, c. 31).

94. II Esztergom, a. 7, compare with Esztergom, a. 52g (*RHM*, II, 356); Stephen's Laws, i:30.

95. II Esztergom, a. 5, compare with Szabolcs, a. 20; Stephen's Laws, i:30; Esztergom, a. 52b.

96. II Esztergom, a. 16; see synod of Trosle (Trosleianum), anno 909, cap. ix, Mansi, *Concilia*, XVIIIA, 263ff.

97. Cf. Concilium Vernense, anno 755, cap. xv: "... ut omnes homines laici publicas nuptias faciant, tam nobiles, quam ignobiles;" *ibid.*, XII, 577ff.

98. See Concilium Rotomagense, a. 1072, c. 14: married clerics may not function as clerics, Mansi, *Concilia*, XX, 34ff.; and Synod of London, a. 1102, c. 22, *ibid.*, XX, 1149ff.

99. II Esztergom, a. 16, and compare with the Fourth Lateran Council, a. 1215, c. 51, Mansi, *Concilia*, XXII, 1038.

100. Cf. II Esztergom, art. 15.

101. *Ibid.*, art. 14.

102. *Ibid.*, art. 1.

103. *Ibid.*, aa. 2-3; Stephen I's *Leges*, a. ii:17.

104. It enacted law "ex auctoritate Apostolici;" cf. *RHM*, II, 373. A. Brackmann, "Die Ursachen der geistigen und politischen Wandlung Europas im 11 und 12 Jahrhundert," *HZ*, 149 (1934), 229ff.

105. *RHM*, II, 371f., preface.

106. *Ibid.*, II, 371f., aa. 1-2, and 6-7.

107. *Ibid.*, aa. 3-5. Kumorovitz, *art. cit.* (1980), 96f., and notes 5 and 9, and p. 98, note 13. For a different view, cf. B. Hirsch-Reich, "Joachim von Fiore und das Judentum," in P. Wilpert (ed), *Judentum im Mittelalter* (Berlin, 1966), 228ff.

108. *Chronicon pictum*, c. 142.

109. *Ibid.*, c. 144.

110. "Quo statuto consilio principes reversi sunt. Cumque Grak regi dixisset, quemadmodum statuerant...;" *ibid.*, I, 423,25-28, meant no direct communication between the king and the nobles. On *comes* Grak, see Knauz, I, 65, and Fejér, I, 482; II, 423. For a different interpretation, cf. F. Makk, *Magyarország a 12. században* (Hungary in the 12th century) Budapest, 1986), 60ff.

111. "Dicebant autem duci: 'Domine dux! rex insidiatur tibi et capere vult te.' ... Hoc autem audiente (sic! = audientes) ambo iuvenes et lascivi congregaverunt exercituum." Cf. *SSH*, I, 422,33-35; I, 423,4-7.

112. This is the reason that there are two references made to Stephen I's *Leges* in Tarcal: "Nam quis ambigat a sancto patre nostro Stephano, viro quippe Apostolico, legem populo nostro datam;" *RHM*, II, 359,11-13. And, "... prefati regis sanctae memoriae Stephani legalem textum recensuit;" *ibid.*, II, 360,5-7.

113. The emperor had to intervene between the monarch and the opposition; "venit in confinium Hungariae, ut colloquium cum rege haberet et inter eos pacem firmaret." Cf. *SSH*, I, 430,3-5.

114. *Ibid.*, I, 429,4-9.

115. "Post hec rex reduxit ducem ad pacem;" *ibid.*, I, 430,8-10.

116. Cf. M. Gallus, *Chronicon Polonorum*, ii:29, in *MGHSS*, IX, 456. On the background, cf. D. Obolensky, "Relations between Byzantium and Russia, eleventh to fifteenth century," *Thirteenth International Congress of Historical Sciences, Moscow, 1970* (Moscow, 1970), 1ff.

117. *Chronicon pictum*, c. 147.

118. Gallus, *Chronicon*, ii:29.

119. *Chronicon pictum*, c. 147.

120. Ekkehardi *Chronicon*, anno 1108, in *MGHSS*, VI, 242.

121. *SSH*, I, 427,22-23.

122. *Ibid.*, I, 427,20-21.

123. "Rex eum suscepit ad pacem;" *ibid.*, I, 427,22-23.

124. "... et dabat ei rex omnia ad venandum necessaria;" *ibid.*, I, 427,25-27, with nothing said about the *ducatum*: the princely one-third granted to him earlier (c. 142).

125. *Chronicon pictum*, c. 148; Knauz, I, 88.

126. "... quod insidias preparasset, ut interficeret regem," *ibid.*, I, 428,4-5.

127. "Reverentissimi episcopi et alii boni principes ... intercesserunt pro eo apud regem;" *ibid.*, I, 428,10-15.

128. *Ibid.*, I, 428,17-31.

129. "... nec cornix iurare posset, cum sit animal irrationale;" *ibid.*, I, 428f.

130. *Ibid.*, I, 429,4-9.

131. Otto of Freising, *Chronicon*, vii:13, *MGHSS*, XX, 254.

132. Dandalo, *Chronicon*, ix:10:11, in Muratori, *Scriptores*, XII, 259; and ix:10:16, *ibid.*, XII, 264f.

133. Th. Spalatensis *Chronica*, c. 17, in Schwandtner, *Scriptores*, III, 532ff.; Ekkehardi *Chronicon*, anno 1108.

134. Cf. G. M. von Knonau, *Jahrbücher des deutschen Reiches unter Heinrich IV und Heinrich V*, vol. VI (Berlin, 1907; rep. 1965), 83ff.; I. Kapitánffy, "Magyar bizánci kapcsolatok Szent László és Kálmán uralkodásának idejében (Hungaro-Byzantine contacts in the days of St. Ladislas and King Coloman)," *Acta historia Szegediensis*, 75 (1983), 19ff.

135. Cosmas of Prague, *Chronica Bohemorum*, iii:22, *MGHSS*, IX, 31ff.; F. Palacky, *Würdigung der alten böhmischen Geschichtsschreiber, rev. ed.* (Prague, 1869), 1ff., 16f.; Wattenbach, II, 203ff.; Annalista Saxo, anno 1108, *MGHSS*, VI, 746f.; Wattenbach, II, 256ff.

Wattenbach, II, 203ff.; Annalista Saxo, anno 1108, *MGHSS*, VI, 746f.; Wattenbach, II, 256ff.

136. Cosmas, *Chronica*, iii:22, *MGHSS*, IX, 112f.; F. Palacky, *Geschichte von Böhmen*, vol. I (Prague, 1844), 335ff. On the background of Palacky as a historian, see the series of three articles in *Catholic Hungarians' Sunday*, Youngstown, Ohio, Jan. 15, 22 and 29, 1984. *Chronica principum Poloniae*, *MPH*, III, 428ff., c. 15; M. Gallus, *Chronica Polonorum*, ii:29, *MGHSS*, IX, 423ff.; G. Labuda, "Bazoar Anonymus Gallus krónikájában (Some comments on the Chronicle of the anonymous Gallus)," *Századok*, 104 (1970), 173ff.

137. "... rex Ungarorum Colomanus, super reges universos suo tempore regentes litterali eruditus;" Gallus, ii:29; *Chronica principum Poloniae*, c. 15; Mügeln, c. 49, *SSH*, II, 193ff.

138. Freising, *Chronicon*, vii:13, *MGHSS*, XX, 254,23-24.

139. Cosmas, *Chronica*, iii:25.

140. "Post autem rex cepit egrotare graviter et habebat quendam medicum Latinum nomine Daconem, cui nimium credebat;" *SSH*, I, 430,3-34.

141. *Chronicon pictum*, c. 150; Gy. Kristó, "XI-XIII századi epikáink és az Árpádkori írásos hagyomány (Hungarian epics of the 11th-13th centuries and the written historical tradition of the Arpadian age)," *Ethnographia*, 83 (1972), esp. 57ff.

142. It must have been II Esztergom, a. 2, *RHM*, II, 373, that provided legal basis for the blinding order; cf. *SSH*, I, 430,11-13.

143. *Ibid.*, I, 430,11-20.

144. "Ductus est autem dux Almus in monasterium suum in Demes;" *ibid.*, I, 430,27-29.

145. *Ibid.*, I, 430f.

146. *Ibid.*, I, 431,22-26, and 33-37; I, 432,2-6.

147. *Ibid.*, I, 432,6-15.

148. "... de equo et cervice fracta mortuus est. Et canes eius qui sequabantur ipsum, devovaverunt carnes eius et ossa;" *ibid.*, I, 432,16-23.

149. "... legatione in Pannoniam functus;" Ekkehard, *Chronicon*, anno 1115, *MGHSS*, VI, 249,3-4.

150. *Ibid.*, VI, 251,30-38 (anno 1116).

151. Cf. *Chronica monasterii Gasinensis*, anno 1110, *ibid.*, VII, 778.

152. Cf. "Coronatio Romana," *MGHLL*, II, 66.

153. Cf. "Acta coronationis," *ibid.*, II, 72.; L. E. Boyle, "The *De regno* and the Two Powers," in J. R. O'Donnell (ed), *Essays in Honor of Charter Th. Pegis* (Toronto, 1974), 237ff.

154. Ekkehard, *Chronicon*, anno 1116, *MGHSS*, VI, 251,19-39. Mansi, *Concilia*, XXI. 121ff.; 129ff.; and 135f.

155. Péterffy, I, 52.

156. Knauz, I, 72.

157. According to a document issued in 1124, "anno nono regni mei," by Stephen II, the death of Coloman may be dated as of 1116; cf. Szentpétery, *Regesta*, I, no. 51.

158. *RHM*, II, 360,5-7.

159. Péterffy, I, 44; Katona, *Hist. critica*, III, 482.

160. Cf. Tellenbach, *Libertas*, 196.

161. *Chronicon pictum*, c. 152.

162. *Ibid.*, cc. 145 and 147; Hodinka, 60Aff., and 67A (anno 1099).

163. Cf. Szentpétery, *Regesta*, I, nos. 35 and 36.

164. *SSH*, I, 433,12-18. K. Bosl *et al*, *Eastern and Western Europe in the Middle Ages* (London, 1970), 125ff.

165. *Chronicon pictum*, c. 147; Szentpétery, *Regesta*, I, no. 51.

# IV

# Primogeniture: Stephen II

Potentiores regni Stephanum Colemanni
filium in regem coronaverunt.

*Chronicon pictum*, c. 153

Of the two Hungarian chroniclers who discussed Hungarian events in the twelfth century, and whose record only survived in the *Chronicon pictum,* [1] one must have been a King Coloman sympathizer, — the other, a Coloman hater —, but they among each other regarded the idea of centralized monarchy as essential for the maintenance of spiritual and temporal order of the country. [2] For example, the pro-Coloman chronicler wrote about Stephen II, Coloman's son, that though he was young, he was fit for the throne; "erat adhuc inpubes, sed spiritus eius in membris eius." [3] And yet, his record of the king's reign does not support his assertion. In recording it, the chronicler simply stressed the need for a strong monarchy. On the other hand, the anti-Coloman chronicler noted — in relying upon a biblical quote: "confirmatum est regnum in manibus eius," — that Béla II the Blind (who had been blinded by Coloman, so that Béla could not hinder the succession of Stephen II, Coloman's son, to the throne) made the realm strong under his rule. [4] That is, the blind monarch was determined to keep tight reins of kingship — with the aid of his outspoken and witty queen of Serbian birth. [5]

In this manner the two chroniclers who faced each other like two cherubim in the Holy of Holies, attempted to counterbalance the influx of western ideas — that undermine royal authority — entering the realm with the crusaders during the mid-twelfth century. Although they attempted to realize their goal by different methods, the two chroniclers wanted to preserve the record of strong (centralized) kingship in the country. Their narratives remain written proof that the

developing Hungarian intelligentsia, — still young and inexperienced — took a part in the "progressive" French
(western) intellectual trend(s), but it developed ideas on its
own to become a member in the, at times contradictory,
cultural commonwealth of western Europe. [6]

About Stephen II (1116-31), the son of Coloman the
Learned, the Hungarian chroniclers have diverse opinions.
Simon de Keza, for instance, did not even mention his name,
because he reported that, as Coloman's successor, it was
Béla who ruled, whom they had buried at Fehérvár. Furthermore, upon the death of Béla, it was Géza who had possessed
the throne for twenty years, whom they also had buried at
Fehérvár. [7] The chronicler of the *Chronicon Budense*, or,
as he is known, for example, to L. Erdélyi, the Chronicler-of-
Óbuda, [8] did mention Stephen, Coloman's son, by saying
that he had ruled for eighteen years and five months; in 1131
he died and was buried at Várad. [9] The eighteen years plus
months would date the reign of Stephen II between 1114
and 1132, but the chronicler left out of his consideration a
decree isssued by Stephen II in the year of 1124, "anno nono
regni mei," that is, in the ninth year of his reign. Consequently, one may date the death of King Coloman as of
1116. [10]

The reign of Stephen II was described at some length
by the Chronicler-of-Stephen III in the *Chronicon pictum*.
He emphasized at the beginning of his report that the "potentiores regni" — the mighty ones of the realm, — did
crown Stephen II king, who, tough awfully young, had already possessed a strong soul (will-power?). [11]

The reader has the impression that it was because of the
king's young age, "adhuc inpubes," that the chronicler
emphasized his immediate coronation by the mighty lords
of the realm. During the ninth year of his reign (the document referred to above was a decree issued by him to confirm the privileges the cities in Dalmatia had obtained from
King Coloman), he visited the seacoast, where he was hon-
orably received by the population. [12] Upon his return from
the seacoast he had campaigned against Poland, and, simultaneously, began negotiations with Czech court. [13] The
chronicler says that he seemed to try to appease the mighty
lords of his realm by starting talks with the Czechs on the

Olsava stream that, at that time, had formed the Hungaro-Czech border.

The course of politico-diplomatic events, however, took a different turn. The chronicler says that an individual named Solt, who had previously been expelled from Hungary and fled to the Czech court, had stirred up trouble for his former master. Before the start of negotiations Solt sent a secret communication to Stephen II to warn him that the Czech prince had plans to take him captive during the (forthcoming) talks. [14] But Solt dispatched a message to the Czech duke also telling him to take care and arm himself and his men because the Hungarian king was going to capture him during the forthcoming talks. [15]

The Czechs, being angry and drunk, had armed themselves, the chronicler reports, [16] and Solt, the traitor, sent another messenger to the king: let the monarch order a detachment of (royal) archers to surround the camp of the duke. The king, himself being a man of temper, "ut fuit impetuosus," had taken action without consulting with his council (a rather revealing comment from the chronicler who in a previous paragraph had said that Stephen II was a ruler who in spite of his youth had learnt the art of self-control) to realize Solt's recommendations. [17]

The results were to be foreseen. The Czechs saw the approaching archers, turned on them and pursued them to the royal camp. [18] The chronicler depicted as worthless, "vilissimi," the Cuman and Székler archers, whose unexpected defeat (at the hands of; flight from the field from the Czech troops) endangered the king's personal safety causing him to leave the camp site in a hurry. [19] The question may be asked, of course, whether the Cumans were identical with the Petchenegs, [20] who, as updated Hungarian research maintains that, indeed, they were [21] trusted friends of the monarch. [22] Some of the Cuman-Petchenegs have joined the king's council, [23] where they, and other members of the council, were sitting (on their stools) while consulting with the king. [24]

For someone who had mastered the art of self-control, Stephen II had acted foolishly on the Czech-Hungarian border, [25] because it is evident from the report of the chronicler that he went there without previous consultation with,

and without the consent of, his advisors. [26] The king had
behaved irresponsibly on the grounds that he had accepted
in good faith (or, out of sheer laziness) the unrequested mes-
sages of a traitor expelled from the realm. [27] Stephen II
actually let a traitor, whom he most probably did not even
know, direct him. The very fact that the king could not order
members of his entourage to arm themselves and stand up
to the approaching Bohemian troops [28] (who must have
behaved just as irrationally), only proves that the son of the
book-lover king was unfit for the crown, or for the leadership of his country. [29]

The chronicler must have altered by now his opinion
about Stephen II, who, the chronicler wrote, [30] did have
a rather high regard for himself: wise like Salomon; strong
as Samson; and heroic like David (all of the Old Testament),
though, in the words of the chronicler, he was, really, no
match for them at all. [31]

The king was, however, fortunate because of Palatine
Janus, son of Urosa, who had his camp pitched at a distance
from the king's, and had staged a counterattack thoroughly
destroying the Bohemian forces. [32] It may have been this
unexpected encounter that caused the Czech chronicler,
Cosmas of Prague, to observe that the Hungarians were the
inhabitants of a very powerful and rich country, capable
of resisting the entire world. [33] Proud were they but naive,
remarked the canon of Prague, because they had spoken
contemptuously with the Czech duke; [34] another source provided a similar though less well balanced account of these
events. [35]

Janus the Palatine reported the unexpected victorious
outcome of this struggle to Stephen II who, though overjoyed,
was unhappy that the body of Solt, who had caused all the
trouble (!), could not be found among the dead on the battlefield. [36] On the other hand, perhaps on account of the
prelude to the battle and the treachery of Solt; perhaps because of the firm stand taken by the Palatine, the Hungarian nobles now decided to observe the personal habits of the
young king who, as a bachelor, had been leading an irregular
life. They had asked, on his behalf, for the hand in marriage
of the daughter of Guiscard of Apulia. [37]

The *Chronicon pictum* does not mention it, but another

contemporary source, the anonymous clerical biographer
of Archbishop Conrad of Salzburg by providing perhaps
less reliable but still valuable information, does say that, in
1118, the Hungarians had entered southeastern German
territory (Ostmark), whereupon markgrave Leopold, who
was in charge of the military defense of the area, invaded
Hungary with his Czech auxiliaries, and occupied Vasvár. [38]
(The cleric wrote "castrum ferrerum," that could also mean
Kismarton alias Eisenstadt.)

It is most probably here that one may find a clue to the
planned Hungaro-Czech meeting on the Olsava, but prevented from taking place by the treachery of Solt. The fact
that the margrave had broken into Hungarian territory with
Czech help leads to the conclusion that the successful treachery
of Solt was not Solt's own idea, but resulted from the encour-
agement and plan of the Czech duke's advisors, whose interests must have been served by keeping the king from conducting peaceful negotiations with their lord. [39] The Salzburg
biographer reports that the representatives of the Hungarian
king had to discuss, under pressure from Salzburg, but with
the archbishop's representatives, the release of prisoners of
war captured, and the return of the booty taken in Leopold's
campaign into Hungary. [40]

The correlation of the fact that it was not the concerned
margrave, but the archbishop's representatives who had
negotiated on behalf of the margrave with Stephen II shows
that someone had a bad conscience. It was the margrave who
invaded Hungarian territory after he had issued accusations
against the Hungarians, and it is likely that at the Hungaro-
Czech talks the prelude to, and the outcome of the Hungarian encounter with Leopold would have been discussed —
and appeared in a different light. [41] The Salzburg biographer's remark that Stephen II had only agreed to the
peace terms after the archbishop had his armed forces placed
into operation against him, should be seriously considered. [42]
The archbishop would not leave his protege in the lurch
while to the Hungarian king it may have seemed to daring
to go to war with a prince of the Church. As a matter of fact,
when the cathedral in Salzburg burnt to the ground, Stephen
II hurried to the archbishop's aid by sending church vest-
ments and gold and silver to Salzburg. [43]

Was it the treachery of Solt? Was it the direct intervention of the archbishop of Salzburg in Hungarian politics?
It remains a fact that Stephen II did not enjoy a very high
reputation among his own, and the king must have had low
prestige before his nobles. [44] The poorly planned campaign
against Kiev ending in a disaster in 1123, [45] proved only
how weak the king's position must have been on the domestic
front. [46]

Yaroslav, prince of Vladimir, and Bezen, prince of
Ruthenia had invited Stephen II to enter Russian soil, in order
to avenge, the chronicler reports, the defeat his father had
suffered there on a previous occasion. [47] It is evident from
the chronicler's description that this recent Kievan affair
had not been too popular with the nobles; and, when the
king actually gave orders for the attack of a Ruthenian fort,
the nobles holding a council meeting, "ad consilium
regis,"[48] literally refused him obedience. They had threatened
the king, who did not think out his plans too clearly, with
dethronement, — unless he gave orders to withdraw from
Kievan territory. "Nos barones" (We, your barons), do not
lay siege to the fort; if it pleases you, Lord, *Domine*, you
besiege the fort yourself. But we go back home, and elect
another king; "et nobis regem eligemus." [49]

The wording of the text implies that the council (or, at
least the nobles who were in attendance on the monarch)
regarded the king as already dethroned, and they, members
of the council, felt free to elect another king. Stephen II
did quickly changed his mind, and although he had accomplished little, returned home and saved his throne. [50]

It is important to note that the nobles' decision to de-
throne their monarch was taken after the death of the
Ruthenian prince Bezen, who had been assassinated. [51] The
nobles could no longer find any reason, nor could they think
of any legal pretext for prolonging their campaign on Kievan
territory. [52] But they may also have been concerned about
the safety of their king in a hostile country, as it is quite evident
from the recorded verbal exchange between Stephen II and
a *baro*, named Cosmas de Pázmány. [53] The opposition
organized and led by Baron Cosmas seems to have been concerned though that the king, like his father before him, would
attempt to extend his authority (and influence) over Kievan-

Ruthenian soil, thereby increasing royal authority and personal prestige. Cosmas and his barons could not consent to the realization of such a plan (or, at least, an idea). [54]

Stephen II had to vent his frustations and decided to fight a war in Poland, — the chronicler noted that the affair took place some three years after Kiev, — while the king's private armies harrassed the lands of the Bulgarians and of the Serbians. [55]

And yet, the events discussed here may have had an entirely different background. The barely fifteen year old Stephen II had, right at the beginning of his reign, entered into war with Venice. The doge of Venice, Ordelaphus Phaledro, had, with a large naval force attacked the seacoast of Dalmatia held by Hungary in order to regain the city states for the republic. The island of Arbe had immediately surrendered to Phaledro, when the doge and his council had promised to respect the ancient rights, customs and privileges of the island. The doge and his retinue confirmed their promises with an oath. The doge's forces occupied Zara and Bielograd, though the garrison at Zara had put up a fierce struggle. On the other hand, Archbishop Manessess of Spaleto had preserved Hungarian rule in his city-state.

Doge Phaledro now had ordered that hostages be taken from the conquered city republics, and had Bielograd refortified. In order to crown his accomplishments, the doge had reassumed his title, Prince of Croatia-Dalmatia, [56] — with the approval of the German emperor. [57]

Stephen II's nobles were most unwilling to renounce the Dalmatian conquests of King Coloman so quickly. [58] One may wonder, of course, whether the term "Hungarian nobles" used by the chronicler may denote the government council of the realm? [59] Now the king and the council began to plan a new campaign for the reconquest of the seashore, and to do that they wanted to make certain of a Hungaro-Czech political-diplomatic background. That must have been the reason for the meeting between Stephen II and Vladislas I of Bohemia, that had been arranged for the king by the nobles. [60] (The chronicler wrote "placuit regno" meaning most probably members of the government council, "potentiores regni." [61] ) The same meeting that had been prevented from taking place by the Czech duke's advisors through the manipulations of Solt. [62]

It is against the background of these precautionary arrangements that the Hungaro-Venetian war began. Sergius,
Stephen II's reeve, led a naval attack upon the island of Arbe
to reclaim it. Protected, however, by Venetian galleys, Arbe's
citizens defeated the forces of Sergius (who must have landed;
there was a land battle), had captured and burnt his ships.
The reeve and his troops had been captured, but the Arbe
population decided to let Sergius and his troops go home
in peace. As a precautionary counter measure, Doge Phaledro
had placed Zara under a naval siege, with some assistance
from Byzantium — and the German court. The Hungarian
viceroy (banus) of Croatia now took command of the military
operations to protect Zara, but he, too had suffered defeat;
Zara was recaptured by Venice. Venice also occupied Spaleto,
Sebenico and Trau, thus extending full Venetian control
of the Dalmatian seacoast. [63]

Stephen II had tried again to retake Zara. The attack
had been so forceful that the doge hurried in person to the
defense of the fortified city — to suffer defeat and be killed
in action. The remains of his troops fled to the city, which they
helped to defend against the Hungarian viceroy. The citizens
of Zara now arranged for the son of the dead doge to go as
ambassador seeking an armistice with the viceroy. [64]

For the next five years, peace had prevailed between
Hungary and the Venetian republic. After that, Stephen II
had attacked Dalmatia anew, and the Dalmatians who bore
the financial burden laid upon them by Venice with great
difficulty, had decided to seek Hungarian rule; they
submitted, one by one, to the Hungarian king. In return,
Stephen II renewed, one by one, the privileges granted by
his father to the city republics. Only Zara held out against
a Hungarian takeover. But two years later, because of a
Venetian counteroffensive, Venice had regained control of
Dalmatia. [65]

It must have been the renewed conflict(s) with Venice that
held the Hungarian nobles back from supporting the king
in the Kievan campaign. The nobles, that is, the government
council, wanted no two front war on their hands. [66]

It is of some interest to note the appearance of (royal)
court army commandos: *falangos* (*sic!* = *felanges?*) *aulicorum*
by the chronicler. [67] Previously, Keza had used this expres-

sion, [68] following, most probably, the vocabulary used by the author-compiler of the *Annales Altahenses.* [69] In other words, the chronicler claimed that the nobles had not taken part in the aimless and irrational devastation of neighboring (Russian, Polish, Bulgarian) territories. Were the words of the chronicler to correspond to the political-military reality in Hungary of the 1120's, then it must be assumed that a king of the blood of Árpád needed private troops to have an armed force to carry out his intentions, and the king had to find employment (and pay-compensation) for his undisciplined and, evidently underpaid troops. There is a striking suspicion in the mind of the reader that Stephen II was not only a very insignificant person as a king, but was also a weak ruler, whom the lords of the realm had tolerated on the throne only because he was an Árpád, whose reign assured continued legitimacy in the royal succession. [70]

Legitimacy in royal succession did not, however, mean that the monarch could abuse his people's confidence. His bad conscience made Stephen II almost paranoid (as a person), who only saw traitors and opponents in everyone near him. He did many evil things a king was not supposed to do, wrote the chronicler. [71] He had, for instance, a lady (not a mere woman) named Christina burnt alive, probably for political reasons. [72] (It may have been she, though, who had disclosed the secret military plans of the king to the Byzantine court. [73] )

Stephen II had shown no mercy toward his opponents and political enemies. "Et super homines cocturas cum stercore equino faciebat fieri," saying, in fact, that he had dry horse manure burnt over the heads of some people enclosed in a small compartment. [74] On the other hand, he had, for instance, appeased the monks of Pannonhalma by restoring the fishing rights of the abbey. [75]

After the disaster of Kiev and the rather shaky political arrangements made with Venice, Stephen II had tolerated little questioning of his policies. [76] He must have tried to divide his opposition. [77] He did rely upon human torture to assure submission of his opponents to his will (and policies); he could make them testify against themselves. [78] His opponents must have hated, but also feared him.

It must have been the plan of the king's judicial system

to use force, — to obtain evidence from the accused, — that they let hot wax from burning candles drip into the rectum (anus) of the accused (defendant), as it to say that they kept the candle burning until it burnt itself out. [79]

Could the king have been such a scarred person? Did he have such a negative opinion of the constitutionality of his royal office? The question ought to be asked, of course, how did the chronicler obtain all this information? Did he base it upon written documentation, — or, on hearsay? Did the chronicler talk to and with individuals who had gone through, and survived, such an interrogation process? If he did, did he openly sympathize with the victims? — or, though telling the truth, he did enjoy collecting damaging information about the uncultured son of the learned king, whom he, the chronicler, hated so much? [80]

As if to preempt further arguments, the chronicler reports that Prince Álmos, who had previously been blinded by King Coloman, [81] was alive and lived in fear of his life; for that reason, he had sought protection at the Byzantine court. [82] A political exile Álmos became, the emperor's protegee, and many Hungarian dissenters had grouped around him in Byzantium. [83] Although the chronicler does not tell it here (he will tell it somewhere else), the main core of the story was that the court had granted political exile status to the blinded Álmos, and Álmos' son, Béla (Álmos was named Constantius at the court), and that was the reason that Stephen II prepared for war with Byzantium. [84]

The emperor, John II Comnenus, was unwilling to extradite his princely refugees, [85] and war begun. [86] The troops of Stephen II had invaded the empire, occupied and destroyed Belgrade, took Nis and Sardica (Sofia), and went as far as Helipolis. The surprised emperor had to seek refuge himself in Helipolis. The war must have broken out unexpectedly, probably without a previous declaration of war, as the Byzantine court was not prepared for it. It may seem that it was important for Stephen II to have his (private mercenary) troops preoccupied constantly with warring. That may also be the reason why the war did not end with the death, in exile, of Álmos. [87]

Because of political reasons, — the deeds of this king were recorded by the chronicler of the age of King Stephen

III, when relations between the Hungarian court and Byzantium were rather strained, [88] — the chronicler did not provide the whole background, but reported on his own hostilities had been resumed with the Byzantines. The war began, he wrote, because of the ill meant remarks made by Emperor Mauritius about the Hungarian monarch in front of Mauritius' empress, Pyrisk (Irene), daughter of Ladislas I of Hungary (and aunt of Stephen II); the emperor had referred to the Hungarian king as to his slave, and when his empressed had made a protest, Mauritius slapped her. [89]

Now, it may be that wife-slapping, wife-beating were characteristic habits of the age; and yet, careful reading of the Latin "castigavit" transliterates the term as having-had-a-quarrel-with; was angry-at-someone, etc., or, if the translation of the Latin sentence in the text as "chastized her," had "severely criticised her," would, perhaps be more appropriate. [90]

The other remark of the chronicler: (1) the Greeks had feared the Hungarians like thunder from the heavens; (2) mothers on Byzantine soil had their crying babies silenced by repeating to them the name of King Stephen; (3) seven hundred Frank knights had accompanied the king on his Byzantine campaign, and the king had an unpleasant exchange of angry words with the emperor; finally (4), the "Greeks" had thoroughly defeated the Hungarian forces, and many a decent Hungarian died in the encounter, etc., may only prove that the chronicler used any information at his disposal to describe Stephen II in the darkest terms and in most compromising situations. [91]

The Byzantine armies had regained the initiative in the war and staged a counteroffensive; all the Hungarian high command could do was to hold its line of defense along the Danube. Setephel the Palatine was the commander of the king's troops [92] (Stephen II had fallen ill [93] ), but the defense against the renewed Byzantine (counter-)attacks did not go well. The Greeks had staged a pincer-movement, in part at the Haram stream and had totally destroyed the Hungarian forces there. And they had, in part, crossed the Danube near Bazis and surprised the unsuspecting Hungarian main army — with its exposed, undefended flanks. For a second time, the Hungarian high command had suffered a humiliating defeat.

Hundreds of dead Hungarian bodies lay decomposed in the bloody stream of the Karasso. But, the Byzantine court played politics and did not follow up its victories. It only occupied Fort Haram (Chram), had Barancs refortified, though, in some skirmishes took possession, and command, of the Serem region. [94]

When the king had regained his health, [95] he had ordered a new offensive against the Greeks, and, aided by the Czechs, attacked Fort Barancs — defended effectively by Kurtikios, its Byzantine commander. Stephen II's troops did, however, carry the day, took the fort, burnt it to the ground and captured most of the Greek garrison. At this point, the imperial court decided to take serious military action, with the emperor leading the campaign in person. The imperial troops easily reconquered Barancs, though, hoping for a peaceful solution, did not pursue the recapture of the Serem region. It is the chronicler's expressed opinion that lack of food and foddler provisions forced the emperor to withdraw from the field early, but not before he had laid a trap for the irresolute Hungarian king. So, when Stephen II had crossed the Danube again, he had to, on the Byzantine side, face imperial troops ready to battle with him. The emperor's plan did work; after some lengthy negotiations a Hungaro-Byzantine peace treaty could be signed by the year 1130. [96]

The chronicler told his story and had his reader almost convinced that Stephen II had really, next to his birthright, no qualifications for occupying the throne. But the chronicler made his assertions in such a crude and harsh manner that he overreached himself. The reader began to doubt his reliability. For instance, although the chronicler had the information, he did not tell that the "Greek" war had broken out because of the propaganda made by the Hungarian political exiles at the Byzantine imperial court and because Álmos had requested, and hope to receive, Byzantine imperial protection (diplomatic and military) against his own brother and king). [97] But the situation did change when Álmos died abroad, and they had taken his body home on royal orders, so that they may bury him at Fehérvár. [98] It was at that time that the emperor and Stephen II finally made peace. [99]

The chronicler made no mention of it, but it is conceivable that this Hungarian-Byzantine treaty had prepared the way for the eventual return of Béla the Blind into public life, and for the marriage of Béla to a Serbian woman. The nobles let their king know that, after the death of Álmos, Álmos' son was still alive. A bishop Paul and a reeve Othmar brought the news to Stephen II, who rejoiced. Now he had an heir to the throne. [100]

Stephen II had now asked for the hand in marriage of the daughter of Uros, grand-supan of Serbia, for the blind prince. The king wisely wanted his successor to have a queen who, through her family ties, would direct her royal husband in the diplomatic labyrinths of the Byzantine court. [101] In due course of time a son, Géza, was born to the young couple, [102] for whom the king had assigned a place to live in Tolna county, and granted them an annual income. [103]

Undoubtedly, the monarch had rejoiced when Béla the Blind had a son, [104] but the question remains, did he have honest intentions? Did Stephen II pay his respect to his dead brother by recognizing the right of his dead brother's son, Béla, to succeed him on the throne? Or, did the king acknowledge Béla as his successor because he wanted to irritate and anger his opposition of those nobles who had previously left him in the lurch during the Kievan campaign and had him threatened with dethronement were he not to comply with their demands? [105]

The chronicler of the *Chronicon pictum* did admit that prior to his receiving news about Béla the Blind, the nobles decided (the text speaks of the nobles' resolution as if made by the realm: *regni*, implying again that they were members of the government council [106]), that, upon the death of Stephen II, it would be Saul, son of Sophia, the king's sister, who would inherit the crown. [107] Probably, Stephen II made, at first, no objection to Saul's succession, [108] — except perhaps it hurt him that he had no son of his own to inherit the throne from him, [109] — but he must have been deeply disturbed by the political movement in the realm, that is, the plans of the nobles who could hardly have awaited his death, so that they may elect a creature of their own choice and liking to the throne. [110]

The chronicler did say that, at that time, the king was

gravely ill at Eger, near death,[111] and the "traitors" (*traditores*, a term not used by the chronicler before) chose the reeve Bors and (an individual named) Ivan as king.[112] The chronicler's composition is clear; his text is readable, but what he says is disturbing. He does not even mention the name of the traitors, but speaks only about the two individuals being elected king (in singular: "in regem electi sunt.")[113] Was it possible to make a royal reeve and most probably a member of the king's family, known only by his first name, *king?*

The chronicler did not address the question. His scanty report described the situation without mentioning at all the surrounding circumstances. But he said that after the king, Stephen II, had regained his health and had ordered that Ivan be beheaded (Bors, the reeve, fled to Byzantine territory), they decided[114] that, henceforth, no close member of the royal family can enter the grounds of the royal household,[115] as if to reveal thus the fact that the "traitors" (who, exploiting the illness of the king, had other(s) elected to kingship), either had belonged to the close family circle of the monarch, or had come from the ranks of his trusted friends.[116]

There is another circumstance that can throw some light upon the reasoning and identity of these "traitors;" the chronicler had previously reported that the king listened to the advice of the nobles and on grounds that his marriage with the daughter of Robert Guiscard remained childless, had agreed to acknowledge blind Béla as his heir to the throne.[117] This may prove that the traitors did not come from, nor did they belong to, the ranks of the nobility; nor were they members of the government council.

On the other hand, the conclusion may be drawn from the assertion of the chronicler that nobody was allowed to enter the royal court,[118] and from the remark that Béla the Blind did not confide in man, but placed his trust in the Almighty, that Béla the Blind had obtained the crown as the result of a power confrontation with, rather as a sign of good will from, King Stephen II.[119] Although the monarch did not prevent, he certainly did not help his cousin ascend to the throne.

The last paragraph devoted to Stephen II in the *Chronicum pictum* speaks of the final months of his reign that had been spent in sheer physical agony.[120] The king died in a monk's habit. [121] The already very ill monarch must have spent the last weeks of his earthly life among his, one may say, overappreciated, but still pagan, Cumans. [122] They buried him, in a monk's habit, at Várad. [123]

The chronicler's handling of the reign of Stephen II remained uneven. He did mention major and minor episodes from the life of the king, rather than to render an honest report about his accomplishments. It can be, of course, that recording the all available information could have depicted the monarch in an even worse light. [124] One cannot help the feeling that Stephen II, though not a bad person, was a naive individual, an irresolute weak character that made him less fit to rule. He not only would not order his nobles around, but he could not even control his own self. [125] Being dressed in a monkish habit on his deathbed may have helped saving his soul, but did not absolve him from the misdeeds of his thoughtless reign.

NOTES

1. Cf. *SSH*, I, 217ff., esp. cc. 142etc.; Horváth, *Stílusproblémák*, 270ff., and 315ff. F. Makk, "Megjegyzések II Béla történetéhez (Some remarks on the history of Béla II)," *Acta historica*, 40 (Szeged, 1972), 31ff.; idem, "Megjegyzések II István történetéhez (Some remarks on the history of Stephen II)," *Memoria Hungariae*, I, 253ff.; the *Chronicon pictum* was written in 1358, *SSH*, I, 239,2-5, by an anonymous compiler. Cf. G. Karsai, "Névtelenség, névrejtés és szerzőnév középkori krónikáinkban (Anonymity and authorship of medieval Hungarian chronicles)," *Századok*, 97 (1963), 666ff.; however, Gy. Kristó argued in his masterful essay, "Anjou-kori krónikáink (Hungarian chronicles of the Angevin age)," *ibid.*, 101 (1967), 457ff., that Canon Mark de Kalta and a Franciscan friar were the compilers; Pintér, I, 341ff., named Canon de Kalta as the author and described him as a well educated chronicler of the early Hungarian renaissance. Horváth, *Műveltség megoszlása*, 18ff., and 198f., spoke of Kalta as a chronicler of the renaissance, who (had) compiled the works of earlier Hungarian chroniclers. Idem, "Die ungarischen Chronisten aus der Angiovienzeit," *Acta linguistica*, 21 (1971), 321ff.; Horváth, 27f., spoke of Kalta as a writer with theological education and good style active at the court of Lewis the Great of Hungary (ob. 1382); see also D. Dercsényi, *Nagy Lajos és kora* (Age of Lewis the Great) (Budapest, 1942), 61ff., and G. Stadtmüller, "Die ungarische Grossmacht des Mittelalters," *HJB*, 50 (1951), 151ff.; E. Mályusz, "A Képes Krónika kiadásai (Various editions of the Chronicle)," *Memoria Hungariae*, I, 167ff. On Background, see Hóman-Szekfű, I, 366ff.; L. Elekes *et al*, *Magyarország története 1526-ig* (Hungarian history until 1526) (Budapest, 1961), 95.

2. See, e.g., c. 152, *SSH*, I, 433,2-12, and c. 160, *ibid.*, I, 446,10-22.

3. *SSH*, I, 434,4-8; the writer-compiler of the Chronicle commented on the

material obtained "ex diversis cronicis veteribus, earundem veritatem ascribendo et falsitatem omnino refutando" (*ibid.*, I, 239,9-12), as if to support F. Heer, *Europäische Geistesgeschichte*, 2nd ed. (Stuttgart, 1965), 96, who said that the objective of the medieval chronicler was "die geschichtliche Rechtfertigung der alten Welt."

4. *SSH*, I, 446,14-22.

5. *Ibid.*, I, 447,2-26.

6. The Hungarian Anonymus had a French education — see his preface, *ibid.*, I, 33f.; Macartney, 63f., and he wanted to stay away from "falsis fabulis rusticorum vel a garrulo cantu ioculatorum" (*SSH*, I, 33f.), as he based his report(s) on "certa scripturarum explanatione et aperta hystoriarum interpretatione" (*ibid.*, I, 34,2-3). Cf. J. Győry, *Gesta regum — gesta nobilium* (Budapest, 1948), 42f., though his argument concerning possible Spanish influence upon Anonymus is less convincing — *ibid.*, 55 and 92f.; Pintér, I, 212 and 219ff. Anonymus stressed the "election" of the first Hungarian ruler (in the 890's); cf. *SSH*, I, 39f. Gy. Kristó, "Szempontok Anonymus gestájának megítéléséhez (Some remarks on the historical value of Anonymus' gesta)," Separatum from *Acta historica*, 66 (Szeged, 1979), 45ff.

7. Cf. Keza, *Gesta*, cc. 65 and 66, *SSH*, I, 183,12-15.

8. Cf. Erdélyi, *Kultúrtörténet*, I, 69ff.; Marczali, *Geschichtsquellen*, 54ff. *SSH*, I, 434S plus insert, marked ***, *ibid.*, I, 434f. The Buda Chronicle was the first book printed in Hungary, in 1473 — cf. the facsimile edition by V. Fraknói (ed), *Chronicon Budense: Budai Krónika* (Budapest, 1900); Pintér, I, 468ff., printed by Andreas Hess at Buda. See J. Fitz, *Hess András, a budai ősnyomdász* (Andreas Hess, first printer at Buda) (Budapest, 1932), 81ff.; idem, *A magyar nyomdászat, könyvkiadás és könyvkereskedelem története* (History of printing, publication and book trade in Hungary), 2 vols. (Budapest, 1959-67), I, 101 and 112ff.; Z. Soltész, "Milyen tervekkel és felszereléssel jöhetett Budára Hess András? (What were the plans, what the equipment of Andreas Hess at Buda)," *MKSz*, 90 (1974), 1ff.

9. *SSH*, I, 434S,4-9.

10. Szentpétery, *Regesta*, i, no. 51; Fejér, II, 80; Cosmas of Prague, *Chronica*, iii:42, *MGHSS*, IX, 122,39-40; Manitius, III, 461ff.

11. "... erat enim adhuc inpubes, sed spiritus eius in manibus eius;" *SSH*, I, 434,6-8, possibly a reference to Ps. 118, 109 (Vulgate): "anima mea in manibus meis semper." Gy. Pauler, *A magyar nemzet története az árpádházi királyok alatt* History of the Hungarian nation under the Árpáds), 2 vols., 2nd ed. (Budapest, 1899; repr. Budapest, 1983), I, 225f.

12. *SSH*, I, 434,8-11; J. Koller, *Historia episcopatuus Quinqueecclesiarum*, vols. 1-3 and 7 (Pest, 1782-84, 1812), I, 187; Katona, *Historia critica*, III, 399.

13. *SSH*, I, 434f.; Cosmas, *Chronica*, iii:42; Pauler, I, 227ff., and 333.

14. *SSH*, I, 435,6-20.

15. *Ibid.*, I, 435,20-24.

16. "Bohemi ergo, sicut furibundi et bibuli, ...;" *ibid.*, I, 435,25-26.

17. *Ibid.*, I, 435f.; as Cosmas put it, "unde dux ille ad placitum distulit ire;" *MGHSS*, IX, 123,4.

18. *SSH*, I, 435f.; Cosmas, *Chronica*, iii:42, *MGHSS*, IX, 123,5-24.

19. "Rex ... cum paucis celeriter equitavit versus Hungariam;" *SSH*, I, 436,6-8.

20. Pauler, I, 233.

21. F. Makk, "Megjegyzések II István történetéhez (Some comments on the reign of Stephen II)," *Memoria Hungariae*, I, 251ff.; idem, *Magyarország*, 106ff.

22. *SSH*, I, 444f.

23. *Ibid.*, I, 444,24-26.

24. *Chron. pictum*, c. 159; P. Ransanus, *Epithoma rerum Hungarorum*, ed. P. Kulcsár (Budapest, 1977), 118f., ind. xiv.

25. *SSH.*, I, 435,2-6; Cosmas, *Chronica*, iii:42, *MGHSS*, IX, 123,13-15.

26. "... fecit sicut Solth dixerat, sine suorum consilio;" *SSH*, I, 435,33-34. And yet, Cosmas says, the nobles, too, should be blamed, — *MGHSS*, IX, 123,2-3.

27. *SSH*, I, 435,32.

28. The king had to flee for his life: "quia sui absque armis venerant, et qui arma habebant, armare se non poterant;" *ibid.*, I, 436,8-11.

29. *Ibid.*, I, 436f.

30. The chronicler also held a low opinion of Solt: "semper inique cogitationes auctor, qui per iniquitatem suam de Hungaria fuerat expulsus;" *ibid.*, I, 435,7-10.

31. *Ibid.*, I, 436,12-16.

32. *Ibid.*, I, 436,17 - 437,5.

33. *MGHSS*, IX, 122f.

34. "Vae terrae, cuius est puer rex!" Cf. *ibid.*, IX, 123,2.

35. *Annales Gradicenses et Opatowicenses*, c. 58, anno 1116, *ibid.*, XVII, 643ff.; Wattenbach, II, 319. Palacky, *Würdigung*, 52ff.

36. *SSH*, I, 437,7-10; on the disposition of the chroniclers reporting on this, see B. Hóman, *A Szent László korabeli Gesta Ungarorum s annak leszármazói* (Hungarian *gesta* of the age of Ladislas I and its continuators) (Budapest, 1927), 106f.

37. States the Chronicle, c. 154; according to Pauler, II, 231 and 473f., Stephen II had married a daughter of Robert of Capua. M. Wertner, *Az Árpádok családi története* (Family history of the Árpáds) (Nagybecskerek, 1892), 229ff., said that Stephen II may have married Adelhaid, daughter of Henry (II) of Stefflingen, *Vogt* of Regensburg. Hóman-Szekfű, I, 366, mentioned the daughter of *an* Italian Norman count; cf. Hóman, *Ungarisches Mittelalter*, I, 381.

38. Cf. *Vita Conradi archiepiscopi Salisburgensis,* c. 18, *MGHSS*, XI, 63ff., and 73f., written in the 1170's; cf. Wattenbach, II, 299f.

39. It was the Hungarians' fault — see *MGHSS*, IX, 123,1-8.

40. *Ibid.*, XI, 74,2-7.

41. Pauler, I, 227ff.

42. *MGHSS*, XI, 74,12-20. "Er zuerst brachte durch seine Festigkeit und sein persönliches Ansehen einen daurenden Frieden mit den Ungarn zu Stande;" Wattenbach, II, 300. W. Bernhardi, *Lothar von Supplinburg* (Berlin, 1879; repr. 1975), 528f., and 532.

43. *MGHSS*, XI, 75 (c. 20); the cathedral burnt down on May 4, 1127 — cf. *Annales s. Rudberti Salisburgensis, ibid.*, IX, 774, and note 67.

44. *SSH*, I, 437,14-16.

45. See Kievan Annals, a. 1123; Moscow Annals, a. 1123; Tverj Annals, a.1123, in Hodinka, 94Af., 200ABff., and 266Af., respectively; Pauler, I, 231f. On the chronicles, see Marczali, *Geschichtsquellen*, 156f.

46. Cosmas of Prague, *Chronica*, iii:51, saw it differently; cf. *MGHSS*, IX, 126,7-9.

47. "Stephanus volens iniuriam patris sui, regis Colomanni, vindicare;" *SSH*, I, 437f.; Gy. Moravcsik, *Byzantium and the Magyars* (Amsterdam-Budapest, 1970), 78f.

48. *SSH*, I, 438,31 — a meeting different from the one that had been held by the "principes Hungarie," *ibid.*, I, 438,20-22.

49. "... nos in Hungariam recedimus et nobis regem elegimus;" *ibid.*, I, 439,9-11.

50. *Ibid.*, I, 439,15-18.

51. Hodinka, 96A.

52. *SSH*, I, 438,14-22.

53. *Ibid.*, I, 438,30 - 439,4.

54. "Si inter principes tuos eligis, nullus remanet;" *ibid.*, I, 439,4-5.

55. *Ibid.*, I, 439,18-24; Pauler, I, 233.

56. *Chronicon Venetum, MGHSS*, XIV, 71,3-11 (or, in *Archivio storico Italiano*, VIII (Florence, 1845), 152f.); Dandalo, *Chronicon,* ix:11:17, and ix:11:19-20.

57. With the approval and support of the German emperor; cf. G. Meyer v. Knonau, *Heinrich IV und Heinrich V*, 7 vols. (Berlin, 1890-1909; repr. Berlin, 1964-65), VII, 1f., and 91.

58. *SSH*, I, 434-8-11; Pauler, I, 232f.

59. The use of the term, "potentiores regni," may point toward government function — *SSH*, I, 434,4.

60. "Placuit enim regno, ut rex Stephanus cum duce Bohemorum colloquium haberet;" *ibid.*, I, 434f.

61. "Erat enim Solth simperinique cogitationis auctor, qui per iniquitatem suam de Hungaria fuerat expulsus, ... qui tunc ibi sum Bohemis presens erat;" *ibid.*, I, 435,6-11.

62. *Ibid.*, I, 434f.

63. Dandalo, ix:11:21.

64. In Muratori, *Scriptores*, XII, 266 — *annotatio in margine.*

65. Dandalo, ix:12:17.

66. "... et dicamus regi, quia hae omnia absque consilio suorum principum fecit. Cum vero principes venissent ad consilium regis, omnes in duas partes se transtulerunt;" *SSH*, I, 438,27-32; H. Kretsmayer, *Geschichte von Venedig* (*Allgemeine Staatengeschichte*, no. 35), vol. I (Gotha, 1905), 229.

67. *SSH*, I, 439,23-24; or, a similar term, "et flangribus aulicorum," *ibid.*, I, 330,18.

68. Keza, c. 48, *ibid.*, I, 171f.

69. In *Annales Altahenses*, a. 1043, *MGHSS*, XX, 799,29.

70. "Rex autem legittime nobelat (*sic!* = volebat?) ducere uxorem, sed concubinis meretricibus iniunctus erat;" *SSH*, I, 437,11-14.

71. "Rex itaque Stephanus multa mala faciebat, que non debeat in impetu animi sui;" *ibid.*, I, 442,13-15. F. Makk, "Megjegyzések II Béla történetéhez (Some comments on the reign of Béla II)," *Acta historica Szegediensis*, 40 (1972), 31ff., spoke of two parties (parties? = interests groups): one, supporting Álmos — Béla II; the other, promoting the interests of Coloman and Stephen II; also, Elekes, 93.

72. *SSH*, I, 442,16-17.

73. Cf. A. Meineke (ed), *Iohannes Cinnamus: Epitomae rerum ab Ioanne et Alexio Comnenis gestarum* (Bonn, 1836), cited hereafter as Cinnamus, i:5 (12,18-21); Krumbacher, 279ff.; idem, *Fontes byzantini historiae Hungaricae aevo ducum et regum ex stirpe Arpad descendentium* (Budapest, 1984), cited hereafter as Moravcsik, *Fontes*, 194ff.; idem, *Byzantinoturcica*, I, 180ff.; idem, "Les sources byzantines de l'histoire hongroise," *Byzantion*, 9 (1934), 663ff.; Marczali, *Geschichtsquellen*, 130ff. Also, Pauler, I, 475, and note 432.

74. *SSH*, I, 442,17-19. The idea may have been borrowed from Paul to the Romans, 12:20 — in the Vulgate.

75. Cf. Erdélyi, *Rendtörténet*, I, 597.

76. See *SSH*, I, 435,32-24; I, 438,14-20.

77. Which, incidentally, may already have been divided! Cf. *ibid.*, I, 438,30-32.

78. "Timebant autem omnes regem Stephanum...;" *ibid.*, I, 435,37-38.

79. Cereos magnos ardentes in fundamentum hominis stillare faciebat;" *ibid.*, I, 442,19-21.

80. Hóman, *Szent László kori gesta*, 106f.; Hóman-Szekfű, I, 297f.; Heer, *Geistesgeschichte*, 90ff.

81. Albertus Trium Fontium, *Chronicon*, a. 1135, *MGHSS*, XXIII, 832. Cosmas of Prague, Chronica, iii:43, *ibid.*, IX, 124.

82. Cf. *Chronicon Monacense*, c. 52, *SSH*, II, 81,3-4; Macartney, 146.

83. *SSH*, I, 442f.; Meyer, 78f.

84. *Chronicon pictum*, c. 156. Cinnamus, i:4 (CB, 10); I. Bekker (ed), *Nicetas Choniates, Historia: De imperio Iohannis Comneni Porphyrogeniti* (Bonn, 1837), cited hereafter as Choniates, *Iohannis Comneni*, c. 5 (CB, 24); Krumbacher, 281ff.; Moravcsik, *Bizánci források*, 195ff., did name him Niketas Akominatos, but following Choniates' own testimony (CB, 230,22), corrected himself: "es war irrig, ihn, wie es früher üblich war, Niketas Akominatos zu nennen;" see his *Byzantinoturcica*, I, 270; idem, *Fontes*, 257ff.; Marczali, *Geschichtsquellen*, 134ff. Recent edition of the Greek text by I. A. van Dieten (ed), *Nicetae Choniatae Historia* (Berlin-New York, 1975), cited hereafter as Dieten, 17,39-19,2. Also, N. Choniates, *O City of Byzantium*, tr. H. J. Magoulias (Detroit, Mich., 1984) ixff.

85. Choniates, *Iohannis Comneni*, c. 5; Dieten, 17.

86. Chronicle, c. 156.

87. Cinnamus, i:4.

88. Choniates, *Historia: De rebus gestis Manuelis Comneni* (*ed. cit.*, supra, note 84), iv:1; Moravcsik, *Fontes*, 274f. Dieten, 126,46 - 128,27. Chronicle, c. 169; G. Ostrogorsky, *Geschichte des byzantinischen Staates*, 2nd rev. ed. (Munich, 1952), 308f. For some background, see also Walter Map, *De nugis curialium*, ed. M. R. James (Oxford, 1914), diss. ii, c. 7; on Map, see G. O. Sayles, *The Medieval Foundations of England* (London, 1948), 369; A. Gransden, *Historical Writing in England, 550 to 1307* (Ithaca, 1974), 242f.

89. *SSH*, I, 439f.

90. As it may be evident from the text: "quam etiam contradicentem imperator castigavit;" *ibid.*, I, 440,3-4.

91. *Ibid.*, I, 440f.

92. *Ibid.*, I, 441,14, — a German name; cf. Pauler, I, 235.

93. And on such occasions the Palatine had to step in for the monarch; cf. the Golden Bull of 1222, art. 1, Marczali, *Enchiridion*, 134f.

94. Cinnamus, i:4 (CB, 11); Moravcsik, *Fontes*, 197f., and n. 13.

95. He had undergone treatment — see Cinnamus, i:4 (CB, 11,1-2.).

96. *SSH*, I, 442,13-15.

97. He only made a brief reference to it: "... et multi Hungari atrocitate regis Stephani fugierunt ad ipsum;" *ibid.*, I, 443,3-5. Álmos has been a dangerous enemy — cf. *ibid.*, I, 442f.; Hóman-Szekfű, I, 365f.; Csóka, 200f.

98. *SSH*, I, 143,5-9; Canonicus Wissegradensis *Continuatio Cosmae Pragensis Chronica*, anno 1137, *MGHSS*, IX, 143.

99. *Chronicon pictum*, end of c. 156.

100. *SSH*, I, 443,9-21.

101. *Ibid.*, I, 443,21-27.

102. *Ibid.*, I, 443,25-26.

103. "Disposuerat eum rex vivere in Talus (*sic!* ═ Tolna) et dabantur ei regalia stipendia;" *ibid.*, I, 443,29-31.

104. "Gavisus est valde;" *ibid.*, I, 443,28.

105. *Ibid.*, c. 155.

106. "... coniuraverat regnum;" *ibid.*, I, 444,3; Hóman-Szekfű, I, 366.

107. *Chron. pictum*, c. 158, opening sentence. Sophia, a sister of Stephen II, had married Lampert of Hunt-Pázmány; the latter had, in about 1135, established a monastery at Bozók; cf. Szentpétery, *Regesta*, I, no. 59; Fejér, II, 82, and VII-5, 100.

108. L. Erdélyi, *Árpádkor* (Age of the Arpads) (Budapest, 1922), 147; A. Bonfini, *Rerum Ungaricarum decades quatuor,* ed. J. Fógel *et al,* 4 vols. (Leipzig-Budapest, 1936-41), I, 117, agrees. One is to remember, of course, that Bonfini "war unkritisch, nur für die Zeit Matthias (Corvinus) glaubwürdig;" cf. A. Potthast, *Bibliotheca historica medii aevi,* 2 vols.; rev. ed. (Berlin, 1896), I, 163. Pauler, I, 237, disagrees.

109. Stephen II had no children; cf. *SSH*, I, 443,19-21.

110. *Ibid.*, I, 444,9-11.

111. "... contigit autem, ut rex incideret in gravem infirmitatem Agrie ( = Eger), ita ut omnes mortem illi inminere videbant;" *ibid.,* I, 444,6-9.

112. "... inani spe ducti;" *ibid.,* I, 444,9-11.

113. *Ibid.,* I, 444,11.

114. "... et ita statutum est;" *ibid.,* I, 444,16.

115. "... quod de propagine ( = progenie?) sua amplius ad curiam regiam nullus dignus esse iudicaretur intrare;" *ibid.,* I, 444,17-19.

116. *Ibid.,* I, 444,19-23.

117. *Ibid.,* I, 443,19-21.

118. *Ibid.,* I, 444,16-23.

119. "Nec posuit carnem brachi sui' in auditorium, nec habuit fiduciam in homine, sed ad altissimum posuit refugium suum;" *ibid.,* I, 446,10-14. Quote is from Jer. 17:5.

120. *SSH*, I, 444f.

121. "... monachalem habitum ... suscepit;" *ibid.,* I, 445,29-31.

122. Cf. Pauler, I, 233.

123. *SSH*, I, 445,32-33.

124. "Hungari vero villani cum audissent, quod rex in mortis esset articulo, interfecerunt Cunos." Cf. *ibid.,* I, 445,5-7.

125. "Rex itaque Stephanus multa mala faciebat, que non debeat;" *ibid.,* I, 442,13-15.

# V

# Béla II the Blind Struggles for the Throne

Quia vero Hungari semper fluctuant iniuria,
sicut mare salsum, filii namque Leviathan.

*Chronicon pictum*, c. 161

The reign of Béla II the Blind (1131-41) was recorded in four paragraphs by the chronicler of the *Chronicon pictum*, [1] who was the Chronicler-of-Stephen-III, [2] possibly an eyewitness of actual events. [3] The circumstance that the chronicler's King Stephen III was through his father, Géza II, [4] the grandson of Béla the Blind, [5] makes understandable the vehement attack of the chronicler upon (the memory of) King Coloman the Learned, [6] uncle of Béla the Blind, who, the chronicler said, has been responsible for the blinding of Béla and Béla's father, Prince Álmos, younger brother of Coloman. [7]

The prince and his son were blinded, the chronicler wrote, because King Coloman did not trust Álmos and wanted to assure the throne for his own son, Stephen II. [8] Although it can be assumed from the report of the chronicler that in the case of King Coloman and Prince Álmos their hostility had been similar to the strained relationship between King Stephen I and his cousin, Vazul, in the 1030's, [9] the chronicler would not approve of the blinding of the prince, and of the prince's son, on the grounds that, in his opinion, Coloman, in spite of his being a bishop, had not been a King Saint Stephen. [10] Therefore, it may stand to reason that the chronicler began his report on the reign of Béla II by praising the Christian virtues of the monarch; Béla the Blind avoided doing evil and performed many good deeds with perfect humility. [11] The chronicler emphasized it as a fact that the monarch's faith in God was answered by the Almighty Who allowed him to see his children (*recte*: son) succeed him on the throne. The country gained strength in his hands,

and he humbled his enemies. [12] As János Horváth has noticed,
the chronicler who depicted the age of the blind king in biblical terminology projected against an Old Testament background, must have had some theological training. [13]

The blinding of the monarch did, however, disturb the
chronicler much. He included a narrative in the same paragraph that Ilona, Queen of Béla the Blind, whose marriage
to him had been arranged for by the predecessor and cousin
of Béla, King Stephen II, [14] had, with her husband's approval and with the resolution of the barons of the land, held
a meeting of the General Assembly: "congregationem generalem fecit," at Arad-Onod. [15] There, in front of the King
who sat on the throne, but sitting next to him, and in the
presence of their children, the Queen presented to them:
the assembled group, the question of "Why, upon whose advice" had her royal husband been blinded? [16]

It is, by all means, evident from the speech segment quoted
by the chronicler that at the Arad-Onod general assembly
"everyone" had made an appearance: the King's loyal supporters, nobles, old and young men, rich and poor, — as
if by describing attendance the chronicler had attempted to
prepare the reader to understand that the meeting had
"revenge" for its motive. As the narrator had explained it
within the framework of his quote from the speech: reveal
to us the purpose of the blinding and take revenge for our
sake. [17]

The Latin composition of the chronicler, "modo michi
propalate ... in hoc loco vindicantes," leaves, however, no
doubt about the fact that he had here expressed his own
opinion by placing words into the mouth of the queen. [18] Even
in his report on the conclusion of the meeting the chronicler
remained tendentious: members of the assembly, he said,
rose against the barons who had blinded the king. They had
bound and mutilated them. They had, without mercy, executed sixty-eight faithless traitors on the spot. [19] The participating members of the assembly had also ordered that
the properties of the executed traitors be distributed among
the churches. [20]

The chronicler's record of these events unwillingly re-
minds one of the gathering conducted by King Béla I in 1060,
when the monarch had summoned two representatives of

each of the *villae*, the basic units of the country's administration, to appear before him, [21] so that he, through their cooperation, may take serious action against those individuals
in his kingdom who had, at that time, revolted against the
Christian kingship of his older brother and predecessor,
and of himself. [22]

The remark of the chronicler that the Queen had, at the
meeting, appeared with her children may, by all means,
indicate that the gathering of the assembly did not take place
at the beginning of the blind monarch's reign because Béla
the Blind married Ilona only during the last year(s) of Stephen
II's reign, [23] and the royal couple could hardly have had
four children by 1131.[24]

Queen Ilona needed time to survey the reputation (and
the situation) of her royal husband among the nobles, the
hierarchy of the Church, and in the population. She could
only have summoned, through her husband and in her husband's name, [25] the General Assembly [26] when she was
certain that the "barons:" [27] nobles in attendance, and the
people would support her and her husband: the royal couple,
against the, to her perhaps still unknown, but to the nobles
and the people most probably well known, [28] members of
the king's opposition. [29]

In reading the text of the chronicler, — why did they
blind the monarch; and, who had advised the blinding, —
one gains the impression that Queen Ilona did not even then,
at the opening of the gathering, know who really constituted
the group of her husband's enemies. [30] She had to find out,
though, about the composition of the opponents, if she wanted to secure her husband's reign in the realm, together with
the future of their children. [31]

The resolutions of the Hungarian queen of Serbian birth [32]
perhaps wreak of blood feud, but, according to the reasoning of the chronicler, it is evident that the fears of the queen
were not baseless. The Hungarians were always an unruly
folk, and in temperament often behaved like a stormy
sea, [33] the chronicler reports against the background of the
gathering, as they were like the wicked sons of Leviathan,
for they had invited Boris, the illegitimate son of King Coloman the Learned, [34] to enter and occupy the country with
the aid of Polish and Ruthenian troops. [35] Boris had indeed

arrived near the Hungarian frontier (located at the time) at the Sajó river. There he was joined by many of the nobles, "plurimi autem ex nobilibus," who had expressed support for his cause. [36]

The monarch had now gathered his armed forces and moved against Boris. He requested, and obtained, military help from his brother-in-law, [37] Adalbert, margrave of the "Eastern March;" [38] he summoned an emergency advisory assembly of his nobles. This meeting must have been of short duration, and had only one item on its agenda: Did the nobles know that Boris was born out of wedlock and was, consequently, unworthy of the throne? [39]

Interesting it is to note the chronicler's choice of words in recording the emergency meeting. "Proceres autem Hungarie vocati sunt *ad colloquendum* cum rege" (Italics mine). [40] The most important barons of the realm had been invited to have a discussion with the king, — a talk which under no circumstances was a regular, or even a special, session of the General Assembly. [41]

And yet, there is, by all means, a close connection between the General Assembly summoned to Arad-Onod by the Queen, and the royal *colloquium* called for by the monarch to dicuss the claim of Boris (the pretender). The one cannot really be imagined without the other. The chronicler reports that present were at this royal discussion the king's loyal supporters (that is, supporters loyal to the cause: "fideles regni"!), who had remained faithful to the blind monarch. [42] But there were also present, even without participating in the discussion, some not so loyal members of the king's opponents, "infideles et contradictores," [43] who spoke in subdued voices and had evil intentions. "Musitabant incerta et titubantes in duas partes claudicantes." [44] The latter, therefore, did not participate in the talks.

The chronicler recorded that the monarch and his advisors, — close attention ought to be paid to the use of words by the reporter: *proceres*, very important element of society, who had formed the group of royal advisors, *consiliarii regis* (that is, in the full text' "rex autem et consiliarii eius" [45] ) —, did their best to separate the sheep from the wolfs. They decided that, right there and then, they assassinate the traitors. Once again, close attention should be paid to the

chronicler's text; the formerly disloyal and opposing element
of the nobility (of the baronage) now became the traitors:
*proditores*, in the words of the chronicler. [46] He even gave
his reasons for writing by saying that the royal advisors made
the decision before the traitors had time to side with, and
join, Boris (an act that brought the realm into great political
danger), [47] — as if to reveal the sad fact that the majority
of the invited barons gathering at this special *colloquium*,
though not participating in it, — because they did not take
an active part in it —, failed to support the blind monarch. [48]

The traitors did not hesitate for long. They staged a revolt. [49] Although their leader, Lampert, a reeve, [50] was
killed by his own brother, [51] and Lampert's son, Nicholas,
was beheaded; [52] furthermore, several of the lesser leaders
were properly executed by the barons loyal to the monarch, [53]
the conspirators had still attacked the blind king, [54] whose
life was only saved by the quick intervention of the lords
faithful to him. [55] The rebels had an organized leadership, [56]
but their leaders, as, for example, Samson, the father of the
reeves Thomas and Torda, had been not very effective in
their carrying out the revolt. [57]

Although Samson had proposed, the record says, that
those present at, but not participating in, the meeting, orally
abuse the king, the proposal could not be realized because
of poor planning and incoordinated timing. [58] When Samson had approached the king to tell him to his face that he
should enter a monastery for life just as his father (blinded
Prince Álmos had done) and leave the kingship to his lord
(*domino tuo!*) Boris, [59] the nobles (and knights) loyal to the
monarch [60] fell upon Samson, ran him down to the river Sajó,
where the reeve, in endeavoring to cross it, fell quickly in
it, and because of the heavy armor under his clothing,
drowned. [61]

The barons loyal to Béla II now decided to make an end
to the Boris affair. They dispatched a delegation to the commander of the Polish and Ruthenian troops supporting Boris,
who, the Polish chroniclers tell us, was the Polish king,
Boleslaw III himself, [62] to enlighten him: the Hungarian
Crown did not belong to a Boris born out of wedlock, but,
by right, it belonged to Béla the Blind, who reigned with
the consent of the people of the entire country; "et ipse regant
cum consensu tocius regni." [63]

The observation of the chronicler is important because it stressed two factors: (1) The barons of the realm who had continued their discussion with the monarch in the royal tent set up on the bank of the Sajó river, did not only defend, by risking their own lives, their royal lord, but had excluded the, by then already identified, opposition members from further discussion. (2) They had dispatched a delegation not to Boris, but to the commander of the Polish and Ruthenian troops who supported Boris, to let the commander know that they: the barons, had favored their king who alone held the right to the Crown: *quod de iure regnum habere debeat.* [64]

There was to be no appeal against their statement. Were the Polish commander of the Polish-Ruthenian troops to continue his support of Boris, born out of wedlock, they had warned him that they would regard him as a traitor, too, to their country's just cause. [65]

It should be noted that, in contrast with the report of the Hungarian chroniclers: "miserunt ad ducem Ruthenorum et Polonorum, qui pro Boricho venerunt," [66] it was the Polish chroniclers who admitted that it was their king, Boleslaw III, who went to Hungary to aid the cause of Boris. [67]

The members of the delegation dispatched by the barons to the commander of Boris' auxiliary troops succeeded in their mission. The contemporary Czech chronicler, a canon of Wishegrad and the first continuator of Cosmas of Prague, [68] reports that Hungary's sightless monarch, *coecus rex*, by resisting him had surprised Boleslaw III who, and whose armies, left the realm in a hurry [69] (though, in this instance, the Hungarian chronicler used the plural: leaders [70] ). Now Béla II turned against the stubborn, still conspiring Boris [71] and had him defeated in a battle. [72]

The chronicler implied that in this latter military engagement, fought on the feast of Mary Magdalen (July 22), the king had no difficulty destroying Boris' forces, since the pretender had only some Polish auxiliaries left at his disposal. The royal troops had captured Polish war booty, and returned home in triumph. [73] Thereby Béla the Blind and his supporters were able to consolidate their position. [74]

One has the definite impression that the chronicler by reporting on the revenge of the Queen had somehow pre-

dated his chronology of events. There existed a serious con-
notation between the meeting at Arad-Onod and the special
sessions called for by the monarch near the Sajó river, where
they had discussed the demands made by Boris and the probability of civil war. The Queen had, in her husband's name,
summoned the gathering at Arad-Onod because she knew
about the planned and, most probably already held, meet-
ing(s) between her royal husband and the nobles, where, she
feared, the numerous opposition of the king — one ought
to call them traitors — could easily gain the upper hand,
and because she wanted to prevent the outbreak of their armed
resurrection — aimed at her husband. [75] As if she had tried
to influence the nobles (who had been summoned anew by
the king) to attend a colloquium, because she wanted to save
the king's life and secure the future of their sons for and
on the throne. [76]

In the fall of the same year, Sobieslav, Czech brother-
in-law of Béla the Blind, had invaded Silesia and devastated
it with fire and sword. [77] In the spring of the following year,
the Czech-Polish encounter continued, though, through
the efforts of Sobieslav, Béla the Blind had requested and
obtained the support of the emperor, Lothair III, who
promised to smooth over the troubles the blind king had had
with the Polish ruler. [78]

Boleslaw III now had political and military troubles
brewing with Kiev, whereupon he, too, went to the German
court at Merseburg to request the emperor's good services
on his behalf. The answer of the imperial court was diplomatic: were Boleslaw III to cease hostilities with the Hungarians and Czechs, the emperor might be willing to act on
his behalf. [79]

Béla II was thus able to neutralize the Polish king as his
political and military opponent. [80] Nor had Béla the Blind
to fear much from Boris because already in 1134, Béla II
had a strong armed contingent placed at the disposal and
command of Yaropolk of Kiev, when the latter had made
his military move against Chernigov. [81] Yaropolk was the
uncle of Boris. [82] Béla the Blind had made his ally a prince,
from whom Boris could have hoped to obtain the most promising and strongest support. [83]

The blind monarch slowly consolidated his hold of the

throne. He extended his authority over Bosnia — a portion of Serbia. Upon the death of Vodin (alias Michael, grand prince of Serbia), various claimants began to fight for pre-dominance, and the Byzantine court, too, intervened in the rather chaotic Serbian domestic situation. [84]

The Byzantine emperor had the son of Vodin, Prince George, captured and had him taken to the Byzantine court in order to extend his claim over a large portion of Serbian territory. [85] The Serbs, however, living near the Bosna river decided to secede from the jurisdiction of the Vodin family, now under the control of the Byzantine court, and placed themselves under the authority of the Hungarian king, whose queen was the daughter of a former grand-supan of Serbia. Consequently, as a result of this, Béla the Blind had, in 1137, named his five year old son, Ladislas, governor of the new region, but had also extended his authority over Rama, an-other portion of Serbia. [86] Rama remained for a long peri-od of time the part of Bosnia. Béla II now assumed the title of the King-of-Rama, a title his successors held until 1918. [87]

The final years of the blind monarch were characterized by religious devotions, performance of pious deeds, some family hardship, and human tragedy. In 1137, he had the bodily remains of his father, Prince Álmos, transferred back to Hungary, and had him buried at Fehérvár. [88] He had restored the monastery of Dömös, founded by his father. [89] He also frequented the abbey church of Pannonhalma for de-votions. The abbot of Pannonhalma only recently had the church rebuilt after a fire, and the king contributed to the costs of reconstruction and attended the re-consecration of the church building in 1137. [90]

In 1139, Béla II the Blind sent twenty pounds of gold to Bishop Otto of Bamberg, the apostle of Pomerania,[91] to-gether with gold and silver ecclesiastical utensils and vest-ments. [92] News of his generosity quickly spread abroad and had only strengthened his reputation as the monarch who "became king despite his blindness, and guided his kingdom through the eyes of faith." [93] Next to his four sons a daughter, Sophia, was born to him, [94] and he had her engaged, at the age of eight years, to Frederick, the two year old son of Emperor Conrad III, in the spring of 1139. [95] The Hun-garian princess was raised on German soil. Queen Ilona died by then, and the blind king, now a widower and tortured by sorrow and physical pain, began to drink. [96] Béla II died on February 13, 1141. They buried him in Fehérvár. [97]

## NOTES

1. *Chronicon pictum*, cc. 160-63, in *SSH*, I, 446,52; Gy. Kristó - F. Makk, "Krónikáink keletkezéstörténetéhez (On the formation of Hungarian chronicles), "*Történelmi Szemle*, 15 (1972), 198ff.; F. Makk, "Megjegyzések a II Géza kori magyar-bizánci konfrontáció kronológiájához (Some remarks concerning the time-sequence in the Hungaro-Byzantine conflict of the times of Géza II)," *Acta historica Szegediensis*, 67 (1980), 21ff.; and, his previous article, *ibid* (1972), 39, note 58.

2. J. Horváth, *Stílusformák*, 255ff.

3. Cf. J. Győry, *Gesta regum — gesta nobilium* (Budapest, 1948), 21f.; G. Constable, "The Structure of Medieval Society According to the *Dictatores* of the Twelfth Century," *Law, Church and Society: Essays in Honor of Stephen Kuttner*, ed. K. Pennington et al (Philadelphia, 1977), 253ff.

4. *Chronicon pictum*, c. 169.

5. *Ibid.*, c. 164; Katona, *Historia pragmatica*, I, 617ff.

6. *SSH*, I, 419,8-11; I, 421,13-17.

7. *Ibid.*, c. 150; Alberici Trium Fontium *Chronica*, anno 1135, *MGHSS*, XXIII, 832.

8. The reason may be, indirectly, rendered by the chronicler, *SSH*, I, 429,10-13; *Annales Aegidi Brunsvicenses*, anno 1135, *MGHSS*, XXI, 13. Béla II was, through his son, Géza II, the grandfather of Stephen III — cf. *Chronicon pictum*, cc. 158 and 160.

9. *Ibid.*, c. 69; Stephen I's *Vita minor*, c. 7, *SSH*, II, 399; Hartvic's *Vita s. Stephani regis*, c. 21, *ibid.*, II, 430; my book, 21f., and 142, note 1.

10. Cf. *Chronicon pictum*, cc. 143 and 149, and compare with the more positive opinion held by Simon de Keza, *Gesta Hungarorum*, c. 64, *SSH*, I, 182f.; on Keza, see Macartney, 89ff.; Gy. Györffy, *Krónikáink és a magyar őstörténet* (Early Hungarian history in the Hungarian chronicles) (Budapest, 1948), 126ff., and 148ff.; J. Gerics, "Adalékok a Kézai Krónika problémáinak megoldásához (Additional remarks for solving the Keza question)," *Annales Universitatis de Rolando Eötvös nominatae*, sectio hist., 1 (1957), 106ff.; Csóka, 599ff. J. Szűcs, "Társadalom-szemlélet, politikai teória és történetszemlélet Kézai Simon Gesta Hungaroruma-ban (Social outlook, political ideas and a specific view of history displayed in Keza's Gesta Hungarorum)," *Századok*, 107 (1973), 569ff., and 823ff., who argued that Keza, chronicler of the thirteenth century, wrote history from the point of view held by the lesser nobility, in order to stress loyalty to the king. A similar argument was presented by Gy. Kristó, "Kézai Simon és a XIII századvégi köznemesi ideológia néhány vonása (Simon de Keza and his attitude toward the outlook of the lesser nobles in the late thirteenth century)," *ITK*, 76 (1972), 1ff.

11. "... omnenmque numerum malorum exercitationi humiliter adherebat;" *SSH*, I, 466,7-10, and a quote follows from Jer. 17:5 (Vulgate).

12. *SSH*, I, 446,14-22, — ending in a quote from Ps. 77:66.

13. Horváth, *Stílusproblémák*, 270ff.

14. *SSH*, I, 443,9-32 (c. 157). Bishop Paulus who spoke on behalf of Béla the Blind before Géza II, was the ordinary of Győr — cf. Fejér, II, 109 and 110, — and became bishop of Veszprém and Csanád; cf. *ibid.*, II, 118. Reeve Othmar, another spokesman of Béla the Blind before the king, was mentioned in a 1124 document, when he met with the abbot of Garamszentbenedek — *ibid.*, 67; Szentpétery, *Regesta*, I, no. 65, though listed as *dubiae fidei*.

15. "... habito consilio regis et baronum fidelium congregationem fecit generalem;" *SSH*, I, 446,24 - 447,1. On the location of Arad-Onod, *ibid.*, I, 447, note 1. It was a special meeting, "habito consilio regis et baronum fidelium," different from the annual gathering held by the king on August 20, the feast of King St. Stephen of Hungary; cf. the Golden Bull of 1222, art. 1, in *RHM*, II, 412ff. According to Kristó-Makk, *TSz* (1972), cc. 160 and 161 of the *Chronicon pictum* represent two strands (providing conflicting information).

16. "... regina ... dixit autem ad populum universum: 'Omnes fideles, nobiles, senes et iuvenes, divites ac pauperes, audite. Cum cuique vestrum Deus visum dederit naturalem, volo audire, cur dominus noster rex oculis sit privatus, et quorum consilio hoc sit actum?' ...;" *SSH*, I, 447,1-14. Keza, c. 65, had nothing to say. The scene has some similarity with 3 Kings, 16:11 (Vulgate).

17. *SSH*, I, 447,19-22; L. Elekes, *A középkori magyar állam megalapításától annak bukásáig* (The medieval Hungarian state, from its beginning to its fall) (Budapest, 1964), 74.

18. *SSH*, I, 447,15-17.

19. "... irruit omnis populus super illos barones, quorum consilio rex obcecatus fuerat. ... Sexaginta autem et octo prophanos ibidem crudeliter occiderunt...;" *ibid.*, I, 447,19-25, — a serious defeat of the opposition?

20. Insuper omnis illorum possessio ecclesiis cathedralibus est divisa;" *SSH*, I, 447,25-26.

21. *Chronicon pictum*, c. 95. "... de singulis villis ... vocarentur duo seniores facundiam habentes ad regis consilium. ... Rex autem et episcopi cunctique proceres...;" *ibid.*, I, 359,20-26.

22. *Ibid.*, I, 359f.; Keza, c. 59, on the "Christian" politics of Andrew I and Béla I, *ibid.*, I, 180. Also, Andrew I's *Constitutio ecclesiastica*, aa. 1-4, *MPL*, 151, 1257f.; my book, 73f., and 176, note 11.

23. *SSH*, I, 443,21-25.

24. At the time Stephen II died, Béla and Ilona had but one child — see *ibid.*, I, 443,25-26.

25. *Ibid.*, I, 446,24-26.

26. *Ibid.*, I, 447, 1.

27. *Barones - principes?* The Hungarian chronicler made no distinction between *barones maiores*, who were summoned personally to the King's council, and *barones minores*, summoned through the reeve! Cf. F. W. Maitland, *The Constitutional History of England* (Cambridge, 1911), 80; B. Lyon, *A Constitutional and Legal History of Medieval England* (New York - London, 1960), 411.

28. Béla the Blind had lived in constant fear of his life during the reign of Stephen II. "Bela ... in Hungaria occulte tenebatur a principibus propter furorem regis;" *SSH*, I, 443,9-12.

29. "... quorum consilio hoc sit actum?" *Ibid.*, I, 447,14.

30. "... eos fideliter in hoc loco vindicantes, nobis de ipsis finem date;" *ibid.*, I, 447,15-16.

31. The Queen took part in the assembly together with her children: "venit regina cum filiis suis et sedit circa regem;" *ibid.*, I, 447,3.

32. "... filia Uros comitis magni Servie;" *ibid.*, I, 443,23-24, and 442, note 4: filia est Uros magni supani Rascie. As Katona, I, 568, said: "Bela ... coniugem sumpsit, patria Macedonicam."

33. "Quia Hungari semper fluctuant iniuria, sicut mare salsum;" *SSH*, I, 447, 28-30; F. Makk, '"Megjegyzések II Béla történetéhez (Some remarks concerning the reign of Béla II)," *Acta historica Szegediensis*, 40 (1972), 31ff.

34. Albericus, *Chronica*, a. 1135, *MGHSS*, XXIII, 832.

35. On Boris, see Otto of Freising, *Chronicon*, vii:21, *ibid.*, XX, 259,30-35; A. Lhotsky, "Otto von Freising: seine Weltanschauung," in his *Europaisches Mittelalter* (Vienna, 1970), 64ff. Also, Canon of Wishegrad, *Continuatio* of Cosmas of Prague, a. 1132, *MGHSS*, IX, 138; Moravcsik, *Byzantium*, 78.

36. "Plurimi autem ex nobilibus;" *SSH*, I, 447f.

37. Adalbert married Hedwig, a sister of Béla II - cf. Freising, *Chronicon*, vii:21; Katona, I, 567f.; E. Patzelt, *Österreich bis zum Ausgang der Babenbergerzeit* (Vienna, 1946), 116f.; W. Bernhardi, *Lothair von Supplinburg* (Munich, 1879; repr. Berlin, 1975), 530, and 539ff.

38. Cf. *MGHSS*, XX, 359,35-37; Adalbert was the son of the saintly Leopold III, margrave of Austria. Cf. Cosmas of Prague, *Chronica*, iii:51, *ibid.*, IX, 126,6-8.

39. "... si scirent Borichium adulterum esse vel filium regis Colomanni?" Cf. *SSH*, I, 448,17-19. On the background, see Choniates, *Iohannis Comneni*, c. 5, in Dieten, 17; Moravcsik, *Fontes*, 267; Chalandon, 17f., and 83ff.

40. *SSH*, I, 448,11-16.

41. "Interrogavit eos rex, ... fideles autem regni responderunt;" *ibid.*, I, 448,16-20.

42. Note that the chronicler did emphasize loyalty to the cause: *fideles regni* (that is, the realm), and not to the king! Cf. *ibid.*, I, 448,19-20.

43. *Ibid.*, I, 448,24-25.

44. *Ibid.*, I, 448,25-27.

45. *Ibid.*, I, 448,27-28.

46. *Ibid.*, I, 448,27-35.

47. "... ut ibidem interfecerent proditores, ne ... traditores se transferrent;" *ibid.*, I, 448,31-33.

48. That is why "rex ... et consiliarii eius, quantum in ipsis erat, segregaverunt edos ab agnis;" *ibid.*, I, 448,27-30, evidently, a reference to Matthew, 25:32.

49. "Orta est igitur seditio;" *SSH*, I, 448f.

50. Lampert, a descendant of the family of Hun-Pázmány, had married a sister of Ladislas I - cf. Fejér, VII-5, 102, 105; J. Karácsonyi, *A magyar nemzetségek a XVI század közepéig* (Hungarian noble families to the mid-16th century) (Budapest, 1901), 184f.; - he established the monastery on his family estate at Bozouk, see Szentpétery, *Regesta*, I, no. 59; Fejér, II, 82f., and VII-1, 100f.; among the witnesses there were Magnold (Moynholt) and Ákos - see Knauz, I, 81f.

51. *SSH*, I, 449,2-8.

52. *Ibid.*, I, 449,8-10.

53. *Ibid.*, I, 449,10-12; Pauler, I, 477, n. 438; Knauz, I, 81f. (no. 54); L. Fejérpataky (ed), *Oklevelek II István korából* (Documents dating back to Stephen II) (Budapest, 1895), 36 and 44.

54. *SSH*, I, 449,12-15.

55. *Ibid.*, I, 449,15-16.

56. *Ibid.*, I, 449,16-18; Samson was the father of Thomas and Torda, both mentioned in a document, dated 1193; cf. Knauz, I, 143f.

57. *SSH*, I, 449,19-24.

58. *Ibid.*, I, 449f.

59. "Domino tuo Borich;" *ibid.*, I, 450,7-13.

60. Among them John, son of Otto, royal chancellor; cf. *ibid.*, I, 450,15-19, whose signature appeared on a royal writ of 1138 - Szentpétery, *Regesta*, I, no. 63.

61. "... pre gravimine lorice natare non potuit;" cf. *SSH*, I, 450f.

62. See *Chronicon principum Poloniae*, c. 15, in A. Bielowski (ed), *Monumenta Poloniae historica*, 6 vols. (Lvov-Cracow, 1864-93; repr. Warsaw, 1960-61), cited hereafter as *MPH*, III, 457ff.; also, *Annales Polonorum*, in *MGHSS*, XIX, 624.

63. *SSH*, I, 451,11-19; for background, see the *Annales Gotvicenses*, anno 1135, *MGHSS*, IX, 602.

64. *SSH*, I, 451,17-18.

65. Cf. M. Gallus, *Chronica Polonorum*, ii:29, *MGHSS*, IX, 956.

66. *SSH*, I, 451,12-14.

67. See *Rocznik Malpopolski*, anno 1131: "Boleslaus intrat Ungariam et prelium cum Ungaris commisit," *MPH*, III, 152.

68. Wattenbach, II, 207.; K. Jacob, *Quellenkunde der deutschen Geschichte im Mittelalter*, 2 vols. (Berlin, 1943-49), II, 109.

69. "Cum suis perterritus, expectata nocte fugam iniit;" *MGHSS*, IX, 138,23-24.

70. *SSH*, I, 451,20-21.

71. "Borich autem cum multitudine populorum venit pugnare regem;" *SSH*, I, 451,24-25 — meaning the undisciplined segment of the population?

72. *Ibid.*, I, 451,26-29.

73. *Ibid.*, I, 451f.; *Cont. Claustroneuburgensis I*, anno 1134, *MGHSS*, IX, 612.

74. *SSH*, I, 452,2-16, and that he had richly rewarded their loyalty.

75. v. Mügeln, *Ungarnchronik*, c. 51, *ibid.*, II, 199,10-12; Macartney, 144ff.; A. Lhotsky, *Quellenkunde zur mittelalterlichen Geschichte Österreichs* (Graz-Cologne, 1963), 311f.

76. Quite effectively; "... facta igitur hac voce irruit omnis populus super illos barones, quorum consilio rex obcecatus fuerat." Cf. *SSH*, I, 447,19-21.

77. *MGHSS*, IX, 138,23-24. He was married to Adelhaid, one of the sisters of Béla the Blind; on this, also Katona, I, 547f.

78. *Ibid.*, IX, 139,23-36; *Annales Magdeburgenses*, a. 1135, *Annalista Saxo*, a. 1135; Bernhardi, 568f. On Bishop Peter, legate of Béla II to Lothair III, cf. *MGHSS*, IX, 139, anno 1134; *Vita Conradi*, c. 18, *ibid.*, XI, 63ff.

79. *MGHSS* IX, 141,27-44.

80. *Ibid.*, IX, 139,37-45.

81. Cf. *Annales Kievanses*, 1111-74, in A. Hodinka (ed), *Az orosz évkönyvek magyar vonatkozásai* (Data of the Russian annals related to Hungarian history) (Budapest, 1916), 99A; on the Annals, see Marczali, *Geschichtsquellen*, 154ff.

82. *SSH*, I, 429 (c. 149).

83. *MGHSS*, XX, 259,30-32.

84. Choniates, *Iohannes Comneni*, c. 5; Dieten, 17,39-18,66; Moravcsik, *Fontes*, 268.

85. Ostrogorsky, 301f., in ref. to W. Regel (ed), *Fontes rerum Byzantinorum*, 2 vols. (Petrograd, 1892-1902), II, 334.

86. Katona, *Historica critica*, III, 503f., and 522; Szentpétery, *Regesta*, I, no. 64. Pauler, I, 244f.

87. On the titles of the Hungarian kings, cf. *RHM*, II, 245; Katona, *Historia pragmatica*, I, 581; Erdélyi, *Művelődéstörténet*, II, 159f., and 197.

88. Cf. Canon of Wishegrad, *Continatio C. Pragensis*, anno 1137, *MGHSS*, IX, 143.

89. Szentpétery, *Regesta*, I, no. 63 (anno 1138); *Chronicon pictum*, c. 148.

90. Szentpétery, *Regesta*, I, no. 61; B. L. Kumorovitz, "A középkori magyar 'magánjogi' írásbeliség első korszaka (The first stage of medieval Hungarian 'private' documentation)," *Századok*, 97 (1963), 5ff., esp. 11.

91. See Herbordi *Vita Ottonis ep. Babenbergensis*, i:37, in *MGHSS*, XX, 717f.; or, a remark made in one of the bishop's sermons, *ibid.*, XX, 769.35, and note 14. On Herbord, see Wattenbach, II, 187ff.

92. W. BERNHARDI, *Konrad III* (Munich, 1883; rep. Berlin, 1975), 105ff.; *Acta Sanctorum*, Iulii I, 335ff.; Giesebrecht, IV, 186ff.

93. *MGHSS*, XX, 717,46-47.

94. *SSH*, I, 446,23-24.

95. *MGHSS*, XX, 718,17-21; or, *ibid.*, IX, 145, anno 1139.

96. *SSH*, I, 452 (c. 162).

97. *Ibid.*, I, 452 (c. 163).

# VI

# Géza II in the Report of the Chroniclers

Respexit autem Dominus Hungariam
et dedit propugnatorem gradientem
in multitudine fortitudinis sue.

*Chronicon pictum*, c. 164.

The reign of Géza II (1141-62) was discussed in an out-line of five paragraphs by the compiler of the *Chronicon pictum*, cc. 164-68, who had placed the record into a prop-er historical prospective. [1] The anonymous compiler of the *Chronicon pictum*, in contrast with Simon de Keza who wrote a line and a half about King Géza II, [2] or, in contrast with the truncated report in the *Chronicon Budense*,[3] known as the Chronicler-of-Óbuda, [4] relied on earlier trustworthy material to describe the Hungaro-German encounter in about 1146. [5] He narrated Hungarian-related events of the Second Crusade by mentioning the sojourn of German and Frankish armies through the country.[6] His data were confirmed by the assertions of Otto of Freising, [7] and the report of Odo de Deogilo. [8]

The Hungarian chronicler-compiler kept silent, how-ever, about the Russian policy of the royal court in the Kiev-Halich area, and said nothing about continued relations with Byzantium, or about principles of policy, or a military show-down with the Greeks. [9] The Hungaro-Byzantine diplomacy still rested on the matrimonial policies of the Hungarian court. [10] The chronicler also left out details of Hungaro-German politics. It may have been the time factor; the compiler began his work in 1358, but made use of the news-material provided, in this instance, by the twelfth century Hungarian chronicler. [11] On account of the lack of reliable information, perhaps, the chronicler(s) did not even men-tion the Hungaro-German and Hungaro-Byzantine politi-cal-diplomatic triangle that had existed; [12] the formation and reality of this condition meant that the court of Géza II found itself caught between the millstones of two imperial diplomacies. The Hungarian court has been on the black lists of intriguers of both imperial courts, running a race against time and space with the imperial advisors on various occasions. [13] Did the chronicler(s) say, — without actually providing evidence or knowing much about it, — that because of the intelligent foresight of Géza II, and in spite of foreign intrigues, there was a Hungarian foreign policy, and the king was able to defend the country's diplomatic interests? [14]

It must have been due to the lack of reliable newsmaterial that the chronicler(s) remained silent about the settlement policy of the king in Transylvania. In accordance with this policy, Franks from the Mosel valley and western Flemish peasants were invited and welcomed by the monarch to settle down in the heavily wooded lands of the southern counties of Transylvania. Those settlers cultivated the land and introduced a systematic forestry culture there. Among the settlers it was the (Hungarian speaking) Széklers and the Cumans who, as mounted constabulary force, maintained law and order. [15]

On the other hand, the failure of the chronicler(s) to say anything about the arrival and settlement in the realm of the new religious orders, as, for instance, the Cistercians, during the reign of Géza II, is difficult to comprehend. [16] After all, it was the Hungarian court that had assured the Cistercian order of its rights and privileges in the country. [17]

## 1. *The Early Phase of the Reign of Géza II*

The record in the *Chronicon pictum* began with the description of the reign of Géza II. The Lord gave the Hungarian people a protector in the son of Béla II the Blind: Géza II, crowned king on the feast of St. Cecilia. The Lord guided the hand of the young monarch in order to confirm him in his office and place peoples under his rule. He allowed the king to put other rulers to flight with his sword. [18]

The reliability of this rather exalted description is, however, lessened by the mentioned date of Géza's coronation; the feast of St. Cecilia falls on November 22 in the ecclesi-

astical calendar, while, — parallel on the same page in the
Szentpétery edition of the text —, the author(-compiler) of
the *Chronicon Budense* placed the coronation date "quarto
Kalendas Martii," that is, February 25 (1141), on *Invocabit*,
the first Sunday of Lent in that year, and two days after the
death of Béla II the Blind; "duobus diebus post mortem
patris." [19] (The editor's remark that one should, instead of
*IIII*, read *XIV* in the text, "nam dominica Invocabit anno
1141 die Februarii fuit," is unnecessary and out of place. [20]
The marginal note of the editor that the feast of Cecilia occurred on February 22, is, in fact, incorrect.) It is very un-
likely that two days after the death of the king, and on the
first Sunday of Lent, they would have held a royal coronation, unless, of course, the situation of the young monarch
was so desperate that, in order to save his throne, they had
to crown him: Géza II, immediately. [21]

The dating by the Cecilia feast is, on the other hand,
made easier by the fact that it was listed in the calendar of
the Pray codex, [22] — though not listed in the calendars of
sacramentaries used in fourteenth century Hungary, and
examined by Dom Polycarp Radó. [23] Still, reliance upon
the feast of St. Cecilia in determining the date of the coronation could not be decisive on the grounds that the feast reaches
back to the early Christian period (the saint may have died
a martyr in the days of Marcus Aurelius [24] ), and the compiler of the *Chronicon pictum* must have attached too much
importance to the feasts of the universal Church in placing
historical events, such as the date of a royal coronation. [25]

Keza provided not even a clue for the time of the coronation, [26] and Henry of Mügeln's *Ungarnchronik*, c. 52, only
stated, — following, most probably, the outline of the Chronicler-of-Óbuda, — that, when Béla the Blind died, they
crowned his son, Géza, king: "da wart sein sun Geysa zu kunge
gekorn und gekront." [27] The correct reasoning may be that,
after the death of the father the Hungarian nobles recognized
Géza II as their king (the chronicler's remark: "transactis
duobus diebus post mortem regis," may support this point
of view [28] ), though they delayed the coronation until November — of that year. Important it is that Géza II became
king after the death of his father, and they had crowned him
king in the same year, in 1141. [29]

At the beginning of his report the chronicler recorded the military encounter with the Germans. He wrote that a German knight, Rapolt by name ("Rapolt vero miles Alamanus"), was able, because of the treachery of the reeve, Julian ("probitate Iuliani comitis"), to occupy Fort Pozsony, thereby creating a dangerous situation for the Hungarian monarch. The young king, "Rex adolescens," would not tolerate this situation, and led an army against the German troops who were devastating the country along its border. [30]

For a survey of the newsmaterial so unexpectedly appearing, and out of context with the previous contents of the columns in the *Chronicon pictum,* one has to depend upon German sources, as, for instance, the report of Otto of Freising, Cistercian monk and bishop-historian, who has described events in detail, though with a strong anti-Hungarian bias. It is he who wrote in his *Gesta Friderici Imperatoris* (of his nephew, Emperor Frederick I Barbarossa), [31] that Henry the Proud of Bavaria warred against Bishop Henry of Regensburg, "gravissimam guerram agitabat," and was supported by Ottokar, margrave of Styria. During this war some nobles, "quidam milites," invaded Pannonia and, listfully, occupied fort Pozsony, the place that had earlier been besieged and taken by the emperor. [32] Otto of Freising wrote *Boson* for Pozsony, or he used the term *Bresburc,* [33] as he mentioned indeed the previous siege and capture of Pozsony by Emperor Henry IV in his other book, *Chronicon de duabus civitatibus.* [34]

The former siege took place in the year 1103, during the reign of Coloman the Learned, when Coloman's younger brother, Prince Álmos, had fled to the German court for help, — and Henry IV had given in to Álmos' request by occupying Pozsony. [35] The chronicler remarked that the German ruler sensing the odd nature of the situation, — Álmos requested, after all, aid against his own king and brother —, had the fort returned to its rightful owner, King Coloman. [36] It is the opinion of Otto of Freising that the second Hungaro-German confrontation had developed in about 1146, or, in about the mid-1140's. [37]

The cause of this German hostility toward the Hungarians may date back to 1140, when Sobieslav of Bohemia died and the Czechs elected his younger brother duke, — instead

of Vladislav, son of Sobieslav. Vladislav sought refuge with
his uncle, Béla the Blind of Hungary, and the new duke of
Bohemia, Sobieslav II (Sobieslav's younger brother) grew
angry with Béla II. When Boris, Coloman's illegitimate son,
turned to the new duke of Bohemia for military support and
political sympathy against his own king, Sobieslav II recommended Boris to the German emperor, Conrad III, who hated
the Hungarians and supported Boris — against Géza II. [38]

Conrad III did not openly support the pretender — it
would have been a bad example set for his vassals to follow, —
and the impatient Boris now had troops recruited in the east
German territory (= Ostmark, to be Austria by 1156), under the leadership of Henry Beugen and Leopold Plaien,
to prepare for a sudden attack upon the fort of Pozsony. [39]

It was the contact of Boris with Conrad III that made
Géza II to create a new political relationship by establishing
diplomatic ties with Duke Welf VI of Bavaria, the political
foe of the emperor. [40] The countermove by the monarch
was not necessary, however; in the mid 1140's, Conrad III
was fully preoccupied with plans for the second crusade. [41]

Certain individuals from among the defenders of Pozsony
had escaped in time before the siege; many were, however,
captured by the imperial troops, though nobody was killed.
"Nonnulis occisis" had the Germans taken the fort. [42] The
Hungarian monarch now had ordered an immediate inquiry
into the occupation of the fort by hostile forces, and given
orders for the recapture of Pozsony. It may be interesting
that the German chronicler spoke of the "multitude of Hungarians" holding the fort, instead of troops, thus to express
his contempt for them. [43] The investigating team sent out
by the king did determine that it was not the garrison, but
the inhabitants of the town of Pozsony who had their town
handed over to the emperor, because they wanted to appease
"their lord, Boris." [44] They were not interested in the German emperor; they were not much concerned about the leader of the German troops; they simply took a liking to Boris —
the illegitimate son of Coloman. [45] As Otto of Freising pointed
out, Boris was willing to use any means, and anybody's help,
to obtain the Hungarian crown for himself, [46] on the ground
that he thought he had the right to succeed to it. [47] That
is why he requested German aid and bribed some German

knights, and (might have) paid sums of money to Pozsony's leading citizens; Boris wanted to have their support and sympathy for his cause. [48]

The king now moved his troops toward Pozsony and laid siege to the fort (and the town). [49] Here the German chronicler made some derogatory remarks about the "primitive" Hungarian military strategy and tactics, including weapons, — "diversis instrumentis tormentorumque geberibus," which they used, though, as Otto of Freising admitted, they also were excellent archers. [50] Pozsony's German garrison must have had an easy victory in taking the fort and the town with it; now, they seemed to lack both courage and determination to defend it. They were probably surprised that the young Hungarian ruler had taken countermeasures so quickly in order to challenge them over the possession of the fort. [51]

Interesting is the remark made by the chronicler that although the German *dux* was responsible for the planning and the siege of Pozsony, he in the meanwhile left it and returned to Bavaria. Without him the German garrison left behind (in the lurch) had to surrender the fort, after Géza II promised to pay them three thousand pounds of gold. [52] The chronicler did not say why Géza II paid the usury sum, but noted that the monarch was quite angry about the payment. The king most probably felt bound by his conscience to make good the previous promise for payment by Boris in paying it. Géza II wanted to preserve the credibility of his family's good name. [53]

King Géza II must have had, therefore, his reasons for being vary about the Bavarian duke in east German lands. The chronicler spoke of a *dux Noricum*, translated here as duke of Bavaria in a sense that the duke, Henry Jasomirgott was the brother of Otto of Freising. [54] (It ought to be remembered that both the chronicler: Otto of Freising, and the duke, Henry Jasomirgott (after 1156, duke of Austria) were half-brothers of the German king-emperor, Conrad III; they were the sons of the same mother. The father of Conrad III was Frederick of Büren, duke of Swabia, the first husband of Agnes, daughter of Emperor Henry IV; Otto of Freising and Henry Jasomirgott were fathered by Agnes' second husband, Leopold III, eastern margrave. [55] )

It is known that Austria became a duchy on September

17, 1156, when Frederick Barbarossa issued the *Privilegium minus*, [56] and when Henry Jasomirgott received an enlarged area of the old *Ostmark*, east of the Enns, as his duchy, with the understanding that the duke of Austria was not obliged to participate in the imperial diet, not was he to provide fighting personnel for the emperor's army, — unless, of course, the emperor needed troops for the defense of south-eastern, that is, Austrian, territory. [57]

The Hungarian chronicler looked upon these events from a different point of view; according to him, Géza II had been unwilling to tolerate the outrageous capture of Pozsony by the German forces, and led an army against the Germans who, at this time, were also devastating the Hungarian frontier. The emperor did not participate in the campaign in person, but dispatched a large force against the Hungarian king. To quote the *Chronicon pictum*, he sent all of his available forces against the Hungarians. [58]

The opponent of Géza II was, therefore, Henry Jasomirgott, *dux Austriae*, the freshly baked duke of Austria. [59] This statement in the chronicle may incidentally prove that at least this portion of the chronicle was written before 1156, unless, of course, the editor-compiler of the text had altered the narrative to make it correspond to the reality of the 1150's. According to the Hungarian source, Jasomirgott had with him the troops of Saxony and Bavaria in his campaign against Géza II. [60] Jasomirgott was also the guardian of Henry the Lion who, after 1156, had added, at the emperor's pleasure, Saxony and Bavaria to his landholdings. [61] To complete the picture, one may remark here that Gertrude, the mother of Henry the Lion, married, upon her husband's death, Jaso-mirgott, whereby the latter had become the step-father of Henry the Lion inheriting, temporarily at least, the duchy of Bavaria. [62]

The gathered German forces on the Hungarian border were confident of their strength (the Hungarian source reports), as they stood in formation like giants facing the forces of Géza II. But the king placed his trust in God and put his armed forces in a fighting order of battle, to move against the enemy. His priests and levites and other clergy turned to God with confidence and fear in their hearts, and prayed for the intercession of the Mother of God in behalf of their cause. It was, after all, under her protection that King St. Stephen had placed his country. Now the young monarch full of faith and confidence in the justness of his cause had entered the battle, ' "et totus alacer ibat in proelium," — with a joyful speed (of youth). [63]

There are two conclusions that may be drawn from the short annotations of the chronicler. One, that Géza II did believe in the rightousness of his cause and, for that reason, knew that the Almighty was on his side. The king had tremendous faith in God, the chronicler wrote. [64] Second, the love of the Mother of God and her cult must have been widespread and very strong in the country. [65] The king's loving confidence in the Mother of Christ was only strengthened by the notion that King St. Stephen had earlier placed the country under her special protection. [66] It had nothing to do with political religion. It simply meant that the young monarch, *rex adolescens*, and his advisors were confident of the justness of their cause and had asked for divine help for the defense of their country and its people from an outsider's attack. [67]

It may be of some importance that Otto of Freising who really could not be accused of being friendly toward Hungary, drew a fair and positive picture of King Géza II — the "enemy." He wrote that, before the battle, the young king visited the nearby village church to receive on the occasion, "ad hoc instituta," the blessing of his bishops. [68] The monarch was so young, the chronicler said, that there, in the village church and before the battle, they made him a knight, and girded his waist with a sword. [69]

Before the battle began, a spy, Guncel by name, who spoke Hungarian and German equally well, entered the king's camp to announce the arrival of German troops and to advise the king to attack before the enemy forces had established a battle formation. [70] From the German chroniclers it is known that the Hungarian king took a large armed force with him, — though the number of seventy thousand troops rendered by the chronicler must be too high. [71] Even though there were seventy-two districts ( = royal fort - counties) in Hungary at this time, [72] the number of seven thousand and two hundred troops in correspondence with the number of county districts must be far more convincing. After all, all those troops had to be equipped, trained, and regularly fed. Géza II camped on the German side of the border, on the plain between the Danube and the Lajta. The region was called *Virwelt* (sic!) in German. [73]

In the Hungarian order-of-battle, Ban(us) Bélus, uncle of the king, [74] commanded the main force behind the monarch together with the reserves, which, according to the German record, numbered some twenty thousand men. [75] What may be interesting in the situation and in the formation of the Hungarian line of defense is that the imperial military intelligence (it must have totally malfunctioned) failed to report immediately the entry of a larger Hungarian fighting force into German territory. It may seem that the Hungarian troops were not expected to appear on the German side of the border, and Géza II did possess the element of surprise — and selected his own field of military engagement — long before the battle had begun. [76]

Otto of Freising insisted, however, that the Bavarian forces were on the ready, and the duke of Bavaria summoned a war council to decide what countermeasures to take in the developed situation. Some members ot that council recommended that they attack immediately the Hungarians in order to wipe them out entirely; some suggested that they await further developments on the Hungarian side. Let them penetrate at first German territory in a depth of two German miles ( = *duo Teutonica milaria*) from the border on the bank of the Fischa stream. [77]

It can be that the Bavarian military advisors had assumed that it would have been too risky to launch a pre-emptive strike on Hungarian territories; in the meanwhile, the reconnaissance units of Géza II's forces put haystacks on fire thereby revealing their presence in the country. On the Bavarian side, they gave it the interpretation that their troops had already defeated the Hungarians who out of sheer desperation put their own camp on fire. [78]

Jasomirgott's military high command must have been unable to judge clearly the situation. It seems that, from the Bavarian point of view, they had been expecting an easy victory and made no preparations for a serious clash with the forces of the young and inexperienced Hungarian monarch. They could not have imagined that the other side

may also win in a battle. Was it not Géza II who had to play
a large sum to the garrison of Pozsony to surrender the fort,
when the garrison was prepared to leave anyway? Was it not
the fort and the town of Pozsony that were played into the
hands of the Germans by the local inhabitants who sympathized with the political ambitions of Boris? Was it not the
king who had paid the sum of money because Boris had tried
to establish a political-military foothold in the northwestern
part of the country? All of these questions and arguments
were, must have been, beyond the curiosity and understanding of the advisors of Jasomirgott. Somehow the entire
Hungaro-Bavarian encounter of the mid-1140's bore witness
to a high degree of heedlessness and to a thorough misunderstanding of the basic political issues in Jasomirgott's camp.[79]

Assuming that they already defeated the Hungarian forces,
the duke of Bavaria, though he was, according to the chronicler, a cautious person, — "mente audax, sed more impatiens, manu fortis," — pushed all precaution aside and rushed
at the troops of Géza II. Although his men followed the duke
loyally, he had caused a great deal of confusion among his
own troops. In his great hurry, he ran over his own archers
before he turned on the two Hungarian army units, one of
which led by the king, the other commanded by his uncle,
Ban Bélus.[80]

It may be interesting to note the probable contradictions
made by one of the chroniclers. If the Hungarians were already defeated, or, if they had already burnt down their camps
out of frustration, how could it have been that, suddenly,
two Hungarian armies stood face to face with the attacking
duke of Bavaria? Or, did the chronicler attempt to imply that
the military newsgathering service of Jasomirgott had done
a poor job, indeed?

The troops of Géza II did not run away, but stood firmly
against the attack. Their lines of defense wavered some at
first, but gradually Jasomirgott's main units broke ranks.
Some of his troops had actually fled from the field. The duke
did not realize that his troops did break away because a dark
cloud of dust covered the sky. In fact, under the cover of dust
the Hungarian troops staged a counterattack and drove a
wedge between the staff of the duke and the rest of his forces.
The same cloud of dust also prevented Géza II from captur-

ing the duke, who fled from the scene and did not stop his flight until he reached the gates of Vienna; "in vicinum Vienis ... declinavit." [81]

The Hungarian chronicler made the "worthless" Széklers and the "unreliable" Cuman auxiliaries of Géza II responsible for the temporary wavering of the Hungarian line of defense in the battle on the grounds that they, especially the Széklers, "sicut oves a lupis," had run from the field scarred. Their flight had caused some confusion in the ranks of Géza II, and it could have happened that, in the heat of the battle, the Bavarian forces gained a temporary initiative and advantage over the troops of Géza II. [82]

It speaks well for Ban Bélus and the self discipline of his troops that victory fell to Géza II; some seven thousand Bavarian dead remained in the battle field. [83] Otto of Freising reported that numerous German nobles and an uncounted multitude of men on both sides died in the engagement. [84] The remark of the Hungarian chronicler that the battle broke the backbone of the enemy because thereafter no troops from Bavaria harrassed Hungarian peasants cultivating their fields along the border, must, however, be accepted with caution. [85]

The Lord indeed freed the country from the dragon; and, the young monarch glorified God with a thankful heart. [86] The culmination of the entire episode may have been that Count Rapolt, who had, by treachery, carried out the occupation of Pozsony (regardless of the fact that it was the German speaking citizens of the town who in their loyalty to Boris had committed treason), and who had initiated the entire diplomatic and military affair on the border, was captured in the battle of "Virwelt" on the Lajta. And the otherwise unknown Count Otto was also captured by a certain reeve named Gabriel. [87]

The chronicler's report closed with a rather impertinent note: after all this, hunger broke out that caused suffering and death in the country for many among the population. The place of this sentence in the body of the chronicle text if fully out of context. The fault may lay with the mid-fourteenth century editor-compiler of the *Chronicon pictum.* [88]

NOTES

1. Cf. *Chronicon pictum*, cc. 164-68, in *SSH*, I, 453ff.
2. Keza, c, 66, *ibid.*, I, 183,14-15.
3. *Ibid.*, I, 453S,4-9 (c. 164); in the "Óbuda" version, there are no corresponding cc. 165-67 at all.
4. Cf. Erdélyi, *Kultúrtörténet*, I, 115.
5. *Chronicon pictum*, c. 165.
6. *Ibid.*, c. 166. V. G. Berry, "The Second Crusade," in M. W. Baldwin (ed), *The First Hundred Years*, vol. I of *A History of the Crusades*, ed. K. M. Setton, 4 vols. (Philadelphia, 1955etc.), 463ff.
7. Otto of Freising, *Chronicon*, vii:34, in *MGHSS*, XX, 266,39-41; idem, *Gesta Friderici*, i:30-31, *ibid.*, XX, 368f.; A. Lhotsky, "Otto von Freising: seine Weltanschauung," in his *Europaisches Mittelalter* (Vienna, 1970), 64ff.
8. Odo de Deogilo (Deuil), *De profectione Ludovici VII in orientem*, ii, in *MGHSS*, XXVI, 59ff., or in *MPL*, 185, 1201ff. There are two classics on the topic worth reading: F. von Sybel, "Über den zweiten Kreuzzug," *Zeitschrift für Geschichtswissenschaften*, 4 (1845), 197ff., and, G. Füffer, "Die Anfange des zweiten Kreuzzuges," *HJB*, 8 (1897), 391ff. See also Mayer, *Kreuzzüge*, 108.
9. *Chronicon pictum*, c. 167, *SSH*, I, 460, notes 2 and 3.
10. *Ibid.*, I, 439f. (c. 156); C. Grot (in Russian:), *From the History of Ugria and the Slavs in the Twelfth Century* (Warsaw, 1889), 26f., reasoned that the marriage between John II Comnenus of Byzantium and Piroska (Pyrisk: Iréne), the daughter of Ladislas I of Hungary, diminished the feeling of distrust between the two states.
11. Cf. *SSH*, I, 239, c. 1; J. Horváth, *Stílusproblémák*, 270ff.; also, Gy. Kristó. "Anjou-kori krónikáink (Hungarian chronicles of the Anjou age)," *Századok*, 101 (1967), 457ff.; Gy. Kristó - F. Makk, "Krónikáink keletkezéstörténetéhez (On the origins of the Hungarian chronicles)," *Történelmi Szemle*, 15 (1972), 195ff.
12. Freising, *Chronicon*, vii:28; Gebhardt, I, 295ff.
13. As Hampe, *Kaisergeschichte*, 148, note 2, possibly in reference to Freising, *Gesta Frederici*, iii:6 and 20 (*MGHSS*, XX, 419 and 428, respectively), esp. ned, the emperor's Hungarian policy depended upon his relations with Byzantium. One is to remember, of course, that Freising's *Gesta* was "eine Verh lichung Friedrichs, ... nicht ohne offiziösen Anstrich;" cf. K. Jacob, *Geschichte der deutschen Literatur im Mittelalter*, 2 vols. (Berlin, 1943-49), II, 90.
14. The chronicler(s) may have said that because he (they) wrote that "Dominus respexit Hungariam et dedit propugnatorem gradientem in multitudine fortitudinis sue;" *SSH*, I, 453,4-7.
15. See the grant of Andrew II to "Hospitibus Theutonicis Ultrasilvanis datum," anno 1224, who "vocati fuerant a piissimo rege Geysa avo nostro;" *RHM*, II, 421,5-6; Marczali *Enchiridion*, 145; Szentpétery, *Regesta*, I, no. 413; Hóman-Szekfű, I, 398f.; Hóman, *Ungarisches Mittelalter*, I, 417.
16. *Ibid.*, I, 405ff.; Hóman-Szekfű, I, 388ff.; R. Békefi, *A czikádori apátság története* (History of the abbey at Cikádor) (Pécs, 1899), 4f., and 28, saying that it was Béla the Blind who had planned, but Géza II who had invited the order to settle in the realm. Also, E. Schwartz, "750 Jahre Stift St. Gotthardt in Ungarn," *Cisterzienser Chronik*, 45 (1933), 97ff.
17. Cf. Szentpétery, *Regesta*, I, no. 137 (anno 1183!); L. J. Lekai, *The White Monks* (Okauchee, Wisc., 1953), 38; idem, *Cisztercita lelkiség* (The Cistercian spirit) (Eisenstadt, 1982), 7ff.

18. *SSH*, I, 453,11-15.

19. *Ibid.*, I, 453S,4-9.

20. *Ibid.*, I, 453, note 2.

21. *Ibid.*, I, 453,9-10.

22. Cf. K. Kniewald - F. Kühár, *A Pray-kódex sanctoráléja* (The sanctoral cycle in the Pray codex) (repr. from *MKSz*, Budapest, 1939), 13, though Radó, *Libri liturgici*, 37 and 39 failed to mention it; see also P. Radó, *Index codicum manu scriptorum liturgicorum bibliothecarum regni Hungariae* (Budapest, 1941), nos. 2, 16, 20-40, etc.

23. Radó, *Libri liturgici*, 58ff.

24. See Funk-Bihlmeyer, *Kirchengeschichte*, I, 61.

25. Kniewald-Kühár, 13, and their observation that "die Messordnung und besonders der Messkanon im Pray Kodex ist einer frankisch-benediktinischen Vorlage aus der Diözöse Arras (Combrai) oder Umgebung, vielleicht aus der Abtei Corbie entnommen." Idem, *A Pray-kódex miserendje* (The order of the Mass of the Pray codex) (repr. from *Theológia*, Budapest, 1939), 37 and 43f.

26. Keza, c. 65.

27. *SSH*, II, 197,6-7.

28. *Ibid.*, I, 453S,8-9 ( =*Chronicon Budense*, c. 164).

29. "... in die sanctae Ceciliae principis coronatus est;" *ibid.*, I, 453,9-10 ( ( =*Chronicon pictum*, c. 164).

30. *Ibid.*, I, 453f. ( *Chronicon pictum*, c. 165, only). Also, *Continuatio Admuntensis*, anno 1146, *MGHSS*, IX, 581; and, *Annales Reichersbergenses*, a. 1146, *ibid.*, XVII, 461.

31. *Ibid.*, XX, 351f.; E. F. Otto, "Otto von Freising und Friedrich Barbarossa," *Historische Vierteljahrschrift*, 31 (1938), 27ff.; Jacob, II, 89f.

32. *MGHSS*, XX, 368 (i:30); *Annales Reichersbergenses*, a. 1146, *ibid.*, XVII, 461; *Cont. Claustroneuburgensis II*, anno 1146, *ibid.*, IX, 614, and *Cont. Claustroneub. III*, a. 1146, *ibid.*, IX, 629.

33. *Ibid.*, XX, 368,12; *ibid.*, IX, 614 and 629; *Continuatio Zwettlensis*, a. 1147, *ibid.*, IX, 538.

34. Freising, *Chronicon*, vii:34, *ibid.*, XX, 254,99, and note 10. P. Lehmann, "Die Vielgestalt des 12 Jahrhunderts," *HZ*, 178 (1954), 225ff.

35. *MGHSS*, XX, 368 (i:30); J. Spörl, "Wandel des Welt- und Geschichtsbildes im 12 Jahrhundert," *Unser Geschichtsbild*, 2 (1955), 99ff.

36. "... ad propria rediit;" *MGHSS*, XX, 368,25-29.

37. Idem, *Chronicon*, vi:34, *ibid.*, XX, 266; *Continuatio Claustroneuburgensis II*, a. 1146, *ibid.*, IX, 614; Bernhardi, 496.

38. Freising, *Chronicon*, vii:34; *Vincentii et Gerlaci Annales*, anno 1140, *ibid.*, XVII, 654ff.; Wattenbach, II, 320f.; W. von Giesebrecht, *Geschichte der deutschen Kaiserzeit*, rev. ed., ed. W. Schild, 6 vols. (Meersburg, 1929-30), IV, 404.

39. *MGHSS*, XX, 368,14-25.

40. *Ibid.*, XX, 368,25-29; Giesebrecht, IV, 449ff.; F. Palacky, *Geschichte vom Böhmen*, I (rev. ed., Prague, 1844), 393ff. On Palacky the historian from the Hungarian point of view, cf. Hóman-Szekfü, V, 366 and 403; from the Slav point of view, see Ch. Wojatsek, "F. Palacky and the Intellectual Leaders of Hungarian Society," *Catholic Hungarians' Sunday*, Youngstown, Ohio, Jan. 15, 22 and 29, 1984.

41. Mayer, *Kreuzzüge*, 96ff.; Hampe, *Kaisergeschichte*, 133f.; G. Constable, "The Second Crusade As Seen by Contemporaries," *Traditio*, 9 (1953), 213ff.

42. Freising, *Gesta Friderici*, i:30.

43. *MGHSS*, XX, 368,16-17.
44. *Ibid.*, XX, 368,18-19.
45. *Ibid.*, XX, 368,19-23.
46. *Ibid.*, XX, 259f. (*Chronicon*, vii:21).
47. *Ibid.*, XX, 368,21.
48. The scheme did not work; cf. *ibid.*, XX, 368,29-31.
49. *Ibid.*, XX, 368,23-25.
50. *Ibid.*, XX, 368,24; "... das ungarische Volk besass seine Kriegsverfassung doch mehrere Vorzüge vor der Deutschen. Der Wille des Königs verfügte unbedingt über die Streitkrafte des Reiches." Cf. Bernhardi, 497.
51. E. Zöllner, *Geschichte Österreichs*, 4th rev. ed. (Munich, 1970), 68ff.
52. *MGHSS*, XX, 368,25-29.
53. *Chronicon pictum*, c. 165.
54. *MGHSS*, XX, 368,30.
55. Gebhardt, I, 293f.
56. Cf. Freising, *Gesta Friderici*, ii:32, *MGHSS*, XX, 415, and note 36; Simonsfeld, 470ff., and 471, n. 175; H. Mitteis, *Der Staat des hohen Mittelalters*, 8th ed. (Weimar, 1968), 255f.; H. Hantsch, *Geschichte Österreichs*, 5th rev. ed., 2 vols. (Vienna, 1969), I, 70ff.; Zöllner, 72ff.; Patzelt, 124ff.
57. *MGHLL*, IV, Const. I, 220; Doeberl, IV, n. 31a; Jacob, II, 94; Mitteis, 255, note 3; H. Fisher, *Medieval Empire*, 2 vols. (1892; repr. New York, 1969), II, 35ff.
58. *SSH*, I, 456,25-29.
59. "Henricus autem, quidam dux Austrie;" *ibid.*, I, 454,9-10. H. Fichtenau, *Beitrage zur Mediavistik*, 2 vols. (Stuttgart, 1975-77), II, 194ff.
60. *Ibid.*, I, 454,11-13; the chronicler "erzahlt nicht bloss einzelne Ereignisse, sondern die einzelnen Epochen zu charakterisieren versteht;" cf. Marczali, *Geschichtsquellen*, 80.
61. *SSH*, I, 454,13-17.
62. Hampe, *Kaisergeschichte*, 128f.; Giesebrecht, V, 76ff.
63. *SSH*, I, 454f.; Marczali, *Geschichtsquellen*, 76.
64. "Rex autem ... posuit spem suam in Deo;" *ibid.*, I, 454,21-23.
65. "... invocabat clementiam Dei, genitricis Virginis Marie, cuius patrocinio beatus rex Stephanus Hungariam specialiter commendavit;" *ibid.*, I, 455,5-8. F. Kühár, *Mária tiszteletünk XI és XII századi emlékei a liturgiában* (Remembrance of the Mother of God in 11th-12th century liturgy in Hungary) (Budapest, 1939), 3ff.
66. Cf. Hartvic, *Vita s. Stephani regis*, c. 22, in *SSH*, II, 431,10-13.
67. See, e.g., the sermons of Pelbart of Temesvár (ob. 1504) on King Stephen, in F. Brisits (ed), *Temesvári Pelbárt műveiből* (Selections from the works of P. T.; Latin text with Hungarian translation), vol. VI of *Magyar irodalmi ritkaságok* (Rare pieces of Hungarian literature), ed. L. Vajthó (Budapest, 1931), 94ff.; on Pelbart, cf. S. V. Kovács (ed), *Temesvári Pelbárt válogatott írásai* (Selections from the writings of P. T.) (Budapest, 1982), 411ff.; I. Dám, *A Szeplőtelen Fogantatás védelme Magyarországon a Hunyadiak és Jagellók korában* (Defense of the Immaculate Conception in late medieval Hungary) (Rome, 1954), 24ff.
68. Freising, *Gesta*, i:32, *MGHSS*, XX, 369,38-41.
69. "... rex autem accinctus est gladio et gloria Domini apparuit super eum;" *SSH*, I, 455,9-11.
70. *Ibid.*, I, 455,17-28; *Continuatio Claustroneuburgensis II*, anno 1118, *MGHSS*, IX, 612.

71. "... 70 pugnatorum milia;" *ibid.*, XX, 369,33.

72. *Ibid.*, XX, 369,14-15; the Moscow Chronicle said that the Hungarians had, in 1152, seventy troops (?) plus three army contingents under their king's command. Cf. Hodinka, 248A+B; also, Kievan Annals, anno 1151, *ibid.*, 172A.

73. "... qui Teutonica lingua Virvelt...;" *MGHSS*, XX, 369,34-35; or, *Vierfeld*, cf. *Continuatio Claustroneuburgensis III*, *ibid.*, IX, 633. Bernhardi, *Konrad III*, 494ff.

74. "Tunc avunculus domini regis Bele ban nominatus...;" Cf. *SSH*, I, 456,19-21 (also, the correction of Bel*e* to Bel*us*, *ibid.*, I, 465,33).

75. *MGHSS*, XX, 369,44.

76. *Ibid.*, XX, 369,44-46; Bernhardi, 497f.

77. *MGHSS*, XX, 369,46-50.

78. *Ibid.*, XX, 369,50-52; Bernhardi, 499ff.; H. Vollrath, "Konrad III und Byzanz," *Archiv für Kulturgeschichte*, 59 (1977), 321ff.

79. Otto of Freising depicted the situation in more favorable terms: "... itaque dux (i.e. Austriae) est enim manu fortis, mente audax, sed morae impatiens, subdito arma corripuit, ... sed praecipitanter advolans in hostem ruit;" *MGHSS*, XX, 369f.

80. *Ibid.*, XX, 370,1-7. H. v. Eicken, *Geschichte und System der mittelalterlichen Weltanschauung*, 4th ed. (Stuttgart-Berlin, 1923), 46f.

81. *Ibid.*, XX, 370,8-14.

82. *SSH*, I, 456,6-19.

83. *Ibid.*, I, 456,19 - 457,3.

84. Cf. Reising, *Chronicon*, vii:34.

85. *SSH*, I, 457,6-12.

86. *Ibid.*, I, 457,12-15. M. Ritter, "Studien über die Entwicklung der Geschichtswissenschaft," *HZ*, 107 (1911), 237ff., esp. 264ff.

87. *Ibid.*, I, 457,15-20.

88. "Post hec diebus illis fames afflixit Hungariam, que magnam partem hominum in morte obsorbuit." Cf. *ibid.*, I, 457,21-24.


## 2. *Hungary during the Second Crusade*

> Caesar iter faciens Iherosolimam per Hungariam, non Christi preregrinus apparuit, sed potius iram tyrannidis predonis exercuit.
>
> *Chronicon pictum*, c. 166.

Otto of Freising in the thirty-first chapter of the first book of his Deeds of Frederick Barbarossa provided a colorful picture about Hungary of the time. [1] He recorded conditions of 1146 and 1147, [2] and his report was fairly reliable in that (1) during the second crusade he traveled through the realm himself and wrote his report as an eyewitness. [3] (2) Henry Jasomirgott, duke of Bavaria (and later, of Austria), who paid close attention to Hungarian politics and kept constant watch over developments in Hungary, was his brother. [4] And yet, Freising was not an objective reporter; he was quite subjective and partial, though he depicted Hungarian conditions in a manner that showed Hungary as a self-confident and strong national commonwealth so thoroughly changed since the days of Coloman the Learned that, as a commonwealth, it must have been the opposite of the then still feudal German empire. [5]

In the fields of common law, constitution and social conditions, the realm and the empire must have been different.[6] Therefore, it is no surprise that Otto of Freising had thoroughly examined the conditions in Hungary. [7] As far as it may be known, it was for the first time that, aside from the English, a country's constitution, its public and social institutions formed the subject of a historical investigation on the continent.

Although research and the tone of Freising's investigations were filled with contempt and scorn, [8] reading him one has the growing suspicion that he was resentful of the great domestic authority of the Hungarian monarch, in this instance, Géza II. [9] But the chronicler and imperial relative must also have been jealous of the country's productive agricultural lands and rich forests; he compared them to (ancient) Egypt and to paradise. [10] Freising had overcome his embarrassment with scorn and contempt with which he handled and spoke about conditions in Hungary; and yet, the essence of his assertion was that though the realm of the Magyars was a barbarous land, life there was as simple and happy as in paradise; where conditions surrounding royal authority and public law and order were ideal. [11]

In the narrative of Freising the determination of geographical directions was rather extraordinary; they were off by some forty-five degrees. According to him, for example, Bulgaria was located toward the east (of Hungary); the Patzinaks and Cumans toward the northeast, and Rama (Bosnia) toward the southeast of Hungary; the Poles and the Russians (Kievans) lived toward the north. [12] Freising most probably regarded the flow of the Danube, in this instance, the lower Danube, as a straight continuation of the west to east (from Vienna to Vác) stretch of the river, and assumed that it flowed directly east instead of southeast. [13] The

Cumans he called *falones*, [14] a designation he used before
in his opus on the Two Cities. [15] From Freising's point of
view, the *gens Hungarorum* (Hungarians) moved from Scythia
to Pannonia "Avaris eiectis," after they had expelled from
there the Avars. [16]

The inhabitants of the realm, Freising continued, were
of crude speech and lived without culture; raw and uncultured the Hungarians were, and that was no wonder because
the Huns had lived there before, who, according to Jordanes,
were the descendants of unclean spirits and of women of
ill pleasures; "ex incubis et meretricibus orti fuerunt." [17] Already on those grounds the Hungarians had created a bad
impression. Physically, they were small of stature and, next
to their language, their customs, too, were primitive. [18] Freising compared them to the Avars who ate raw and putrid
meat, [19] and looked upon it as an incredible example of
divine patience that Providence had such a beautiful country
provided for these human monsters, "talibus hominum
monstris." [20]

Otto of Freising was indeed harsh, in his report, on this
realm and its population. And yet, he, in the same paragraph
changed his tone. He admitted that the Hungarians were
cunning like the ancient Greeks, because they would not
undertake major projects, nor make major decisions, without lengthy and thorough discussions among themselves. [21]
Although their town and villages were, he wrote, in most
deplorable condition, — they built their homes out of reed,
sometimes out of wood; only a few stone buildings could he
find in the entire country, — the Hungarians spent the entire summer and fall under tents in the open country. One
may, therefore, assume that they had plenty of time for discussion among themselves (like the ancient Greeks). Lives lived
under tents in the open were communal lives, where there
existed a need for mutual leadership. [22] When the nobles
gathered, in fact, at the royal court for discussions, they
brought their seats: *stella* ( = stools) with them because they
wanted to have a serious talk — among themselves and with
the king — over matters of public concern. [23]

Interestingly, Freising reported, the Hungarian nobles held
their talks with the king, or in the monarch's presence, while
sitting down on their seats (stools), and not standing erect

in their king's presence. [24] And yet, they did not dare even
to whisper in the presence of their king, nor did they ever
contradict the king in any manner. [25]

For the purpose of administration, the realm was divided
into seventy-two or more districts. Thereby Freising unin-
tentionally provided one of the oldest available data concerning the number of county districts in the realm. [26] Every
district had its own court of law, and of the fines paid to that
court, two-thirds belonged to the king, and one-third went
to the district reeve. [27] Only the king was allowed to mint
money and collect tolls. [28]

The person of the monarch was protected by public
confidence. Were any of the nobles to insult him even in
the least manner; were even news spread about by someone
that a noble (any nobles) had (in any manner) insulted the
king, or the king's good name, the (a) representative of the
royal court, be he the most insignificant royal freeman, could
arrest the noble(s) thus indicted and could, — among, or
in front of, the others, — put the noble(s) thus indicted into cuffs, and/or torture him without a trial. [29]

In more important judicial matters the king could act
and pronounce a sentence himself. In his presence the accused
party could not defend himself. The monarch judged (decided) in any case that was brought before him without further
cooperation from the accused party. [30]

When called for by the monarch, people entered military
service. Nine free peasants in a village provided for the training, arms, and food supply for the one of themselves (in a
rich countryside, seven peasants did the same for the eighth
selected from among themselves), and sent him to fight in
the king's armed forces. The others — the nine, or seven
peasants, — stayed at home to cultivate their fields and tend
their animals. A nobleman had to have serious reasons for
remaining at home in time of a general insurrection. [31]

There were many foreigners: *hospites*, in the king's
household, frequently mentioned as noblemen; and, as high
nobility: *principes*, who formed the king's body guard. [32] The
Hungarians were not only an ugly folk, Freising continued
his report, but had crude armaments. Only from foreigners
could they have learnt about military tactics, or obtain better
weapons. [33] They were no heroes; even heroism they had

to learn from the German knights, from whom they must have taken over some improved fighting techniques and more improved arms. [34]

Emperor Conrad III's participation in the second crusade was discussed at length in the *Chronicon pictum* in a somewhat irritated tone. [35] Interestingly, the compiler of this segment of the *Chronicon Budense* made no mention of it at all. [36] The Hungarian chronicler(s) recorded that the emperor passing through Hungary as a crusader did not behave (or, travel) like a knight of Christ who brought peace with him; instead, he came like a thief and behaved like a tyrant. [37] He had false intentions (here the chronicler spoke of a petition: *petitio stimulara inventa*) in gaining entry into the realm and forcing its people to pay for the expenses of his crusade. [38] The chronicler made the point that no Hungarian bishop, — in the text: *ecclesia*, which could mean a parish, though a "diocese" would be a more appropriate term to use, — and no abbot had escaped the financial extortions of the emperor. The compiler of the *Chronicon pictum* made no further explanation of his assertions except that it was out of fear that the country's churchmen had made payments to the pilgrim emperor; "peregrinanti caesari pre timore pecunia offeretur." [39]

Did the emperor force the ecclesiastics of the realm to make payments to him? If he did, on what grounds did he obtain those payments? Did Conrad III request financial aid on the grounds that he was a Christian knight on a pilgrimage? Or, did he make fiscal requisitions as a military commander, whose armed forces had to be provided for with food, supplies, and fodder for the animals when traveling through the land? The chronicler's remark that only "petitionis simulacione inventa auditum" had the emperor entered Hungary, [40] could imply that the emperor and King Géza II had reached an agreement, or, had, at least, arrived at an oral understanding with each other.

The question remains though whether the Hungarian court assured free passage for the imperial crusaders through the realm in that the king had agreed that the crusaders could, for payment, purchase food and fodder from the population, but Emperor Conrad III decided to, — or his troops had, — abused their host's hospitality?

Or, did the crusaders request food and supplies, and free lodging from the ecclesiastics in the realm because they were "pilgrims"? [41] Could it be that the imperial crusaders had purposefully abused the oral understanding reached with the Hungarian court on the grounds that they could force the high churchmen to provide for their needs? After all, uncooperative ecclesiastics could face hostile retributions from a frustrated and starving army moving through their backyards. The answer to these questions may be found in Freising's remark who said that a large multitude of people had joined the crusading army of the emperor while passing through Hungary. [42] If true, the situation must have gotten out of control (of the Hungarian court), and the "multitude" now had to be fed and provided for.

It is against this background of the ("irresolute" and) unpleasant behavior of the German crusaders that the Hungarian chronicler described in the best of colors the passage through Hungary of Louis VII, king of the Franks. [43] Géza II maintained personal contact with the Frankish monarch, the chronicler reported, as if to emphasize the difference between the behavior of the German and Frankish crusaders. [44] Géza II must have learnt a lesson from his experience with the imperial pilgrims. He was more strict with the Franks. He kept, in a friendly manner, a steady eye upon the armies of Louis VII during their entire sojourn in the realm. [45]

The chronicler described the Frankish monarch as a prominent and honorable person, a worthy pilgrim of Christ, who received an honorable reception in the realm of the Hungarian king. Louis VII was the personal guest of Géza II, who overwhelmed his guest with gifts and kindness, but accompanied him personally during the passage of the crusaders through the country. [46] At the same time, the two kings became related to each other. [47]

One has to read between the lines in order to grasp the true meaning of this report. The Frankish king "a rege Geycha honeste conducitur" until he and his crusaders reached and crossed the southern Hungarian border. The passage of the crusaders must cause no damage to the country; they are expected to go through "praeter omnem regni molestiam Hungariae." [48] One has the impression that though Géza II truly liked the Frankish monarch, — and, it is known that

Louis VII was indeed a kind and pleasant person who possessed many virtues, [49] — his friendship toward the Franks
must have had other: political and military, reasons as well.
He accompanied the Frankish troops passing through the
realm because he wanted to keep them under observation,
in order to prevent another devastation of the country and
humiliation of its people by another foreign ruler. The conclusion drawn by the Hungarian chronicler is that Géza II
had provided food for the Frankish crusaders in transit, —
and this after the devastation of the realm by the previous
multitude of crusaders, — so that he thereby prevent an
economic destruction of the realm (and the psychological
devastation of its people) and of church lands. [50]

Two observations may be drawn from this conclusion: (1)
The devastation of the country by Conrad III's army must
not have been as damaging as the chronicler described it;
and yet, another "plague of the locusts" could certainly have
distroyed the Hungarian economy during the sixth year of
Géza II's reign. The statement attached by the chronicler
to the end of the previous paragraph: "post haec diebus illis
fames afflixit Hungariam," [51] should, perhaps, be placed
here in the text on the grounds that, at the beginning of Géza
II's reign, the economy stood indeed on weak foundations
on account of bad weather and poor harvests. [52]

(2) Another irresponsible, — unplanned, — economic
policy, be it related to prilgrim adventures or pious Frankish
crusaders, especially if connected with newer devastation
of the countryside by foreigners, would have led the country
toward an economic brink. It could have placed the economic
foundations of Géza II's rule in great danger at a time when
the monarch's opponent, Boris the pretender, was still alive
and had tried everything, — he had requested imperial
sympathy; Frankish military aid, or even Byzantine diplomatic appreciation of his position, — to undermine the throne
of his king not for the sake of national interest, but to fulfill
his own selfish goal. [53]

It came to the monarch's attention that Boris had recently
joined the entourage of Louis VII, and had entered Hungary. [54] Boris was by this time well known to the chroniclers
of the age; besides the Hungarian sources, Otto of Freising [55]
and Odo de Deogilo spoke of him in connection with the

crusade of Louis VII. [56] The Byzantine chroniclers paid him attention on grounds that Boris had turned to the Byzantine court for political support and even military aid against his own king. [57] It must have been no coincidence that Boris died during a Greek military expedition conducted against Hungary in the year of 1155. [58]

In 1147, Géza II requested the extradition of Boris from his Frankish guest and now relative. It was not decent, he told Louis VII to protect someone who had frequently in the past threatened the life and throne of his sovereign. [59]

The real meaning and importance of Géza II's petition rested, however, with the fact that many of the Hungarian nobles had encouraged Boris to go home and challenge the king on his home grounds. They, the nobles, would, in turn, recognize him as lord and desert the king. [60] That is why Boris went "home" anonymously; as an obscure member of the entourage of the Frankish monarch he crossed the border. [61] After they had discovered his true identity, Boris turned to Louis VII for protection and support. [62]

The Frankish crusader-knight king said no to the request of his host. "Noverit rex, quod domus regis quasi ecclesia (est);" anyone who had asked the king (of the Franks) for protection was like one who had sought protection from the (in a) church. [63] The position of Louis VII was made easier, and Géza II's situation more complicated by the unnecessary reasoning of the Hungarian king's delegate who in his talk with the Frankish monarch had stressed the point of view that the Church would not identify itself, nor extend support to someone who was born out of wedlock; "ut adulterinam progeniem ecclesia non communicat." [64] The pretender remained in the Frankish camp under the protection of Louis VII. [65]

It is worthwhile to compare the Hungarian and Frankish reports of these events. The Hungarian chronicler added the remark that Boris made no use of the occasion. During the cover of the (following) night he fled the camp of Louis VII, and murdered the groom of the Frankish royal stables because the groom had attempted to prevent his departure from the camp. [66] One has the rather awkward suspicion that the Frankish king had, during his sojourn in the country, placed Boris under protective surveillance; Boris revolted against such treatment and sought a way out of his detention by fleeing from the royal entourage. Judged by the chronicler's report, one cannot really assume that Boris was intelligent enough to understand that his being in the protective custody of the Frankish monarch had been intended for his own good: to assure him personal safety.

The annotations of the Frankish chronicler present, on the other hand, a different version of the situation. It is known about Odo de Deogilo that, like Otto of Freising, he, too, had accompanied his royal lord on the second crusade and returned home with him in 1149. [67] Deogilo had attempted, of course, to depict his lord in the best possible colors. His report on Boris was different from the Hungarian point of view in various aspects. [68] According to Deogilo, the Frankish monarch did not make a decision by himself in the case of Boris, but had it discussed with his advisors. Louis VII regarded Géza II as a relative and friend, but extradition of someone who had sought the king's protection was a different matter. He could not extradite Boris to Géza II on account of the pilgrim's law, *quod deceret peregrinum*. As a Christian knight, Louis VII was obliged to protect people in trouble, even if such an individual, be he a pretender to the throne of the host's country, had caused considerable disturbance elsewhere. [69]

Boris had left Hungary together with Louis VII. [70] Deogilo's statement only asserts the opinion expressed above that the pretender had killed the Frankish royal groom of the stables because he wanted to escape from the protective custody the Frankish monarch had forced upon him, — or, rather, a custody Boris had brought upon himself. [71]

Deogilo made another remark that described Géza II in even less pleasant colors. The chronicler said that the king had made such an impossible request to his royal lord that it could not have been dealt with properly. "Ob huc multa immo vix credenda promittit." [72] Géza II had only ruined his own situation and compromised himself in front of his Frankish guest and the nobles by having made a personal appearance in the camps of Louis VII; King Géza had tried to bribe the advisors of Louis VII to make them agree to the extradition of Boris. [73] It is, therefore, understandable that the Frankish monarch, — who had, until then, enjoyed the hospitality of, and his new family relationship with the Hungarian host, — now had to ask for the opinion of his nobles, for their advice concerning Boris. [74]

It is evident from the usage of the words, *non valet*, that the thoughtless personal interference of Géza II in the Boris affair had not only backfired, but it strengthened Louis VII in his resolution that he deny his host's personal and yet political request. [75] It is more than likely that the Frankish royal advisors did not appreciate at all the sudden attempt of the Hungarian host to bribe them: the advisors of the visiting monarch, with gifts. [76]

Deogilo also confirmed another statement made by the Hungarian chronicler by reporting on it differently. The emperor, Conrad III, had indeed made his requisitions in Hungary during the crusade, but, Deogilo said, those requisitions were made and carried out legally and only because Géza II had permitted the emperor to realize them. Aside from the fact that the Church did escape the requisitions, the king, Géza II, was in no position to challenge by military means the imperial crusaders entering his realm. [77]

The main problem with Deogilo's assertion is that he placed too heavy an emphasis upon the term *peregrinus*: the emperor's pilgrim status when entering the realm, as if to say that a Christian monarch (Géza II) could not really go to war with (or, against) a fellow Christian ruler (Emperor Conrad III) on a crusade to fight the non-Christian infidel in the Holy Land. Deogilo's defense of his own thesis in saying that Conrad III had appeared on the western Hungarian border "as emperor," *valde imperaliter engressus est*, as the ruler of western Christendom, whose request for food and lodging for his troops no fellow Christian monarch could deny, remains, to this writer at least, unconvincing. [78] Conrad III had placed emphasis upon his title as emperor in front of the Hungarian king because he was, at this time, in war with him. Deogilo admitted this much, thereby confirming the annotations by some German sources that it was pretender, Boris, who had caused all the trouble. The chronicler of the *Continuatio Admuntensis — pars Annalium Austriae* reports that Boris "pecunia fixit," had bribed some Germans so that he may, with their aid, obtain the Hungarian throne. [79]

Deogilo's remark that Conrad III had entered Hungarian soil as the emperor: "sicut opportuit et decuit principem, ingressus est Hungariam," points toward a note previously made by Otto of Freising, [80] who in a different context wrote that Emperor Frederick Barbarossa had, as emperor, ruled all over Europe. [81] On these grounds, the emperor could demand and obtain the assent of the Hungarian king (or, of any Christian monarch) to the passage of imperial troops (crusading armies) through his realm, and to requisition food and lodging from the people of the country for those troops. [82] Deogilo stressed the point of view that Louis VII was not the emperor, but just another Christian ruler who could make no similar demands for himself from the Hungarian ruler. [83]

Deogilo's argument that Géza II had let himself be taken advantage of, because he thereby prevented an armed attack by the emperor's crusaders on his country, is, on the grounds that Boris had already persuaded Conrad III to carry out an invasion of Hungary, such a clear late addition to the text, that it can be ignored. [84] Deogilo admitted it himself that Boris had turned to the Frankish king (for sympathy and support) only after he had been turned down by the German court with a similar request. [85]

It was his respect for the imperial title and position, and not his fear of Boris that caused Géza II to provide for the emperor's crusade and to support the men of Conrad III with fodder and shelter during the passage of the crusaders through the realm. [86]

### NOTES

1. See his *Gesta Friderici Imperatoris*, i:31, in *MGHSS*, XX, 368f.; Marczali, *Geschichtsquellen*, 150ff.

2. For background, cf. Mayer, *Kreuzzüge*, 96ff.; Haller, III, 73ff.; and, the 'reaction' of John of Salisbury to the crusade, — see his ep. 145, *MPL*, 199, 133ff., esp. 134bc and 137cd.

3. See Prologue to the *Gesta*, in *MGHSS*, XX, 351,18-25; H. Strzewitzek, *Die Sippenbeziehungen der fresinger Bischöfe im Mittelalter* (Munich, 1938), 208, spoke of Otto of Freising as the greatest 'Austrian' representative of medieval chroniclers.

4. He gave his daughter, Agnes, in marriage to Stephen II of Hungary — cf. appendix to the *Gesta*, anno 1167, *MGHSS*, XX, 492,15; *continuatio Zwettlensis*, a. 1166; *continuatio Claustroneuburgensis II*, a. 1165; *continuatio III*, a. 1166, *ibid.*, IX, 538, 616, and 630, respectively.

5. *Ibid.*, IX, 369,12-22 (*Gesta*, i:31); "Obwohl das ungarische Volk damals noch in halbwildem Zustande lebte, ... besass seine Kriegsverfassung doch mehrere Vorzüge vor der deutschen. Der Wille des Königs verfügte unbedingt über die Streitkrafte des Reiches, ohne, wie in Deutschland, an die Bestimmung von Reichsfürsten gebunden zu sein." Cf. Bernhardi, *Konrad III*, 497.

6. "Noch wirkte das Feudalsystem nicht schlechthin zersetzend. Alles hing davon ab, ob machtvolle Persönlichkeiten die Krafte zusammenzuballen und zu steigern verstanden;" cf. Hampe, *Hochmittelalter*, 240, and, the remarks of Gebhardt, I, 645ff.

7. "Sed antequam de egressione huius gentis dicamus, breviter quaedam de ipsius terrae situ nationisque ritu praelibanda videntur;" *MGHSS*, XX, 368,31-33.

8. "Sunt autem predicti Ungari facie tetri, profundis occulis, statura humiles...;" *ibid.*, XX, 369,3-4.

9. *Ibid.*, XX, 369,17-20.

10. *Ibid.*, XX, 368,34-38.

11. "Crebras vero barbarorum irruptiones passa, haud mirum, si moribus aut lingua agrestis manet et insula;" *ibid.*, XX, 368,45-47.

12. *Ibid.*, XX, 368,41-45.

13. "Attingitur ab oriente, ubi Sawa famosus fluvius Danubio recipitur...;" *ibid.*, XX, 368,41. Compare with the Idrisi world map, "Weltkarte des Idrisi," in Ch. H. Hapgood, *Maps of the Ancient Sea Kings*, rev. ed. (New York, 1979), 10. no. 5, and 180; on Idrisi (Edrisi, ob. 1166), see J. Lelewel, *Géographie du moyen age*, 4 vols. (Brussels, 1852-1857; repr. Amsterdam, 1966), I, 92ff., a brilliant Moor at Ceute who spent many years at the court of Roger II of Sicily. Cf. B. Penrose, *Travel and Discovery in the Renaissance* (Cambridge, Mass., 1967), 8.; I. Elter, "La Hongrie dans la géographie descriptive d'Idrisi (1154)," *Acta historica*, 82 (Szeged, 1985), 53ff.

14. *MGHSS*, XX, 368,44.

15. Cf. Freising, *Chronicon*, vi:10, *ibid.*, XX, 233,48.

16. *Ibid.*, XX, 233,44-45.

17. *Ibid.*, XX, 369,1, and the reference, "quod alibi latius a nobis dictum est" (*ibid.*, XX, 368,47), to Jordanes, *Getica*, xxiv:122, in *MPL*, 69, 1251ff.; or, Muratori, *Scriptores*, I-1, 187ff. There is, also, a previous reference in Freising's *Chronicon*, iv:16, *MGHSS*, XX, 203.

18. "... moribus et lingua barbari et feroces;" *ibid.*, XX, 369,4.

19. "... postmodum Avarorum crudis et immundis carnibus vescentium conculcationi...;" *ibid.*, XX, 369,1-2.

20. "... divina patientia admiranda sit, quae, ne dicam hominibus, sed talibus hominum monstris tam delectabilem exposuit terram;" *ibid.*, XX, 369,4-6. A Lhotsky, "Die Historiographie Ottos von Freising," in his *Europaisches Mittelalter* (Munich, 1970), 49ff.

21. "In hoc tamen Graecorum imitantur solertiam;" *MGHSS*, XX, 369,6-8.

22. *Ibid.*, XX, 369,8-10.

23. See Rogerius, canon of Várad, *Carmen miserabile*, c. 4, *ibid.*, XXIX, 547ff.; or, in *RHM*, I, 258ff.; or, Schwandtner, *Scriptores*, I, 292ff.; Pintér, I, 730f.; Wattenbach, II, 478ff.

24. *MGHSS*, XX, 369,10-12.

25. "At omnes sic principi suo obsequantur, ut unusquisque, ne dicam manifestis illum contradictionibus exasperare, sed et occultis susurris lacerare nefas arbitretur;" *ibid.*, XX, 369,12-14.

26. "... cum regnum per 70 vel amplius divisum sit comitatus;" *ibid.*, XX,

369,14-15, and compare with the entry in the Kievan Annals, anno 1152 (Iptius MS), in Hodinka, 172A, and with the Moscow Chronicle, anno 1152, *ibid.*, 248A+B.

27. *MGHSS*, XX, 369,15, and compare with Coloman's Synod of Tarcal, art. 78, in *RHM*, II, 369.

28. "... nullusque ... rege excerpto, monetam vel theloneum habere audeat;" *MGHSS*, XX, 369,16-17.

29. *Ibid.*, XX, 369,17-20.

30. "... nulla accusato excusandi licentia datur, sed sola principis voluntas apud omnes pro ratione habetur;" *ibid.*, XX, 369,20-22.

31. *Ibid.*, XX, 369,22-27.

32. *Ibid.*, XX, 369,27-28.

33. *Ibid.*, XX, 369,28-30.

34. "... quondam non kinnatam sed quasi extrinsecus affixam virtutem trahentes;" *ibid.*, XX, 369,30-32.

35. *Chronicon pictum*, c. 165, and Freising, *Gesta*, i:44, *MGHSS*, XX, 375. Also, *Continuatio Claustroneuburgensis III*, anno 1148, *ibid.*, IX, 629; Berry, *loc. cit.*, 483f. J. Hannenheim, *Ungarn unter Béla II und Geisa II in seinen Beziehungen zu Deutschland* (Hermannstadt, 1884), 146f.

36. *SSH*, I, 457ff.; Bernhardi, *Konrad III*, 592, on behalf of Boris; Giesebrecht, V, 449ff.

37. Conrad "vero non Christi peregrinus apparuit, in qua non pacem, sed potius iram tyrannidis predonis exercuit;" *SSH*, I, 458,2-5; Bernhardi, 599.

38. "... a regno ... pecuniam non modicam extorsit;" *SSH*, I, 458,5-8. Confirmed by the *Annales Disibodi*, anno 1147: "Counradus rex Ungariam intrat, ... igne praedaque vastat universa;" *MGHSS*, XVII, 27.

39. *SSH*, I, 458,12-14. "Der Marsch durch Ungarn ging ohne wesentliche Störungen vor sich;" Bernhardi, *Konrad III*, 600.

40. *SSH*, I, 458,5-7.

41. "... ita nulla mater ecclesia sive monasterium totius Hungarie remaneret, de quo pecunia non extraheretur;" *ibid.*, I, 458,9-12.

42. The answer may be provided for by Freising, *Gesta*, i:44: "Tantam autem post se multitudinem traxit, ut et flumina ad navigandum camporumque latitudo ad ambulandum vix sufficere videretur;" *MGHSS*, XX, 375,9-10.

43. "... rex Francorum venerabiliter et, ut decet Christi peregrinum, subsecutus;" *SSH*, I, 458,15-17.

44. "... a rege Geycha honorabiliter susceptus est;" *ibid.*, I, 458,17-19. On the chroniclers' style of writing, see F. Blatt, "Sprachwandel im Latein des Mittelalters," *Historische Vierteljahrschrift*, 28 (1934), 22ff.

45. *SSH*, I, 458,19-28, and Odo de Deogilo, *De profectione Ludovici VII regis Francorum in orientem*, lib. II, in *MGHSS*, XXVI, 61, or *MPL*, 185, 1205ff.; Marczali, *Geschichtsquellen*, 158. It would make an interesting study to compare the educational backgrounds of the Hungarian and Frankish chroniclers; cf. A. Önnerfors, "Geistige Ausbildung und lateinische Ausdrucksfahigkeit der skandinavischen Gelehrten im Mittelalter," in A. Zimmermann (ed), *Methoden in Wissenschaft und Kunst des Mittelalters*, vol. VII of *Miscellanea mediaevalia* (Berlin, 1970), 92ff.; or, the comments of P. Lehmann, *Erforschung des Mittelalters*, vol. V (Stuttgart, 1962), 275ff.

46. "... a rege Geycha honeste conducitur;" *SSH*, I, 458,23-25.

47. "... conpaternitatis vinculo regi Geyche sociatur;" *ibid.*, I, 458,20-21.

48. *Ibid.*, I, 458,25-26.

49. Deogilo, *De Profectione*, lib. I, *MGHSS*, XXVI, 61, and the writ of Pope

Eugenius, in Freising, *Gesta*, i:35, *ibid.*, XX, 371f.

50. "... et tali dilectionis nodo internexo multis muneribus a rege ... conducitur;" *SSH*, I, 458,21-25, though, Deogilo wrote that the Hungarians paid too much money to the emperor's troops — in order to escape harrassment! Cf. *MGHSS*, XXVI, 62,50-52.

51. *SSH*, I, 457,21-22.

52. "... que magnam partem hominum in morte absorbuit;" *ibid.*, I, 457,22-24.

53. King Géza II "... audivit, quod Borich, adulterius regis Colomanni, esset in comitatu regis Francie;" *ibid.*, I, 458,30-33. On Boris, see Freising, *Gesta*, i:30, in *MGHSS*, XX, 368,19-24.

54. *SSH*, I, 458,28-33.

55. See Freising, *Chronicon*, vii:21: "Boricius, qui et ipse Colomanni ... Rutenorum seu Chyos regis filia natus discebatur;" *MGHSS*, XX, 259,27-31.

56. *Ibid.*, XXVI, 62,7-14.

57. Cinnamus, iii:11; Moravcsik, *Fontes*, 208.

58. Cinnamus, iii:19; F. Chalandon, *Jean II Comnène et Manuel I Comnène* (Paris, 1912), 54ff., and 413f.

59. *SSH*, I, 458f.

60. *Ibid.*, I, 459,11-16.

61. *Ibid.*, I, 458,28-33.

62. Boris "statim ad pedes regis Francorum se prostravit vitam ab eo et veniam rogaturus;" *ibid.*, I, 459,17-19.

63. *Ibid.*, I, 459,27-34.

64. *Ibid.*, I, 459,34-38.

65. *MGHSS*, XXVI, 63,27-33; the *Chronicon pictum* provided a different rendering of this — see *SSH*, I, 459f.

66. *Ibid.*, I, 460,4-10.

67. He became, by 1152, the abbot of St. Denis. Cf. *Historia pontificalis*, c. 43, in *MGHSS*, XX, 544; Deogilo was regarded as an honest person — cf. B. Kugler, *Studien zur Geschichte des zweiten Kreuzzuges* (Stuttgart, 1866), 11, although the compiler of the *Historia pontificalis* noted that Odo had weakened ecclesiastical influence among the common folk; cf. *MGHSS*, XX, 544,46-47.

68. *Ibid.*, XXVI, 63,24-26.

69. *SSH*, I, 459,5-11.

70. *MGHSS*, XXVI, 63,34-35.

71. "... et ipse manus sequentia evasit...;" *SSH*, I, 460,9-10.

72. *Ibid.*, I, 459,27-34.

73. *Ibid.*, I, 458f.

74. *Ibid.*, I, 459,5-7.

75. "Cumque hoc rex Francorum audisset, dixit...;" *ibid.*, I, 459,26-27.

76. It is evident from Odo's remark, "deinde post oscula, post amplexus, statuunt, pacem; ... quo facto rex nostre Hungarum laetum dimisit;" *MGHSS*, XXVI, 63,23-26.

77. *Ibid.*, XXVI, 62,50-52.

78. *Ibid.*, XXVI, 61,9-17. W. Kienast, *Deutschland und Frankreich in der Kaiserzeit*, 3 vols. (Stuttgart, 1974-75), II, 259ff.; H. Vollrath, "Konrad III und Byzanz," *Archiv für Kulturgeschichte*, 59 (1977), 321ff.

79. "... valde imperialiter egressus est, et nacali apparatu et pedistri ecercitu; et bene habeat eum tunc Hungaros inimicos;" *MGHSS*, XXVI, 62,42-44.

80. *Ibid.*, XXVI, 62,45-46.; H. v. Eicken, *Geschichte und System der mittelalterlichen Weltanschauung*, 4th rev. ed. (Stuttgart, 1923), 368ff.

81. Freising, *Chronicon*, vii:34: "... quatenus auctoritate imperiali, ad quam totius orbis spectat patrocinium;" *ibid.*, XX, 266,34-35. Bernhardi, *Konrad III*, 494ff.; Kienast, II, 345ff., though pointed out that the imperial title, *imperium mundi*, has met the disapproval of the intellectuals of the age, *ibid.*, II, 417ff. On this, also John of Salisbury, *Policraticus* (Webb edition), iv:2 (or, *MPL*, 199, 514f.); J. B. Morrall, *Political Thought in Medieval Times* (London, 1958), 41ff.

82. "Nam petitionis simulatione inventa aditum ... non modicam extorsit;" *SSH*, I, 458,5-8. Deogilo, in *MGHSS*, XXVI, 62,48-50.

83. *Ibid.*, XXVI, 62,14-15. The imperial chancellor, Rainald of Dassel, spoke contemptuously of Louis VII as mere *regulum*; cf. C. C. J. Webb, *John of Salisbury* (London, 1932), 150, in ref. to John of Salisbury's remark recorded in his *Opera omnia*, ed. J. A. Giles, 2 vols. (Oxford, 1948), I, 332, no. 189.

84. *MGHSS*, XXVI, 62,50-52.

85. *Ibid.*, XXVI, 62,52-54.

86. "Cuius caesaris precessum egregius rex Francorum venerabiliter et, ut decet Christi peregrinum, subsecutus, a rege Geycha honorabiliter susceptus est." Cf. *SSH*, I, 458,14-19. It would be interesting to compare it with the study by M. Ritter, "Studien über die Entwicklung der Geschichtwissenschaft: die christlich-mittelalterliche Geschichtschreibung," *HZ*, 107 (1911), 237ff., esp. his remarks on Otto of Freising, *ibid.*, 264ff.

# VII

# The Attitude of Géza II toward Byzantium and the Roman See

Post haec autem rex Geycha dedit ducales expensas
fratribus suis Ladizlao et Stephano duxitque
exercitum in Rusciam super Lodomerium ducem...

The view prevailed at the Hungarian court that upon his departure from the country with the troops of Louis VII,[1] Boris would seek further understanding and support on Russian soil.[2] Therefore, Palatine Belus, uncle of the king,[3] attempted to establish relations with the family of grand prince Minoslavo, alias Mistislav, of Kiev by asking for the hand in marriage of Euphrozina, daughter of the grand-prince. The marriage took place, and Boris received no aid from Kiev.[4]

The Hungarian monarch, however, paid an exorbitant price for this political alliance. On account of his new relatives he was involved in lengthy wars with the family of his father-in-law. Grand-prince Mistislav could not have been better served by a defensive alliance that rested on a marriage contract with the Hungarian monarch. In 1146, the year of the German attack on Pozsony but before the entry of the armies of the Second Crusade into the land,[5] Izjaslav, brother-in-law of Géza II and son of Mistislav, took over rather unexpectedly the grand-duchy held, by customary law, by George Dolgorukij of Suzdal, uncle of Izjaslav . During the next five years, from 1146 to 1152, Izjaslav requested military aid on six different occasions from his Hungarian brother-in-law;[6] and, on two of those occasions, the king led his army himself to help out *his* brother-in-law.[7]

According to the Russian sources, it was Dolgorukij who defeated Izjaslav and occupied (rather, regained) Kiev. Izjaslav now sought refuge in Ladomer.[8] (Ladomer lay northeast of the Carpathians and north of the Dniester, with its western portion located in the northeastern section of Galicia, somewhat southeast of Kiev. Halich lay on the right hand side of the Dniester in the eastern section of Polish Galicia. [9] ) During the winter of 1149, Géza II dispatched several thousand cavalry to the aid of his brother-in-law; in fact, Polish troops also joined the Hungarian forces. In order to avoid another attack, Dolgorukij established contact (and alliance?) with the Cumans and with Vladimir, duke of Halich, a former ally of Géza II. [10]

On the grounds that Vladimir was a former military and political ally of the king, the two of them avoided direct confrontation; in fact, following the advice of the Hungarian and Polish military commanders, the Russian princes made peace with each other and, in the meanwhile, Hungarian and Polish troops sent to Kiev, quietly returned home. By 1150, Dolgorukij of Suzdal took possession of the grand-dukal throne of Kiev and kept Izjaslav away from his territories. The Russian sources imply that Izjaslav received wrong advice from the commanders of the armed forces of his brother-in-law; without the aid of the Hungarian and Polish troops, Izjaslav was unable to resist politics and military pressure of the cunning prince of Suzdal. [11]

The interesting side of the affair was that it was not so much Prince Dolgorukij, but his friend, Vladimir of Halich, who had humbled Izjaslav. It may be that the duke of Halich wanted no direct military encounter with the armed forces of his former political and military ally, the king of Hungary. But by now a situation had developed in which the humiliated Izjaslav was seeking aid from Géza II once more. The Hungarian expedition was led directly by the king against Vladimir who withdrew from the field because he wished to avoid a direct military confrontation with the king. [12] Vladimir had little hope of breaking through the ring of besieging Hungarian forces, so he had thought of a listful plan. He had bribed the nobles who had formed the entourage of King Géza II. They in turn had, during the siege of the fort, carefully warned their monarch of the quickly approaching cold Russian winter. Time went by fast, they told him, the feast of St. Demeter (held October 26 according to the calendar of the Pray codex) was at hand. [13] Freezing weather would set in soon enough, and the troops had no equipment for a winter campaign. Let the king break up the siege! In-

deed, it was only in the spring of 1151 that a decisive battle
had developed, in which Hungarian troops had helped Izjaslav to recapture Kiev and repossess his princely throne.[14]

The Hungarian forces went home, and without them
the prince felt lonely and afraid of a diplomatic-military
trap being laid out for him by his opponents. At least, that
is what the chroniclers tell us by recording that Izjaslav had
once more requested, and received, military aid from Géza
II; however, before the arrival of Hungarian reenforce-
ments his opponents had attacked Izjaslav who had no choice
but to meet them in battle without Hungarian aid. Although
he had been wounded in the battlefield, Izjaslav, fighting
without outside aid, had defeated his enemies.[15] Géza's
troops dispatched for the aid of Kiev and arriving late were
now attacked by Vladimir of Halich — and fully destroyed.
Vladimir could not, most probably, even stand the idea of
Izjaslav's keeping his throne with outside help, coming from
his Hungarian brother-in-law. [16]

In 1152, another request for aid came from Izjaslav,
and now Géza II had in person led the entire Hungarian
armed force comprising seventy-three contingents, to Kiev. [17]
Incidentally, the Russian chronicler's information concerning the number of contingents in the Hungarian army of
1152 provides valuable information on the seventy-two districts
(= counties) of territorial administration of the realm; and,
on the existence of the Hungarian royal bodyguard that
accompanied the monarch into military action. [18] The result of the campaign was to be forseen; Géza II and Izjaslav
had totally destroyed the forces of Vladimir of Halich near
Przemysl. Vladimir himself died of wounds received in the
battle a few months later, and, with his death, Kiev had lost
its most powerful opponent. After the death of Vladimir,
Izjaslav of Kiev had no further need for military aid from
his brother-in-law.[19]

In discussing these political-military events in Kiev, two
features may stand out; one, why was it necessary for Géza
II to waste such energy, time, and manpower to aid, almost
without interruption, his Kievan brother-in-law? To aid him
at a time when Géza II himself had his problems with the
German emperor and had to keep under control a friendly
Frankish king moving with crusading troops across the realm.

Was Géza II really so much concerned about the possible political contact of Boris?

Second, out of which resources had the Hungarian monarch paid for the major and minor military operations of these Kievan campaign? He must have needed food for his troops, fodder for the horses, and fighting equipment. Did the Hungarian troops fighting on Kievan soil steal their food and supplies? Or, did they make forced requisition from the native population? If the observation made by Otto of Freising that nobody during meetings with the Hungarian monarch would dare contradict the king, they had savagely punished anyone who dared to speak ill of the ruler, or about the ruler's decisions, and could, in fact, execute the (unfortunate) person so concerned, [20] were correct, it only could mean that though he had listened to his advisors, Géza II made his own decisions, but considering the young age of the monarch, he remained under the influence (and tutelage) of his uncle, Palatine Belus. It was the ruler's Serbian-born uncle who had been so afraid of Kiev, about the probability of a Kievan-Byzantine connection, and a possible Kievan contact with pretender Boris. [21]

It may be here that one may seek an answer to the question asked before. It was not the ruler, but the ruler's uncle, Belus the Hungarian Palatine, who determined foreign policy for the realm, just as it was he who arranged for the marriage contract of Géza II with the daughter of the grand prince of Kiev. [22] The crusading armies had already travelled through the land; [23] the Byzantine court had been preoccupied with the expected threat resulting from the crusades — the consequences of a successful Frankish crusade in the near East, in the former territories of the empire —, [24] and, in order to prevent even the probability of a Kievan-Byzantine alliance aimed at Hungary (that would have only furthered the political interests and military chances of Boris), Géza II had to go to the aid of the grand prince of Kiev and keep him in the sphere of interest of the Hungarian court. On those grounds, the Palatine of Serbian birth, who on account of his family ties had dreaded any relationship with Byzantine politics, had to have, as uncle to the king, a free hand in directing and shaping Hungarian diplomacy. [25] Were he unable to avoid a military confrontation with the Byzantine court, he had to neutralize even the possibility of development of a Kiev-Byzantium diplomatic-military axis east of, and probably aimed at, Hungary. [26]

Was the political-military clash with Byzantium unavoidable? In all probability, it was, and for various reasons. When he had ascended to the imperial throne in 1143, Emperor Manuel Comnenos made a statement promising the restoration of territories that had once belonged to the Roman empire. He regarded himself as a twelfth century Justinian, the worthy successor of Constantine the Great. Because of his political and military troubles with the Turks, Manuel could not expand his policies toward the east, so he decided to develop relations instead with the German court. [27]

In 1143, it was not a strong willed emperor who had ruled the German empire; Conrad III did have a formidable domestic opposition, and the Germans may have seemed to be an easy diplomatic prey to the Byzantine court. [28] But there was another reason for concern at the Hungarian court: the Hungarian family ties of the Byzantine emperor. Because of his mother, Manuel had extended his political and diplomatic interests to Hungary; [29] through his first wife, Irene, alias Bertha of Sulzbach, he attempted to build firm relations with the court of Conrad III. [30]

Manuel had his foreign diplomacy oriented toward the west; he could not do otherwise at a time when the outline of a new European policy was in the making, and when the power status of the Byzantine empire had rested upon its hold of the Mediterranean. [31] Relations with the west were, however, disturbed by the second crusade, [32] on the grounds that, because of the influence of Bernard of Clairvaux, [33] both the king of the Franks and the German imperial court were involved in it. [34]

Manuel disapproved of the idea of a crusade; in case of victory the Christian states of the near East, as, for example, Antioch, the archenemy of Byzantium, would become stronger; [35] participation by the German court in a crusade would only weaken ties with the Byzantine court; expected cooperation of the Frankish court with the Germans would effect relations between the Norman king of Sicily and — Byzantium. [36]

Manuel and his German brother-in-law had not met before the crusade, [37] and the Greek disliked the Frankish
king, [37a] because Louis VII was a friend of Roger II, Norman king of Sicily. [38] In Franco-Norman circles they had
openly discussed the probability of besieging Byzantium. [39]
The Byzantine emperor had thought of a possible way out
of the conflict: he would, upon their arrival at Byzantium,
have the crusaders transported immediately to Asia Minor
and make, at the same time, their leaders take an oath to
him promising that they would hand over to him all of the
areas they had planned to conquer in the near East. [40]

In order to realize his goal, Manuel had planned to occupy
Dalmatia and encounter the hostility of the court of Géza
II. He had thought of occupying the Italian south also,
wherefore the Normans, not friends of the Greeks, grew
angry at him. [41] In the summer of 1149, the emperor had
crossed the Adriatic near the southern portion of the Italian peninsula, but a strom on the sea made an end of his
plan; he now turned against Serbia. [42] If he could not defeat Roger of Sicily, he at least devastated Serbian territory,
from Rigómező to the Morava river. [43] The grand supan
of Serbia was a relative of Géza II, — the mother of King
Géza was the daughter of the grand supan, — who requested Hungarian aid against — Byzantium.

Roger II of Sicily had supported the Hungarian and
Serbian courts; [44] Louis VII of the Franks was the ally of
Roger II, [45] so was Bernard of Clairvaux who had constantly
preached a crusade against the "schismatic" Byzantines. [46]
What Belus the Palatine had feared, had now happened:
Byzantine greed and Serbian diplomatic incompetence had
created a state of war between Hungary and Byzantium.
Only the German emperor, Conrad III, could have smoothed
over the trouble in the alliance, but he died in 1152 (during
preparations for the crusade). [47]

In 1150, Manuel attacked Serbia from another direction; he had the land devastated from east to west, to the
Drina stream, where he was halted by the Serbian forces
and their Hungarian auxiliaries, whom he had attacked and
destroyed without any hesitation. [48] In an episode of this
military expedition the emperor and the Hungarian reeve
Bágyon had fought a duel on horseback; although the reeve

hit Manuel so heavily on the head that he had warped his vizor, the emperor, without even flinching, tore the sword from the hands of the reeve and — had captured him! [49] This episode seemingly underlines the correctness of the German chronicler's observation that the Hungarian method of warfare ( = fighting?), weapons ( = their quality), were, must have been, out ot date by then. The reeve had most probably patiently awaited that the emperor fall dead, or at least unconsciously from his horse, but his opponent, presumed dead or unconscious, tore instead his own sword from his own hands. [50]

In the following year, the Serbian grand supan submitted to the Byzantine court. [51] If the grand supan had witnessed the duel between Emperor Manuel and Reeve Bágyon, or had received news of its outcome, he must have had no choice but to surrender to his opponent. Hungarian troops fighting in Serbia must have proved to be useless against the Byzantine forces. It may be, of course, that Géza II did not dispatch his best troops for the aid of Serbia; he must have been much too preoccupied with his Kievan expeditions. [52]

In early 1151, Géza II was ready for a military encounter with Manuel, but the Hungarian bishops opposed his military undertaking; the king was told to his face that hostilities with Byzantium were his fault; members of the hierarchy failed to conceive the idea that the king turned against Byzantium on account of his family ties with Serbia. They expressed concern that, were those hostilities to continue, the country would lose the war. Géza II had no choice but to abandon his war plans. [53]

In the following year, it was the Byzantine emperor who began a new campaign against Hungary at a time when Géza II was much too busy with Kievan politics. The emperor, however, behaved with dignity, in a knightly fashion: he did not invade the country immediately, but at first notified the monarch about his intentions. [54] The latter was told in writing that his country was going to be invaded because it had sided with Serbia in the previous campaign. [55] What the emperor did not mention in his letter was that Boris the pretender had also joined the Byzantine armed forces. [56]

During the invasion Manuel had the Serem region devastated and fort Zimony (Zeugminon) besieged and captured; the garrison of the fort, bareheaded and with ropes around their necks, appeared in front of him, but he spared their lives. The Byzantines did rob the town and had a part of the population transferred to a region south of the Save river. It was now that Géza II and Palatine Belus were returning home from their annual military expedition against Kiev, and forced Manuel to withdraw from Hungarian territory. The emperor sent the captured booty across the Save river, though he himself stayed in the region in order to offer a battle with the Palatine. Belus avoided a direct military confrontation near Barancs (Branizova) because he wanted to attack the imperial forces form their flank. And Boris, who had been taken along by the emperor on this expedition, now had the Temes area plundered, though the armies of Géza II had him expelled from the region; Boris had fled to the southern bank of the Danube. Now the emperor crossed the river in order to strike at Barancs; after he had scored three victories, he still awaited a major attack from the main Hungarian army, but Géza II had offered peace instead; and, Choniates reports, peace was concluded, though it proved to be of a short duration. [57]

Frederick I Barbarossa became in 1152 the new German ruler, [58] whose intention it was to challenge and conquer the realm of Géza II. The German princes were, however, not too impressed with the plan, and the invasion of Hungary did not take place. [59]

In 1153, the armies of Géza II and Manuel faced each other again across the Danube, though war was avoided because, Cinnamus reports, the Hungarian king wanted peace. Rumors about Hungarian troop movements along the Danube persisted, however, to make the emperor hurry back to the frontier; and yet, there were no hostilities. [60] Rather, at this time, Géza II felt threatened by the fact that Manuel's mother was Pyrisk (Piroska:Irene), the daughter of Ladislas I of Hungary, [61] — the emperor was the grandson of Ladislas and the great-grandson of Béla I of Hungary (ob. 1063). [62] The father of Géza II was Béla II the Blind, [63] son of the blinded Prince Álmos, [64] who in turn was the son of Géza I (ob. 1077), [65] a ruler not recognized by the Holy See. [66] Géza I was the brother and predecessor of Ladislas I, [67] — and Géza II was the great-grandson of Géza

I, who was the brother of the Greek emperor' grandfather. [68]
When Géza II's younger brother, Stephen (a favorite of Belus
the Palatine), [69] the future anti-king, Stephen IV, [70] was
seeking political refuge at the Byzantine court, [71] although
the king had, the chronicler reports, assured a princely al-
lowance for both of his younger brothers, [72] Manuel, imperial uncle and political mentor to Prince Stephen, had
moved with an army agains Géza II. [73] The Hungarian king
had offered peace, regardless of the fact that the Byzantine
court refused to repatriate some ten thousand Hungarian
prisoners of war from the previous campaigns, [74] but the
probability of a Hungaro-Byzantine confrontation remained.

In 1154, Manuel placed his nephew, Andronicus Comnenos, in charge of the governments of Nis (Naissos) and
Barancs (Branitzova); in a secret dispatch the nephew had
promised to hand over both cities to Géza II, if the king expressed willingness to aid him to obtain the imperial throne.
The new governor's treacherous act was reported to Manuel,
who knew that Géza II, acting according to a secret agreement with Boris, governor of Bosnia, and aided by his Czech
and Saxon mercenaries, had the Danube crossed and was
on the move toward Belgrade. The regional Byzantine forces
began to harrass Géza II, but the later had defeated them
and had some of the armed Hungarian adherents of Prince
Stephen captured. (Boris the pretender was not among the
later; he had died earlier in an armed skirmish with Cumans
who had earlier invaded Hungary). Manuel was able to retain Belgrade, though the fort's garrison was in the midst of
preparations for surrendering to the Hungarian monarch. [75]

Cinnamus alone recorded all of this. Choniates provided a
different report, as if viewed from another point of view:
Manuel had destroyed the army of Géza II, with the emperor
in person directing military operations against him. After
the Byzantine victory peace was concluded, and Barancs
and Belgrade remained under Byzantine jurisdiction. [76]

The difference between the reports and interpretations
of the two Byzantine chroniclers may be explained by the
fact that Géza II had not been able to conquer Belgrade
because the flooded waters of the Danube prevented him
from crossing the Save on time. The emperor had pursued
him from a distance, and, simultaneously, had ordered that

one of the imperial military commanders, Johann Cantacuzenus, harrass the Bosnian auxiliaries of the Hungarian
king, — possibly to weaken (or destroy) the Bosnian troops, —
then to reach and attack the center of Géza's main army. But
commandant Cantacuzenus was too ambitious a person to
carry out such a simple command; instead of attacking the
Bosnian auxiliaries, he directly charged the main force —
to be trapped and destroyed by Géza II. It may seem that
some of the Hungarian exiles fighting on the Byzantine side
all perished in this battle. [77]

Cinnamus reports that in the spring of 1156, Manuel
had plans for a new invasion of Hungary, but because of the
peace petition of King Géza, he had concluded a five year
truce. According to this truce, the king had to return to
Byzantine prisoners of war. (As if it were Hungarian policy
to take a large number of prisoners and use them as "means
of diplomatic exchange" during negotiations with Byzantium.)
The king had, in fact, returned some of the booty captured
in the last military campaign. [78]

It is known, however, from another source that during
the summer of 1156, Manuel did request the support and
aid of the German monarch for a renewed attack upon Géza
II. Relations between Frederick I Barbarossa and Manuel
Comnenos were not too cordial. Frederick I had claimed,
on the grounds of Roman law, the hegemony of a universal
empire. [79] He did oppose Byzantine claims to south-Italian territory. He was angered by the fact that the Greek
emperor held similar plans for world predominance. [80]

In about the mid-1150's, Manuel planned, — together
with the German monarch, if possible; without him, or, if
necessary; against him, if needed —, a military campaign
in the Italian south because he wanted to retake that portion of territory for Byzantium. From Ancona to Tarento,
the area had to be under Byzantine jurisdiction and influence. [81]

The new Norman king of Sicily had, however, defeated
the proud Greeks at Brundisi. The defeat suffered at the
hands of the Normans must have reminded Manuel that
he was, really, an enemy of the German court. With papal
aid in the field of diplomacy he now concluded peace with
William I, Norman ruler of Sicily, and gained a free hand

in his forthcoming negotiations (to prevent the outbreak of hostilities; or, was it war, he feared?) with Frederick Barbarossa. [82]

It must have been at this stage of diplomatic activities and military development that Géza II, who wished to weaken the political situation of the Byzantine court, had expressed a sudden interest in recalling his brother, Prince Stephen, — who had lost his political footing among the Greeks, — from Manuel's court. Géza's plan (and brotherly consideration?) had miscarried, however, because of the stiff resistance of the nobles at the court. They had warned the monarch that the homecoming of the prince would only lead to civil war. [83] Obviously, the prince, who could not go home, now had applied for refuge and support at the German court. He told Emperor Frederick that his own brother, King Géza II, had been threatening his life. [84]

It may seem that it was the nobles who had feared a possible reconciliation between the king and the prince. It was, at any rate, characteristic of the intensified confrontation between Géza II and his brother that Manuel Comnenos had dispatched ambassadors to the German court in order to commend the Hungarian prince to the good will of Frederick Barbarossa. [85] The Byzantine emperor had also requested that, before the month of September (1156), the German court begin a war with Géza II, in order to divert the king's attention from the planned south-Italian policy of Byzantium, and from its diplomatic goals in Asia Minor. [86] As if success of the Greek policy in Italy would have depended upon the (enforced) neutrality of the Hungarian monarch. The German court may have sympathized with Prince Stephen (most probably, they saw through the clever diplomatic scheme of Manuel), but paid no attention to him, or to Manuel. Frederick Barbarossa simply asked King Géza II to recall his brother from exile and welcome him at home. [87]

The king now sent Bishop Gervasius (Gyárfás) and Chief Justice Heidrich as delegates to the German court with gifts. The purpose of their delegation was, first, to deny the accusations made by the prince against his brother and king, and, second, to declare that it was the prince who had caused the controversy between the German and Hungarian courts. [88] After he had received the delegation, the emperor ceased supporting the prince. [89]

It is true, of course, that by this time Frederick Barbarossa had made plans for the siege of Milan, and the Hungarian delegation in order to tone down the sharpness of their reply to the German court, — Géza II still had to face a difficult situation at home; he needed, if not the support, but at least the sympathy of the German court, — had agreed to the German request that the Hungarian court provide six hundred excellent archers for Frederick Barbarossa. [90]

It may be assumed that recognition of a Hungarian prince was not worth risking the aid to be received from the Hungarian monarch, not to mention the fact that imperial support for anyone who, without a cause, rebelled against his own sovereign, would only have presented a poor example for the German ruler's own vassals to follow.

The chronicler reports that the Hungarian auxiliary force of some six hundred archers consisted of horsemen, Saracens and archers. [91] The siege of Milan ended with the total destruction of the city by 1162, when they had plowed under its territory. [92] (Just as the Romans had plowed under the area of Carthage after the third war and placed a curse on anyone who would dare rebuild it. [93] ) Many of the inhabitants of the destroyed city fled to Hungary — probably expecting fair treatment — to the church province of Kalocsa, where they established settlements such as Kabul and Nagyolaszi (Franca-villa; Mangelos). [94]

Prince Stephen, incompetent and greedy, could have no rest. He turned to Manuel in the hope that, at this time, he would find him in a more appreciative mood. Manuel had indeed married his niece to the prince, whose personal circle at the Greek court now comprised Hungarian political exiles. [95] Among the latter was Prince Coloman, son of Boris the pretender; the court had named him Constantine and appointed him to a high office. Encouraged by the court's attention to his brother's needs, Prince Ladislas (Stephen's younger, and King Géza II's youngest brother) decided to flee from Hungary to seek political exile at the court of the Byzantine emperor. [96]

There must have been another reason also for the flight of Ladislas from the realm. At home, Géza II was a strong handed ruler who did provide for his younger brothers, but did not let them participate in the political and military decision making ( = leadership) of the country. [97] On account of his personal behavior and strictness, Géza II had many enemies; it can easily be surmised that groups of political dissenters were formed in the realm around both princes, Stephen and Ladislas, who were leading their own princely lives in their separate princely households in the country, away from the royal court. They actually opposed and openly criticised the king's person and his policies. [98]

Géza II had placed and kept under surveillance the residential households of both of his younger brothers, — it was the king who paid for their upkeep, — for the sake of the domestic-political and military interests of the country. Bearing in mind that his kingship had, since its beginnings, rested on constitutional foundations, [99] Géza II must have notified his brothers about his decision to keep both of them under constant supervision. On the other hand, the princes must have regarded the king's precaution as gross personal insult (of their freedom and integrity), and did their best to circumwent it. Both princes had conspired against their own brother, the king (it can be explained on psychological grounds), and decided to irritate him more. Stephen and Ladislas were too immature and spoiled children to realize that their older brother was, after all, king of the country, and through their irrational behavior they only advanced the cause of the Byzantine emperor.

It also happened about this time that Géza II had the Dalmatian city state of Zara retaken from the Venetian republic; [100] and it may be that the German emperor's victory over Milan (in 1158), in which the archers of the king ("copiae Ungarorum, ferme 600 sagittari electi") had, together with others, participated, whetted the diplomatic appetite of the Hungarian monarch. [101] The diplomatic-military aid thus provided had, however, its own political price tag: Frederick Barbarossa now invited the Hungarian episcopate to attend the "synod" of Pavia in order to support the anti-pope, imperial candidate, against the legitimate pontiff, Alexander III. [102]

The English pope, Hadrian IV, died in 1159, and Alexander III, the former Cardinal Bandinelli, was the political opponent of the emperor because two years earlier, at Besançon, Roland Bandinelli, then legate of Hadrian IV, had shown too much self-confidence in front of Frederick Barbarossa.[103] Although Hadrian IV had excused himself and his legate's behavior ("beneficium non feudum, sed bonum factum ... imponere"),[104] relations between Rome and the emperor worsened. Only the death of the pontiff had, slightly, eased the situation.[105]

In the election following the death of Hadrian IV, there were two candidates for the papal throne: Roland Bandinelli, Cardinal and papal chancellor, one time legate,[106] and Octavian Monticelli, who was a distant relative of the English and Frankish royal families.[107] Bandinelli had taken the name of Alexander III, while Monticelli that of Victor IV. Rahewin discussed in detail the twofold papal conclave from the German point of view.[108] Gerhoch of Reichersberg, in his *De investigatione antichristi* provided a more reliable information by saying that Alexander was elected in accordance with canon law by a majority of the assembled Cardinals; "maior et potior apparuit numerus cardinalium, qui in cancellarii Rolandi electionem consenserant."[109] Alexander III was installed in his office on September 18, and consecrated two days later by three of the cardinals.[110] Within eight days of his consecration, he placed Monticelli (Victor IV), whose consecration was held October 4, under excommunication. As Alexander III noted in a letter, Monticelli would not have dared to behave in such manner without the knowledge and consent of the emperor,[111] who knew that Hadrian IV had plans to excommunicate him before he died.[112] Bandinelli, the former papal chancellor and right-hand man of Hadrian IV, would have carried out the policy.[113] On the grounds that he regarded himself as supreme guardian of the secular interests of the Church, the German monarch attempted, however, to create a legal basis for interferring at the highest level in the affairs of the Roman See;[114] even Bandinelli had recognized him in such a role.[115] Frederick Barbarossa held the legal jurisdiction to terminate the condition persistent in ecclesiastical leadership, — there were two popes, — by summoning a church synod.[116]

The monarch based his views on the two-swords theory used in the defense of spiritual and secular interests by stating that only Pope and Emperor could use those swords in protecting divine and secular rights. Because the Church had two visible heads, he called a synod where the question could be settled. In addition to the German hierarchy he had invited the Frankish, English, Danish (below in the text, Spanish replaced Danish) and, *atque*, Hungarian bishops, who, gathered together, shall, "remoto omni seculari iudicio," investigate the issue of the papal election(s) of 1159. [117]

Attention ought to be paid to the reply of Bandinelli to the German court. Although he had realized that the German monarch was the defender of the Church who must be respected on account of his position, one must honor God more than man. The defender of the Church did mobilize the episcopal hierarchies of five countries to bring forth a decision in the papal election question without the knowledge of the Roman pontiff, [118] but failed to invite the pontiff to the synod, and failed to treat him as a spiritual leader. [119] The Lord gave Peter and his successors the power to govern and supervise the Church. Rome could not recognize the authority exercised by the German monarch in ecclesiastical affairs. The Holy See had to live by its tradition, and Alexander III could not go to Pavia to attend a church gathering that had been summoned without his knowledge and consent. [120] They in Rome viewed with skepticism the political-diplomatic chess game of the German court, by which the court utilized dissent in high ecclesiastical circles in order to obtain, for itself, leadership in and over the Church. [121] The court placed the burden of decision making upon the participants of the gathering; it made the bishops responsible for the outcome of their negotiations, though it promised to accept their judgment as valid. The gathered churchmen will answer to God for their behavior. [122]

Frederick Barbarossa had no reason to worry about the outcome of decisions reached by the synod; only those German bishops and churchmen went to Pavia who had been loyal to the court and who certainly would vote for Victor IV, the protege of the monarch. [123] The sixty-fifth chapter of the fourth book of the *Gesta Friderici* clearly stated, however, that the Hungarian hierarchy and the representative(s) of Géza II were not present at the "synod" called by the German court; nor were the delegates of the Frankish, English,

Danish and Spanish courts in attendance. [124] The contemporary English chronicler, William of Newburgh, stated frankly that only the imperial bishops had appeared at the synod. [125] Rahewin insisted in the seventieth chapter of the fourth book that the Hungarian king had in a letter and through his delegates identified himself with the synod's decisions. [126] In view of the fact, however, that Rahewin did not mention the Hungarian ruler by name, — reference to the king's writ and the royal delegates could be a later addition to, an unsuccessful falsification of, the text, — it can be stated that Géza II had not only not identified himself with the "synod" at Pavia, but he had maintained no contact with the bishops who had participated in it. [127]

From the list of names published in Rahewin, IV:67, the names of the English, Frankish, Czech, Danish and Hungarian rulers have been left out. Therefore, these rulers could not have, even through delegates, participated in the church gathering held at Pavia. [128] In the second list published by Rahewin of names of those who have signed the resolutions of the gathering at Pavia, the first six churchmen: one patriarch and five German bishops, were recorded by name. The next fourteen signators were, — with the exception of Guido, archbishop-elect of Ravenna, and King Henry II of England —, listed only by official rank, without a name. [129] He did state, for example, that the king of the Hungarians had "by letter and through his delegates" agreed, *consensit*, to the resolutions reached at the synod. [130] The names of the signators did not appear on the official synodical transcript. [131] (Rahewin reported about Guido earlier that he had been appointed archbishop to Ravenna (by the German court) to succeed Anselm of Ravenna. [132] )

The first roster of signators in Rahewin, IV:67, mentioned by name no member of the Hungarian hierarchy, [133] nor did the letter of Eberhard of Bamberg to Archbishop Eberhard of Salzburg say anything about the delegates of the Hungarian monarch, [134] though the bishop spoke of some fifty, *circiter 50*, ecclesiastics assembled in Pavia. [135]

The "synod" of Pavia was and remained a German domestic affair, [136] serving the personal interests of the German monarch; in the words of John of Salisbury, "quis hunc brutis et impetuosis hominibus auctoritatem contulit, ut pro arbitrio principem statuant super capita filiorum hominum?" [137] In his letter to Eberhard of Salzburg, Lukács of Esztergom had asserted his determination to work for preserving the faith of his flock and the integrity of ecclesiastical leadership in the realm — "et unitate ecclesiae unitis." [138] The primate of the Church in Hungary did not tolerate German imperial interference in church affairs. [139]

Arnold of Lisieux noted that the emperor did hurt his own cause by siding with the anti-pope: "non ne princeps ille, cui similem a multo tempore Roma non habuit ... a die susceptionis Octaviani divino coepit iudicio reprobari." [140] Provost Henry of Berchtesgarden reported to his ecclesiastical superior, Eberhard of Salzburg that they had to gain the adherence of the Frankish, Spanish and Hungarian courts to the resolutions reached at the synod in Pavia. The emperor had to send ambassadors to the monarchs so mentioned. He did indeed dispatch the bishop of Prague to the Hungarian king. [141]

If the delegates of the Hungarian king and bishops had been participating in the deliberations at the synod in Pavia, why was it necessary for the emperor to send the bishop of Prague to Géza II to request the monarch to consent to the resolutions of the synod?

The imperial ambassadors had visited their respective destinations. [142] It is known, however, from another source that Géza II had dismissed the bishop of Prague with an indirect answer. [143] Without the knowledge and the consent of his nobles and bishops, the ambassador was told by the king, he was unwilling to make important decisions. [144] It must have been for the first time that Géza II had direct contact with a representative of the synod of Pavia. On the other hand, the king cordially received the legates: Cardinal-bishop Julius of Palaestrina, and Cardinal-deacon Peter, of Pope Alexander III at his court. [145] Thus, it would be difficult to accept the accuracy of the emperor's assertion that the Hungarian king had Victor IV recognized as pope. (The emperor made this statement to Pilgrim, patriarch of Aquileia). [146]

The Hungarian court also notified by correspondence both Louis VII of the Franks and Eberhard of Salzburg of his decision, made upon the advice of Archbishop Lukács,

that he supported Alexander III. He promised both king
and archbishop military aid against Frederick Barbarossa,
if necessitated by the hostile behavior of the latter. [147] Therefore, Rahewin's angry outburst that the Hungarian king
had never had much confidence in the emperor, may make
sense. [148] But Rakewin also said that the German court had
quickly overcome the resistance of Géza II, and they had,
in fact, exchange ambassadors. [149] In the summer of 1161,
the emperor sent Provost Sigfried of Paderborn to Géza II,
in order to negotiate (1) some church matters; (2) the possible marriage of a Hungarian princess to a son of the margrave of Thuringia; and (3) the participation of some Hungarian army units (archers) in the emperor's campaign(s). [150]
Frederick Barbarossa must have recognized the fact that
Géza II, though no friend, remained an honest opponent. [151]

Pope Alexander III did not remain thankless toward
Géza II. He granted the king the right to hand over the
pallium in person to his country's new archbishops. [152] It
was not permitted in Hungary to appeal to the papal curia
without the king's written permission; nor could papal delegates enter the country without permission of the court. [153]
The monarch had, in turn, agreed that he would not depose bishops without a trial by, and the consent of other
bishops; nor would he transfer high churchmen without
their consent and the permission of Rome. [154] Géza II would
not abuse the income derived from vacant episcopal sees
for temporal and political purpose(s). [155]

The text of the oath taken by Géza II before the papal
legate is lost. It is possible, however, that the Ecclesiastical
Constitution issued by Stephen III in 1169 (or, in 1171) did
renew and confirm the promise made by Géza II. [156]

Géza II died on May 31, 1162. [157] They buried him at
Székesfehérvár. [158] From the cultural-historical point of view,
it was during his reign that the first Frankish Cistercians had
entered the realm in order to settle permanently at Cikádor; [159]
the Canons of Prémontré had established their first Hungarian community at Garáb in the county of Nógrád. [160] The
Knights of St. John of the Cross had opened their first hospital and home for the elderly in Abony near Esztergom on
the Danube. The knights received five wagon loads of fire-
wood annually from the royal forest in the hills of Pilis. [161] The

order also took over and directed the house for Hungarian
pilgrims in Jerusalem. [162]

## NOTES

1. Cf. Odo de Deogilo, *De profectione Ludovici VII regis Francorum in Ori-
entem*, ii, in *MGHSS*, XXVI, 62,50-54. For the full text, see the one in the Columbia
Records of Civilization series, edited, with an English translation by V. G. Berry
(New York, 1948); Marczali, *Geschichtsquellen*, 158.

2. The question is, of course, how, and under what conditions did he leave
the realm? – cf. *SSH*, I, 460,7-10.

3. Bélus (= Belus *banus*), "frater reginae Helenae;" cf. *ibid.*, I, 456, note 3.
Name mispelled in text: "... tunc avunculus domini regis, Bele (sic!) ban nominatus." Cf. *ibid.*, I, 456, 19-21; on the office of the *ban(us)*, and its dignity, see
the Hungarian Golden Bull of 1222, art. 30, *RHM*, II, 412ff.

4. *Chronicon pictum*, c. 167, *SSH*, I, 460, and notes 3 and 4: Kievan Annals,
anno 1149 and 1150, Hodinka, 106A, and 132A; idem, 92f. Volodimir, the younger brother of Izjaslav, married the daughter of Bélus – cf. *ibid.*, 90. in ref. to the
Kievan Annals, a. 1150, *ibid.*, 130A. Pauler, I, 347ff. F. Makk. "Megjegyzések
Kálmán külpolitikájához," *Acta Szegediensis*, 67 (1980).

5. *Chronicon pictum*, c. 165.

6. Hodinka, 90f.; Kievan Annals, aa. 1148, 1149, 1150 and 1152. *ibid.*, 103Af.,
106AB and 106B and 108A, 124Af., and 168Aff., 168B.; Gy. Kristó. "Kiev a magyar
krónikákban (Kiev in the Hungarian chronicles)," *Tiszatáj*, 36 (1982), 61ff. Ivo
Dujcev, "Die Bedeutung der mittelalterlichen slawischen Literatur für die byzantinische Studien," in V. Vavrinek (ed), *Beiträge zur byzantinischen Geschichte
im 9-11 Jahrhundert* (Prague, 1978), 317ff.

7. *Ibid.*, M. F. Font, "II Géza orosz politikája, 1141-52 (The Kievan policy
of Géza II, 1141-52)," *Acta Szegediensis*, 67 (1980).

8. Kievan Annals, anno 1149, *ibid.*, 106A; Moscown Annals, anno 1149, *ibid.*,
210A and 210Bf.; Gy. Moravcsik, *Byzantium and the Magyars* (Amsterdam-
Budapest, 1970), 79. Székely, *Magyarország története*, II, 1198ff.

9. See maps in P. Váczy, *A középkor története* (Medieval history), vol. II of
B. Hóman (ed), *Egyetemes történet* (Universal history), 4 vols. (Budapest, 1935-37),
672; in F. Somogyi and L. Somogyi, *Faith and Fate: Hungarian Cultural History*
(Cleveland, Ohio, 1976), 51; and, in Hóman-Szekfű, I, 448.

10. Cf. Kievan Annals, a. 1149, Hodinka, 108A; Moscow Chronicles, a. 1149,
*ibid.*, 212B.

11. *Ibid.*, anno 1150, 212A✝Bff.; Kievan Annals, a. 1150, *ibid.*, 118A✝Bff.

12. Kievan Annals, anno 1150, *ibid.*, 124A and 122Bf.; 148AB; Moscow
Chronicle, a. 1150, *ibid.*, 225B.

13. Kievan Annals, a. 1150, *ibid.*, 126A; F. Kniewald - F. Kühár, *A Pray kódex
sanctoraléja* (The 'Proper of the Saints' in the Pray codex) (Budapest, 1939), 37:
feast held on Oct. 26. The authors cited the "Frankish" strand of the church
calendar, *ibid.*, 54.

14. Moscown Chronicles, a. 1150, Hodinka, 224ABf.; Kievan Annals, a. 1150,
*ibid.*, 146A✝B.

15. Moscow Chronicle, a. 1151, *ibid.*, 238A and 236Bf.

16. *Ibid.*, 240A✦Bf.

17. Kievan Annals a. 1152, *ibid.*, 168Aff.; Moscow Chronicle, a. 1152, *ibid.*, 242A✦Bf.

18. *Ibid.*, 172A, and compare with the report on the statusquo of the realm under Béla III, in *RHM*, II, 245f.: "unusquisque comitum LXXII semel in anno regem Hungariae procurat;" and, with the report of Otto of Freising, *Gesta*, i:31: "regnum per 70 vel amplius divisum sit comitatus." Cf. *MGHSS*, XX, 369,14-15.

19. Moscow Chronicle, a. 1152, Hodinka, 242A ✦ Bff.; 262Aff.; Kiev Annals, a. 1152, *ibid.*, 168Aff.

20. *MGHSS*, XX, 369,17-20; on Freising, cf. K. Jacob, *Quellenkunde der deutschen Geschichte im Mittelalter*, 2 vols. (Berlin, 1943-49), II, 89f.; Marczali, *Geschichtsquellen*, 150ff.

21. Hodinka, 90 and 92, most probably in reference to the Kievan Annals, a. 1150, *ibid.*, 130A.

22. *Ibid.*, 92; Kievan Annals, a. 1150, *ibid.*, 124B — God bless our brother-in-law, the king; cf. *ibid.*, 114A. Also, *SSH*, I, 460,11-17.

23. *Ibid.*, c. 166.

24. Cinnamus, ii:12; Mayer, *Kreuzzüge*, 104ff.; W. von den Steinen, *Der Kosmos des Mittelalters*, 2nd ed. (Bern-Munich, 1967), 213ff.

25. Cf. Regel, *Fontes*, II, 334.

26. Moscown Chronicle, aa. 1149 and 1152, in Hodinka, 210A✦Bff., and 242ABff.

27. Manuel Comnenus, *Novellae const.*, *MPG*, 133, 773; and, compare with Cinnamus, v:10.

28. W. Ohnsorge, "'Kaiser' Konrad III: zur Geschichte des staufischen Staatsgedankens," *MIÖG*, 46 (1932), 343ff.; Hampe, *Kaisergeschichte*, 128ff.; 128, note 3; Bernhardi, 323ff., and 355f.; Giesebrecht, IV, 378ff.

29. Hóman-Szekfű, I, 371ff., in reference to the entry in the *Chronicon pictum*, c. 156: "imperatrix Constantinopolitana, filia regis Ladislai, nomine Pyrisk;" *SSH*, I, 439,25-27. Moravcsik, *Fontes*, 338; Krumbacher, 389.

30. Cf. Freising, *Gesta*, i:23, *MGHSS*, XX, 363,6-12; also, his *Chronicon*, vii:28, *ibid.*, XX, 263,30-32. "Das Werk ist in seiner pessimistischen Stimmung ein getrauer Ausdruck für die wirrenvollen Zeiten Konrads III;" Jacob, *Quellenkunde*, II, 89; also, Bernhardi, 412f.; Giesebrecht, IV, 390f.

31. *Ibid.*, V, 99f., and IV, 390ff.; Ostrogorsky, 302f.

32. Cf. Pope Eugenius III announcing a crusade, in *MPL*, 180, 1064f.; E. Caspar, "Die Kreuzzugsbullen Eugens III," *Neues Archiv*, 45 (1924), 285ff.; V. C. Berry, "The Second Crusade," in Baldwin, *Hundred Years*, 463ff.

33. Who, with irresistable force before him drove the sentiment of Europe; cf. W. Williams, *Saint Bernhard of Clairvaux* (London, 1935), 288. L. Grill, "Die Kreuzzügsepistel St. Bernhards ad peregrinantes Jerusalem," *Studien und Mitteilungen des Benediktinerordens*, 67 (1956), 237ff. The letter of Bernhard to the Frankish monarch, in Freising, *Gesta*, i:41, *MGHSS*, XX, 373f.; Bernhardi, 455ff., and 520f.; Giesebrecht, IV, 428ff.

34. Haller, III, 74ff.; G. Constable, "The Second Crusade As Seen by Contemporaries," *Traditio*, 9 (1953), 213ff.; Bernhardi, 517ff., and 533f.; Giesebrecht, IV, 438 and 440f.

35. S. Runciman, *A History of the Crusades*, 3 vols. (Cambridge, 1951-54), II, 264ff.; the letter of Pope Eugenius III to the king of the Franks, in Freising, *Gesta*, i:35, *MGHSS*, XX, 371f.; K. Heilig, "Ostrom und das Deutsche Reich um die Mitte des 12 Jahrhunderts," in his *Kaisertum und Herzogsgewalt im Zeitalter Friedrichs I* (Leipzig, 1944), 159ff.

36. Cf. Deogilo, iii, *MGHSS*, XXVI, 63,47-64,10; Freising, *Gesta*, i:33, *ibid.*, XX, 370; Giesebrecht, IV, 446, 447f.; Ostrogorsky, 304f.

37. Bernhardi, 616; Kienast, I, 197f.

37a. Deogilo, iii, *MGHSS*, XXVI, 65,22-27. Manuel wrote a letter to Louis VII; cf. Bouquet, XVI, 9; Cinnamus, ii:11, reports that Manuel made peace with the Turks — F. Chalandon, *Jean II Comnene et Manuel I Comnene* (Paris, 1912), 244ff.

38. Freising, *Gesta*, i:24, and 53 (33); *Annales Cavenses*, a. 1147, *MGHSS*, III, 192; *Historia ducum Venetorum*, a. 1147, *ibid.*, XIV, 75; Bernhardi, 605, and 618f.

39. Deogilo, iii, *MGHSS*, XXVI, 66,17-21; Cinnamus, ii:17; v. d. Steinen, 316ff. Deogilo spoke of "Constantinopolis ... moribus subdola, fide corrupta;" *MGHSS*, XXVI, 67,76; Bernhardi, *Konrad III*, 618f.; Giesebrecht, IV, 503f.

40. *MGHSS*, XXVI, 67,23-34; also, *ibid.*, XVI, 82, anno 1147; W. of Tyre, xvi:19 and 20; *Historia pontificalis*, c. 24, in *MGHSS*, XX, 534.

41. Deogilo, iv (text in Berry); Roger's fleet sailed from Ottranto to Corfu, where he left a garrison behind — cf. Freising, *Gesta*, i:33, *MGHSS*, XX, 370; Bernhardi, 814ff.

42. Cinnamus, iii:7-9; Michael rhetor, in Moravcsik, *Fontes*, 128ff.; C. Neumann, *Griechische Geschichtsschriber und Geschichtsquellen im zwölften Jahrhundert* (Leipzig, 1888), 72ff.; Choniates, *Manuelis Comneni*, ii:7; v. Mügeln, c. 53; Giesebrecht, IV, 505.

43. Manuel had attacked the Hungarian "water bastion;" cf. F. Dölger (ed), *Regesten der Kaiserurkunden des oströmischen Reiches*, Reihe A, Abt. I-2 (Munich-Berlin, 1924-65), II, no. 1383, a reference to Cinnamus, iii:10 (Moravcsik, *Fontes*, 205f.), and Choniates, *Manuelis Comneni*, ii:7; Freising, *Gesta*, i:59.

44. Cinnamus, iii:6.

45. *MGHSS*, XXVI, 67,21-23, and 67,28-34. B. Kügler, *Studien zur Geschichte des zweiten Kreuzzuges* (Stuttgart, 1866), 146f.; Giesebrecht, IV, 505ff.

46. See the letters of Bernhard to the Frankish king and the pope, — and the papal reply, — respectively, in Freising, *Gesta*, i:41 and 48; also, i:46-47; Rassow, *loc. cit.*; Bernhardi, *Konrad III*, 520f.

47. Freising, *Gesta*, i:63, in *MGHSS*, XX, 389; Giesebrecht, IV, 522ff.; Bernhardi, 892ff.

48. Cinnamus, iii:7.

49. Cinnamus, iii:9 (Moravcsik, *Fontes*, 203f.); Ephraemus, "Manuel Comnenos, 38 Years," *ibid.*, 329f., and Patriarch Michael's speech in front of Manuel, *ibid.*, 149; Choniates, Manuelis Comneni, ii:7, Dieten, 92,29-93,71; Moravcsik, *Fontes*, 269f.

50. *MGHSS*, XX, 369,28-32; H. Prutz, *Kulturgeschichte der Kreuzzüge* (Berlin, 1883; repr. Hildesheim, 1964), 397ff.

51. Cinnamus, iii:9, in Moravcsik, *Fontes*, 204f.

52. *SSH*, I, 460,11-20.

53. Advised for resistance, but not for war; cf. Choniates, *Manuelis Comneni*, ii:7.

54. Cinnamus, iii:10. In Moravcsik, *Fontes*, 205.

55. *Ibid.*; Choniates, *Manuelis Comneni*, ii:7.

56. Ita tunc quidem Borichius in Graeciam euasit; sed Hungariam iterum, ut videbimus, turbavit;" Katona, *Historia pragmatica*, I, 597, in ref. to Deogilo, ii: "Noster (that is, rex), autem Boricium satis honeste secum habens de Hungaria educit;" *MGHSS*, XXVI, 63,33-35. Cinnamus, iii:10-11; Choniates, *De imperio*

*Ioannis Comneni*, c. 5 (CB, 24f.; Dieten, 17); F. Makk, "Megjegyzések a II Géza kori magyar-bizánci konfrontáció kronológiájához (Remarks on the time-sequence of the Hungaro-Byzantine hostilities in the days of Géza II)," *Acta Szegediensis*, 67 (1980), 21ff.

57. Cinnamus, iii:11; Choniates, *Manuelis Comneni*, ii:7; description of the Serem-region: 1) as the richest part of Hungary; 2) well populated; 3) fort Zimony built there, — *ibid.*, CB, 25,6-8, and 122,19-23; Dieten, 18 and 92.

58. *MGHSS*, XX, 391 (*Gesta*, ii:1 and 3); *Chronica regia Colonensis*, a. 1152, *ibid.*, VI, 407; H. Simonsfeld, *Jahrbücher des Deutschen Reiches unter Friedrich I (1152-58)* (Munich, 1908; repr. Berlin, 1967), 39ff.; Giesebrecht, V, 4f.

59. *MGHSS*, XX, 395,55-57, and n. 97 in ref. to *Gesta*, i:25; had it taken place, "so hätte Friedrich wenigstens auf diese Weise Ungarn gegenüber das Ansehen des Reiches zur Geltung gebracht;" cf. Simonsfeld, 109; Giesebrecht, V, 11f.

60. Cinnamus, iii:12 (Moravcsik, *Fontes*, 209).

61. Cinnamus, i:4 (CB, 9,23-10,8; Moravcsik, *Fontes*, 195); Iohannes Zonaras, *Epitomae historiarum*, ed. Th. Büttner-Wobst (Bonn, 1897), xviii:24 (Moravcsik, *Fontes*, 101); *SSH*, I, 439f. Louis Bréhier, *Vie et mort de Byzance* (Paris, 1946), 262ff.

72. *Ibid.*, I, 358ff. (*Chronicon pictum*, cc. 94-96).

63. *Ibid.*, I, 446,23.

64. *Ibid.*, I, 446,6-7.

65. *Ibid.*, I, 394ff.; *Chron. pictum*, c. 124.

66. See my book, 84ff.

67. *SSH*, I, 403,30.

68. Ladislas I; cf. J. Gerics, "Judicium Dei a magyar állam XI századi külkapcsolataiban (Judicium Dei in the foreign relations of the Hungarian realm of the 11th century)," in Mezey, *Athleta*, 111ff.

69. *SSH*, I, 461f.

70. Ban(us) Belus (*ibid.*, I, 456,33), "... avunculus domini regis;" cf. *ibid.*, I, 456,19-20, that is, Géza II was the son of Queen Ilona and Béla II the Blind — *ibid.*, I, 456,42.

71. Choniates, in Bekker, CB, 165,3-9.

72. *SSH*, I, 460,11-14

73. Cinnamus, iii:19; Choniates, in Bekker, CB, 123,4-11.

74. Cinnamus, iii:12.

75. Cinnamus, iii:16-17. (Moravcsik, *Fontes*, 210f.)

76. Choniates, *Manuelis Comneni*, iii:1, Dieten, 100,46-102,87.

77. Cinnamus, iii:19 (Moravcsik, *Fontes*, 210.; Ephraemius, *Chronicon*, ibid., 330ff.

78. Cinnamus, in Meineke, CB, 130-34.

79. Freising, *Gesta*, i:25; ii:50; iv:7, *MGHSS*, XX, 447f.; *MGHLL*, sectio IV, Const. 1, 271, no. 191; Kienast, II, 334f.

80. Cf. Manuel, *Novellae Constitutiones*, in *MPG*, 133, 773; also, Cinnamus, v:10.

81. Cinnamus, iv:15; Choniates, *Manuelis Comneni*, iii:1-2; Ostrogorsky, 306f.

82. Cinnamus, iv:11-13; William of Tyre, xviii:8; *Annales Casinenses*, cont. I, *MGHSS*, XIX, 311; *Annales Reichersbergenses*, anno 1156, *ibid.*, XVII, 466; Simonsfeld, 450f., and 458.

83. There is an indirect reference to this in Keza, c. 68, *SSH*, I, 183; see also Freising, *Gesta*, ii:54-55; iii:12, in *MGHSS*, XX, 424,6-16, and note 52. On the marriage of Stephen (IV) to a Byzantine princess, see Choniates, *Manuelis Com-*

*neni*, iv:1 (Moravcsik, *Fontes*, 274), in Dieten, 126,46-128,27; and Gerhoch of Reichersberg, *De investigatione antichristi*, i:68, in *LdL*, III, 358; Katona, *Historia pragmatica*, I, 604ff.

84. Simonsfeld, 437.

85. Cinnamus, iii:19 (Moravcsik, *Fontes*, 211f.); Freising, *Gesta*, ii:31, *MGHSS*, XX, 414,41-44.

86. Idem, ii:53, and ii:49, and 52. Bernhardi, 494ff. On Boris, see Choniates, *Manuelis Comneni*, iii:20. Manuel had to struggle for the interests of his family, and for the survival of the empire; cf. William of Sicily to Manuel, in Cinnamus, iv:15, and Freising, *Gesta*, ii:49, and iii:6; Simonsfeld, 438f., and 558f.

87. *MGHSS*, XX, 423f.; Simonsfeld, 560f., and note 127.

88. *MGHSS*, XX, 424,7-20; "de castro ferrero:" Eisenstadt, cf. *ibid.*, XX, 424, note 52; Simonsfeld, 603, and note 20.

89. *MGHSS*, XX, 424,21-27.

90. Cf. Vincent of Prague, *Annales*, *ibid.*, XVII, 667; furthermore, see *ibid.*, IX, 160, anno 1157; Freising, *Gesta*, iii:13, — they were actually sent, cf. *ibid.*, iii:25. Compare with Cinnamus, v:1 (CB, 202); Hungaro-German relations were still not relaxed. Cf. Holtzmann, *art. cit.* (1926), letter one; Freising, *Gesta*, iii:25, in *MGHSS*, XX, 430,48-49.

91. Freising, *Gesta*, iii:36.

92. *MGHSS*, XX, 310, anno 1161.

93. See Polybius, *Histories* (Loeb Classics), 39:3-5.

94. Katona, *Historia critica*, III, 723; Hóman-Szekfü, I, 398f.; Hóman, *Ungarisches Mittelalter*, I, 417f. Nagyolaszi ( = Francavilla; Mangelos) mentioned by Ansbertus, in *Fontes Austriacrum SS*, V, 19, and 23f., and by Rogerius, *Carmen*, c. 26, in *SSH*, II, 568,11-15; Giesebrecht, V, 251ff.

95. Cinnamus, v:1 (Moravcsik, *Fontes*, 214f.).

96. Choniates, *Manuelis Comneni*, iv:1.

97. In the words of the chronicler, "rex Geycha dedit ducales expensas fratribus suis Ladislao et Stephano duxitque exercituum in Rusciam," *SSH*, I, 460,11-15, that is, he took care of both during a (or, the) Kievan campaign; the king did provide for them, but he alone, without his brothers, led his armies into Kiev.

98. "Qui non multo post regno privatur, et Ladislaus frater defuncti regnum invadit;" *Continuatio Claustroneuburgensis II*, a. 1162, *MGHSS*, IX, 615.

99. He immediately succeeded upon his father's death; cf. *Chronicon pictum*, c. 164.

100. Choniates, *Manuelis Comneni*, iv:1; Moravcsik, *Fontes*, 274ff.

101. Cf. Funk-Bihlmeyer, II, 120f.; Gebhardt, I, 310f.; Giesebrecht, V, 189ff.; P. Munz *Frederick Barbarossa* (Ithaca, N.Y., 1969), 186ff.; my paper "Did Géza II of Hungary Send Delegates to the 'Synod' of Pavia, 1160?" *Annuarium Historiae Conciliorum* (Augsburg, 1984), 40ff.

102. "A quo habet, si a domno papa non habet imperium?" Cf. Freising, *Gesta*, iii:10, *MGHSS*, XX, 422,10; also, *ibid.*, XX, 420, n. 46; Kienast, I, 198ff.; H. Beumann, "Die Historiographie des Mittelalters als Quelle für die Ideengeschichte des Königtums," *HZ*, 180 (1955), 449ff.

103. "Beneficium non feudum, sed bonum factum ... imponere;" Freising, *Gesta*, iii:22, *MGHSS*, XX, 429,3-4; also, the exchange of letters between Bamberg and Salzburg, *ibid.*, XX, 462f. Compare with C. S. Lewis, "Imagination and Thought in the Middle Ages," in his *Studies in Medieval and Renaissance Literature*, ed. W. Hooper (Cambridge, 1966), 41ff.

104. See correspondence recorded by Freising, *Gesta*, iv:16-17, *MGHSS*, XX, 454f.; Haller, III, 142ff.; Kienast, II, 426f.; Beumann, *art. cit.*, esp. 472ff.

105. Card. Boso, *Gesta pontificum*, in Duchesne, II, 351ff., or, in J. Watterich (ed), *Vitae pontificum Romanorum ab ex saeculo IX usque ad XIII*, 2 vols. (Leipzig, 1862), II, 281ff.; Freising, *Gesta*, iv:66 and iv:52; M. W. Baldwin, *Alexander III and the Twelfth Century* (Glen Rock, N.J., 1968), 43ff.; Haller, III, 145f.

106. Freising, iv:52, 53 and 55; Funk-Bihlmeyer, II, 117ff.; R. W. Southern, "Pope Hadrian IV," in his *Medieval Humanism* (New York — Evanston, 1970), 243ff.

107. Freising, *Gesta*, iv:50; on Monticelli, *ibid.*, ii:21; Peter of Blois looked down upon Monticelli — "auctor schismatis toto tempore vitae suae congregaverat opes et divitias, ut quietem Ecclesiae perturbaret;" *MPL*, 207, 142; Southern, *Medieval Humanism*, 105ff.

108. Lhotsky, *Quellenkunde*, 120; idem, *Europäisches Mittelalter*, 58ff.; Jacob, II, 89f.

109. Gerhoch of Reichersberg, *De investigatione antichristi*, i:53, *LdL*, III, 305ff., though he was no friend of the emperor; cf. his *De aedificatione Dei*, c. xii, *MPL*, 194, 1228f.; nor did he sympathize with Bandinelli — see P. Classen, *Gerhoch von Reichersberg* (Wiesbaden, 1960), 193ff., but changed his opinion when he saw that Monticelli was a dishonest person — *LdL*, III, 384 (i:68).

110. Cf. *MGHSS*, XVIII, 28; Jaffé, *Regesta*, II, 147; letters of Bandinelli in *MPL*, 200, 71d, and 73b.

111. *Ibid.*, 200, 88d-89a.

112. Gerhoch, *De investigatione*, i:56, *LdL*, III, 367.

113. *MPL*, 200, 89bd.

114. Freising, *Gesta*, iv:56; *MGHLL*, IV, const. 1, 182, *and* 185.

115. Jaffé, *Regesta*, II, no. 10597; Watterich, II, 383.

116. To summon such a synod was the prerogative and duty of the emperor; cf. Freising, *Gesta*, iv:55.

117. *MGHSS*, XX, 476,26-27.

118. Duchesne, II, 401; Freising, *Gesta*, iv:53; *MPL*, 200,90ff.

119. As it is evident from a letter of the emperor; cf. Freising, *Gesta*, iv:55.

120. *Ibid.*, iv:51, summarized by Jaffé, *Regesta*, II, no. 10587; Gerhoch said that the synod was a good idea — see *De investigatione*, i:56-57, and 58.

121. *MGHSS*, XX, 475,16.

122. Freising, *Gesta*, iv:56.

123. *MGHSS*, XX, 476,24-27.

124. *Ibid.*, XX, 479,29-32; though neutral, Rahewin, through the documentation he provided (*Gesta*, iv:66), supported Octavian.

125. Cf. Katona, *Historia critica*, III, 717f., in ref. to William of Newburgh, *Historia regum Angliarum*, R. S. 82,1-4 (London, 1884-89), ii:9; Sayles, 281; Grandsen, 263ff.

126. *MGHSS*, XX, 487,6.

127. *MGHLL*, sectio IV, const. 1, 190.

128. Freising, *Gesta*, iv:67.

129. *MGHSS*, XX, 486f. The list recorded a multitude of abbots and prelates in attendance together with a "mob" of Lombards; it also recorded the princes of the empire.

130. *Ibid.*, XX, 487,6.

131. Freising, *Gesta*, iv:15.

132. Idem, iv:3.

133. For the "first list," cf. Freising, *Gesta*, iv:67, *MGHSS*, XX, 482,3-44.

134. *Ibid.*, XX, 487,20-49.

135. *Ibid.*, XX, 487,22-23, — "episcopis circiter 50."

136. William of Newburgh, ii:9. G. Constable, "The Abbots and Anti-Abbot of Cluny during the Papal Schism of 1159," *Revue Bénédictine*, 94 (1984), 370ff.

137. *MPL*, 199, 39b; on Salisbury, see Sayles, 368f.; Salisbury did say that the two swords belonged to the Church — see his *Policraticus*, ed. C. C. J. Webb, 2 vols. (Oxford, 1909), II, 22, n. 16; Hugh of St. Victor, *De sacramentis et fide Christiana*, ii:2,4, in *MPL*, 176, 418c, held a similar opinion.

138. Fejér, II, 161, dated it 1161; A. v. Meiller (ed), *Regesta arhciepiscoporum Salisburgensium* (Vienna, 1866), no. 171.

139. Katona, *Historia pragmatica*, I, 614.

140. *MPL*, 201, 36bc; Watterich, II, 469f. Eberhard of Bamberg said that the Frankish king would not recognize either of the candidates until he received word from the emperor; cf. *MGHSS*, XX, 487,39-40.

141. *Ibid.*, XX, 488,47-49.

142. Freising, *Gesta*, iv:74.

143. The continuator of Cosmas named Géza II king of the "Huns;" *ibid.*, IX, 161,30-34.

144. *Ibid.*, XVII, 679,25-28; Pauler, I, 295ff.

145. Duchesne, II, 403; Fejér, II, 160. Card. Peter returned to Rome by Dec. 21, 1160 — Jaffé, *Regesta*, I, no. 10637, and Card. Julius returned by Feb., 1161, *ibid.*, I, nos. 10657, 10678 and 10679.

146. See *MGHLL*, sectio IV, const. 1, 196.

147. Szentpétery, *Regesta*, I, no. 95; Bouquet, *Recueil*, XVI, 27, note 89; Katona, *Historia critica*, III, 732; Kienast, I, 201.

148. *MGHSS*, XX, 491,2-4.

149. *Ibid.*, XX, 491,4-6; the problem is that Rahewin simply "updated" Einhard's previous remark — see Einhard, *Vita Caroli Magni*, c. 16, *ibid.*, II, 451f.

150. Cf. Doeberl, IV, 195ff. (no. 41); Giesebrecht, V, 276.

151. Giesebrecht, V, 271, said that since Géza II died in 1161, Sigfried visited the court of Ladislas II (!); however, Géza II died in 1162 — cf. Pauler, I, 381, in ref. to the *Annales s. Rutperti Salisburgenses*, anno 1162, *MGHSS*, IX, 776, to cite but one of the many references of Pauler, I, 637, note 493.

152. Jaffé, *Regesta*, I, no. 10682.

153. Gerhoch, *De investigatione*, i:68, *LdL*, III, 385, a situation in correspondence with conditions in Sicily; cf. *MGHLL*, sectio IV, const. 1, 588ff. (no. 413).

154. *RHM*, II, 382f.

155. Fejér, II, 180f.; Péterffy, I, 63; Mansi, *Concilia*, XXI, 35f.

156. Szentpétery, *Regesta*, I, no. 118.

157. See *Continuatio Admuntensis*, anno 1162, *MGHSS*, IX, 583; *Continuatio Claustroneuburgensis II*, anno 1162, *ibid.*, IX, 615; *Continuatio III*, anno 1162, *ibid.*, IX, 630.

158. *SSH*, I, 460,28.

159. Cf. R. Békefi, *A czikádori apátság története* (History of the Cistercian abbey at Cikádor) (Pécs, 1899), 6f., and 28; L. J. Lekai, *The White Monks* (Kauchee, Wisc., 1953), 216.

160. See A. Oszvald, *A magyarországi középkori premontrei apátságok* (Religious communities of the Canons of Prémontré in medieval Hungary) (Budapest, 1939), 10f.; G. Schreiber's 66 page article, "Praemonstratensenkultur des 12 Jahrhunderts," *Analecta Praemonstratensis*, 16 (1940), 41ff.

161. Knauz, I, 132; E. Reiszig, *A jeruzsálemi szent János lovagrend Magyarországon* (The Knights of St. John in Hungary), 2 vols. (Budapest, 1925-28), I, passim.

162. Szentpétery, *Regesta*, I, no. 100.

# VIII

## The Mid-Twelfth Century View of History in the Background of Hungarian Politics

*Absit autem a sacrosancta Ecclesia talis macula et ruga, qualis nomine curiae notatur!*

Gerhoch of Reichersberg

During the mid-twelfth century two authors, Otto of Freising and Gerhoch of Reichersberg pointed to the intellectual-religious features in the political background of their age. Of these two Otto, the Cistercian monk and bishop of Freising, was the more famous, who was being referred to by his contemporaries as the most distinguished chronicler of the century.

Otto of Freising in his universal history discussed the meaning of contemporary events. A relative of the Hohenstaufen and a descendant of the Babenberg family, he, as a monk, had studied theology and religious history at Paris for several years. As the half-brother of Conrad III (elected because Conrad seemed to be, as the opponent of Henry the Proud, the weaker party), he expected the imperial court to revive the centralized form of government for the empire. Otto maintained close relations with the court and had access to official court information when, between 1143 and 1146, he wrote his universal history, *Chronica sive historia de duabus civitatibus*. He reworked his opus in 1156-57, but did not essentially alter its contents, nor did he go beyond the events of 1146. It is known in the version in which he sent it to his nephew, Frederick Barbarossa, the elected and anointed successor of Conrad III. Otto of Blasien continued the opus until 1209, in the early thirteenth century.

Literary historians say that the monkish bishop who had become a chronicler was a serious scholar, who did a thorough work in research, and wrote a well composed, clear narrative of history. He preoccupied himself with various topics;

he may have been the first medieval chronicler who superseded the annalistic approach dating back to the Carolingian age in his search for a new method of writing history.

Otto of Freising wrote history by focusing on the whole picture of his age. And yet, he may be spoken of as a dilettante, instead of a scholar, who was not free from, nor afraid of, a certain kind of naivite. He was very subjective, for instance, in his approach toward the imperial court. He could not observe events clearly; was unable to see through the almost constant political intrigues that surrounded the diplomatic objectives of Conrad III and Frederick I. His style; the structure of his writing, in fact, are most similar to the editorial style and structure of composition of the "Chronicle of the Emperors" (*Kaiserchronik*). Even the basic concept of his work, the idea of change: *Veränderlichkeit*, lacks originality on the grounds that is shows striking resemblance to the fundamental concept of the Chronicle of the Emperors, even though he in his letter of dedication addressed to the Emperor placed in front of the book, recommended his opus as "liber de mutatione rerum" to the interested reader.

Otto of Freising said that "miser mundi rotatus," constant misery and trouble were the order of things in the world. He identified his notion of misery with the system of the *civitas terrena*, whose development and essence were characterized by almost continuous decline and constant change. Suffering was life upon the earth, because earthly distress had a meaning in that it brought the moribund inhabitants of this earth closer to the realm of God, the world of the *civitas Dei*. As if one were to listen to the ideas of the great Latin church father Aurelius Augustinus (St. Augustine), who in one of his commentaries on the Psalms has revealed a similar concept. By the rivers of Babylon we sit and weep because we remember Sion; we deserve our exile; here we are, it is our fate, because we went astray; we ignored the laws of the Creator and failed to keep his commandments. The difference is, however, that the church father in his magnificent City of God had further expanded this trend of thought, the change of earthly things and timely decay.

The history of the terrestrial world proved that constant change, *mutatio rerum*, was characteristic of every earthly event. This is why a Christian was longing for the final change

of his status, when entirely free of all earthly goods he could
live in a spiritual sphere; therefore, he attempted to perfect
his terrestrial ideas in his earthly life. Amidst terrestrial
conditions, however, such a permanent alteration could only
mean the constant cyclical change in the power structure
of earthly authorities: "translationes imperii," when terrestrial power: authority, over mundane matters is being transferred from one people to another, from country to country.
So it was with the Greeks; Alexander the Great inherited
world predominance, as did, after him, the City of Rome.
St. Augustine, and, in a similar fashion, Otto of Freising,
explained that such a hypothesis was based upon the second
chapter of the Book of Daniel, and it created quite an echo
among the church fathers. Continuing this trend of thought
Otto of Freising remarked that though the history of Rome
formed an epoch of the rule of law and of creative jurispru-
dence, Roman rule gradually changed to the predominance
of the Franks, Lombards, and to the activities of the eastern
Frankish (German) tribes. Since the birth of Christ only
Christian rulers had dominated the world, therefore, the
City of God identified itself with the sphere of existence of
the Church and of Christian ideas.

The world picture of the Cistercian monk and bishop
of Freising becomes Christocentric European. He identifies
the concept of the last *translatio imperii* with the growth
of spiritual power effective over the policies of the City of
God, and the German empire. So, the idea of transfer of
power becomes the representative ideological outlook of the
age, a kind of realization of the "translatio sapientiae,"
transfer of wisdom, that made possible the expansion and
growth of human knowledge.

Human learning originated in the east, in Babylon,
wrote Otto of Freising, because it was there that human
learning of things had grown into knowledge (of things).
From Babylon, knowledge has reached Egypt because of
Abraham who found refuge there from famine in his native
land. As Iosephus mentioned it in his book about Antiquities,
Abraham had offered in return for Egyptian hospitality
to teach them the mathematics and astronomy of the Baby-
lonians. Before the sojourn of Abraham to Egypt, the two
fields of knowledge were unknown there.

In his interpretation of Iosephus' annotations, Otto of Freising continued his trend of thought by saying that in such a manner human wisdom was being transferred from the Kaldi (Chaldaeans) to Egypt; and, from the Egyptians to the Greeks. From the latter the Romans took over and preserved universal human knowledge, which was being cultivated and developed, though not without fault, in his own age during the twelfth century by scholars and learned individuals, such as Berengar, Manegold, and Anselm, the priest of Laon. "Ab urbe quippe ad Grecos, a Graecis ad Francos, a Francis ad Longobardos, a Longobardis rursum ad Teutonicos derivatum, non solum antiquitates senuit, sed etiam ... sordes multiplices ac defectus varios contraxit."

Monks played a role in the cultivation of knowledge because they had already readied themselves for the spiritual — intellectual life, and done much for the common good. The monastic movement, too, had its beginnings in Egypt; it spread to Gaul and to the Teutonic countries, as if to prove that knowledge from the east had been expanding toward the west.

In politics, Otto of Freising discussed the controversy between the pope and the German emperor *vs.* the background of relations between religion and politics (=state and Church), God and His creatures. The two powers, *regnum* and *sacerdotium*, could not exist without each other for the duration of mundane existence; therefore, the two must learn not to struggle constantly, but to cooperate with each other in a peaceful manner. The spiritual responsibility of the Church exercised in the field of *cura animarum* has become, Freising wrote, an acknowledged historial fact since Constantine the Great. But the Church had the right to play a leading role in the events of the world. For this reason, attention will have to be paid to the behavior of ecclesiastic in temporal politics. Were secular leaders to deny the need for spiritual services, an unavoidable clash between *civitas Dei* and *civitas mundi* would occur. The "secular" element must ask for a part, and must actually play a role in the service of spiritual institutions. The emperor was lord and protector of the world: "auctoritate imperialii, ad quam tocius orbis spectat patrocinium." Christian Rome was the symbol of the empire, *sacrum imperium*. Church and state ( = religion and politics) were but tools in the hands of God. Consequently, world history had to become the theater of activities on earth of divine Providence.

Otto of Freising discussed the role of salvation by dividing its history into three chronological stages: "triplex status," in the eighth part of his work. "Civitas perversae triplex aeque status invenitur, duorum primus ante gratiam, secundus tempore gratiae fuit et est, tertius post presentem vitam erit."

The first stage lasted from Adam's fall to the birth of Christ. The second is to last until the end of times, when, in this Christian epoch: *tempus gratiae*, cooperation between Church and state must materialize. Together, they establish the earthly realm of God.

In the reigns of Constantine the Great and Theodosios the Great religion and politics became, indeed, almost identical — the terrestrial realm with the Christian empire, *imperium Christi*. "Nam de duabus civitatibus, sed pene de una tantum." The main obligation of these two powers was to preserve their accomplished identity. "Nemo autem nos Christiani imperium ab ecclesia separare putet, cum duae in ecclesia Dei personae, sacerdotalis et regalis esse noscantur." The identity of the Christian empire and of the Church ought not be rent asunder.

That is the reason why the bishop of Freising condemned the political confrontation between Pope Gregory VII and the German king, Henry IV. The initial conflict of the investiture controversy only hurt the cause of Christian unity. Nor did it serve the needs of human salvation. Although he spoke with respect and love about the Roman pontiff, — "Salerni defunctus beatae memoriae summus pontifex Gregorius," — he criticised the political attitude of the pope: "quod papa super papam, sicut rex super regem positus fuerat, taedet memoriae." It was the confirmed opinion of Otto of Freising that the two swords, symbols of spiritual and temporal authority, originated from God, and, for this reason, two hands ought to handle the two swords. Freising thereby literally contradicted the ideas of his contemporary and confrere, Bernard of Clairvaux, whose conviction it was that both swords, the "temporal" sword, too, served the cause and interest of the Church; and, for this reason, the pope alone had to handle both swords.

In the opinion of Otto of Freising the misinterpreted usage of the two swords (who could yield it and when?) made co-operation between Church and state impossible, and made more difficult the realization of the City of God on earth. Even so, it was mainly due to the prayers of the monks, he wrote, that the devil was unable to gain control of the world, though even the most ardent prayers of the monks could not prevent the ongoing confrontation between the political factions in the empire.

The third stage of human salvation is to occur "post praesentem vitam," when the goals of this terrestrial life will be realized in the world to come. "Porro quia civitas illa duabus parietibus compacta ex angelis constat et hominibus." The bishop of Freising concluded his opus in the spirit of his episcopal colleague, St. Augustine, and with the words of Augustine by saying that events of world history could only have one aim: to make certain that God's rule spread over the world. "Sicut ex scriptura sacra docemur, civitas Christi ... civitate mundi, ... sub antichristo passura erit."

The continuation of the Augustinian ideal by Otto of Freising to the effect that good and evil constantly confront each other, and yet, the good must prevail, may also be evident from a scene recorded in the 161st paragraph of the *Chronicon pictum*. There the Hungarian nobles supportive of their monarch, Béla II the Blind, told firmly the Polish ruler who had been aiding Boris, the illegitimate son of King Coloman the Learned (ob. 1116), that he was wrong to help the opponents of their king. The kingship belonged to Béla the Blind on the grounds that he ruled the country with the approval and support of its people; "non decet vos contra iniustitiam querere regnum homini adulterino, nos enim scimus, quod de iure regnum habere debeat Bela, et ipse regnat cum consensu tocius regni." (It is of little concern here, but the point may be made that the Hungarian chronicler spoke only of the leader of the Ruthenian and Polish troops already on Hungarian soil and supporting Boris; it was the Polish chroniclers who revealed that the 'leader' was really their king, Boleslaw III.)

Gerhoch of Reichersberg was a representative author of this age, who had urged the inner spiritual renewal of the Church in his writings. The basic idea of his works was to encourage his clerical colleagues that they adhere to the teaching *of* the Church and present a good example to the laity *in* the Church. He supported the case of the popes. Gerhoch belonged to the German clerical-intellectual stratum that had attempted to orient the ecclesiastical policy directed by laymen of the imperial court toward Rome. In his books he was preoccupied with the view held by leading German churchmen of the 1122 Worms Settlement, though he paid detailed attention to the principles, laid down in the concordat, concerning church and imperial relations. He wanted to know about the impact of the concordat upon the clergy and lay people *vs.* the background of the feudal institutions of the age.

Gerhoch criticised the papal policy of Frederick Barbarossa, and the emperor's personal behavior toward the Roman See. Gerhoch discussed and acknowledged the unjustified demands of the ecclesiastics toward the imperial court, though he was not afraid of criticising the papal curia. In his opinion the popes over emphasized their demands to intervene, any time and anywhere, in mundane politics. In his last book, *De quarta vigilia noctis*, a work he wrote as a political exile, when he was ill, he assured Pope Alexander III of his personal loyalty, but could not resist in making the remark that the clergy should show more appreciation of the laity, so that together they may, within the framework of the ecclesiastical organization, realize their personal cooperation. The prerequisite for such cooperation was, he wrote, that both clergy and laity remain in their own spheres of proper activities. Let the priest be preoccupied with the souls of his fellow men and administer the sacraments to them; let him be concerned with secular politics only to a very limited extent.

Gerhoch with his assertions actually supported the views of his contemporary: the pope-eater revolutionary Arnold of Brescia, who openly maintained that the faithful must not support clergymen who have grown rich in worldly goods. The temporal wealth perpetuated by the clergy was, after all, the property of temporal rulers who only shared their wealth with the laity, and with clergymen who were too much interested in secular matters. The Church was a spiritual institution, and, as such, it should not claim secular wealth and values.

In his later studies, as, for example, in *De aedificatione Dei*, written between 1126 and 1132, Gerhoch simply criticised the acceptance of the episcopal *regalia* from the hands of the emperor on the grounds that their usage led to evil habits. The acceptance of *regalia* actually forced the elected, but not yet consecrated, bishop to accept the government of, and care for, the temporal wealth of his diocese from the hands of the emperor, in the court of the emperor, after he had taken his oath of loyalty to the emperor. Gerhoch said that the bishop-elect became, by having taken his oath prior to his consecration as bishop of the Church, a vassal of the emperor, *homo imperatoris*, and it was as an imperial vassal that he took over his episcopal office.

The provost of Reichersberg recognized the fact that a bishop, or an abbot, who fulfilled high church functions in the empire, could not be the emperor's enemy, nor could he be the emperor's personal opponent. He even acknowledged it as a necessary evil that a bishop readied to take over his office, — or, an abbot his monastery, — had to assure the imperial court of his good intentions by taking the oath of loyalty to it. But the bishop-elect by accepting the *regalia*: authorization to oversee the temporal goods of the bishopric, from the hands of the emperor, had taken upon himself certain responsibilities toward the emperor, thereby recognizing the latter as his temporal overlord, to whom he, the bishop, now owed mundane services. Such feudal obligation, as, for example, a vassal's military commitment to his feudal lord, were contrary to the spirit of the bishop's spiritual vocation.

A consecrated bishop could not utilize church goods, or income, for providing military support to the emperor because, in accordance with canon law, church property and episcopal revenues could only be spent (1) for the maintenance of the diocesan clergy; (2) for the upkeep of church buildings in the diocese; (3) for the support of widows and orphans, and (4) for the bishop's personal expenses — including care for visitors and the poor at his court.

The secular investiture: temporal authority placing a man of the Church into a non-secular position, or office, of high personal responsibility, could have only caused confusion. After all, the cross used at the episcopal investiture was the symbol of the ordinary's spiritual authority, as it was the symbol of Christian humility. This is why the bishop's cross had to be carried in front of him; in front of the emperor they carried the flag because it symbolized temporal authority to punish criminals. The root of the problem was that while the Jewish clergy held both spiritual and temporal power, the Christian priests could function even in their spiritual capacity only within limits imposed upon them by the secular authority.

In the 53rd paragraph of *De investigatione antichristi*, Gerhoch discussed the circumstances surrounding the papal election of 1159, when the imperial party at the conclave elected an antipope, Victor IV, against the constitutionally chosen pontiff. Gerhoch recognized the legitimate pope, but complained that Pope Alexander III, even though he had been invited, failed to attend the ecclesiastical gathering in Pavia (1160), summoned (by the emperor) to debate the case of the two popes. Even Our Lord, wrote Gerhoch, descended to our wretched human level when He had appeared among the disciples who had doubted His resurrection. Even Peter, prince of the Apostles, took humbly and in good faith the public correction the Apostle Paul had sorted out for him.

In other words, Gerhoch accused the legitimate pope of false pride in ecclesiastical politics without realizing that Alexander III may have had serious reservations about attending the "synod" of Pavia. According to Gerhoch, even a pontiff may err, and in a case of papal error the entire matter must be negotiated carefully by the parties concerned. Were the pontiff unwilling to subject his person ( =office?) to the resolutions of a church synod, he ought to be corresponding in the matter with leading churchmen and temporal lords.

Gerhoch recommended that the Church function properly in public life ( =*publica functio*), without overestimating the need for temporal goods. He said that the Church should rather lose its temporal wealth than to get involved in politics. In the twenty-fifth chapter of the *Aedificatio Dei* Gerhoch explained that it was not the obligation of the Church to serve the world. The Church had to serve, however, the spiritual needs of the world. Being subservient to secular needs and/or interests, the Church would severly curtail its supernatural mission. On the other hand, Gerhoch criticised the ideas of Pope Paschal II who said that the Church ought to, once and for all, renounce all of its temporal goods.

It is known that the pontiff wanted the German episcopate to surrender their temporal wealth (chattel) to the court of the emperor; therefore, the provost of Reichersberg made a distinction between wealth legally belonging to the Church, and other unnecessary acquisitions by the Church of wordly goods. The latter only endangered the supernatural interests and spiritual vocation of the Church and compromised its position in society. The bishop should not, for the sake of his spiritual vocation, take, for instance, upon himself the fulfillment of feudal military obligations. In his book, *De ordine donorum Sancti Spiritus*, Gerhoch stated his conviction that the spiritual and temporal lords should remain hostile to each other until they secure for themselves the use of all privileges in the empire. The temporal lords abuse the spiritual benefits of the Church, but churchmen, too, make provocative demands from their secular counterparts.

These differences had to be worked out in detail. The bishop-elect, who had already taken his oath to the emperor, should have a free hand in the administration of church goods which, really, formed a part of the wealth of the empire. The resolutions laid down in the Worms settlement that the new bishop had to be elected in the presence of the emperor, or his representative, was no longer observed in the times of Gerhoch. The idea that the elected bishop gained temporal authorization *per sceptrum* was, by then, a forgotten custom. Nor could the upper clergy interfere in secular politics; their obligation consisted of crowning the ruler who had been elected by the people, as if to breathe a soul into the royal office.

It had been customary for the people to elect their bishops and the pope, and the validity of their election was recognized by the temporal authority. The only problem, remarked Gerhoch, was that the Roman pontiffs had been able to secure the support of the people by the payment of good money to them. The Romans, however, would not have raised such high fiscal demands from the Holy See had they not known that the Church had at its disposal funds from which to meet their demands.

Members of the college of Cardinals, too, had been guilty, because their pride knew no limits. They had forgotten about the essence of their vocation and neglected to see to it that the visible head of the Church and the emperor would not continue fighting each other, but learn to cooperate with one another, in the spirit of good will.

It may be mentioned though, from an outside point of view, that the ideas of the two German writers placed, for instance, into a sharp focus the cooling trend that had characterized the mental disposition of King Géza II of Hungary (1141-62) toward the advisors of Frederick Barbarossa during the mid-twelfth century. Géza II tolerated no interference in his political and religious affairs from the courtiers of a foreign ruler, — be that ruler the emperor himself.


NOTES


This chapter is an altered version of the paper, "Mid-Twelfth Century View of History in the Writings of Otto of Freising and Gerhoch of Reichersberg," published in *East European Quarterly*, 21 (1987), printed here with the permission of the editor.

See Otto of Freising, *Chronicon de duabus civitatibus, libri octo*, in MGHSS, XX, 118ff.; idem, *Gesta Friderici I Imperatoris, libri quattuor*, ibid., XX, 347ff., the last two chapters of which were completed by his secretary Rahewin; cf. Wattenbach, *Geschichtsquellen*, II, 271ff., who spoke of his master as his "nutritor" (iv:14). M. Ritter, Studien über die Entwicklung der Geschichtswissenschaft: die christlich-mittelalterliche Geschichtsschreibung," *Historische Zeitschrift*, 107 (1911), 237ff.; H. Grundmann, "Geschichtsschreiber im Mittelalter," *Deutsche Philologie im Aufriss*, 26 (1952-29), 1273ff. A. C. Krey, "William of Tyre," *Speculum*, 16 (1941), 149ff., made a comparison between Otto of Freising and his contemporary chroniclers; B. M. Lacroix, "The Notion of History in Early Medieval Histories," *Medieval Studies*, 10 (1948), 219ff., an impressive and educational essay, and A. Lhotsky's original contribution, "Die Historiographie Ottos von Freising," in his *Europäisches Mittelalter* (Vienna, 1970), 49ff.

According to K. Jacob, *Quellenkunde der deutschen Geschichte im Mittelalter*, 2 vols. (Berlin, 1943-49), II, 89, Otto of Freising 'hat ... auf augustinischer Grundlage und mit philosophischer Durchdringung die weltgeschichtliche Entwicklung zu begreifen gesucht." On Freising and his background, see also H. Simonsfeld, *Jahrbücher des deutschen Reiches unter Friedrich I* (1152 bis 1158) (Munich, 1908; repr. Berlin, 1967), 92f., and 233ff.; and, W. v. Giesebrecht, *Geschichte der deutschen Kaiserzeit*, rev. ed., ed. W. Schild, 6 vols. (Meersburg, 1929-30), V, 86ff.

Otto of Freising dealt with the movement "of human knowledge based upon written evidence" from east to west in his letter of dedication addressed to the emperor, *MGHSS*, XX, 116f., and in the preface of his opus, *ibid.*, XX, 118,6-44, and said that the notion of *mutabilitas* and the concept of *translationes imperii* were connected, *ibid.*, XX, 118,20-30. In the center of change(s) and among the multitude of peoples stood the emperor, "quoniam data est a Domino potestas vobis, et virtus ab Altissimo, qui interrogabit opera vestra, et cogitationes scrutabitur;" *ibid.*, XX, 116,23-24. He explained his idea of historical progress (of knowledge) from Assyria through the Medes and the Persians toward the west — finally reaching Rome —, in his writ to Regenald, chancellor to the emperor, *ibid.*, XX, 117,34-39; A. Hauck, *Kirchengeschichte Deutschlands*, 6 vols., 9th ed. (Berlin, 1958), IV, 509f.

Otto's idea that the emperor was lord of the world and its defender, cf. *Chronicon*, vii:34, may have been connected with the events of 1146, when Boris, the illegitimate son of Coloman the Learned of Hungary, requested aid from Conrad III; cf. *Gesta*, i:31; W. Bernhardi, *Konrad III* (Munich, 1883; repr. 1975), 494ff.; or, W. Kienast, *Deutschland und Frankreich in der Kaiserzeit*, 3 vols. (Stuttgart, 1973-75), I, 345ff. Quotes from *MGHSS*, XX, 278,40-44, and 295,39-40. Rome predominated the world, but beyond the frontiers lived the barbarians and the Greeks, *ibid.*, XX, 351ff. Otto made no direct mention of the Hungarians, though placed them among the barbarians — in *Gesta*, i:32. A fifth century prayer for Good Friday identified the barbarians with the pagans asking God that He may let them acknowledge Christian predominance: "respice ad Romanum benignus imperium, ut gentes, quae in sua feritate confidunt, potentiae tuae dextera comprimantur;" *Missale Romanum*, feria VI in parasceve; F. Cabrol, in *Dictionnaire d'árcheologie chrét. et de liturgie*, VI, 1776ff.

The intellectuals of the age, — Kienast, I, 417ff., — did not like the imperial title, *imperium mundi*; John of Salisbury said that it was not the emperor but the regional prince who "tamen legis nexibus dicitur absolutus." Cf. C. C. J. Webb (ed), Iohannes Saresberiensis *Policraticus*, 2 vols. (Oxford, 1909), iv:2. For a counterargument, see Bernard of Clairvaux in his letter addressed to Pope Eugenius III, epistola 256, in *MPL*, 182, 464, Bernard who had very much controlled contemporary public opinion — see W. Williams, *Saint Bernhard of Clairvaux* (London, 1935), 288. H. A. Myers, "The Concept of Kingship in the 'Book of Emperors' (Kaiserchronik)," *Traditio*, 27 (1971), 205ff. H. U. Ziegler, "Der Bamberger Erzpriester Gotebold, Hauptkraft in der Beteuerkundungstelle Bischof Eberhards II (1146-70), Hermanns II (1170-77) und Verfasser von Urkunden Friedrich Barbarossas," *Mitteilungen des Institutes für österreichische Geschichtsforschung*, 92 (1984), 35ff.

Otto of Freising was angry at Gregory VII because "sedemque Hiltiprando, archidiacono suo Gregorius dictus est, relinquit," at a time when the Roman pontiff could only be elected with the consent of the German court, *MGHSS*, XX, 246,17-19; W. v. d. Steinen, *Der Kosmos des Mittelalters*, 2nd ed. (Bern-Munich, 1967), 200ff. The City of God on earth remained invincible because "als Führer der Christenheit, der Ecclesiae, standen die Kaiser an der Spitze des Abendlandes;" cf. F. Heer, *Die Tragödie des Heiligen Reiches* (Vienna-Zurich, 1952) 143. The comparison with Saint Augustine is based on the brief text of his *De civitate Dei*, xv:2; cf. F. E. Cranz, "De civitate Dei, XV, 2, and Augustine's Idea of Christian Society," *Speculum*, 25 (1950), 215ff., following the interpretation of H. Leisegang.

"Der Ursprung der Lehre Augustins von der Civitas Dei," *Archiv für Kulturgeschichte*, 16 (1925), 127ff. Note the remark made by Augustine himself, "nam fuisse et futurum esse non est aeternum. Et dum loquimur et inhiamus illi, attigimus eam modice toto ictu cordis." Cf. J. Bernhardt (ed), *Augustinus: Confessiones*, 3rd ed. (Munich, 1966), ix;10.24.

The idea that human progress (historical-cultural) has made its headway from *east to west* appears also in medieval Hungarian chronicles. Keza, c. 4, mentioned Hunor and Magor, sons of Enoch, first wife of Nimrod, after the flood to stress the origins of the Magyars and their migrations from *east to west*; cf. *SSH*, I, 144,5-17. Anonymus said that the Huns *or* Magyars descended from Hunor and Magor who, in the Maeotid marshes, had come across a miraculous doe, had captured the daughters of the prince of the Alans and took them to wife; *ibid.*, I, 34,19-20, 35,6-7; I, 114,18-20. S. Tóth, "Megjegyzések Toynbee magyar őstörténeti koncepciójához (Comments on Toynbee's idea of Hungarian origins)," *Acta historica Szegediensis*, 71 (1981), 13ff., in ref. to A. Toynbee, *Constantine Porphyrogenitus and His World* (Oxford, 1973), 708ff. The two families became a great nation and moved *west* to Scythia; *SSH*, I, 41,21-22; I, 145,17-18. Because of the continued increase of their population, they decided to invade further *western* areas: "occidentales occuparent regiones;" *ibid.*, I, 147,8. They fought their way through the Petchenegs, White Cumans and the territory of Suzdal, and ravaged further *west* the region of the Ruthenians and Black Cumans, and reached (by moving *west*) the Tisza river, *ibid.*, I, 148,7-10, where they settled down and established a country of their own; *ibid.*, I, 257,14-19.

Anonymus most probably followed quite closely an earlier composition identified as "T" by Macartney, 35f., 67, etc., and Regino of Prüm's *Chronicon*; cf. *MGHSS*, I, 536ff., esp. the years of 889, 894 and 901. Regino "verdient unsere Beachtung als einer der frühesten Versuche die Weltgeschichte zu einer ziemlich ausfolgreichen Erzählung zusammenzufassen;" Wattenbach, I, 260; Hóman-Szekfű, I, 293ff.; Hóman, *Ungarisches Mittelalter*, I, 297f., and 302f.; Gy. Kristó, *Korai levéltári és elbeszélő forrásaink kapcsolatához* (Connection between early Hungarian narrative sources and archival material), vol. XXI of *Acta historica Szegediensis* (Szeged, 1966), 13ff., and 23.

The Huns who had gone *west* had disappeared from the historical scene after the triumphs of Etele (Attila), his marriage to a Byzantine princess and ultimely death; cf. *SSH*, I, 155ff.; also, I, 276ff. But the Hun nation came back to life: its fifth generation had reentered the *west* by occupying the inheritance of its ancestors; *ibid.*, I, 162f.; H. Homeyer, *Attila der Hunnenkönig von seinem Zeitgenossen dargestellt* (Berlin, 1951), 36ff. They were now the Magyars, *SSH*, I, 39f.; their leader, Álmos (Chronicle, cc. 26 and 27) had led them *westward* of the Etil (Volga), west of Suzdal and Kiev. "Terram intraverunt Ruscie, que vocatur Susdal. Postquam ... usque ad civitatem Kyeu transierunt;" *ibid.*, I, 42, 5-9. When the prince of Kiev attacked them with the aid of seven Cuman chiefs, Álmos defeated the prince (Anonymus, c. 8), who now had advised Álmos to move further *west*, into Pannonia; "versus occidentem in terram Pannonie descenderent," *ibid.*, I, 45,6-8, because Pannonia had belonged to Etel, the forefather of Álmos. Cf. *ibid.*, I, 35,7-19. There is a Polish source that says that the Magyars had entered Pannonia "per Russiam et Tartariam;" cf. A. Bielowski (ed), *Monumenta Poloniae historica* 6 vols. (Lwov-Cracow, 1864-93), I, 489f. Among the twelfth century Polish cources, see *Rocznik Malpolski*, anno 1132, *ibid.*, III, 152; the *Chronica principum Poloniae*, c. 12, did mention Boleslaw III by name; *ibid.*, III, 457ff. Quotation is from the *Chronicon pictum*, *SSH*, I, 451,16-20.

Gerhoch of Reichersberg did attempt "wie wening es einem Manne seiner Richtung möglich war, das Problem von Imperium und Sacerdotium grundsätzlich und befriedigend zu lösen;" Jacob, *Quellenkunde*, II, 95. Wattenbach, *Geschichtsquellen*, II, 308ff.; A. Dempf, *Sacrum imperium*, 4th ed. (Munich-Vienna, 1973), 252, said that "der Ruhm, den Otto von Freising besitzt, gebührt eigentlich seinem Zeitgenossen und Landsmann Gerhoch von Reichersberg." See further H. Fichtenau, "Studien zu Gerhoh von Reichersberg," *Mitteilungen des Institutes für österreichische Geschichtsforschung*, 52 (1938), 1ff. (who spelled Gerhoch without a *c*). It is a must to read the 53 page essay by J. Stülz, "Propst Gerhoch von Reichersberg," *Denkschriften der kaiserlichen Akademie der Wissenschaften*, phil.-hist. Klasse, 1 (Vienna, 1850), 113ff.; or, the original essay by H. H. Jacobs, "Studien über Gerhoch von Reichersberg: zur Geistesgeschichte des 12 Jahrhunderts," *Zeitschrift für Kirchengeschichte*, 50 (1931), 315ff. Before his election, Lothair III did renounce some rights of investiture; cf. *Narratio de electione Lotharii*, in *MGHSS*, XX, 511.

On the controversy between Gerhoch and the imperial court, see E. F. Otto, "Otto von Freising und Friedrich Barbarossa," *Historische Vierteljahrschrift*, 31 (1938), 27ff. In order to understand the situation properly, one has to turn to Gerhoch himself: in his *Opusculum de aedificatione Dei*, c. 12, *MPL*, 194, 1228ff., he discussed the circumstances surrounding the transfer of regalia and emphasized the point of view that no high ecclesiastic may use church funds for feudal purposes, *ibid.*, 1231ff., c. 13. On dividing the income of the bishop, c. 14. Gerhoch's last major work is the *De quarta vigilia noctis*, in *MGH Libelli de lite*, ed. E. Dümmler, 3 vols. (Hannover, 1891-97), III, 503ff.; P. Classen, *Gerhoch von Reichersberg* (Wiesbaden, 1960), 273ff. Nobody can reclaim ecclesiastical property; nor can churchmen demand more wealth (and property), – cf. *De aedificatione*, c. 25, *MPL*, 194, 1257ff. It was during the winter of 1141-42, during his journey to Rome, that Gerhoch wrote his *De ordine donorum Sancti Spiritus*, of which selections appeared in *Libelli de lite*, III, 273ff.; Classen, *Gerhoch*, 98ff.

It ought to be pointed out though that, from the Hungarian point of view, Géza II and his court were very much concerned about the ecclesiastical policy of Frederick I Barbarossa. On this, see my article, "Did Géza II of Hungary Send Delegates to the 'Synod' of Pavia, 1160?" *Annarium Historiae Conciliorum* (Augsburg, 1984), 40ff.

# IX

## Stephen III Retains the Throne and Maintains Position Between West and Southeast

> ... regnavit Stephanus annis XI, mensibus novem,
> diebus tribus. Quo quidem imperante Ladislaus
> dux sibi usurpat regnum et coronam. ... Post
> istum Stephanus frater suus coronam usurpat.
>
> Keza, *Gesta Hungarorum*, cc. 67-68

When Géza II died, it was his "son of age," the fifteen year old Stephen III, who succeeded him. [1] The new king was a child in years and in spirit, the late maturing type, without a determined personality; [2] as if they had thoroughly neglected the upbringing of children at the Hungarian court. [3] Civil war, greed and vicious jealousy must have prevailed among members of the ruling family, — a situation from which only the nobles drew political benefits and the court politicians of the German and Byzantine, Czech and Polish monarchs, whose natural-diplomatic interests it served to undermine the existence of the Hungarian royal family so preoccupied with its own petty problems. The younger members of the Árpád dynasty were perhaps unable to comprehend that they through their behavior had only aided the cause of their opponents. [4]

The attitudes of the spoiled and utterly irresponsible younger brothers of Géza II (they were undisciplined; anyone could influence them), must have caused the early death of Géza II, [5] and near ruin to the entire country. [6] It may have been no coincidence that a sister of Géza II, Sophia, became a religious at Admont abbey (where she died in 1150). [7] The nobles who had already turned against Stephen III before, and especially after his coronation, had held him in a very low estem. [8]

One may assume that the Kievan queen of Géza II,

Euphrozina, the daughter of Grand Prince Mistislav of Kiev, was more than careless about the upbringing of, and educating the children. [9] The early childish behavior of the well disposed Stephen III may prove this point of view; his attitudes, however, underwent a change for the better during his reign. [10] Only the younger brother of Stephen III, Prince Béla (the later Béla III) received the proper upbringing at the Byzantine court that enabled him to hold his own on the royal throne and to become an important and respected ruler of the Árpád dynasty. [11]

It is unfortunate that so little is known about the queen of King Stephen III, the daughter of Margrave Henry II of the *Ostmark*. It is to be feared that she was not the mature and self-assured person who might have influenced the behavior of her royal husband. [12] On the other hand, Prince Béla had married a real royal consort in Anna ( Agnes) of Chatillon, who not only stood loyally by her husband, but shared his political and diplomatic troubles. [13] It speaks well for the personal wisdom of Béla III that, upon the death of his queen, he married once again a royal princess, Margaret, the widowed daughter of Louis VII, king of the Franks, by his second wife. A widower married a widow. Béla undoubtedly tried to improve on his Hungaro-Frankish relations through this marriage, searching, at the same time, for a life-partner who would support him in his royal obligations. [14]

Emperor Manuel Comnenos of Byzantium, the imperial uncle of King Stephen III, had, however, entertained different ideas concerning royal succession to the Hungarian throne. [15] Manuel held, and had the news spread, that in Hungary it was not the king's son, but the younger brother of the deceased monarch who succeeded to the throne. [16] Consequently, the emperor now supported the candidacy of Prince Stephen, son of Géza II and thus an uncle to Stephen III, for the throne against Stephen III who, in the meanwhile, had been crowned king of Hungary. Prince Stephen was the husband of Maria, daughter of Isaac Comnenos, brother of Manuel. [17]

When he heard the news about the death of Géza II, Manuel had immediately ordered his troops on the march and dispatched Prince Stephen to go from Sofia to Harám-

vár (on the Hungaro-Byzantine border) for the purpose of
recruiting, with gifts and promises (or, by threats), support
for the cause of the Byzantine emperor on Hungarian soil. [18]
At the same time, Manuel dispatched delegates to the court
of Stephen III, — whom he, incidentally, by having sent
ambassadors to him, had acknowledged as king of Hungary —, in order to remind the king of the *senoritas* rule
in royal succession. According to this rule, the right of succession to the Hungarian throne belonged to the younger
brother, and not to the son, of the deceased king. [19]

The real cause for this reasoning, and for sending ambassadors to Stephen III, may have rested with the imperial
constitution issued by Manuel Comnenos upon his succession to the imperial purple. In this constitution the emperor
stated that he regarded himself as the fullfledged successor
of Constantine the Great, Theodosios and Justinian, and
had set as the goal of his reign, the restoration of the territorial integrity of the Roman (not eastern Roman) empire. [20]
Because he had a need for, Manuel had to form a claim to
the Hungarian throne on the grounds that the road toward
restoration of the empire led through Hungary. [21]

The viewpoint presented by the Byzantine ambassadors
at the court of Stephen III must have been convincing enough
to make the majority of the Hungarian nobles (in fact, the
majority of the royal reeves led by *Ban* Bélus) to recognize
as correct the emperor's arguments and accept them as valid,
*were* Manuel to make Prince Ladislas, — Prince Stephen's
younger, Géza II's youngest, brother —, king, instead of
Prince Stephen, the uncle of Stephen III. The ambassador
accepted the recommendation made by the nobles and royal
reeves, and Ladislas II now became a Byzantine stooge on
the Hungarian throne. [22]

Stephen III, the constitutionally elected and crowned
monarch of the realm, now fled to Pozsony in the Hungaro-
German border region, where he still had supporters, and
had hoped that the German emperor, Frederick Barbarossa,
would not abandon him. [23]

The constitutional position protected by law of King
Stephen III indeed caused Archbishop Lukács of Esztergom, primate, who had the right to crown the kings of Hungary, [24] to refuse anointment and coronation to Ladislas

II, a Byzantine pawn on the country's throne. [25] Archbishop
Mikó of Kalocsa, a proponent of Byzantine politics in the
realm, performed, unconstitutionally, the coronation of
Ladislas II, instead of the archbishop of Esztergom. The
latter, by being Mikó's ecclesiastical superior, excommunicated the unsubordinate Kalocsa archbishop and placed
the entire church province of Kalocsa under the interdict. [26]

Ladislas II, an immature child now sitting on an usurped
throne, demanded with a drawn sword in his hand from
Archbishop Lukács that he withdrew the previous excommunication. The archbishop did nothing of the sort. He refused to obey the political and physical threats of a Greek
stooge: an unlawfully crowned anti-king; but, for his refusal,
Ladislas II had the primate placed under house arrest and
in prison. [27] Only on Christmas day (1164, the first day of
the new year [28] ), did he relent and freed the archbishop,
and that because of the intervention of Pope Alexander III.
Archbishop Lukács refused, however, to give in. From his
place of detention he hurried to the Esztergom cathedral,
where on Christmas day, he had the altar stripped of all
ornaments and declared that the interdict remained in force.
And, in the presence of the stunned anti-king, he begged
the Almighty that He convert Ladislas II from his evil ways,
or punish him within the next forty days. [29]

The prayer said and the curse pronounced by the archbishop had come through. Ladislas II died within twenty
days, after hardly half a year in office. [30] During his reign,
it was his younger brother, Prince Stephen, who held the
title of heir to the throne and held, as his source sustenance,
one-third of the realm's territory; the Byzantine chronicler
had referred to him as *urum* (= little lord in Hungarian). [31]

In January, 1164, Stephen IV became the new anti-king; [32]
and, the real: constitutional monarch, Stephen III, had
bidded his time in Pozsony awaiting in vain the possible intervention on his behalf of the German imperial court. [33] Or,
probably, he wisely had hoped that the situation that surrounded the rise of both anti-kings would, in due time, come
to an end. It was Mikó of Kalocsa, again, who crowned
Stephen IV. [34]

According to a later papal letter, the coronations performed by the Kalocsa archbishop — in spite of the order

of the primate in Esztergom to the contrary —, lacked constitutional value not because they had not been carried out by and through an unauthorized church official, but on the grounds that the country already had a lawfully crowned and anointed monarch in the person of Stephen III. [35] Archbishop Lukács had no other choice but to excommunicate the archbishop of Kalocsa, who now went to Rome to bring unfounded charges against Lukács of Esztergom. [36]

Lukács granted another forty-day grace period to the new anti-king to mend his ways and alter his position. As noted, however, by the former English schoolmate of the archbishop, the "breath of the archbishop" killed the (new) anti-king. [37] By June, 1164, Stephen IV's early supporters staged a revolt against him at a time when the allies of King Stephen III, — with the Csák family among them —, made a counterattack upon, and defeated the "uncle," — the elder Stephen IV, aged thirty-one, [38] — in the battle of Fehérvár. The latter fled from the battle grounds toward the ferry-site at Pest, when, at Giod, a woman the wife of Elek, recognized and delivered him into the hands of the king, the sixteen year old Stephen III. The lawful monarch restored his thirty-one year old uncle to freedom under the condition that the latter would not set foot on Hungarian soil again. [39]

It is an interesting comment on the affair that it is mostly known from von Mügeln's *Ungarnchronik*, who, probably, relied upon the then still available written and oral documentation of the times in entering this episode into his narrative. [40] As if the editor(s) of the *Chronicon pictum* were unwilling to record anything favorable and positive about the activities of the young but well disposed Stephen III, [41] who must have grown a good deal during his (enforced) stay at Pozsony in the winter months. Only a socially self-assured and mentally mature monarch could afford to treat his rebellious uncle, — who had caused considerable damage and anguish; who had attempted to have the monarch, his royal nephew, deposed or assassinated, thereby bringing the realm to the brink of civil war —, with kindness, and request only that he leave the realm for ever. [42]

The victories of Stephen III over his opponents forced Manuel, the head culprit in the Byzantine witch kitchen of international diplomacy, to make concessions to Stephen III.

The emperor realized in time that the king stood on solid political and military grounds; he now had to face an angry and self-assured monarch, whose main weapons were idealism and determination. Manuel acted instantly. He now offered to make Béla, the king's younger brother, heir to the Byzantine throne by marrying his own daughter to him. The emperor only requested that Stephen III hand over the Serem region (= the area south of the Danube and north of the Save river), together with Dalmatia —, both former possessions of the Byzantine empire. The Hungarian monarch and his nobles accepted the imperial offer, — after all, the anti-king, Stephen IV, was still alive —, and Béla had left for the Byzantine court. [43]

It was about at this time that Stephen IV had visited the German court at Parma, Sicily, offering his services to the German emperor. The anti-king wished to make his country an imperial fief; [44] however, being aware of the almost constant fiscal difficulties of the German court, Stephen III now promised the payment of five thousand marks of silver to Frederick Barbarossa. [45] The king wanted to neutralize the offer previously made by his uncle to the emperor, and to outwit his nobles, who had formed a conspiracy against him, [46] —and who were, not without irony, referred to as *barones* by the compiler of the *Chronicon pictum*. [47]

The financial overtunes made by Stephen III to the German court may have been unnecessary. The uncle's visit to Parma ended in failure, and, shortly thereafter, Stephen IV had appeared before the Byzantine court to pay his respect to Emperor Manuel. The royal uncle must have been the most irresponsible, and irresolute, person, indeed.

The Greek ruler was less selective than the German one. The record has it that Stephen IV soon after attacked his own country with Byzantine troops, — that, incidentally, included many Hungarians —, and suffered defeat. Thereupon Manuel, who had no other choice, — or, wished to use the defeat of the anti-king as an excuse to intervene in Hungarian affairs —, sent an army commanded by Andronicos Kontostefanos against Stephen III. [48] The Byzantine forces proceeded toward Bács (north of the Danube), and, the Byzantine source reports, the people of the area went out in great numbers in order to greet the Byzantine army as (their) liberators. [49]

The background for this development must have consisted of the fact that, by then, Prince Béla had departed for the Byzantine court, where he soon became *despotes*: official heir to the imperial throne, and the emperor now wanted to obtain — by forces since it seemed to be unobtainable by peaceful means —, the Serem region that had formed Béla's territorial inheritance. [50] Now Stephen III had to face a serious fiscal-political and military situation at home in that his mother, the dowager Queen Euphrozina had, in fact, intervened on his behalf with her son-in-law, Vladislas, duke of Bohemia, [51] who had then been elevated to the dignity of Czech kingship by Emperor Frederick Barbarossa in 1158. [52] Although his troops had been ravaging Hungary, the duke, now king, still provided aid for Stephen III. One of the sons of Vladislas was married to one of Stephen III's sisters, and another sister was engaged to the second son of Vladislas. [53]

Emperor Manuel wisely changed tactics. He met in person with the Czech ruler in order to inform him that the Byzantine court wished no war, but only to obtain, and to take possession of the territorial inheritance of Prince Béla, now Byzantine *despotes*. Manuel requested the understanding and support of Vladislas, and, to show good will, had ordered redeployment of his troops along the southern side of the Danube. [54] Stephen IV, who was not even informed about the diplomatic proceedings between Manuel and Vladislas, had remained on Hungarian soil with some Byzantine troops, whose command rested, however, with Nicephorus Khalufes, who had fled in the meanwhile with some of the troops across the river into Byzantine territory. Left in the lurch, Stephen IV had no other choice but to follow the example of his commander and let the Moravian-Czech armies of Vladislas occupy his abandoned camp. [55]

Under the personal influence of his Czech brother-in-law, Stephen III now signed a peace treaty with Manuel's court. The Hungarians had agreed to the surrender of the Serem region for good and of Dalmatia to Manuel, while the emperor promised to withdraw his troops and support from the anti-king, and to acknowledge Stephen III as the legitimate monarch of Hungary. [56] The treaty was signed in 1164. [57]

Upon the completion of the Byzantine takeover of Dalmatia, Emperor Manuel broke his solemn oath by permitting the Hungarian anti-king, Stephen IV, to remain in the Serem region with a Byzantine army commanded by Michael Gabras. (The region now lawfully belonged to Manuel; but the anti-king's sojourn there became unlawful.) Because the emperor had evidently broken his oath, Stephen III, rather thoughtlessly ordered an attack upon Fort Zimony in the Serem region in early 1165. [58]

The point ought to be made that although Stephen Neman(ia) of Serbia was, most probably at this time and against his own will, forced to submit to the authority of Manuel's court, [59] the Hungarian monarch by ordering the latest attack had acted foolishly and without planning. The clumsy Hungarian riverboats were easily pushed back and held at bay by the Byzantine river fleet on the Danube at Zimony, while the uncoordinated attack on the fort (taking place without an official declaration of war) actually played into the hands of Manuel, who now could, as he did, accuse Stephen III of bad faith, and rightfully organize a military alliance against him. Venice, the Russian princes, the German emperor and Henry of Austria had joined the Byzantine court-alliance against Hungary, and Manuel himself was gathering his forces for an invasion of the realm. [60]

Michael Gabras and Joseph Bryennius, commanders of the Greek forces at Zimony, easily stood their ground, and the Byzantine fleet took control of the Danube. The situation changed only when Stephen IV died (unexpectedly, on April 11, 1165), and the Byzantine garrison surrendered the fort upon his death. [61] The Greek chroniclers report that Stephen III had bribed the anti-king's personal servants to poison their lord, and the victorious Hungarian troops now in possession of the fort threw the naked body of Stephen IV in front of the main gate, where it remained unburied for days. [62] The body was, eventually, taken to a church in town, and later given a Christian burial at Székesfehérvár. [63]

The overconfident and grossly irresponsible Hungarian commander, George by name, and a royal reeve by office, wasted too much time and effort on humiliating the dead body of the anti-king, and could not prevent the Byzantines, — after the latter had recovered from the initial surprise —, from recapturing the fort of Zimony. During the siege, reeve George began negotiations for terms of surrender, but during the talks the Greeks scaled the walls and took the fort by storm. George's garrison had been caught by surprise and massacred mercilessly. The emperor who had directed the offensive in person, had the captured reeve imprisoned. [64]

It was now King Stephen III's turn — the king must have been fully "unreadied," ill advised as to the real situation at Zimony —, to make a promise under oath to renounce permanently those territories which, legally, had formed Béla's inheritance and had, legally, belonged to Manuel. The chronicler reports on this occasion that Manuel could not repress a cutting remark by saying that since Dalmatia was already in his possession and the Serem only now recaptured, what, indeed, had the Hungarian court to surrender to him? [65]

The emperor now had his daughter, Maria, the fiancé of Béla, named as his heir to the imperial throne, and had members of the imperial court swear an oath of homage to Béla *despotes*. [66] At the same time, some Hungarian nobles who had formed the entourage of Béla at the Greek court, decided to make their prince also Hungarian king already during the lifetime of Stephen III, the brother of Béla. Understandably, the king became very angry and ordered, — again, without thinking, and without any military and diplomatic preparation —, his reeve Dénes, commander of the royal forces, to use force to recover Serem from the Byzantines. Stephen III and his advisors must have, by this time, become paranoid on account of the constant politicking of the Byzantine court; they must have assumed that the emperor had planned, again, the overthrow of the legitimate Hungarian monarch. Reeve Dénes had defeated Michael Gabras, now Greek governor of Zimony, and ordered that the bodies of the fallen Byzantine enemies be gathered into a huge mound of a heap for a Christian burial. The reeve had, the chroniclers report, placed a cross on the top of the burial mound. [67]

The emperor was surprised by the defeat of his Zimony garrison and immediately dispatched three armies to take revenge. The Byzantine forces were formally headed by Béla himself, though actual command rested with three army commanders headed by one of three, Alexander Aksukhos, father-in-law of Manuel's brother. Another Byzantine army led by Leo Vatazes broke into Transylvania, but quickly withdrew from there. A third army, under the command of Iohannes Ducas, invaded through the Borgo pass and caused some awful bloodshed and massacre among the population along the border. Before he withdrew from the region, commander Ducas had a huge cross made out of bronze erected on the frontier with the inscription that read: "It was here that the heavy hand of Mars and of the Romans struck the Hungarian nation in the reign of the divine Augustus Manuel." [68]

The fact that there were three Byzantine armies simultaneously entering the realm may prove that Manuel had at this time been prepared for a takeover of the realm, as he was willing to install Béla (*despotes!*) as king of Hungary before Béla would become his heir on the imperial throne. In order to understand the situation we must realize that Henry Jasomirgott, brother-in-law of Stephen III (his daughter, Agnes, was the queen of Stephen III), had visited on behalf of Frederick Barbarossa, the court of Manuel in Sardica to act as a diplomatic trouble-shooter and to bring about, if at all possible, a Hungaro-Byzantine peace treaty. Jasomirgott's efforts did not remain fruitless, and a Hungaro-Byzantine truce of a short duration was arranged. [69]

The Hungarian court gave orders, however, to invade Dalmatia; their invading army commanded by Onod, a royal reeve, repossessed the Dalmatian city states in the hinterland, with the exception of Trau, Spaleto and Sebenico; they defeated the Byzantine governor, Nicephorus Khalufes, and destroyed an army in neighboring Bosnia. [70] It may have been at this stage of events that Stephen III suggested peace negotiations to the imperial court, but Manuel, hoping for the Byzantine recapture of territories in Dalmatia, assumed that only a new military campaign would provide a lasting solution for his military-diplomatic problems with Hungary. [71]

The chroniclers report that, in 1167, Manuel fell off his horse, [72] and he, and his advisors, regarded it as a bad omen that in the Forum of Constantine in the capital the statue of Rome fell down, though the statue of Hungary remained standing. Manuel had the statue of Rome restored, but the one of Hungary removed from its place (on grounds that by changing them around he may cause the (military) downfall of Stephen III). Then, he dispatched his uncle, Andronimos Knostephanos, with an army against the Hungarians. [73]

It may be of some interest to note, — perhaps as an episode in connection with the exchange of statutes on the Forum of Constantine as recorded by Choniates —, that when Manuel had finished his speech in front of his troops (before the battle), there suddenly appeared a Hungarian horseman near his camp and, just as suddenly, the horseman and his horse fell down, both facing the ground. When told about the incident, the emperor was jubilant; he looked upon it as a good sign. By having changed around, — that is, one restored, the other one removed —, the statutes on the forum he may have assured the Hungarians' defeat in the forthcoming battle. [74]

Manuel's latest military-diplomatic maneuvering did not find the Hungarian court unprepared. And yet, the Hungarian army some fifteen thousand strong and commanded by Dénes (= Gyónis; Dionysius) and by thirty-seven county reeves, [75] was unable to prevent the Greeks from crossing the Save river, though, the chronicler reports, Manuel gave orders to cancel any military action that had been planned for July 18, [76] because his court astrologers had predicted a great disaster as the outcome of the battle to be fought on that day. [77] The situation, however, developed differently. The sight of the burial mound of the dead who had fallen in 1166 had encouraged Andronikos' forces to seek revenge upon the Hungarians and attack them immediately. Their attack came at a time (of the day) when the overconfident Hungarian leaders (and men) were drunk from wine; they did not expect the Byzantines to invade so soon. [78]

The Greek chroniclers record it that, like a black cloud, the (drunk) Hungarian knights in full black armor holding their lances by side, and armor plates covering the heads and bellies of the horses, approached the Byzantine line of defense. [79] Andronikos awaited their approach calmly with his Italian and Serbian mercenaries in the center, while he delegated command of the right (Byzantine) wing to Andronikos Lampardas, who was in control of Greek, Turkish and some German mercenary troops. The Byzantine left wing must have been weak, as it was commanded by various officers, such as Coccobasilieus and Philocoles; among the latter, Demetrius Branas did distinguish himself. [80]

The strategy of Contostephanos to break up the Hungarians' formation by staging a sham attack in the field had accomlished nothing. Now the Byzantine left- and right-wings began a simultaneous attack. The Hungarian left flank backed down, but the right flank stood its ground and in fact demolished the center of the Byzantine left-wing. [81] In the decisive moment of the battle Reeve Dénes attempted to strike out at the Byzantine center (of defense), but Lampardas was quicker than Dénes. His troops (= the Romans) stood their ground and turned to slaughter the "barbarians." After their lances broke and their swords fell to pieces, they began to clubber to death the unfortunate enemy: "miserorum capita clavis contundebant." [82] As Choniates (correctly) observed, it was the use of iron cudgets (= clubs: *clava*) by the Byzantine troops against the barbarians that had decided the outcome of the battle, because the Hungarians (=barbarians) were not prepared for the use of cudgets in close combat. [83] Manuel's forces have won the battle. [84]

The "Huns" (=Hungarians) have fled the field in disarray leaving thousands of dead, including five royal reeves and some eight hundred knights, behind in the field. [85] The Greeks (=Romans) collected two thousand pieces of personal armor, a lot of helmets, shields, swords, from the field. They had also captured the Hungarian royal standard. [86] When news came that fresh Austrian troops were approaching the field, the Byzantines crossed the Save in a hurry in order to retreat to the safety of their own territory. [87] During their quick withdrawal they still had time to demolish the fort of Zimony, but the Serem region remained, in spite of the impressive Byzantine victory, under Hungarian control. [88]

Stephen III did not cease warring with Manuel. Perhaps he knew that the emperor had plans for the conquest of Egypt, a plan that would divert his attention from the Hungarian border region. [89] Stephen III now began the reconquest of Trau, Spaleto and Sebenico on the Dalmatian seacoast, where the inhabitants received him with joy and acknowledged him as their sovereign. [90] Zara, too, followed their example. [91] The Dalmatian expedition remained, however, an ill conceived affair, without any organized plan. The Hungarian court made no preparations for a permanent conquest and defense of the territory. It was Venice that now unexpectedly reclaimed and occupied Zara, while Trau and Spaleto were retaken by Byzantium. [92] On the other hand, the loss of Zara to the Venetian republic did not prevent Stephen III from establishing an alliance with Venice in 1171, during the renewed Venetian-Byzantine naval campaign. [93]

Lack of proper planning, missed financial opportunities and limited fiscal resources were the characteristics of the reign of Stephen III. Because of the almost constant warfare at home and abroad, the king had to abuse the territorial and financial resources of the Church. [94] Walter Map remarked that Archbishop Lukács had besought the king with tears in his eyes not to repossess ecclesiastical land illegally. His warning had, however, no effect, and the archbishop had to excommunicate the dissolute monarch. [95]

Stephen III could not afford the loss of church support. Therefore, he made a pilgrimage to Esztergom in order to reconcile himself with the archbishop, and to open negotiations with him. Lukács did not await the arrival of the monarch in Esztergom, but went ahead to meet him and absolve him before that. It has been recorded that when the archbishop met the king, he broke out in tears and continued to cry, for he knew then that Stephen III would die soon, within a year of time. [96]

Reconciliation with the archbishop and negotiations with the Church did have a pricetag, but they also brought forth many positive results. In the presence of the papal legate, Cardinal Manfred, Stephen III did issue an Ecclesiastical Constitution, in which he renewed the promises his father had made to the Church (in Hungary): (1) He, the king, will not depose, or transfer, any (Hungarian) bishop, or abbot, without the approval and consent of the Roman See. (2) He, the king, will not name a secular person (=layman) as caretaker for a vacant episcopal see or goods, or for monasteries, but only qualified clergymen, who needed little provisions for their own personal maintenance. (3) The king would use the income of a vacant bishopric of monastery only for (a) the support and upkeep of the episcopal residence and the house for canons (of the cathedral chapter); (b) or, for the support and aid of the poor, the widows and orphans. (4) The king will not confiscate ecclesiastical property and landholdings (chattel) of the Church, except in times of need, when, for example, the enemy had entered and threatened the realm's security and territorial integrity, and even then with the consent of the local ordinary. [97] (5) The king will not depose, or transfer, prelates or abbots of monastic communities without due canonical procedures. The issuance of the Ecclesiastical Constitution may have occurred in the year of 1171,[98] or, as early as 1169. [99]

The chronicler recorded that in 1172, Henry Jasomirgott of Austria and Henry the Lion had begun their journey to the Holy Land, and their boat leaving Vienna had reached Hungarian soil at Moson. There, they were greeted by Florentinus, a royal ambassador (of Stephen III) who had orders to accompany the noble guests to the royal court in Esztergom. [100] During the night of March 4 (1172), and upon the arrival of the foreign dignitaries at the royal court, Stephen III died unexpectedly. [101]

Arnold of Lübeck seems to have known that the monarch had been poisoned; "nam ipse nocte rex veneno, appotiatus, *ut dicunt* (italics mine), a fratre suo," recorded the chronicler who, according to W. Wattenbach had to have access to reliable newsmaterial, though provided, probably, a somewhat less reliable report on events in a far away country.[102] Still, the timing of the event was very precise. The king died, when his foreign visitors from the west had reached the royal court in Esztergom. [103] The remark of Arnold that, astonished, the foreign visitors did not quite know what to do, — one may add: what to expect to happen next —, must have been no empty excuse. [104] This political-diplomatic murder was not only expected, but entirely unnecessary. The monarch died young, unsuspecting, and without a will at a time when his queen had been expecting their child. [105]

Emperor Manuel had done it again. Perhaps he was afraid that King Stephen III's foreign visitors, who were en-route in an official capacity to the Byzantine court ', "sed legatione functus imperatoris ad regem (!) Graecorum Manoe pro filia

ipsius filio matrimonio socianda," — could obtain a preliminary report on Byzantine politics from the Hungarian
ruler, who must have had a good idea s to what was going
on in Byzantine court circles.[106] Manuel must have feared
that Stephen III would depict him in less pleasant colors in
front of the western guests. Someone, who had a bad conscience, had to be suspicious and untrusting of anybody alive.

The evil hand of the Byzantine emperor reached too far.
Manuel could not forgive Stephen III that the king (young and
inexperienced) was able to keep his throne in an almost
constant struggle between two emperors, from the west and
from the southeast, and with his own uncles, and with his
own brother.[107] In fact, Stephen III dared, at least from
the Byzantine point of view, to regain Serem and, temporarily, though with the approval of the population, retain
the hinterland in Dalmatia as well for the Hungarian
Crown.[108]

<br>

### NOTES

1. "Loco eius coronatur Stephanus filius eius magnus;" cf. *SSH*, I, 461,3,
*and*, 461,29.

2. He just could not make any decisions — see his vacilations with the Byzantine
court, in Cinnamus, v:5-8; Moravcsik, *Fontes*, 214f.

3. On the queen's sons, see *Chronicon pictum*, c. 160.

4. Choniates, *Manuelis Comneni*, iii:1 (CB, 165,3-8), or, in Dieten, 100,46-
102,87; Moravcsik, *Fontes*, 274ff.

5. On Géza's birth, see *Chronicon pictum*, c. 160, in *SSH*, I, 446,23-24; on
his death, *ibid.*, I, 460,21-29. Géza II died in his thirty-second year; cf. *Continuatio Claustroneuburgensis II*, anno 1162, *MGHSS*, IX, 583; furthermore, cf.
*ibid.*, IX, 615, 630, and 776.

6. "... in cuius imperio dux Ladislaus filius regis Bele ceci usurpavit sibi coronam;" *SSH*, I, 461,4-8. "Post hunc ... Stephanus frater eius usurpavit sibi coronam;" *ibid.*, I, 461,14-15, and compare with Keza, c. 67, *ibid.*, I, 183; or, with
v. Mügeln, *Ungarnchronik*, c. 54, *ibid.*, II, 200.

7. Cf. Katona, *Historia critica*, III, 532; idem, *Historia pragmatica*, I, 569f.
(On Katona, and on G. Pray, see Hóman-Szekfű, V, 278.)

8. Cinnamus, v:1; v. Mügeln, c. 54; F. Makk, "A XII századi főúri csoportharcok értékeléséhez (Importance of group-struggle among the nobles during the
twelfth century)," *Acta historica Szegediensis*, 71 (1981), 29ff.

9. *Chronicon pictum*, c. 167, *SSH*, I, 460, note 3; Katona, *Historia critica*, III,
560f.

10. Idem, *Historia pragmatica*, I, 625ff., in reference to Cinnamus, v:5.

11. Cinnamus, v:6; Choniates, *Manuelis Comneni*, iv:1, in Dieten, 128.

# Stephen III

195

12. *Continuatio Claustroneuburgensis II*, anno 1165: "Stephanus rex Hungariae duxit uxorem Agnem, filiam Henrici ducis Austriae;" cf. *MGHSS*, IX, 616; Katona, *Historia pragmatica*, I, 618f.

13. Engaged at first to the daughter of Manuel — see Cinnamus, v:5; Choniates, *Manuelis Comneni*, iv:6 (Dieten, 137); however, he married, upon orders received from Manuel, Anna (=Agnes) Chatillon; cf. *ibid.*, iv:8 (in Dieten, 170), and Cinnamus, vi:11; Alberici Trium Fontium *Chronica*, in *MGHSS*, XXIII, 849; Katona, *Historia pragmatica*, I, 659f.

14. "Hic viduus ea, viduam;" *ibid.*, I, 661, in reference to *Ex gestis Henrici II et Richardi I*, in *MGHSS*, XXVII, 108, and compare with the report on the Hungarian status-quo of the times, in *RHM*, I, 245f.

15. Choniates, *Manuelis Comneni*, iv:1.

16. Cinnamus, v:1, and, previously, i:4. On this, also E. Jakubovich - D. Pais, eds., *Ó-magyar olvasókönyv* (Old Hungarian Reader) (Pécs, 1929), 50. In 1160, it was Béla I; Ladislas I in 1077 (had) inherited the throne — cf. Keza, c. 58-59 and 63; *Chronicon pictum*, cc. 92 and 131; F. Makk, "Contributions a l'histoire des relations hungaro-byzantines au XIIe siècle," *Acta antiqua Academiae Scientiarum Hungariae*, 29 (1981), 445ff.

17. Choniates, iv:1; *Chronicon pictum*, c. 169; oddly enough, Walter Map says that Lukács had crowned Stephen III king, — see Wright, ii:7; v. Mügeln, c. 54.

18. Cinnamus, v:1 (CB, 211-215); Choniates, *Manuelis Comneni*, iv:1.

19. Cinnamus, v:1 (and i:4), though, it ought to be pointed out, he did also confuse Stephen IV with Stephen III! Cf. Cinnamus, iii:19 (CB, 132); Choniates, *Manuelis Comneni*, iv:1.

20. Cf. his *Novellae constitutiones*, *MPG*, 133, 773, and his letter to Stephen III, in Cinnamus, v:10.

21. See H. Decker-Hauff, "A legrégibb magyar-bizánci házassági kapcsolatok kérdéséhez (Essay on the oldest Hungaro-Byzantine marriage contacts)," *Századok*, 81 (1947), 95ff.

22. Cinnamus, v:1; during the reign of Stephen III, "dux Ladizlas filius regis Bele Ceci usurpavit sibi coronam dimido anno;" *SSH*, I, 461,4-8.

23. Choniates, *Manuelis Comneni*, iv:1; v. Mügeln, c. 54: "do floh der kunig stephan Geyse sun, gen Presburg, do yn die Vngern liessen." *SSH*, II, 200,13-14; Freising, *Gesta*, may have been referring to this, *MGHSS* XX, 491,35-36; Pauler, I, 376ff., and 636.

24. Letter of Pope Innocent III to Archbishop John of Esztergom, in *MPL*, 216, 50c. "Strigoniensis ecclesiae praeiudicium fieret quominus Hungarici reges ab archiposcopis eiusdem ecclesiae semper debeant coronari," with the privilege originating in Rome: "salva semper apostolicae sedis auctoritate, a qua Hungarici regni corona processit." *Ibid.*, 216, 51a, and 216, 50a and d.

25. The circumstances are evident from the papal writ, published by W. Holtzmann from codex 144, fol. 24, of the Tortosa Kapitalbibliothek, in his "Alexander III und Ungarn," *Ungarische Jahrbücher*, 6 (1926), 397ff.

26. Archbishop Lukács had no other choice, but to excommunicate the insubordinate archbishop of Kalocsa; a letter by Pope Alexander III disclosed that open hostility prevailed between the two Hungarian high churchmen; cf. Holtzmann, *loc. cit.*, 401f., third letter; also, the writ by Alexander to the Hungarian king on the friction between Lukács and Andrew of Kalocsa, in W. Holtzmann, "XII századi pápai levelek kánoni gyűjteményéből (Twelfth century papal correspondence taken from canonical collections)," *Századok*, 92 (1959), 414f. Evidently, Rome had to intervene — see Innocent III to the archbishop of Esztergom and chapter, dated Sept. 15, 1204, and his letters of May 9 and 15, 1209, respectively,

in *MPL*, 215, 413ff.; 216, 50ff.

27. See the writ dated May 15, 1209, to John of Esztergom, *ibid.*, 216, 51a; F. Kemp, *Die Register Innozenz' III: eine palaeographisch-diplomatische Untersuchung* (Rome, 1945), 87ff.

28. On this, H. Grotefend, *Zeitrechnung des deutschen Mittelalters und der Neuzeit*, 2 vols. (Hannover, 1891-92), I, 205f.; A. v. Brandt, *Werkzeug des Historikers*, 2nd ed. (Stuttgart 1960), 36ff.

29. Wright, 73f., ii:7; v. Mügeln, c. 54. Lukács was born *de genere Gutkeled* of the Bánffy family of Alsó-lendva; cf. Knauz, I, 214. Only later did Bánffy become a family name; cf. L. Balics, *A római katholikus egyház története Magyarországon* (History of the Roman Catholic Church in Hungary), 2 vols. in 3 (Budapest, 1885-90), II-1, 127.

30. Cf. Mügeln, c. 54, *SSH*, II, 200f.; "... usurpavit sibi coronam dimidio anno;" — *Chronicon pictum*, c. 169. Its compiler placed his death on Feb. 1, 1172 (!), *ibid.*, I, 461, though it occurred "die xix Kal. Februarii," that is, on January 14, 1163, on a Sunday: *feria prima*; cf. *ibid.*, I, 461, note 3.

31. Cinnamus, v:1. Moravcsik, *Fontes*, 215, and note 57.

32. *SSH*, I, 461,14-17, and note 3.

33. *Ibid.*, II, 200,13-14; Cinnamus, v:1. Moravcsik, *Fontes*, 214f.

34. Mügeln, c. 55; Choniates, *Manuelis Comneni*, iv:1; Holtzmann, *art. cit.* (1926), first letter.

35. Letters of Innocent III of Sep. 15 and Nov. 2, 1204, in *MPL*, 215, 413ab and c; 215, 464bc.

36. The Holy See was, however, impressed with Kalocsa and had him emancipated from charges brought against him by Esztergom — cf. Holtzmann, *art. cit* (1926), second letter; it was Andrew of Kalocsa who represented Hungary at the Third Lateran Synod, cf. *MGHSS*, XXII, 217.

37. Wright, ii:7; Katona, *Historia pragmatica*, I, 651f.

38. *Ibid.*, I, 655f., — "in festo Geruasii et Protasii" (that is, June 19, 1163); cf. *SSH*, I, 462,2-6. Cinnamus, v:5; *Annales Posonienses*, 1172, *ibid.*, I, 127; Pauler, I, 642, note 515.

39. *SSH*, II, 201,13-19; Cinnamus, v:5.

40. *SSH*, II, 91f.; Lhotsky, *Quellenkunde*, 311; D. Dercsényi, *Nagy Lajos kora* (The age of Lewis the Great of Hungary (Budapest, n.d.), 26 and 143. F. Somogyi-L. F. Somogyi, "The Medieval University of Pécs," in S. B. Vardy (ed), *Louis the Great, King of Hungary and Poland* (New York, 1986), 221ff., on the intellectual climate in fourteenth century Hungary.

41. Cf. J. Horváth, *Stílusproblémák*, 278., and 272f.

42. Mügeln, c. 55.

43. *Ibid.*; Choniates, iv:1 (CB, 166f.); Cinnamus, v:5 (CB, 211-15); Moravcsik, *Fontes*, 217f.

44. Cf. *Continuatio Sanblasiana*, c. 17, *MGHSS*, XX, 311; Katona, *Historia pragmatica*, I, 657f.; Stephen III did, at this time, maintain good relations with the Doge of Venice. Cf. Dandalo, *Chronicon Venetum*, ix:15,15, in Muratori, *Scriptores*, XII, 287f.

45. *MGHSS*, XX, 491, anno 1164.

46. "... multi nobiles Hungariae corruerunt;" *SSH*, I, 462,5-6. J. Gerics, "Das Ständewesen in Ungarn am Ende des 13 Jahrhunderts," in R. Vierhaus, ed., *Herrschaftsverträge, Wahlkapitulationen, Fundamentalgesetze* (Göttingen, 1977), 129ff.

47. On *baro* and *barones maiores* (greater men: *homines maiores* in the feudal

sense) who paid their dues directly to the king; on *baro, homo* (small men who paid their dues through the reeve); on the fact that the "greater men" when serving in the army brought up their retainers under their own banners, while the "smaller" served under the reeve, — cf. F. W. Maitland, *The Constitutional History of England* (Cambridge, 1911), 64ff.; Gy. Bónis, *Hűbériség és rendiség a középkori magyar jogban* (Feudalism and the feudal order in medieval Hungarian law) (Kolozsvár, 1947), 287ff., and 485, wrote that the *barones* developed (in Hungary) out of the *iobagiones* only in the thirteenth century. Also, P. Engel, "Honor, vár, ispánság: tanulmányok az Anjou-kori királyság kormányzati rendszeréről (Honor, castle, royal reeves in the system of administration of the Angevin kings in Hungary)," *Századok*, 116 (1982), 880ff., esp. 883f.

48. Cinnamus, v:6 (CB, 215); Moravcsik, *Fontes*, 219.

49. Cinnamus, v:8.

50. Letter of Manuel to Stephen III, *ibid.*, v:6.

51. Cf. *Chronicae Cosmae Agensis continuatio*, anno 1164, MGHSS, IX, 165; also, *Annales Pragenses*, anno 1164, *ibid.*, III, 121.

52. Rahewin reports that in 1158, on his own authority derived from Roman law and without the sanction of the Church, Frederick Barbarossa had elevated his protegé to the dignity of Czech kingship on the grounds that God glorifies the Church through the empire — "Deus per imperium exaltavit ecclesiam;" Cf. *MGHSS*, XX, 424, and 426,47-48; Hampe, *Kaisergeschichte*, 148 and 161.

53. Cf. G. Pray, *Annales regum Hungariae ab anno Christi 997 ad annum 1614 deducti*, 5 vols. (Vienna, 1764-70), I, 136; F. Palacky, *Geschichte vom Böhmen*, vol. I (Prague, 1844), 415ff.; Katona, *Historia critica*, III, 560f. On Pray, see also C. Horváth, 696f.; on Géza II's Kievan wife, see *SSH*, I, 460, note 3.

54. Cinnamus, v:8.

55. *Ibid.*; Vincent of Prague, *Chronicon*, anno 1164, in *MGHSS*, XVII, 681.

56. Cinnamus, v:8.

57. Vincent of Prague, *Chronicon*, MGHSS, XVII, 681 and 683.

58. Choniates, *Manuelis Comneni*, iv:3, in Dieten, 134. Fifty-seven cities had submitted to Ioannes Ducas, ambassador of Byzantium; cf. Cinnamus, v:9.

59. Choniates, Manuelis Comneni, iv:3; Moravcsik, *Fontes*, 277f.

60. Cinnamus, v:12.

61. *Ibid.*, v:13.

62. *Ibid.*, v:13.

63. *SSH.*, I, 462,7-8.

64. Cinnamus, v:15-16; Moravcsik, *Fontes*, 228f.

65. Cinnamus, v:16; R. Browning, "A New Source on Byzantine-Hungarian Relations," *Balkan Studies*, 2 (Thessalonica, 1961), 199ff.

66. Choniates, Manuelis Comneni, iv:1, in Moravcsik, *Fontes*, 281; in Dieten, 128.

67. *Ibid.*, 137 (iv:4); Cinnamus, v:17.

68. Cinnamus, vi:3 (CB, 261,8-11); Moravcsik, *Fontes*, 239, and compare with the poem of an unknown poet, *ibid.*, 193.

69. Cinnamus, vi:4.

70. *Ibid.*, see also *Chronicon Venetum libri VIII*, v, in *Archivio storico Italiano*, vol. VIII (Florence, 1845), 158f. (in *MGHSS*, XIV, 5ff., selections only); Giesebrecht, V, 352ff.

71. Cinnamus, vi:4; Choniates, *Manuelis Comneni*, iv:4, in Dieten, 132,31-136,46; *Chronicon Venetum*, in *Archivio*, VIII, 159; Marcus, *Chronicon Venetum*, c. 44, *ibid.*, VIII, 259; Dandalo, *Chronicon*, ix:15:15-16, and 18, in Muratori, *Scriptores*, XII, 292.

72. Cinnamus, vi:5 (CB, 264,11-17, and 21-24); Moravcsik, 272.

73. *Ibid.*, vi:7; Choniates, *Manuelis Comneni*, v:1, in Dieten, 151f.; Moravcsik, *Fontes*, 283f.; also, v. Mügeln, c. 56, who spoke of "Kunig Belan;" *SSH*, II, 203,2 and 18.

74. Choniates, *Manuelis Comneni*, v:1; Moravcsik, *Fontes*, 285.

75. Cinnamus, vi:7 (CB, 270,17-21).

76. The feast of St. Procopius; cf. Moravcsik, *Fontes*, 286; Choniates, *Manuelis Comneni*, v:2 (CB, 199,14-15); in Dieten, 153; recorded in a fourteenth century (Hungarian) missal — cf. Radó, *Libri liturgici*, 70, and 80.

77. Choniates, *Manuelis Comneni*, v:2; Moravcsik, *Fontes*, 286f.

78. Cinnamus, vi:7 (CB, 272,1-4); Moravcsik, *Fontes*, 243; Choniates, *Manuelis Comneni*, v:3 (CB, 202f.), in Dieten, 155f.; Moravcsik, *Fontes*, 286.

79. Choniates, *Manuelis Comneni*, v:3 (Moravcsik, *Fontes*, 289).

80. Cinnamus, vi:7 (CB, 271); Moravcsik, *Fontes*, 244f. Choniates, *Manuelis Comneni*, v:3.

81. *Ibid.*, Cinnamus, vi:7 in Moravcsik, *Fontes*, 289., and 243f., respectively.

82. Cinnamus, vi:7 (CB, 274,1-2); Moravcsik, *Fontes*, 244f.

83. Choniates, *Manuelis Comneni*, v:3 (CB, 204,4-5); Moravcsik, *Fontes*, 290. In Dieten 156f. On the iron mace(s), and its (their) role in this battle, see also the speech of Archbishop Eustathius in the year 1174, in Thessalonica, in *MPG*, 136, 973ff.; or Moravcsik, *Fontes*, 162; Krumbacher, 536ff.

84. Cinnamus, vi:7 (CB, 274,21-22), and Choniates, *Manuelis Comneni*, v:3 (CB, 204f.); Moravcsik, *Fontes*, 245 and 291, respectively.

85. Cinnamus, vi:7 (CB, 274,7-10); Moravcsik, *Fontes*, 245.

86. Cinnamus, vi:7 (CB, 274,14-17).

87. *Ibid.*; CB, 274,17-19; Choniates, *Manuelis Comneni*, v:3 (CB, 204,14-19), in Dieten, 157. In Moravcsik, *Fontes*, 245 and 290f., respectively.

88. "Dalmatien und Bosnien wie auch das Sirmium Gebiet gelangten unter das Zepter des byzantinischen Kaisers;" cf. Ostrogorsky, 308, who expressed an opinion to the contrary.

89. Cinnamus, vi:9.

90. Choniates, *Manuelis Comneni*, v:4-5, in Dieten, 159,18-168,78; F. Dölger, "Ungarn in der byzantinischen Reichspolitik," *Archivum Europae centro-orientalis*, 8 (1942), 5ff.; Ostrogorsky, 309.

91. Dandalo, *Chronicon Venetum*, ix:15:15; Stephen III's Letter of Privileges of 1167, in *RHM*, II, 376f.; Szentpétery, *Regesta*, I, no. 113, dated it 1169; Fejér, II, 179f.

92. Dandalo, *Chronicon*, ix:15:16.

93. Idem, ix:15:18-19.

94. Katona, *Historia critica*, IV, 141f.

95. James, or Wright, Walter Mapes, ii:7.

96. Katona, *Historia pragmatica*, I, 640f.

97. Walter Mapes, ii:7; Katona, *Historia critica*, IV, 183.

98. *RHM*, II, 383f.; Marczali, *Enchiridion*, 123ff.

99. Szentpétery, *Regesta*, I, no. 118, dated it anno 1169. Fejér, II, 180f. M. Maccarone, "Die Cathedra Petri im Hochmittelalter," *Römische Quartalschrift*, 76 (1981), 137ff.

100. Cf. Arnold of Lübeck, *Chronica Slavorum libri VII*, i:2, in *MGHSS*, XXI, 116f.; Giesebrecht, V, 573ff. A. Kubinyi, "Burgstadt, Vorburgstadt und Stadtburg: zur Morphologie des mittelalterlichen Buda," *Acta archaeologica Academiae Scientiarum Hungaricae*, 33 (1981), 161ff.

101. Cf. *SSH*, I, 462,8-11. On the date of his death, cf. *ibid.*, I, 462, note 5; Katona, *Historia pragmatica*, I, 644f.

102. Cf. *MGHSS*, XXI, 117,18-19. The choice of words used by the chronicler, in this instance: "ut dicunt, a fratre suo," *ibid.*, XXI, 117,19, and note 29, support the opinion expressed by Wattenbach, II, 343.

103. *MGHSS*, XXI, 117,15-17.

104. *Ibid.*, XXI, 117,19-20.

105. *Ibid.*, XXI, 117,22-24.

106. The meeting between the visitors and the Esztergom archbishop did take place, with the nobles present; cf. *ibid.*, XXI, 117,24-28.

107. *Ibid.*, XXI, 117,6-7.

108. Cinnamus, vi:11.

# X

# The Reign of Béla III (1172-1196)

Hic quidem fures et latrones persecutus est
petitionibusque loqui (sic) traxit originem,
ut Romana habet curia et imperii.

*Simon de Keza*

It is surprising that besides some basic data concerning his reign, the compiler(s) of the *Chronicon pictum* said little about Béla III, 1172-96, one of the greatest rulers of medieval Hungary.[1] He persecuted thieves and robbers; in accordance with the examples set by the papal curia and the German court, introduced the custom of making official written petitions.[2] The late thirteenth century chronicler, Simon de Keza, wrote in his *Gesta Hungarorum* that Béla III was named 'the Greek' (Bela Graecus);[3] and, some nobles were quite some time able to keep him out of the country at the court of the Byzantine emperor.[4]

The author-compiler of this passage in the *Chronicon pictum* remains unknown.[5] It seems that Master Ákos, chronicler of King Stephen V, 1270-72, and parish priest in Pest, former court chaplain of Béla IV, 1235-70, and canon at Székesfehérvár, treasurer for king and country, and (in 1261) judge of the Queen's Court,[6] — who did have a brother: *comes* Detre, of some overbearing reputation,[7] — could not have been the author of this particular passage in the text of the Chronicle.[8]

The mid-fourteenth century compiler(s) included some of the (then) available annalistic entries in their opus,[9] in spite of the fact that those entries recorded nothing about the colorful and rich life of King Béla III; they said nothing about his upbringing in Byzantium; his relations with the Greeks — his being a Byzantine *despotes* for a given period of time;[10] recorded nothing about his French marriage,[11] or on his ecclesiastical-monastic contacts with France.[12]

It was he, for instance, who had confirmed the settlement of French Cistercians in the country. The chronicle entry reported nothing on his contacts with the Holy See, or about his military campaigns undertaken on his country's behalf. In other words, the chronicler entries failed to mention events that must have been known to contemporaries, — be it the inhabitants of the realm and/or men of letters at the royal court. [13]

The reign of Béla III must still have been common knowledge during the 1270's, barely seven decades after his death. Stephen V was Béla IV's son and the grandson of Andrew II (1205-35), [14] the great-grandson of Béla III. [15] Or, could it be that the men of letters in mid-thirteenth century Hungary knew too much about the times of the great monarch? They must have been aware of the far less successful and less glorious deeds, — in other words: the shady side —, of the reign of Béla IV, and they choose to remain silent, in fact, attempted to minimize the achievements of Béla III. [16]

It was Béla III who, over a decade, was able to conduct a foreign policy that kept balance between the German west and the Byzantine southeast of European politics. [17] It may be that the grandson, Béla IV, was unable to claim such an accomplishment in his foreign diplomacy, even though he had aimed at restoring conditions and prestige of the age of Béla III. [18]

In spite of all this, the remark by the chronicler concerning petitions (writs) in the country according to the examples set by the papal curia and the imperial court, [19] caused quite a stir among Hungarian historians who are of the opinion that the remark, in this instance, an annalistic entry, referred to conditions prevalent during the reign of Béla IV, but actually depicted those of the days of Béla III. [20]

This assumption rests upon the remark made by Canon Rogerius, author of *Carmen miserabile*, who described the horrors of the Tartar invasion of Hungary (1241-42); [21] and, as a contemporary eyewitness, [22] reported that Béla IV had, upon his succession to the throne, earned the hatred of his nobles by having ordered that they do not discuss any of their problems, nor begin law suits in the royal court (of law), without having petitions handed in to the royal chancellor to request that proceedings start in their particular case, or law suit. [23]

Rogerius noted that the monarch, by establishing it, did imitate the policy in use by that time at the papal curia. [24] In other words, the king let the nobles know that they had to show more respect toward him by not turning directly to him, but to his chancellor with their, frequently petty, or important, affairs, and that they do so in writing — by requesting a writ. [25] Less important matters would, henceforth, be handled by the chancellor, and the monarch could focus his attention on more important problems.

The monarch must have hoped that in such a manner he would have to intervene in only a small number of legal cases involving the nobility, thereby limiting contacts with the nobles, thus increasing the prestige of the king's dignity before them. And yet, the remark in the annalistic entries stated nothing new, really, because legislation dating back to Ladislas I, [26] and Coloman the Learned, [27] made it clear that every lawsuit in the realm, and not only in the royal court, that could lead to legal complications, any important purchase and sale, be it in private or at the public market, had to be placed into writing in front of witnesses. [28] Already by the end of the eleventh century, royal justices had the right and obligation to cite, by issuing a writ, the accuser or the accused, buyer and/or seller, to appear before them. [29]

On account of the scanty Hungarian source material in this age, one has to turn to foreign sources reflecting upon the times of King Béla III. Iohannes Cinnamus [30] and Nicetas Choniates, [31] Byzantine chroniclers, provided detailed annotations on events in the realm. [32] Thomas of Spaleto [33] and Andreas Dandalo of Venice report events in Dalmatia; [34] the Russian chroniclers, especially the annotations by Hypatius of Halich; [35] contemporary Austrian and German chroniclers, [36] together with Arnold of Lübeck's Chronicle of the Slavs provide material for the interpretation of historical happenings in Hungary. [37]

The canonization of Ladislas I is described by his *Vita*, [38] and by Thomas of Spaleto. [39] The reign of King Emory I is commented on by the Major Annals of Cologne, [40] and by Thomas of Spaleto. [41] In addition, one may consult the material of the contemporary royal *Regesta*, together with the preserved royal and ecclesiastical documents of the age. [42]

The deceased Stephen III was the elder brother of Béla III; [43] his younger brother was Prince Géza, [44] all of whom were the children of Géza II, [45] their mother being Euphrozina, daughter of Mistislav of Kiev. [46] Upon the death of his brother, the nobles dispatched an embassy to the Byzantine court to offer Béla, heir of the throne, the Hungarian crown. [47] Béla was already en-route to Hungary when he met with the ambassadors of Sofia. Béla was the former heir of the Byzantine throne. When the emperor, Manuel, had a son born to him out of his second marriage, Béla, until then *despotes*, had no alternative but to leave the Byzantine court. He was not even allowed to marry his fiance, Maria, daughter of Manuel. It was instead Agnes (in Hungarian: Maria), step-sister of the emperor's second wife and daughter of Raynold Chatillon of Antioch, who became his wife. [48]

The emperor had Béla accompanied to Sofia (Sardica) and, before he and the prince departed, he made Béla swear an oath that as long as he lived, he would serve the interests of the Roman ( Byzantine) emperor(s), and remain loyal to the empire. Upon taking the oath, the prince was allowed to proceed to Hungary. [49]

The prince educated at the Greek court was not received with open arms in Hungary. [50] Many were afraid of him on account of his Byzantine upbringing. Archbishop Lukács, the Hungarian primate, turned against him on grounds that the prince gave, as a gift, a cloak to one of his legates. The archbishop looked upon the gift as bribery and let the prince know that he would not anoint or crown him king. [51] Pope Alexander III said in a letter that Béla, the Hungarian king-elect, had, out of sheer goodness of heart, donated a cloak to the archbishop's messenger; that was the reason why Lukács refused to crown Béla. [52]

Euphrozina, Béla's mother, was also against him; she wanted to see Géza, his younger brother, on the throne. It must have been the dowager queen who had contributed to the stubborn behavior of Lukács toward Béla III. The warning of Rome to the contrary, Esztergom supported the dowager queen. [53]

Béla III did not, however, give up so easily. This is evident from the papal letters. The king reconfirmed the church constitution issued by his brother and predecessor, [54] and

requested the Holy See's help and understanding. [55] (When
the king had the provost of Székesfehérvár deposed, Pope
Alexander raised a protest on grounds of this document,
and the king had to back down acknowledging his fault in
the procedure. [56] ) Since the pope himself was unable to
change the mind of the archbishop, [57] the curia decided to
permit the archbishop of Kalocsa to crown Béla III, [58] without, however, infringing upon the right of Esztergom to crown
the Hungarian monarchs in the future. [59] On January 13,
1173, the archbishop of Kalocsa placed the crown upon
the head of Béla III. [60]

The coronation must have been performed by Cosmas
of Kalocsa, whose name appears on what St. L. Endlicher
listed as the fifth article of the 1169 Ecclesiastical Constitution (of Stephen III). [61] The fact ought to be considered,
however, that in the text edited by Duchesne of this constitution, there is only the initial C (archiepiscopus) recorded; [62]
Szentpétery, who dated the document 1171, had recorded
archbishop C(hemma). [63] The diploma of Stephen III issued
for Sebenico, [64] dated 1167 in Marczali, [65] and 1169 in
Szentpétery, [66] is signed by Archbishop Sayna of Kalocsa. [67]
On the other hand, in two documents, both issued in 1169,
Chemma signed as bishop of Eger. [68] Chemma (Sayna) may,
of course, be identical with C(osmas).

Ecclesiastic Andrew (the archenemy of Lukács) was,
since 1169, bishop of Győr, [69] in 1176, he became archbishop
of Kalocsa [70] over the protests of Lukács who was very slow
in granting his approval of the appointment. [71] Soon thereafter Archbishop Andrew was accused of perjury, [72] and
of treason toward the king. [73] The archbishop had a noto-
riously vehement nature; he had, for instance, used physical
force against the clerics of Archbishop Lukács. [74] The latter
now had requested the monarch to depose his rival of the
archbishopric of Kalocsa and to deprive him of his income, —
a request evidently granted. [75] And yet, Archbishop Andrew
was able to return to his office; he apparently had good
connections in Rome. [76] The papal legate who made peace
between the king and the archbishop was Cardinal Walter
of Albano who dared not enter German territory, but had
to reach a decision in a dispute over the arhciepiscopal see
of Salzburg. Encouraged by Béla III, the legate invited

Adalbert of Salzburg, together with Adalbert's rival, — the latter being an appointee of the emperor, — to a special church gathering at Győr. Although the imperial appointee failed to appear, the legate, aided by the Hungarian bishops at Győr had discussed the matter and pronounced Adalbert as the lawful archbishop of the see. [77]

At the Third Lateran Synod, 1179, it was Andrew of Kalocsa who represented the Hungarian hierarchy. [78] His name also appeared as that of a witness on two royal diplomas issued in 1181, [79] and in 1186. [80]

In the interest of domestic peace the king had, temporarily, incarcerated his brother, Géza, who later fled to Austria. [81] He also had, in the public interest, held his dowager queen mother out of circulation, especially after she was excommunicated by the Roman See. [82] The *principes et barones* of the realm had, on the other hand, expressed active and public support of Béla III. [83] That must have been the reason why Géza had departed for Austria. Leopold V of Austria had been married, since 1174, to Ilona the 'var' princess, the younger sister of both Géza and King Béla. [84] The king and prince had, in fact, another sister, Elizabeth, married to Frederick, brother of the duke of Bohemia. [85] Prior to that, the queen of the by now deceased Stephen III had been Agnes, daughter of Henry II, margrave of Austria. [86] So, to Austria Géza had to go and, for the duration of time, there to remain. [87]

Béla III had, because of his family relations and contacts, no alternative but to seek an alliance with Bohemia, [88] — against his Austrian brother-in-law. [89] The king must have taken the rather immature and irresponsible political-diplomatic manipulations of his younger brother rather seriously. Béla III must have been concerned that Géza would, — on Austrian and/or Czech soil, — organize a diplomatic-military coalition against him, the Hungarian monarch who has been, presumably, serving the political and diplomatic interests of the Byzantine court. [90]

This must have been the time when the political wounds caused by Archbishop Lukács were still fresh in memory. Although Béla III held the confidence of the Roman See and harbored no ill feeling toward the archbishop of Esztergom, the flight of his brother Géza to the west must have deeply disturbed him. The chronicler of Milovice has provided a convincing argument. [91]

Austria had only recently become a duchy, and its princely family may have tried to appease the imperial court by following an anti-Byzantine policy toward the east. [92] Béla III most probably knew little about the 1156 *Privilegium minus*; even if he did, he did not regard as important the assertion of the document that the Austrian dukal family enjoy full freedom of action within the political and diplomatic framework of the empire. [93]

In the summer of 1176, Hungarian and Czech troops invaded Austria, and the mercurial Géza now fled to the court of Bohemia. [94] In early 1177, Henry Jasomirgott died, and Géza did not want to await the expected changes in Austrian policy. But, he made the wrong move. Sobieslav II of Bohemia did not show much appreciation for the irresponsible and erratic prince, and he was concerned that Géza had plans to go to the imperial court in order to submit himself and his royal brother's country in vassalage to the German emperor. Sobieslav II remained friendly but determined. He patiently listened to the plans of Géza, then had him surrendered to Béla III. [95]

At this stage of the game the king had some political countermeasures undertaken regarding the princely brother. He had him placed under (house) arrest so that he may cause no more trouble. [96] Incidentally, it may have been at this stage of diplomatic development that the king had his (their) mother, Euphrozina, the dowager queen, exiled to Byzantine territory, where she became a religious in the monastic community for women at Barancs (the chronicle text reads: Bronz). [97] The king had also begun persecution of the political adherents of both the (exiled) queen mother and Géza, with the faithless royal reeve Vata among them, and had ordered that the latter be blinded. [98] (It must have been quite a coincidence that it was *a* Vata who had organized a conspiracy against King Stephen I in the 1030's; [99] now, it was *another* Vata who headed a conspiracy against Béla III, and suffered the same punishment: blinding.) [100]

The king's concern about his brother Géza's seeking contact with the imperial court in order to bring about a diplomatic-military coalition against him, had not been baseless. After Sobieslav II of Bohemia had Géza handed over to the royal Hungarian authorities, Emperor Frederick Barbarossa had the Czech prince (king) punished by removing him from office on the grounds that the prince had behaved badly toward a political exile seeking his help.[101] (It was Emperor Frederick Barbarossa who on his own authority derived from Roman law and without the sanction of the Church, had elevated his protege to the dignity of kingship,[102] on grounds that God glorifies the Church through the empire.[103])

Simultaneously, because he may have wanted to cover up his policies, the emperor concluded a treaty with King Béla III [104] and had his daughter engaged to the eleven year old Emory, Béla's son, [105] whom they had crowned (junior) king for the first time in the year of 1182.[106] It may be, though that it was Béla III who, through this engagement, hoped to assure success for his diplomacy over Dalmatia from the German court. [107]

Béla III had shown respect toward Emperor Manuel also. He had left the emperor in the possession of the Serem region and of the Dalmatian seacoast. In fact, he had aided the emperor against Arslan Kilids, sultan of Iconium, though the emperor had lost that campaign.[108] A document issued in 1230 by "Béla, Junior King" (future Béla IV), to confirm the writ of Béla III awarding Lob and Thomas who had served him so bravely in the campaign on Byzantine soil, bears, most probably, witness to this military operation. [109]

Upon the death of Manuel in 1180, [110] Béla III had turned his attention toward Dalmatia; the city republics of Spaleto, Trau and Zara had submitted to his rule. [111] He placed the seacoast under his reeve Mór ( = Maurus), in order to assure Hungarian predominance over the region. [112] He had also new fortifications built around Zara; [113] and, when Venice headed by the cunning doge Orio Mastropier began a war over the seacoast, his forces could not take the refortified city. [114] The king now nominated Dénes ( = Dionysius) viceroy (*banus*) over the seacoast,[115] and named the prelate Peter to the archbishopric of Spaleto. [116]

Struggle involving succession broke out at the Greek court following the death of Manuel; his son, Alexius, heir and successor, was still a minor. The opposition supported Andronikos Comnenos against the heir, and against the dowager empress acting as regent for her son. [117] (It was Andronikos who, in the recent past, had been dealt with so mercifully by Emperor Manuel. [118] ) Andronikos proved to be a savage, merciless person, who had the empress removed from the regency (and from the imperial court), and, as the uncle of the new emperor, he made himself both guardian and regent for the young Alexios. [119]

The dowager emperess had now turned for aid to Béla III; the king invaded Byzantine territory, occupied Belgrade, Boron (Barancs; Branitchevo), and, during the second campaign, took possession of Nis and of Sofia (in 1183). [121] Out of revenge, Regent Andronikos had the entire imperial family assassinated. [122]

When he occupied Sofia, Béla III decided to capture and take from Sofia the relic of Saint Ivan of Rila, a hermit in tenth century Bulgaria, and had it deposited at the archepiscopal see of Esztergom. By taking the relic with him, the king may have wished to establish the cult of the saint in Hungary. The archbishop of Esztergom, Nicholas, [123] was, however, unwilling to acknowledge the sainthood of Ivan of Rila on the grounds that his name did not appear on the roster of saint of the Church. Ivan's *Vita* says that the archbishop had thereby denied him sainthood, therefore, Nicholas had to be punished. The archbishop went dumb, had no power of speech until he repented and turned to Ivan for intercession. Upon observing this miracle Béla III had the reliquary of the saint decorated with gold and silver, and returned it, with the relic, to Sofia by 1187. [124]

Béla III had in the neighborhood of Nis also captured Vlach prisoners during the same campaign, and had them settle down in Transylvania together with the other Vlach settlers, whom he had earlier defeated and captured. [125] It may have been this group of Vlach settlements that has been pointed out by the Hungarian Anonymus, who has written about the Vlachs fighting with their primitive weapons at Esküllő near Fort Gyelő (Gyalu), [126] There were some other Vlach settlements east of Seben and at Kerc (in Transylvania); Anonymus has also mentioned other Vlach settlers who lived in three villages under their own *kenéz* (elected mayor). [127]

When the Hungarian king attempted to assure himself
of a large and coherent portion of Byzantine territory, the
ruler of Apulia (in the Italian south) had the Byzantine seacoast devasted with his naval forces. [128] Then he, together
with the king of Sicily, had begun a war against Andronikos,
and people in Byzantium had revolted against the latter.
From the sea, a large naval force had reached the empire:
a fleet of two hundred ships of William II of Sicily had captured Thessalonica. It was the intention of William II to
destroy Andronikos, and make himself emperor of Byzantium. [129]

In 1185, the revolution in Byzantium replaced the tyrant
Andronikos with Isaac II Angelos, nephew of Manuel and
the grandson of the daughter of Alexius I. Isaac II wanted
to have peace with Béla III, and asked for the hand in marriage of Margaret, ten year old daughter of Béla III. [130] Isaac
received the hand of Margaret and, for a dowry, the area
beyond the Save and Danube rivers. [131] The Vlachs in the
region contributed herds of sheep for the dowry of the royal
bride. [132] (Reading the reports of the Byzantine chroniclers
the impression may be gained that Isaac II had concluded
a marriage-treaty with the daughter of the Hungarian
monarch because he, at that time, had a constant political-
military turmoil brewing on Cyprus [133] and, simultaneously,
on the Balkans. [134] )

This new Hungaro-Byzantine alliance, on the other hand,
may have been destined to counterbalance a new German-
Norman agreement of Emperor Henry VI and Constance of
Sicily — in favor of William II of Sicily, against Byzantium.[135]
It must have been at this time that dowager Euphrozina left
Branics (Branitchevo) for the Byzantine court, [136] so that she
could enter a convent in Jerusalem. [137] The occasion must
have been ripe for Béla III to request the hand in marriage
of (the younger) Theodora, [138] a request refused by the Greek
court on religious grounds. [139] With the Hungaro-Byzantine
border thus secured, the court now could turn its attention
on the threat from the king of Sicily. Alexios Branas had
defeated William II, who left the Balkans and returned to
Sicily. [140] (But, the Vlachs and the Cumans headed by Asen,
John and Peter, [141] had carried out an uprising against the
empire and established "Bulgaria" with Tirnovo as its capital. [142] )

In 1187, Islam carried a victory over Christian forces and over the remains of the kingdom of Jerusalem at Hattin. The papacy headed by Pope Gregory VIII, proclaimed a crusade for the recapture of the Holy Land.[143] From the Hungarian point of view, this meant that the Venetian republic so preoccupied with preparations for the planned reconquest of Zara on the Adriatic, now concluded a two year truce with the Hungarian king, so that it may concentrate its attention on the new developments in the politico-diplomatic situation in the near East.[144]

Béla III would have been pleased to lead the campaign against Islam in person, but domestic matters, — mostly political-domestic developments in Halich, — directed his attention into different channels of diplomatic communication.[145] In 1187, Yaroslav of Halich had died and, for his successor the nobles of Halich elected Vladimir, Yaroslav's legitimate son who had been fully ignored by his father (though compensated by the father with the city Premysl), instead of Oleg, the natural son of Yaroslav and his heir-designate.[146]

The elected Vladimir was, however, a drunk and a womanizer, and the nobles of Halich called upon Prince Roman, the grandson of Yaroslav and duke of neighboring Ladomer, inviting him to become their leader.

Vladimir now turned to Béla III for help and understanding, and placed himself under the monarch's protection.

Thereupon Béla had crossed the Carpathians and had, both he and his armed forces, accompanied Vladimir to Kiev. When the Hungarian forces approached the city, Roman fled from the region, and Halich submitted — to the Hungarian king. The people of Halich — and of Kiev — did not like, nor did they want Vladimir for their princely ruler. Realizing the unsettled political situation in Halich, Béla III decided to keep Halich for himself, and named his twelve year old son, Andrew, as his governor for Halich. The monarch also made arrangements for the departure of Vladimir and Vladimir's family to Hungary. He had placed the prince and his family under (house-)arrest in the Tower of Visegrád.[147] Now Béla III assumed a new title: *rex Galiciae*, king of Halich.[148]

The newly developed political-military situation in Halich

gained the disapproval of the Orthodox Patriarch of Kiev, who was afraid that the Hungarian monarch would oppress religion and freedom of his Church in the area. [149] Soon thereafter the nobles of Halich turned against the king; it may be that the Hungarians had behaved badly; may be the religious differences were greater than it could have been foreseen. It is possible that language usage caused some serious differences (of opinion). Natives and newcomers must have found it difficult to exchange ideas, communicate effectively, and to establish personal contact. Without such an interaction the administration of the region could have been endangered. Without knowing the language, the Hungarian advisors of the barely twelve year old Andrew must have had difficulties in trying to understand the mentality of the population of Halich. [150]

It may make good sense, therefore, that Vladimir and his family had escaped from their captivity in Hungary (they must have been under very light supervision); and, in Halich, it was Rastislav, the grandson of Vladimir's brother, who gained the upperhand in politics — by heading the opponents of Hungarian rule in the area. [151]

Béla III could not, at this point, remain inactive. He sent an army to aid his son. The leaders of this force dispatched to Russia had forced the native leaders of Halich into taking an oath of loyalty to Andrew, the chroniclers report, and now the Russians made a military move against Rastislav; they had him defeated and captured. Rastislav soon died of the wounds he must have received in the battle. The opponents of Andrew in Halich were lacking unity, and the forceful Hungarian interference had only weakened the remnant of that unity among the Russian nobles. Still, a small group of hard-core opponents remained active in Halich, and Vladimir (who had escaped from his Hungarian captors; also known as Yaroslavich  son of Yaroslav) joined them as their leader. Vladimir-Yaroslavich now requested political sympathy and military aid from the new German ruler, Henry VI. [152] The German court, however, told the by now desperate Vladimir-Yaroslavich to turn for help to the Polish prince, Casimir to regain his hold on Halich. At this point of the diplomatic game, Andrew left Halich and headed for home. [153]

It is more than likely that the Polish prince did not like the possible expansion of Hungarian rule over the area alongside the southeastern Polish border, but he wanted to avoid an open military conflict with Béla III. Through the intercession of the Russian grand-prince, Vasevolod of Suzdal, the Polish Casimir now made peace with Béla III; in fact, they had concluded an alliance. This peace treaty had its own price tag in that Halich remained in the possession of Vladimir-Yaroslavich. [154]

Upon the death of his queen Béla III had asked for the hand in marriage of the eight year old daughter of the Welf duke, Henry the Lion, but they turned down his request. [155] Thereupon, he requested the hand in marriage of Margaret, the sister of Philip II Augustus of France; she was the widow of the late English heir to the throne. [156] Henry, eldest son of Henry II of England, was, from 1170 to his death in 1183, associate ruler with his father; his widow had a large income. [157] Were she to marry the Hungarian monarch: a widow a widower, she would have to relinquish that income. The French court understandably requested a written statement of the annual revenues of Béla III. [158]

An official statement was issued. Its original is still in the National Library in Paris. [159] It enumerates the itemized annual income of the Hungarian king and provides a clear picture of the realm at that time. [160] Béla III had assured a rich annuity for Margaret. In 1186, he married her. [161]

According to the enumeration of this document, the Hungarian monarch held four titles (in the 1180's): he was king of Hungary, Dalmatia, Croatia and Rama (Serbia), meaning that four kingdoms were under his sceptre. [162] His annual income included fifteen thousand marks (gira) received from the German settlers in Transylvania; they had settled there during the reign of Géza II. [163] (This is a feature of the document that ought to be pointed out here on the grounds that the royal titles of Béla III were identical with those held by Béla II the Blind, except that the latter did not receive, as yet, an annual revenue from the German settlers in Transylvania. [164])

The document itself shows that (1) the king's annual income was about 240.000 marks (gira), out of which amount 60.000 marks (gira) came from "new money," that is, the amount gained from the annual exchange of coins in circulation in the realm, and some 30.000 marks from road and river crossing tolls and fair taxes. The annual salt tax was around 16.000 gira; the two-thirds share contributed by the county reeves came about to 25.000 gira, but the reeves also provided 10.000 marks worth of gifts for the king (the reeves were obliged to provide hospitality for the king; to secure gifts of cloth, silk, silver and horses for the Queen and the elder son). The annual land tax paid by the German settlers in Transylvania (it has already been referred to) amounted to 15.000 marks, while the duke of Slavonia owed the monarch the annual sum of 10.000 marks. [165]

The sum total of this itematized list records 166.000 marks (gira) annually; it can be assumed that the peoples of the royal domain, including the free stratum of the population, contributed some 70.000 marks worth of food supply a year for the royal household. [166]

(2) In the ecclesiastical field, the realm had two archbishoprics (according to this document), — those of Esztergom and of Kalocsa. The archbishop of Esztergom had an annual income of 6.000 gira (marks); and under his jurisdiction were the bishop of Eger, with an income of 3.000 marks; the bishop of Vác, 1.500 marks; of Győr, 1.700 marks; and of Nyitra, 1.100 marks. The archbishopric of Kalocsa became united with that of Bács, and its archbishop had an annual income of 2.500 marks. He had under his jurisdiction the bishop of Csanád with an income of 2.000 marks; the bishop of Bihar (whose see was located at Várad-Olaszi) with 1.000 marks; of Transylvania, with 2.000 marks, and of Zagreb, with an income of 1.500 marks. [167]

There were two archbishoprics, at Zara (Jadera), income 500 gira; and at Spaleto, income 400 gira, with ten bishoprics under their jurisdiction(s) in the realm of the Hungarian king in Dalmatia. [168]

Margaret was the daughter of Louis VII, king of the Franks, and his second wife, Constance of Castile (and the daughter of Alphonso VIII of Castile). [169] Thus, through Margaret, queen of Hungary, there had to be some strong Castilian influence in evidence at the Hungarian court, the probable result of which may have been the marriage of the son of Béla III to Constance of Aragon, the daughter of

Alphonso II of Aragon; [170] such an influence may also have created an impact of the Castilian-Aragonese *cortez* upon public life in Hungary after the death of Béla III.[171] For instance, the Castilian-Aragonese influence may be discernable in the prepared text of the Hungarian Golden Bull of 1222, and in the development of circumstances that may have led toward the drafting of that document. [172]

Béla III had not only extended his political-diplomatic activities toward the Byzantine Southeast and the Teutonic West, but had developed relationship resting upon family ties, toward the Iberian southwest, thereby to further the formation of public institutions and that of the economy of his country. [173] It is of some interest to note that upon the death of Emery I in 1204, Queen Constance became the first wife of the German emperor, Frederick II. [174] Constance, Hungarian queen and German empress died in the year of 1222. [175]

In 1189, a new crusading army travelled through the realm led by Emperor Frederick I Barbarossa.[176] Béla III had agreed to the journey of the crusading armies through his kingdom, but had, through prearrangements, set a scale of prices the crusaders had to adhere to in paying the country's population for food supplies and animal fodder. The king promised, however, that he would provide for men and animals of the crusading troops. They set the price of animal fodder for one-hundred horses at one *gira* (mark) that equalled the price of four oxen. Twenty-five horses equalled the price of four oxen. It became the official pay scale and the base price for any business transaction and goods sold for the crusaders in transit in the realm. Béla III had also given orders that all bridges and roads in the country be brought into usable condition; some old bridges had to be rebuilt, and some new ones constructed. [177]

On May 11, 1189, Frederick I left Regensburg by boat and reached the Hungarian border on May 24 across of Pozsony on the right-hand side of the Danube. [178] There he awaited the arrival of his troops. His son, Frederick of Swabia, accompanied him. On May 31, the German crusaders began their sojourn through the country. Shiploads of bread; wagonloads of fodder awaited them. Herds of sheep and oxen were at their disposal. As he reached Esztergom, Béla

III and his queen greeted the emperor. [179] The queen donated a decorated tent to Frederick I, lined from the inside with scarlet wool. The tent was divided into four compartments. In one of these there stood a throne carved out of elephant tusk. In another, a poster bed stood, covered with hand-embroidered covers; a white hunting dog was embroidered on its curtain. This tent, when taken apart, could be transported on three wagons. [180] The monarch donated two silos full of flour to the emperor's men, four of whom, starved crusaders, had entered the silos so hurriedly and greedily that they fell into and suffocated in the flour. [181]

Frederick I had, on the other hand, his son, Frederick, engaged to the daughter of Béla III, and, because of a request from the Queen, obtained the release of Géza, Béla III's younger brother, from his eleven year captivity. The king complied with the request out of respect for the Queen; Géza was released and, in fact, provided with two thousand knights. [182] But King Béla placed his brother under the personal supervision of the emperor, and commanded him to act as a guide for the German crusaders while in transit in the land. Since he could not deny the request of his wife, made through the intercession of the emperor, Béla III did his best to get rid of his irresponsible brother. [183]

Béla III organized a four day hunting party in the honor of his imperial guests, whom he accompanied, followed by some thousand knights, to the summer home of the queen on the island of Csepel (Etzelburg) in the Danube. The king also gave a reception at Acquincum, where, legend has it, Attila the Hun had his headquarters. [184] A tournament of the knights followed the reception and a royal hunt in the hills of Pilis. [185] (This may have been the picture in the mind of the Hungarian chronicler Anonymus in his report of the conquest by Árpád of the mid-Danube region, and of the circumstances surrounding that conquest in the 890's. [186])

In addition to the two thousand knights who had accompanied Géza to the emperor's camp, many Hungarians had joined the crusaders, as, for instance, Ugron Csák, bishop of Győr. [187] The king had kept an eye on the crusaders until they reached the southern Hungarian frontier. Before they departed from the realm, however, he gave them five thousand marks worth of donations: a large amount of sacks of flour, and four camels loaded with gifts. [188] In order to express his appreciation, and acting under the false assumption that because of the narrow rock straits the Danube would not be navigable east of Belgrade, the emperor in return donated all of his ships (upon which he must have made his sojourn from Regensburg to Barancs) to Béla III. [189]

The transit of the crusaders through Hungary may have lasted four weeks. Judged by the remark of the chronicler that at the southern border the emperor transferred all of his ships to the Hungarian monarch, it may be concluded that at least a part of the German crusading force — the emperor and his staff — made the journey on ships and not on horseback. Reaching Byzantine territory the joyful adventure of the crusaders came to an end. A misunderstanding broke out between the emperor and the son-in-law of Béla III: Emperor Isaac Angelos, who demanded an oath of fidelity from the Germans before allowing them to continue their sojourn on Byzantine territory. [190]

It was at Philippopolis that open strife developed between the Germans and the local authorities. Guerilla type attacks were made upon the crusaders, and at Sofia war broke out between them and the population. Béla III did attempt to restore some peace and trust among the two emperors, but remained unsuccessful in his efforts. Thereupon he ordered that his troops that had joined the crusaders return home. [191] The king did not want to hurt his son-in-law, or to ruin the recently improved relationship with Byzantium by supporting a cause that had little to do with Hungarian interests. Still it is known that three royal reeves, and their forces, remained with the German emperor and proceeded with him on their crusade to the Holy Land. [192]

Béla III must have had a good reason for keeping his relations with Byzantium intact. By 1190, the truce with the Venetian republic expired; Venice began to war again, but the Hungarian court did not want to lose the good will of Byzantium. Therefore, when Venice had stirred up public opinion among the population of Arbe, and its navy moved up to Zara, Béla III ordered the naval vassals of the Dalmatian cities into action against Venice. In the naval battle at Cade Trau, the Dalmatian ships had gained the upper hand over the republic, whose leaders now concluded another two year truce with the Hungarian monarch by 1191. Zara remained under the control of the Hungarian king, but Arbe was restored to the republic. Henry Dandalo, the 84 year old and half blind doge of Venice had another war begun with Béla III by 1193, but had accomplished little; although the doge was able capture Pago and its small group of islands in the Adriatic, Dalmatia remained under Hungarian rule. [193]

Béla III appointed Bishop Kalán of Pécs governor of Croatia-Dalmatia making him *banus* of the region beyond the Drava river. For two years the bishop held both positions. As governor, he kept Zara under the rule of Béla III, [194] but after that he had asked to be relieved from his duties. It may be that the bishop was the type of a person who could function in public office only in difficult times; he must have felt out of season in times of relative peace and inactivity. [195] Emery, Béla III's son (and successor) became the new governor of Croatia-Dalmatia in 1194, and on this occasion of his new appointment, he was crowned (junior) king of Hungary for a second time. [196]

Béla III visited Dalmatia in person in order to find out whether conditions there were peaceful enough for his son (who was young and inexperienced) to take over as governor. The monarch also wished to meet with his son-in-law on the Save river. Isaac Angelos had requested Hungarian aid against his enemies: the Cumans and the Petchenegs on the lower Danube, and against the Vlachs and the Bulgarians who had been in the recent past, almost constantly besieging the territories of the empire. [197] Béla III was willing to move his troops in supporting Isaac, but before he could give the orders, Isaac's brother, Alexius, staged a palace revolt and had Isaac deposed. The emperor fled his capital; he was captured and blinded, and they had imprisoned him together with his son. [198]

Was it all Byzantine politics? Did Béla III pursue real politics? The king could not intervene any further in the interests of his deposed and imprisoned son-in-law and he needed to have peace with Byzantium. He had plans for visiting the Holy Land and, to fulfill an earlier vow, for taking up the cross. Before he died, the king had collected a treasure for his crusade to the Holy places — the treasure (together with the father's intention to go on a crusade) was to be inherited by his younger son, Andrew, [199] because he died during preparations made for the crusade on April 23, 1196. [200]

His grave — his big-boned remains next to the burial site of his queen, Anne, — had been unearthed in 1848. In the grave a pilgrim's staff and a ring with Arabic inscriptions were found, and a small silver (home) crown on (the remains of) his skull. [201] Legend has it that he had been poisoned by Bishop Kalán of Pécs, former governor of Croatia-Dalmatia and author of a book on Attila the Hun.[202] Rome did order an investigation, but the charges were unfounded.[203] Béla III's second queen, Margaret, made her own pilgrimage to the Holy Land and died in Ptolemais in the year 1197. [204]

The reputation and fame of Béla III had little to do with glorious military accomplishments; nor did any of his legislative acts come down to posterity. Still, he is one of the outstanding monarchs of European history. [205] His late successor, Béla IV (1235-70), had remarked in one of his official writs that it was his aim to reign in the spirit and to restore conditions in his realm as they had existed during the years of the rule of Béla III. [206] It was at the Byzantine court that he, as heir designate to the imperial throne, acquired the political wisdom of the effective government. He had been prepared with the utmost care for his role in his realm's government. He possessed training and experience when he, unexpectedly, became king of Hungary. [207]

In 1172, the realm and the royal court were functioning in poverty; the land and its government were split into various factions. Béla III had to end the unnecessary struggle for the throne and restore political and social-economic unity in the country. [208] He restored conditions for public confidence in the government, law and order, protection of individual rights and of property. He improved the machinery of day to day administration in the land enabling it to deal with its long range problems on the continental scale. He restored much of the royal domain that had been partitioned away, recreating thereby the territorial and financial base for the regular functioning of the monarchy. He was a firm handed strong monarch. [209]

The letter of Bishop Stephen of Tournai addressed to Béla III bears witness to the love of the king for justice; the bishop wrote to the monarch that he had learnt from the

reports he had received about Béla, how much the king loved
and cultivated justice. Béla III's respect for justice and law-
order had become the reputation of the country and the jewel
of the Hungarian crown. [210] (When Margaret and King Béla
were married, the future queen was accompanied by a French
troubadour who in his poems spoke of the civilized conditions he had experienced when visiting the realm. [211] )

The Hungarian clergy did, at first, dislike the young
monarch. They suspected him of being a Byzantine-Orthodox
church sympathizer. The behavior of the clergy and of Archbishop Lukács toward the monarch did not, however, rest
on solid evidence. Béla III looked upon the interests of the
land and loyalty to the Roman See as aims of his kingship.
Pope Innocent III in one of his letters addressed to King
Emory, son and successor of Béla III, had only praise the
personality and the accomplishments of the king. [212] Nor did
he become a blind tool in the hands of the Byzantine imperial court. [213]

A loyal son of the Church, Béla III made endowments
for the bishopric of Nyitra, [214] for the cathedral chapter
in Zagreb; [215] he also attended to the complaints of the cathedral chapter at Zagreb; [216] provided for the Knights Templar
and Hospitallers. [217] He made donations for the Cistercian
monastery at Heiligenkreuz. [218] He established the Szeben
and Szepes deaneries; [219] made endowments for the upkeep
of St. Theodosios monastery in Jerusalem; [220] created firm
foundations for permanent Cistercian settlements in the
realm. [221] The order has been in Hungary since the days of
Géza II; [222] in 1142, the Cistercians entered the land from
Austria and settled down in Cikádor, in Tolna county, at
what is Bátaszék today. Egres at Tolontál; Zirc in the Bakony
hills; [223] Szentgotthárd in Vas county, [224] and Pilis in the
Heves district became Cistercian settlements. [225]

Béla III established the Cistercian order permanently
in order to provide his kingdom with religious-spiritual services, and to improve techniques and conditions in the country's
agriculture. Soon enough, the Cistercian monasteries of
Egres and Pilis were able create daughter houses at Kerc
in the southeastern border region of Transylvania, and in
Pásztó in Heves. [226] Béla III had granted the order the same
privileges it had possessed in France. [227] Many of members

of the Cistercian settlements in Hungary were French monks.[228]

The monks turned the woodlands into agricultural fields; drained marshes, and established well planned farm communities. Their first monastic communities in Hungary were located in the valleys, and soon those valleys turned into little earthly paradises.[229] The Cistercians did transplant to Hungarian soil the more valuable agricultural achievements they had learnt in France.[230]

In the Cistercian order monks and lay brothers shared in the same treatment; no one despised anyone.[231] The lifestyle of the lay brothers may have differed somewhat from that of the monks in that they prayed less and were given more food to eat. They did not rise for night services in the church; they could sleep all night because they needed their physical strength for work. They worked quietly as cooks, taylors, carpenters, black smiths, or ordinary craftsmen. In silence they harvested the wheat from the fields, or did their work as sacristans, shepherds, or even as forestry guards.[232]

The monks also performed physical work.[233] Were they to write books, they hid their names and their identity.[234] It is known that St. Bernard looked upon a monk's worldly erudition with great suspicion, as he had persecuted empty sophistry.[235]

Béla III welcomed the Canons of Prémontré in his realm, who had settled at Várad, Jászó and Lelész.[236] The monarch also confirmed the letter of donation of thirty-five villages made by his mother for the Knights of St. John.[237]

Foreign, mostly French, influence became evident in church construction in Hungary at this time; on account of fire hazard, they began to replace the wooden roof structures of the Romanesque churches with stone barrel vaulting. The Cistercians built no towers for their monastic churches, but did enlarge them by adding transepts.[238]

## NOTES

1. The compiler of the *Chronicon pictum* has one short entry, c. 171, on Béla III; cf. *SSH*, I, 462f.; Á. Kuncz, "Anjou-kori történetíróink kérdéséhez (Remarks on the chroniclers of the Angevin age)," *ITK*, 68 (1965), 358ff.; A. Tarnai, "A

Képes Krónika forrásaihoz (Sources of the Chronicle)," *Memoria Hungariae,* I, 203ff. Arnold of Lübeck, *Chronica Slavorum,* iv:8-9, *MGHSS,* XXI, 115f., in contrast with the rather depressive picture by Iohannes de Piscina, *De transfretatione Friderici, I, ibid.,* XXIX, 339; Marczali, *Geschichtsquellen,* 149f.; Wattenbach, II, 298; Székely, *Magyarország története,* II, 1238ff.; Gy. Moravcsik, "Die byzantinische Kultur und mittelalterliches Ungarn," *SB der Deutschen Akademie der Wissenschaften zu Berlin,* phil.-Gesch., *1955* (Berlin, 1956), No. 4; Gy. Kristó-F. Makk (eds), *III Béla emlékezete* (Béla III Memorial Volume) (Budapest, 1981), 5ff. Hóman Szekfű, I, 649., and II, 247f.; Hóman, *Ungarisches Mittelalter,* I, 403ff.; Moravcsik, *Byzantium,* 89ff.; L. Thallóczy, "III Béla és a magyar birodalom (The realm of Béla III)," in Gy. Forster (ed), *III Béla magyar király emlékezete* (In memory of Béla III, King of Hungary) (Budapest, 1900), 157ff.

2. *SSH,* I, 462,14-16; L. Szilágyi, "Írásbeli supplicatiók a középkori magyar adminisztrációban (Written requests used by the medieval Hungarian government)," *Levéltári Közlemények,* 10 (1932), 157ff., and in *MIÖG* Erg. Bd. VI, 220ff.; Cs. Borsodi, "800 éves a magyar hivatali írásbeliség," *Századok,* 117 (1983), 450ff.

3. Horváth, *Stílusproblémák,* 350ff.; Marczali, *Geschichtsquellen,* 40ff.; Pintér, I, 275ff.; J. Szűcs, "Kézai problémák (Questions concerning Keza)," *Memoria Hungariae,* I, 187ff.

4. Keza, c. 69, *SSH,* I, 183,23-24.

5. E. Mályusz, *A Thuróczy Krónika és forrásai* (The Thuroczy Chronicle and its sources) (Budapest, 1967), 42; G. Karsai, "Névtelenség, névrejtés és szerzőnév középkori krónikáinkban (Anonimity and authorship of medieval Hungarian chronicles)," *Századok,* 97 (1963), 666ff., and the opposing views of Gy. Kristó, "Anjou-kori krónikáink (Hungarian chronicles of the Angevin age)," *ibid.,* 101 (1967), 480ff.; Gy. Kristó-F. Makk, "Krónikáink keletkezéstörténetéhez (Comments on the formation of Hungarian chronicles)," *Történeti Szemle,* 15 (1972), 198ff.

6. Gy. Györffy, *Krónikáink és a magyar őstörténet* (Early Hungarian history in the Hungarian chronicles) (Budapest, 1948), 152f., and 171ff.; Csóka, 593ff.; Pintér, I, 355ff.; Marczali, *Geschichtsquellen,* 83, note 55 in ref. to I. Decius Barovius, *Syntagma institutionum iuris imperialis ac Ungarici* (Claudipoli, 1593), preface.

7. Györffy, 164 and 165, argument based on two documents issued in 1235, and 1243; cf. Szentpétery, *Regesta,* I, no. 608 and 744; on the intellectual background, Mályusz, *Egyházi társadalom,* 307ff.

8. Csóka, 595 and 596; Györffy, 157, said that Master Ákos could have been responsible for the material what is now in cc. 174-80 of the Chronicle (*SSH,* I, 464-71); v. Mügeln, cc. 53-56, provided detailed information: "darnach wuchs der kunig Bela kunig Stephans des wenigen Pruder, an weyszheit an tudent;" *ibid.,* II, 203,3-4; it may be that v. Mügeln relied upon a text that ended with the reign of Béla III. Cf. Horváth, *Stílusproblémák,* 272., and 279.

9. *Ibid.,* 288f., noting that cc. 169-178 and 180 were, really, annalistic entries; Csóka, 567; E. Mályusz, *V István-kori gesta* (Gesta dating to the years of Stephen V) (Budapest, 1971), 13ff., and, for an interesting comparison, P. Classen, "Res gestae, Universal History, Apocalypse: Visions of Past and Future," in R. L. Benson *et al, Renaissance and Renewal in the Twelfth Century* (Cambridge, Mass., 1982), 387ff.

10. Béla-Alexios: *despotes,* was mentioned in the ruling hierarchy of the court; he did participate in a 1166 church synod, whose nomocanon he approved; cf. *MPG,* 140, 252; N. Wilson-J. Darrouzès, "Restes du cartulaire de Jiéra-Xérocho-

raphion," *Revue des études byzantines*, 26 (1968), 24; Gy. Moravcsik, "Pour une alliance byzantino-hongroise (seconde moitoé du XII siècle)," *Byzantion*, 8 (1933), 555ff.; Cinnamus, v:5.

11. *MGHSS*, XXVII, 108; Cinnamus, i:4, v:1 and 5; Gy. Moravcsik, "III Béla és a bizánci birodalom Manuel halála után (Relations between Béla III and Byzantium after the death of Manuel)," *Századok*, 67 (1933), 513ff.

12. Cf. Szentpétery, *Regesta*, I, no. 137; R. Békefi, *A pilisi apátság története* (History of Pilis abbey) (Pécs, 1891), 126.

13. As, for instance, Andrew II (ob. 1235) wanted to restore monetary values of the days of Béla III — see the Golden Bull of 1222, art. 23: "et denarii tales, sicut quales fuerunt tempore regis Belae;" Marczali, *Enchiridion*, 140a. The epitaph of William, son of Margaret, a sister of Béla III, buried in front of the cathedral in Trau, depicted favorably the domestic conditions prevalent in his uncle's realm; cf. D. Farlatus-I. Coletus (eds), *Illyricum sacra*, 8 vols. (Venice, 1851-1819), IV, 341; Pauler, I, 428; II, 168.

14. *SSH*, I, 470,14-15; I, 467,4-5, respectively.

15. "Andreas filius Bele tertii, qui Andreas coronatus est;" *ibid.*, I, 464,9-10.

16. Béla IV "erat enim vir pacificus, sed in exercitibus et preliis minime fortunatus;" *ibid.*, I, 469,4-5. In 1241, the nobles were not too happy to go to war against the Tartars: let the king defend the realm with his Cumans, they said; see Rogerius, *Carmen*, c. 14. "In hac opinione quam plurimi concordabant;" *ibid.*, II, 561,8-9. P. Váczy, "Anonymus és kora (Anonymus and his age)," *Memoria Hungariae*, I, 13ff., noted that Anonymus wrote about early Hungarian history and not of the reign of Béla III!

17. As exemplified by the attempt of Béla III to act as a go between the German and Byzantine courts in 1189; cf. Ansbertus, *Chronica*, in *Fontes Austricarum*, SS, V, 21f.; or, the exchange of letters between Béla III and Henry II of England, in Fejér, II, 245ff.; F. Makk, "Contributions a l'histoire des relations hungaro-byzantines au XIIe siècle," *Acta antiqua*, 29 (1981), 445ff.; Katona, *Historia critica*, IV, 334f.

18. As, for example, Béla IV aimed at the restoration of conditions in the realm as of the days of Béla III — see Knauz, I, 321f.; Szentpétery, *Regesta*, I, no. 626, and compare with Rogerius, *Carmen*, cc. 3-12, *SSH*, II, 554ff., or *RHM*, I, 255ff.

19. *SSH*, I, 462,15-16; Keza, c. 69, *ibid.*, I, 183,25-26.

20. Gy. Györffy, "A magyar krónikák adata a III Béla-kori peticióról (Data in the Hungarian chronicles concerning written requests in the days of Béla III)," *Memoria Hungariae*, I, 333ff. Székely, *Magyarország története*, II, 1245ff. Still, Béla had emphasized the need of placing into writing all legal matters of private nature — see Szentpétery, *Regesta*, I, no. 130; Fejér, II, 198, or Forster, 345f.; L. Erdélyi, *Árpádkor* (Age of the Árpáds) (Budapest, 1922), 165.

21. See his prefatory note, *SSH*, II, 551f.; or, *MGHSS*, XXIX, 547ff.; Marczali, *Geschichtsquellen*, 113f.; Macartney, 43 and 88; Pintér, I, 730f.; Horváth, *Stílusproblémák*, 239ff.

22. *SSH*, II, 552,18-20, though, actually, he provided an interpretation of historical events; see his first fifteen chapters discussing conditions in the country prior to the Tartar invasion in 1241, *ibid.*, II, 552,61; on the Tartars, *MGHSS*, XXIX, 599; Wattenbach, II, 478f.; A. Dempf, *Die Hauptform mittelalterlichen Weltanschauung* (Munich-Berlin, 1925), 62f., and 83.

23. Rogerius, *Carmen*, cc. 6 and 11, *SSH*, II, 556 and 559.

24. *Ibid.*, II, 559,6-10.

25. *Ibid.*, II, 556,7-10; H. Bresslau, *Handbuch der Urkundenlehre*, 2 vols.; 2nd ed. (Berlin, 1912-31), II, 2f., and notes 2 and 3.

26. See Ladislas I's *Decretum I*, a. 9; *Decretum II*, aa. 7 and 14; *Decretum III*, a. 27; the founding charter of Somogyvár abbey, dated 1091, in Szentpétery, *Regesta*, I, no. 24; Erdélyi, *Rendtörténet*, I, 590ff., and 594.

27. Coloman's Jewis Laws, aa. 2-4 and 7, *RHM*, II, 371f.; Tarcal, a. 33; B. L. Kumorowitz, "Szent László vásártörvénye és Kálmán király pecsétes cartulája (Marketing laws of St. Ladislas and Coloman's sealed legal writs)," in *Athleta patriae*, 83ff.; Horváth, *Stílusproblémák*, 107ff.

28. *RHM*, II, 371, aa. 2-4; Tarcal, aa. 42, 51-56 and 81.

29. *Decretum I*, a. 43; *Decretum II*, a. 13; *Decretum III*, aa. 26-27.

30. Cinnamus, v:1; v:5 and 6; vi:11; vii:3.

31. Choniates, *Manuelis Comneni*, v:8 (in Dieten, 168,79-171,40); idem, *Alexii Comneni*, c. 17; *Andronici Comneni*, i:1; *Isaaci Comneni*, i:4 and iii:4 and 8.

32. Moravcsik, *Bizánci források*, 189ff., and 195ff.; idem, *Byzantinoturcica*, vol. I: *Die byzantinischen Quellen der Türkvölker* (Budapest, 1942), 180ff., and 270ff.; Marczali, *Geschichtquellen*, 130ff.; M. Gyóni, *Magyarország és a magyarság a bizánci források tükrében: Ungarn und das Ungarntum im Spiegel der byzantinischen Quellen* (Budapest, 1938), 114ff.

33. *Historia Salonitarum*, cc. 22etc., in Schwandtner, III, 532ff., or in *MGHSS*, XXIX, 570ff.; Macartney, 40f., and 177f.; Marczali, *Geschichtsquellen*, 116ff.; for background, cf. Matthew of Paris, *Chronica maiora*, R.S., 7 vols. (London, 1872-83), VI, anno 1241; Hóman-Szekfű, I, 648 and 656.

34. *Chronicon Venetum*, ix:15:15etc.; x:1:3etc., in Muratori, *Scriptores*, XII, 292ff.; Marczali, *Geschichtsquellen*, 140f.

35. Cf. Hodinka, 288Aff.

7 36. Cf. Ansberti *Historia de expeditione Friderici imperatoris* — "ist der heute gültige Titel einer Schrift, die einst unter dem Namen eines Ansbert ging," and, actually, consisted of three parts; cf. Lhotsky, *Quellenkunde*, 226 —, in *Fontes rerum Austricarum*, Abt. I: *Scriptores*, 10 vols. (Vienna, 1855etc), cited hereafter as *FRASS*, V, 14ff.; Wattenbach, II, 315; Marczali, *Geschichtsquellen*, 148ff. Also, *Chronica regia Coloniensis*, in *MGHSS*, XVII, 723ff.; Wattenbach, I, 341; *Continuatio Claustroneuburgensis II* and *III*, *MGHSS*, IX, 615ff.; *Continuatio Zwettlensis II, ibid.*, IX, 541ff.

37. Arnold of Lübeck, *Chronica Slavorum*, i:2-3, and iv:8, *ibid.*, XXI, 117f., and 171f.; Arnold had continued Helmold's Chronicle, cf. Wattenbach, II, 343ff.

38. *SSH*, II, 525f., c. 11; *ASS*, Iunii V, 315ff., and 319; J. Gerics, "Krónikáink és a Szent László legenda szövegkapcsolatai (Similarities in the texts of Ladislas' *Vita* and the Chronicle)," *Memoria Hungariae*, I, 113ff.

39. *MGHSS*, XXIX, 575,15-27 (c. 24).

40. *Ibid.*, XVII, 796f., and 808f.

41. *Ibid.*, XXIX, 575; also, Farlatus, V, 80f.

42. Cf. Szentpétery, *Regesta*, I, 40ff., nos. 125-167.

43. *SSH*, I, 462,14.

44. *Ibid.*, I, 460,24-26.

45. *MGHSS*, IX, 583, anno 1162; and, *ibid.*, IX, 615, anno 1162. In the *Chronicon pictum*, Géza is listed before Stephen (III) and Béla (III); cf. *SSH*, I, 460,25-25.

46. *Ibid.*, I, 460,16-17, and note 3; Hodinka, 90, 92 and 93; the Kievan Annals listed the (Hungarian) royal brother-in-law of the Kievan prince; see Hodinka, 124A, 126A and 130A.

47. Cinnamus, vi:11 — Moravcsik, *Fontes*, 246; Choniates, *Manuelis Comneni*, v:8, who compared events and narrated them from a different point of view; he said that Manuel had immediately, upon the death of Stephen III dispatched

Béla to take charge of the Hungarian realm; Moravcsik, *Fontes*, 293; Dieten, 170.

48. *Ibid.*, Alberti Trium Fontium *Chronica*, anno 1167, *MGHSS*, XXIII, 849f. Béla-Alexios and his wife had made a donation for the Knights of St. John in Jerusalem; cf. Fejér, V-1, 284ff.; F. Makk, "Megjegyzések III István történetéhez (Comments on the reign of Stephen III)," *Acta historica Szegediensis*, 66 (1979), 29ff.

49. Cinnamus, vi:11; Choniates, *Manuelis Comneni*, v:8 - in Dieten, 168,79-171,40; compare with v. Mügeln's remark: "der kunig Bela, ... an den hingensich vil Vngern und dynten ym und schriben dem keyser von Krichen, das das kungreich von recht zu vngern sein werde;" cf. *SSH*, II, 203,3-6. On the oath of Béla III, see F. Dölger (ed), *Regesten der Kaiserurkunden des oströmischen Reiches*, Reihe A, Abt. I-2 (Munich-Berlin, 1924-1965), II, no. 1465. Interesting is the entry in the *Annales Posonienses*, anno 1185 (!): "Bela ... de Grecia eductus in regem elevatur;" *SSH*, I, 127, and the writ of Pope Alexander III, in Holtzmann, *art. cit* (1926; and, *Századok*, 1959, 443); Hóman, *Ungarisches Mittelalter*, I, 400f.

50. Isaac II to Pope Celestine III, in Darrouzès, 343, or, Moravcsik, *Fontes*, 251f.; Cinnamus, v:5, though, he did have supporters; cf. *SSH*, I, 183; II, 203; F. Makk, "III Béla és Bizánc (Béla III and Byzantium)," *Századok*, 116 (1982), 33ff.

51. "Ungariorum regem elegistis, ... ei obtentu cuiusdam palli, quod nuncio tuo de mera liberalitate donaverat, quantumque districtum a nobis mandatum receperis, coronam imponere noluisti;" cf. Holtzmann, *art. cit* (1926), 401ff., and note *f*. Possession of royal power depended upon the coronation - see Csóka, 422f., and 557, in following Hartvic's *Vita* of King St. Stephen; Gy. Kristó, "Legitimitás és idoneitás: adalékok Árpád-kori eszmetörténetünkhöz (Legitimacy and aptness: some data on the concept of Hungarian kingship)," *Századok*, 108 (1974), 585ff., and 606ff.; compare with the reasoning of Pope Innocent III, in his letters of Sept. 15, and Nov. 22, 1204, *MPL*, 215, 413ab and c; 215, 464bc, respectively. The remark by Walter Map that "puerum iustum haeredem cum omni solemnitate iniunxit," Wright, 74, does not correspond to reality.

52. A Kubinyi, "Királyi kancellária és udvari kápolna Magyarországon a XII század közepén (Royal chancery and court chapel in mid-twelfth century Hungary)," *Levéltári Közlemények*, 46 (1975), 59ff., esp. 110; L. Mezey, *Deákság és Európa* (Medieval Latinity and Europe) (Budapest, 1979), 139.

53. *SSH*, I, 127,14-16; the sister of Géza and Béla III was married to Adalbert, son of Leopold of Austria; cf. Alberti *Chronica*, anno 1135, *MGHSS*, XXIII, 832. Leopold, son of Jasomirgott, married, in 1174, the sister of Béla III; cf. *Chronicon Austriacum*, in Rauch, II, 225, though (and correctly!) the *Continuatio Claustroneuburgensis* II, anno 1175, mentioned the *daughter* of Béla III, *MGHSS*, IX, 616; Hóman-Szekfű, I, 409. Béla III had two sisters: Ilona, married to Leopold of Austria, and Elizabeth, wife of Frederick of Bohemia (brother of the Czech ruler); cf. Hermann Altahensis, *Geneologia*, *MGHSS*, XVII, 377.

54. Cf. Duchesne, *Liber pontificalis*, II, 444f.; also, *MPL*, 200, 58f.; document mentioned in Duchesne, II, 350, dated 1169; Holtzmann, *art. cit.* (1926), letter four.

55. Innocent III wrote that Lukács had other reasons for refusing the coronation, and Alexander III was unable to change the mind of the archbishop; cf. *MPL*, 215, 413c. Rome was angry with Lukács for having ignored the excommunication of the dowager queen - Holtzmann, *art. cit.* (1926), letter three.

56. "... donec Albensi preposito preposituram, quam ei contra privilegium

ab ipso (sc. Bela III) et antecessoribus suis Romanae ecclesiae datum et sacramento firmatum abstulerat;" Holtzmann, letter three; the conclusion that Béla III did assure Rome of his loyalty is based upon the writ of Innocent III to Emery, *MPL*, 214, 227a. The monarch had shown "specialis dilectionis sinceritatem" toward the Roman See; he behaved properly, "illustris recordationis B. quondam pater tuus Ecclesiae Romanae devotior exstitit;" *ibid.*, 214, 227c. Also, the request of some Hungarian nobles to the pope who (in turn) supported Manuel's policies (that is, Alexander III!), in Fejér, III-1, 91.

57. *MPL*, 215, 413c. Also, Innocent III to John of Esztergom, *ibid.*, 216, 50c, and the writs of Celestine III, dated Dec. 13 and 20, 1191, in Jaffé, *Regesta*, II, nos. 16771 and 16773; Fejér, II, 275 and 276.

58. Innocent III to the Esztergom chapter, *MPL*, 216, 51c; and, earlier, Celestine III, dated Dec. 11, 1191, in Jaffé, *Regesta*, II, no. 16770.

59. *MPL*, 216, 50c; Szentpétery, *Regesta*, I, no. 125; Knauz, I, 123; Fejér, III-1, 92, and VII-1, 166; Katona, *Historia critica*, IV, 228.

60. Chronicle, c. 171; Fejér, II, 436; III-1, 92; Pauler, I, 322. Béla III enjoyed the support of churchmen - see for instance, Knauz, I, 188, and of the former supporters of Stephen III, as, for example, of Ompud (Ampud) the Palatine, and *comites* Dionysius and Fulco; cf. Szentpétery, *Regesta*, I, nos. 108 and 116, 126; Dionysius to become the reeve of Bács - *ibid.*, I, nos. 128, 131, 133 -, governor of the Dalmatian seacoast, *ibid.*, I, no. 136, and *ban* of Dalmatia, *ibid.*, I, nos. 138etc.

61. Cf. *RHM*, II, 384, par. 5; Marczali, *Enchiridion*, 124, printed it without numbering the paragraphs.

62. Duchesne, II, 444f., dated it 1169. Manfred of St. George, cardinal of Velabra and papal legate - cf. Jaffé, *Regesta*, nos. 11422 and 11644, who had issued a charter for the hospital in Esztergom of the Knights of St. John, - *ibid.*, no. 15992, - may be held responsible for (drafting of) the constitution.

63. Szentpétery, *Regesta*, I, no. 118, dated it 1171.

64. Known as "sacramentum;" cf. *RHM*, II, 382, conclusion; Marczali, *Enchiridion*, 126f.

65. *Ibid.*

66. Szentpétery, *Regesta*, I, no. 113.

67. "Hoc autem ... ego Sayna Colocensis archiepiscopus laudo et confirmo;" *RHM*, II, 382, par. 10; Marczali, *Enchiridion*, 127b, par. 7.

68. Szentpétery, *Regesta*, I, nos. 111 and 112.

69. L. Székely, *Az 1171-évi bakonybéli összeírás és I András győri püspöksége* (The 1171 Bakonybél census and the episcopate of Bishop Andrew I of Győr) (Győr, 1914), 32f., in ref. to Szentpétery, *Regesta*, I, no. 119.

70. Walter of Albano spoke of Andrew as Colocensis episcopus," *MGHSS*, XVII, 502, who acted as papal legate; Knauz, II, 192, provided no date.

71. Holtzmann (1926), letter three.

72. "Ipsum a periurio ... immunem denunciamus;" *ibid.*, letter two. "Eum ... predicans ... periurium;" *ibid.*, letter three.

73. "Asseruit se regiam magnitudinem et honorem in nullo penitus offendisse etsi forte, quod ipse prorsus inficiatur, te offendit, offensa eius de levi veniam mereatur?" Cf. *ibid.*, letter four.

74. "... pro violentia manum iniectione in clericos eiusdem Strigoniensis;" *ibid.*

75. "Memoratum arhciepiscopatu ... spoliasti et de sua sede eiciens archiepiscopalibus privasti redditibus;" *ibid.* It may be ironic that the *Annales Posonienses* recorded, anno 1187, that *Stephen* of Kalocsa "deponitur;" *SSH*, I, 127,20;

*MGHSS*, XIX, 505; Radó, *Libri liturgici*, 40, in describing the *Annales* in the late twelfth century Pray codex, ff. 9-9', referred to it as "Chronicon noncupatum Posoniense;" see also Wattenbach, II, 210f.

76. On the archbishop's complaint, see Jaffé, *Bibliotheca*, V, 465, no. 280; Makk in *Századok*, 1982, - a most conscientious study of events.

77. See Walter of Albano's writ to the provost of Reichersberg, in *MGHSS*, XVII, 501 (date:1176); Knauz, II, 192, has no date.

78. *Ibid.*, II, 193; invitation for the Hungarian hierarchy to attend, in Mansi, *Concilia*, XXII, 213, 239, and 458.

79. Cf. Szentpétery, *Regesta*, I, no. 133.

80. *Ibid.*, I, no. 142. In 1188, Paul was the archbishop of Kalocsa - see *ibid.*, I, no. 147.

81. "Dux Geyza exiens Ungariam ... intravit Austriam;" cf. *Annales Posonienses*, anno 1186 (!), *SSH*, I, 127,14-16. The daughter of Jasomirgott, Agnes, was the queen of Stephen III of Hungary; cf. Vitus Arpeckius, *Chronicon Austriacum*, in H. Pez (ed), *Scriptores rerum Austricarum*, 3 vols. (Regensburg, 1721-45), I, 1194. On the name of "Austria," see E. Zöllner, *Geschichte Österreichs*, 4th rev. ed. (Munich-Vienna, 1970), 63.

82. "Mater vero eius tenetur captiva in Bronz;" cf. *Annales Posonienses*, anno 1186 (!), *SSH*, I, 127,16-17, and note 5; *MGHSS*, XIX, 573. Pope Alexander III had accused Archbishop Lukács of having disregarded the dowager queen's excommunication; cf. Holtzmann, *art. cit.* (1926), letter three.

83. As it is evident from a writ of Pope Innocent III; cf. Potthast, *Regesta*, I, no. 3725. It may be that Lukács had, together with some other nobles, as, for instance, Lawrence (cf. Jakubovich-Pais, *ÓMO*, 45 and 46) and Ruben (cf. Erdélyi, *Rendtörténet*, I, 605), supported Géza; Makk, in *Századok* (1982), 36.

84. Cf. *Chronicon Austriacum*, anno 1174, in A. Rauch (ed), *Rerum Austricarum Scriptores*, 3 vols. (Vienna, 1793-94), II, 225; Lhotsky, *Quellenkunde*, 202; furthermore, *MGHSS*, IX, 504, anno 1174; *ibid.*, IX, 630, anno 1174; *ibid.*, IX, 541, anno 1174 *Continuatio Claustroneuburgensis II*, anno 1174, spoke of the daughter of the Hungarian king; *ibid.*, IX, 616. Lhotsky, *Quellenkunde*, 189, even though Frederick Barbarossa must have been preoccupied with his Italian policy; see K. Jordan, *Investiturstreit und frühe Stauferzeit* (Munich, 1973), 145, 147.

85. Cf. Hermannus Altahensis *Geneologia*, *MGHSS*, XVII, 377.

86. *Ibid.*, IX, 630, anno 1166. *Chronicon Austriacum*, anno 1166, Rauch, II, 224.

87. Cf. Thomas of Ebendorf, *Chronica Austriacum*, in Pez, *Scriptores*, II, 709.

88. The two Czech brothers "duas sorores, filias regis Ungariae, duxerant;" Przibico, anno 1174, in *Fontes Bohemicarum*, V, 108.

89. The 'soror' of Béla III was married to Adalbert, son of Leopold of Austria - cf. Albericus, *Chronica*, anno 1135, *MGHSS*, XXIII, 832; Ebendorf, *Chronicon*, in Pez, *Scriptores*, II, 711.

90. Przibico, *Chronica*, in *Fontes Bohemicarum*, V, 110.

91. Cf. Gerlaucus Milovicensis *Chronicon Bohemiae*, anno 1174, *MGHSS*, XVII, 686; also, *Continuatio Claustroneuburgensis III*, anno 1174, *Ibid.*, IX, 630.

92. Pez, *Scriptores*, I, 1194f.

93. Magnus Presbyter of Reichersberg, *Chronica*, anno 1176, *MGHSS*, XVII, 501f.; Erna Patzelt, *Österreich bis zum Ausgang der Babenbergerzeit* (Vienna, 1946), 124ff.; Hampe, *Hochmittelalter*, 241f.; text in Doeberl, IV, 88, no. 31a.

94. *Cont. Claustroneuburgensis III*, anno 1176, *MGHSS*, IX, 630.

95. *SSH*, I, 127,18-19; Gerlaucus, *Chronicon*, anno 1177; he was a continuator of Cosmas of Prague, see Wattenbach, II, 320f.

96. *SSH*, I, 127,14-16; *MGHSS*, XIX, 573, anno 1186.

97. Pauler, I, 417.

98. *SSH*, I, 127,19-21.

99. *Ibid.*, I, 340; my book, 54.

100. "Wata comes caecatur;" *SSH*, I, 127,19.

101. Gerlaucus, *Chronicon*, anno 1177, *MGHSS*, XVII, 689; *Continuatio Claustroneuburgensis III*, anno 1175, *ibid.*, IX, 630; K. Lechner, *Die Babenberger* (Vienna-Graz, 1976), 167f., and 184; Jordan, 147.

102. Cf.Otto of Freising, *Gesta Friderici*, iii:16, *MGHSS*, XX, 426,47-49; Hampe, *Deutsche Kaisergeschichte*, 161.

103. "Deus per imperium exaltavit ecclesiam;" Freising, *Gesta Friderici*, iii:13, *MGHSS*, XX, 424; Hampe, *Kaisergeschichte*, 148. Palacky, I, 472f.

104. On this, see *Annales Marbacenses*, anno 1184, in *MGHSS*, XVII, 162.

105. *Continuatio Zwettelnsis*, anno 1180, *ibid.*, IX, 541; Katona, *Historica critica*, IV, 300.

106. Anno 1182; cf. *MGHSS* XVII, 202; Smiciklas, Codex, II, 192. The German fiance died in 1184 - see *Annales Marbacenses*, anno 1184, *MGHSS*, VII, 162.

107. Cf. Burckhardi Uspergensis *Chronicon*, anno 1181, in *ibid.*, XXIII, 358; and, *Chronica sancti Petri Erfordensis*, anno 1184, *ibid.*, XXIII, 230. The emperor and the Hungarian monarch may have been allies - according to *Continuatio Zwettlensis II*, anno 1181; cf. *ibid.*, IX, 541.

108. Cinnamus, vii:3 (CB, 299). The arguments of D. Obolensky, *The Byzantine Commonwealth* (London, 1971), 160, and of Calandon, 492, probably based on Manuel's speech in 1173 — cf. C. Manasses, in Moravcsik, *Fontes*, 158; Krumbacher, 376ff.; and, on the talk of Patriarch Eustathios, in *MPG*, 136, 973ff.; Moravcsik, *Fontes*, 162f.; Krumbacher, 536ff., — that Béla III's Hungary was a vassal state of Byzantium, remain unconvincing. After all, Béla had only made the promise that he would not fight against the interests of the Byzantine court; cf. the writ of Isaac II to Pope Celestine III, in Moravcsik, *Fontes*, 251f.

109. "Bela Dei gratia rex primogenitus regis Hungariae," that is, during the reign of his father, Andrew II, in 1230; cf. Szentpétery, *Regesta*, I, no. 592; Wenzel, *ÁUO*, VI, 486f., no. 305; Katona, *Historia critica*, IV, 255 (and, V, 568).

110. Choniates, vii:3 (in Dieten, 220,10-222,86). E. Molnár, *A magyar társadalom története az őskortól az Árpád-korig* (A history of Hungarian social formation from ancient times to the age of Árpád), 2nd ed. (Budapest, 1949), 333, may be wrong in saying that during Manuel's reign Greek influence (had) peaked in Béla III's Hungary; even if the gifts of Béla III were looked upon as "dues" by the Greek court, cf. Hóman-Szekfű, I, 413, Cinnamus (CB, 299) said that the Hungarians were considered as the allies of Byzantium!

111. Cf. *Chronicon Venetum continuatio, MGHSS*, XIV, 67f.; Katona, *Historia critica*, IV, 233; Brand, 31, though, according to Dandalo, x:2:3 (Muratori, XII, 311), Zara only in 1190; the *Supplementum ad historiam ducum Venetorum, MGHSS*, XVII, 90, rendered the date of 1186.

112. Katona, *Historia critica*, IV, 280; Szentpétery, *Regesta*, I, no. 134, dated 1182; Smiciklas, II, 179f.; Fejér, II, 172, no. 178.

113. Dandalo, x:2:14-15.

114. Katona, *Historia critica*, IV, 329f.; Szentpétery, *Regesta*, I, no. 147 (anno 1188); Knauz, I, 137. According to the entries in Fejér, II, nos. 200 and 203, it happened in 1187, a date confirmed by Andreas Ventii *bereves*, a. 1187, *MGHSS*, XIV, 72.

115. Szentpétery, *Regesta*, I, no. 138, dated it 1183; Smiciklas, II, 178.

116. Pope Celestine III, dated March 13, 1192; cf. Jaffé, *Regesta*, II, no. 16834; Fejér, II, no. 173; *Pontifices Salonitani et Spalotenses*, in D. Farlati (ed). *Illyrici sacra*, 5 vols. (Venice, 1760-75), I, 335; Thomas Spalotensis, *Carmen*, c. 22 (this time) in *Monumenta spectantia historiam Slavorum meridionalium*, 48 vols. (Zagreb, 1868-1918), XXVI, 72f., c. xxii.

117. Choniates, *De imperio Alexii Comneni*, cc. 1-2 (in Dieten, 223,1-225,55).

118. *Ibid.*, c. 3.; Dieten, 225f.

119. *Ibid.*, c. 16.

120. *Ibid.*, c. 17 (in Dieten, 267f.); S. Kyriakidis, *Eustazio di Tessalonica, la espugnazione di Tessalonica* (Palermo, 1961), 56; Moravcsik, *Byzantium*, 91f.

121. Choniates, *De imperio Andronici Comneni libri duo*, i:1, in Dieten, 277; *Continuatio Zwettlensis II*, aa. 1182, 1183, *MGHSS*, IX, 542; Pauler, I, 327.

122. Choniates, *Alexii II*, c. 18, Dieten, 269, 273f.; idem, *Andronici Comneni*, i:1; Brand, 46, 49. M. Angold, *The Byzantine Empire, 1025-1204: A Political History* (London, 1984), 217f.

123. Nicholas of Esztergom, in Szentpétery, *Regesta*, I, no. 133 (a. 1181), 136 and 138 (a. 1183).

124. Cf. Moravcsik, *Fontes*, 247.; J. Bödey, "Rilai szent Iván legendájának magyar vonatkozásai (The portion of St. Ivan de Rila legend pertinent to Hungary)," *Egyetemes Philologiai Közlöny*, 64 (1940), 217ff.

125. Choniates, *Andronici Comneni*, i:1, in Dieten, 277.

126. Anonymus, *Gesta Hungarorum*, c. 24, *SSH*, I, 65.

127. Idem, c. 44, *ibid.*, I, 90,5-11.

128. Ansbertus Austriensis *Gesta*, in *Fontes Austricarum, Scriptores*, V, 22; Anonymi Caietani *Descriptio*, in P. Riant (ed), *Exuviae sacrae Constantinopolitanae*, 2 vols. (Geneva, 1841-43), I, 151f.

129. Cf. Magnus Presbyter, *Chronicon*, *MGHSS*, XVII, 511; *Chronicon Venetum*, *ibid.*, XIV, 68; Chalandon, 401ff.; Brand, 160ff.

130. Choniates, *De imperio Isaaci Angeli*; *libri tres*, i:4 (CB, 368; Dieten, 367,26-368,46); Georgius Acropolita, *Annales*, c. 8, *MPG*, 140, 997; Dandalo, x:2:3; the Hungarian record speaks of the "soror" of Géza who had married on Byzantine soil, cf. *SSH*, I, 127,6.

131. Fejér, II, 437.

132. *MPG*, 140, 1007f., c. 11. M. Gyóni, "Niketas Akominatos lakodalmi költeménye (The wedding poetry of N.A.)," *EPhK*, 47 (1923), 79ff. Moravcsik, *Bizánci források*, 195, named him Akominatos, but following Choniates' own testimony (CB, 230,22), corrected himself: "es war irrig, ihn, wie es früher üblich war, Niketas Akominatos zu nennen." Cf. his *Byzantinoturcica*, I, 270.

133. Choniates, *Isaaci Angeli*, i:5, in Dieten, 369f.

134. *Ibid.*, i:5, Dieten, 369, 371, 372; and, the writ os Isaac II on the attack by Béla III upon Serbia, in J. Darrouzès (ed), *Georges et Démétrios Tornikés: lettres et discourse* (Paris, 1970), 336ff.; Katona, *Historia critica*, IV, 255f.; M. Gyóni, "A legkorábbi magyar-bizánci házassági kapcsolatok kérdéséhez (On the earliest Hungaro-Byzantine marriage contacts)," *Századok*, 81 (1947), 212ff.

135. Chalandon, 385ff.; Hampe, *Kaisergeschichte*, 210ff.

136. *SSH*, I, 127,20-21 (anno 1186!); *MGHSS*, XIX, 573.

137. Fejér, II, 230.

138. Hóman-Szekfű, I, 412, spoke of the older sister of Manuel who died in 1157; Béla III must have asked for the hand of Manuel's granddaughter; cf. R. Kerbl, *Byzantinische Prinzessinnen in Ungarn zwischen 1050 and 1200, und ihr Einfluss auf das Árpád Königreich* (Vienna, 1979), 148ff.

139. She was a religious who had taken the veil and could not leave the monastery; cf. *MPG*, 137, 1132bc.

140. Brand, 170f.

141. Choniates, *Isaaci Angeli*, in Dieten, 371, 372f., 374.

142. *Ibid.*, 374. Ostrogorsky, 321, 323, and note 3.

143. Cf. Ansbertus, *Gesta Friderici I*, in *Fontes*, SS, V, 14ff. Mayer, *Kreuzzüge*, 129ff.; Ostrogorsky, 323f.; on preparations for the crusade, see the exchange of letters between Henry II of England and Béla III, in Fejér, II, 245ff. Richard of London reported on the meeting of Béla III with the emperor — see his *Itinerarium peregrinorum*, i:20-21, *MGHSS*, XXVII, 199f.; A. Cartellieri, "Richard Löwenherz im Heiligen Bande," *HZ*, 101 (1908), 1ff.; Haller, III, 263ff.

144. Dandalo, *Chronicon*, x:2:20.

145. The crusading knights requested aid from Béla III; cf. Wenzel, *ÁOU*, I, 83f.; Arnold of Lübeck, *Chronica*, iv:8, *MGHSS*, XXI, 171f.; see the 149 page article by S. Riezler, "Der Kreuzzug Kaiser Friedrichs I," *Forschungen zur deutschen Geschichte*, 10 (1870), 1ff.

146. Cf. Godyslaw Basco, *Chronicon Poloniae*, *MPH*, II, 467ff., c. 39; Iohannes Dlugossius, *Excerpta a fontibus incertis*, *ibid.*, IV, 9ff., anno 1188; *Chronica Polonorum*, *MGHSS*, XIX, 563; Katona, *Historia critica*, IV, 369f., and V, 534f.

147. Cf. Halich-Volhynia Annals (Ipatius MS), anno 1188, in Hodinka, 288A-Bff., though, as Hodinka noted, 277ff., the annalists provided no reliable dates.

148. Basco, c. 40, *MPH*, II, 535; Halich-Volhynia Annals, a. 1181; Katona, *Historia critica*, IV, 344f.

149. Basco, c. 41; Hodinka, 298B, anno 1189.

150. *Ibid.*, 288A Bff., a. 1188.

151. *Ibid.*, 302A B, a. 1190.

152. Cf. Matthias Miechovius, *Chronica Polonorum*, iii:22, in P. Pistorius (ed), *Poloniae historiae corpus*, 3 vols. (Basel, 1582), II, 68f.

153. See Basco, c. 42, *MPH*, II, 536f.; Hodinka, 307AB, anno 1190; Gy Kristó, *A feudális széttagolás Magyarországon* (Feudal diversions in Hungary) (Budapest, 1979), 55.

154. Miechovius, iii:26; Basco, 42; Katona, *Historia pragmatica*, I, 678. Also, Vincent of Cracow, *Historia Polonica*, iv:18, and, earlier, iv:15-16, *MPH*, 421, and 412f., respectively; J. Dlugossus of Cracow, anno 1193, *ibid.*, IV, 12.

155. Katona, *Historia pragmatica*, I, 661.

156. Cf. *Gesta Henrici et Ricardi regum Angliae*, in *MGHSS*, XXVII, 108, anno 1186; Poole, 362, note 1; *Chronicon Martini Turonensis*, a. 1186, in E. Martene-U. Durand (eds), *Veterum scriptorum et monumentorum collectio*, 9 vols. (repr. New York, 1968, V, 917ff., esp. 1026.

157. Sayles, 355. G. Brito, *Historia de vita et gestis Philippi Augusti*, anno 1186, in A. Duchesne (ed), *Historiae Francorum coaetanei Scriptores*, 5 vols. (Paris, 1636-49), V, 73.

158. *RHM*, I, 245. Roberti s. Mariani Autissiodorensis *Chronicon*, anno 1186, *MGHSS*, XXVI, 248; R. Parisiensis *Imagines historiarum*, anno 1186, *ibid.*, XXVI, 275.

159. Marczali, *Enchiridion*, 128.

160. Cf. Gervasius Cantuariensis *Chronica maiora*, 2 vols. R.S. (London, 1879-80), I, anno 1186; Gransden, 253ff.

161. *MGHSS*, XXVI, 248,42-43.

162. Cf. *RHM*, I, 245; and compare with note 217, *infra*.

163. "De alienis hospytibus regis de ultrasyluas xv milia marcum; *RHM*, I,

245, a. 6; and, the diploma of Andrew II for "hospitibus Theutonicis Ultrasylu-anis datum," in Marczali, *Enchiridion*, 144ff.

164. Katona, *Historia critica*, III, 522.

165. *RHM*, I, 246, aa. 6-7.

166. "... populus terrae facit uictum plenarium;" *ibid.*, I, 246, a. 8; Marczali, *Enchiridion*, 130, note 8.

167. *RHM*, I, 245f., aa. 2-4; compare with *Census Romanae sedis in Hungaria*, *ibid.*, I, 247 (anno 1192).

168. *Ibid.*, I, 246, a.5.

169. One can perceive a most civil tone from the writ of Henry II, in Fejér, II, 245f., and from the reply of Béla III, *ibid.*, II, 246f.; it was good diplomacy, cf. Katona, *Historia pragmatica*, I, 661f. The *Chronicon pictum*, c. 44, confused her with the Queen of Béla I; cf. *SSH*, I, 298, note 8.

170. *Ibid.*, 463; H. Svrita ( = J. Zurita), *Indices rerum ab Aragoniae regibus gestarum ab initiis regni ad annum MCDX* (Caesaraugustae, 1578), I, 84; H. Blancas, *Aragonensium regum commentarii* (Caesaraugustae, 1588), 153f.

171. For the text of the Golden Bull, 1222, see *RHM*, II, 412ff.; Marczali, *Enchiridion*, 131ff. J. Deér, "Der Weg zur Goldenen Bulle Andreas II von 1222," *Schweizer Beiträge zur allgemeinen Geschichte*, 10 (1952), 104ff.; A. Timon, *Ungarische Verfassungs- und Rechtsgeschichte* (Berlin, 1904), 124f.

172. Hóman-Szekfü, II, 85ff.; J. Szekfü, *Ungarn: eine Geschichtsstudie* (Stuttgart, 1918), 50f.; A. v. Tasnády-Nagy, "Der Geist der ungarischen Verfassung," *Ungarische Jahrbücher*, 22 (1942), 1ff.; A. Négyessy, "The Magna Carta, 1215, and the Bulla Aurea, 1222," *The New Hungarian Quarterly*, 5 (New York, 1965), 135ff.; T. Bogyay, "A 750 éves Aranybulla (The 750th anniversary of the Hungarian Golden Bull)," *Katolikus Szemle*, 24 (Rome, 1972), 289ff.

173. Katona, *Historica critica*, V, 304f., quoting a writ of Andrew II to Rome - cf. Szentpétery, *Regesta*, I, no. 162, and compare it to no. 356; this letter may be *dubiae fidei*, though based upon an authentic document.

174. *SSH*, I, 463,10; Gebhardt, I, 352.

175. Constance married, upon the death of Emery, the German emperor Frederick II, and she died in 1222; cf. Svrita, I, 103; Gebhardt, I, 340 and 352.

176. Arnold of Lübeck, *Chronica*, iv:8; cf. *MGHSS*, XXI, 171f.

177. Cf. *Chronica regia Colonensis*, anno 1189, *ibid.*, XVII, 796.; *Continuatio Zwettlensis*, anno 1189, *ibid.*, IX, 543f.; H. C. Peyer, "Gastfreundschaft und harmonielle Gatlichkeit im Mittelalter," *HZ*, 235 (1982), 265ff.

178. "... qui (quae) vulgo Uieruelt dicitur, ultra Bosonium urbem; cf. Ansbertus, *Gesta*, in *Fontes Austricarum, Scriptores*, V, 15. On Ansbertus, see Lhotsky, *Quellenkunde*, 226f., - the *gesta* actually consist of three parts; on the Ansbertus-Tageno contact, both *ibid.*, and Wattenbach, II, 315f.

179. Cf. Arnold of Lübeck, *Chronica*, iv:8, *MGHSS*, XXI, 171,12-19.

180. *Ibid.*, XXI, 171,21-26. Ansbertus, *Fontes*, V, 19.

181. Arnold, *Chronica*, iv:8, *MGHSS*, XXI, 171,32-36.

182. *Ibid.*, XXI, 171,26-32.

183. See also A. Chroust (ed), *Quellen zur Geschichte des Kreuzzuges Friedrichs I*, vol. V of the *Rerum Germanicarum Scriptores* (series nova); Berlin, 1928), 1ff., esp. 26ff., and 33, 34 and 37f.

184. *MGHSS*, XXI, 171,36-38, and note 28.

185. Ansbertus, *Fontes Austricarum*, V, 19. Also, Hampe, *Kaisergeschichte*.

186. See Anonymus, *Gesta Hungarorum*, cc. 44 and 50, in *SSH*, I, 88f., and 101; on Anonymus, cf. P. Váczy, "Anonymus és kora (Anonymus' historical

background; the times he lived in)," *Memoria Hungariae*, I, 13ff., and Gy. Kristó, "Szempontok Anonymus gestájának megítéléséhez (Some comments on the historical value of Anonymus Gesta Hungarorum)," *Acta historica Szegediensis*, 66 (1979), 45ff.

187. Hóman-Szekfű, I, 414, who became archbishop of Esztergom, *ibid.*, I, 432f.; Szentpétery, *Regesta*, I, no 210. Ugrin, bishop-elect of Zagreb, *ibid.*, no. 140, and bishop of Győr, *ibid.*, no. 152, 155, 172-75; Emery I had to defend Ugrin before the pope in 1199, *ibid.*, no. 187.

188. *MGHSS*, XXI, 172,9-13.

189. *Ibid.*, XXI, 172,13-14; *Chronica regia*, anno 1189.

190. Choniates, *Isaaci Angeli*, ii:3-4; in Dieten, 402, 403f., 408f.; also, Arnold, iv:9.

191. Arnold, iv:12, *MGHSS*, XXI, 173; Ansbertus, *Gesta*, in *Fontes*, V, 28.

192. *Ibid.*, V, 22; Chroust, 51ff., and 61.

193. Dandalo, *Chronicon*, x:2:20-21 and 28; x:3:4; supplement to *Historia Venetorum*, aa. 1186 and 1192, *MGHSS*, XIII, 90f.; supplement to the Justinian Chronicle, anno 1190, *ibid.*, XIV, 90f.; writ of Pope Lucius III, in Jaffé, *Regesta*, II, no. 15196.

194. Smiciklas, II, 264 and 268f.

195. Katona, *Historia critica*, IV, 372f.; J. Koller, *Historia episcopatus Quinqueecclesiarum*, 3 vols. (Posonii, 1782-84; vol. 7, Pest, 1812), I, 304.

196. Katona, *Historia critica*, IV, 369. Master Cathapanus, prelate and royal chancellor (1192-97), at the time of Emery's second coronation - cf. Smiciklas, II, 267; Pauler, II, 8; A. Huber, "Studien über die Geschichte Ungarns im Zeitalter der Árpáden," *Archiv für österreichische Geschichte*, 65 (1884), 156ff.

197. Choniates, *Isaaci Angeli*, iii:8, in Dieten, 434.

198. *Ibid.*, 446f., and 450,58-452,19; Choniates, *Imperii Alexii Comneni fratris Isaaci Angeli libri tres*, i:1, in Dieten, 479 (CB, 597).

199. Cf. letter of Pope Innocent III, dated Jan. 29, 1198, in *MPL*, 214, 8; Potthast, *Regesta*, I, no. 315; Katona, *Historia pragmatica*, I, 692; Hóman, *Ungarisches Mittelalter*, I, 438.

200. See *Continuatio Claustroneuburgensis II*, anno 1196, *loc. cit.*; *Chronicon pictum*, c. 171; Alberti Trium Fontium Chronica, in *MGHSS*, XXIII, 873; *Annales Colonienses maiores, ibid.*, XVII, 808. Also, the Zagreb Chronicle, *SSH*, I, 210f., and 211, note 1.

201. Hóman-Szekfű, I, 417.

202. Pintér, I, 731.

203. Dated June 14, 1198; in Fejér, II, 315.

204. Roberti *Chronicon*, anno 1197, *MGHSS*, XXVI, 257.

205. Hóman-Szekfű, I, 408ff.; L. Thallóczy, *III Béla király magyar birodalma* (The Hungarian realm of Béla III), in the *Magyar Könyvtár* series, ed. A. Radó (Budapest, 1906), 12ff.

206. Cf. Knauz, I, 321f.; in fact, in another document, Béla IV will refer to Béla III as "the great." Cf. Wenzel, *ÁUO*, VIII, 129f., no. 90; also, *ibid.*, VI, 164, no. 104, and Szentpétery, *Regesta*, I, no. 144.

207. Cinnamus, vi:11; Keza, c. 69.

208. Wright, Walter Map, ii:7; Szentpétery, *Regesta*, I, no. 680, - issued by Béla IV, in reference to Béla III.

209. *Ibid.*, I, nos. 126-127, 130-31, 133, 136, 144, etc.; Forster, *III Béla*, 345.

210. Cf. Stephen of Tournai to Béla III, in *MPL*, 211, 334f.; Fejér, II, 189f.; Katona, *Historia critica*, IV, 241f.

211. Cf. *MGHSS*, XXVII, 208.

212. Innocent III on the merits and accomplishments of King Béla III, *MPL*, 214, 227; Fejér, II, 312; Katona, *Historia critica*, IV, 475.

213. Cinnamus, vii:3.

214. Cf. Szentpétery, *Regesta*, I, no. 136 - document most probably prepared by the Cistercians; Fejér, II, 203; Katona, *Historia critica*, IV, 289f.

215. Szentpétery, *Regesta*, I, nos. 131 and 140; Fejér, II, 122 and 188; Smiciklas, II, 179f.; Wenzel, *ÁUO*, XII, 45, and XI, 44.

216. Smiciklas, II, 176ff.

217. Szentpétery, *Regesta*, I, no. 132 (transcript of which in Fejér, II, 382), and no. 155; Fejér, II, 283; Katona, *Historia critica*, IV, 410; J. Delaville le Roulx, *Cartulaire général de l'Ordre des Hospitaliers de S. Jean de Jérusalem* vol. I (Paris, 1894), 222f.

218. Fejér, II, 300; Wenzel, *ÁUO*, XI, 58f., though, Szentpétery, *Regesta*, I, no. 159, says that it is a spurious document.

219. See the writ of Pope Celestine III, dated Dec. 20, 1191, Jaffé, *Regesta*, no. 16774; Knauz, I, 141; Fejér, II, 176; also, the reference made by Card. Gregory, papal legate, *ibid.*, II, 250. E. Mályusz, "Geschichte des Bürgertums in Ungarn," *Vierteljahrschrift für Wirtschafts- und Sozialgeschichte*, 20 (1928), 357ff.

220. Cf. A. Theiner, (ed) *Vetera monumenta historiam Hungariae sacram illustrantia*, 2 vols. (Rome, 1859-60), I, 9f.

221. Szentpétery, *Regesta*, I, no. 137; Fejér, II, 202; A. Békefi, *A pilisi apátság története* (History of the abbey of Pilis) (Pécs, 1891), 126; Katona, *Historia critica*, IV, 288ff.; also, I. Horváth, in *Vigilia*, 39 (1974), 611ff.

222. L. J. Lekai, *The White Monks* (Okauchee, Wisc., 1953), 38. Gy. Györffy, "Les débuts de l'evolution urbaine en Hongrie,' *Cahiers de civilisation médiévale*, 12 (1969), 127ff., and 253ff.

223. L. J. Lekai, "Zirc 800 éve (The 800th anniversary of the Abbey of Zirc)," in D. Farkasfalvy (ed), *Ciszterci lelkiség* (Cistercian spirit) (Eisenstadt, 1982), 7ff.

224. Established in 1183; cf. Péterffy, *Concilia*, II, 275; Szentpétery, *Regesta*, I, no. 505.

225. Békefi, *Pilisi apátság*, 126; Hóman-Szekfű, I, 388ff.

226. Péterffy, *Concilia*, II, 273; Katona, *Historia critica*, IV, 333; E. Fügedi, "Die Entwicklung des Städtewesens in Ungarn," *Alba Regia*, 10 (1969), 101ff.

227. Szentpétery, *Regesta*, I, no. 137; Fejér, V-1, 289; and, II, 202; F. Hervay, "Nyolczáz éves a pilisi apátság (800th anniversary of Pilis abbey)," *Vigilia*, 49 (1984), 830ff.

228. As, for example, the charter of Somogyvár, 1091; cf. Marczali, *Enchiridion*, 100ff.

229. E. Schwartz, "750 Jahre Stift St. Gotthard in Ungarn," *Cisterzienser Chronik*, 45 (1933), 97ff.

230. Lekai, *White Monks*, 209ff.; P. Boissonade, *Life and Work in Medieval Europe* (London, 1949), 132ff.

231. For comparison, see D. Knowles, *The Religious Orders in England* (Cambridge, 1950), 64ff.

232. Lekai, *White Monks*, 145ff.

233. *Ibid.*, 229ff.; O. Ducourneau, "De l'institution et des usdes convers dans l'ordre de Citeaux," *Saint Bernard et son temps*, vol. II (Dijon, 1929), 139ff.

234. Karsai, *Századok*, 97 (1963); H. Beumann, "Die Historiographie des Mittelalters als Quelle für die Ideengeschichte des Königtums," HZ, 180 (1955), 449ff.

235. St. Bernard, *De diligendo Deo*, in *MPL*, 182, 973ff.; idem, *Sermones in Cantica*, esp. sermo 20; cf. *ibid.*, 183, 785ff.

236. Hóman, *Ungarisches Mittelalter*, I, 405ff.; Potthast, *Regesta*, I, no. 293. Om Norbert, see Bernhardi, *Lothair III*, 83ff.; on the Canons of Prémontré, see *Vita Norberti*, cc. 9 and 13, *MGHSS*, XII, 678ff., and *Vita Godfredi*, c. 3, *ibid.*, XII, 513ff.; S. Weinfurter, "Norbert von Xanten - Ordenstifter und 'Eigenkirchenherr'," *Archiv für Kulturgeschichte*, 59 (1977), 66ff.

237. Szentpétery, *Regesta*, I, no. 155.; compare to A. J. Forey, "The Emergence of the Military Order in the Twelfth Century," *Journal of Ecclesiastical History*, 36 (1985), 175ff.

238. Cf. Th. v. Bogyay, "L'iconographie de le 'Porta speciosa' d'Esztergom et ses sources d'inspiration," *Revue des études Byzantines*, 8 (1950), 85ff.; J. Horváth, "Ein weiteres Fragment der Esztergomer Porta speciosa," *Acta archaeologica*, 32 (1980), 345ff.; compare to E. Adam, *Baukunst des Mittelalters*, pt. *II*, vol. 10 of *Ullstein Kunstgeschichte* (Frankfurt/M-Berling, 1963), 38ff.; W. Giese, "Zur Bautätigkeit von Bischöfen und Äbten des 10 bis 12 Jahrhunderts," *Deutsches Archiv*, 38 (1982), 388ff.; and, Ch. Brooke, *The Twelfth Century Renaissance* (London, 1969), 90ff.; K. Bosl *et al*, *Eastern and Western Europe in the Middle Ages* (London, 1970), 175ff.

# XI

# Hungarian Kingship: Legislation, Jurisdiction and Administration

In eadem civitate sub eodem rege duo populi sunt,
et secundum duos populos duo vitae; ... secundum
duos principatus duplex iurisdictionis ordo
procedit.

*Stephen of Tournai*

Atto of Vercelli made a note in his treatise on the letter of Saint Paul to the Romans that a secular prince ( = ruler) received his authority: *auctoritas*, from God regardless whether he was a Christian ruler or a pagan potentate. [1] Ladislas I of Hungary asserted in his letter to the abbot of Montecassino that service of "wordly" events made it difficult for him to work in an honest and close relationship with the visible head of the Church. [2] Wipo, chaplain and biographer of Emperor Conrad II, said that a monarch — in this instance, the emperor himself —, was the vicar of Christ. [3] According to Stephen of Tournai, the "realm" was the Church itself; the ruler was Christ; and, in this realm, the "orders" of the people ( = inhabitants) were constituted by the clergy and laity, in a society that had led a two-fold: spiritual and secular, life guided by clerics and monarch, in accordance with divine and human law. [4]

Peter Damian in his letter addressed to Anno of Cologne, argued that both *regnum* and *sacerdotium* were institutions established by the Almighty, therefore, they needed each other (very much). The privileges and obligations of secular authority to maintain justice and punish offenders, rested upon the commission it received from God. [5] Manegold of Lautenbach explained a similar concept in his writ to Eberhard of Salzburg: "Rex enim non nomen est naturae, sed officii, sicut episcopus..." [6]

It makes good sense that Stephen I of Hungary expressed a very like idea in his *Admonitiones*, a political handbook

addressed to his successors on the throne. The king stated
that the concept of Christian kingship rested upon a relationship with God and faith in, and loyalty to, the Church. [7]
The monarch lived by faith to have strength to behave
properly toward bishops, county-reeves, nobles, and migrants (*hospites*) among his people. [8] The monarch held a
supernatural contact with God, and this supernatural tie
became evident in his dealing with advisors at the court,
and his attitude toward the administrators of ecclesiastical
and secular justice. [9] In accordance with Christian tradition,
King Stephen I wrote, the monarch must be a Catholic,
ruler of his people, anointed and crowned by the bishops
of the country. [10]

The idea of Hungarian kingship formulated by King
Stephen gained confirmation through the legislative acts
of Ladislas I, [11] Coloman the Learned, [12] the decrees of
two synods of Esztergom, [13] and in the ecclesiastical con-
stitutions issued by Andrew I, [14] and Stephen III. [15] Still,
the code of laws of Stephen I; the legislation promulgated
by Andrew I, Ladislas I, Coloman the Learned, and Stephen
III, and the articles of the church synods firmly agree that
the (Hungarian) ruler, though he made the final decision, [16]
could not take decisive (religious-political) action without
proper consultation with members of the hierarchy and
the consent of the nobles, — very much like a Benedictine
abbot, [17] or, earlier, Pepin I, king of the Franks. [18] On
the other hand, it was the privilege of a dying Christian
monarch to make his reeves swear oaths of loyalty to his successor. [19]

The Hungarian monarch, therefore, had to be Catholic — his titles were *christianissimus rex*; *rex magnificus*, —
and could not become a selfish tyrant. [20] A king unworthy
of his office could be dethroned; [21] however, they would
not tolerate an unlawful conspiracy against the monarch:
were someone, in fact, to know about such a conspiracy but
fail to report it, they would punish him canonically, sentence him to death, while confiscating all of his chattel in
a secular court of law. (It may have been characteristic of
conditions in the realm at this time that an intriguer who
had spread false rumors — about the king's politics, or his
death —, had a similar fate awaiting him. [22] ) The ruler

was the defender of the faith and of the Church, [23] for whom the clergy had offered prayers, [24] and who could, together with his reeves, attend Mass in a tent chapel on Sundays and holidays. [25] The king had punished those who refused to accept the verdict handed down by the regional ordinary (in an ecclesiastical court of law); and, it was the monarch who had obtained from the bishop the names of all excommunicated persons (in a particular bishopric). [26]

The monarch is the guardian and multiplier of ecclesiastic wealth; were someone to doubt the legal valid standing of ecclesiastical landholdings (and chattel), they excommunicate him. [27] Church prebends and privileges established by King Stephen I were to remain in effect, but offices and privileges granted, or determined, by his successors (could) revert to the royal court. Were, however, a parish or a monastery to receive such a privilege, only surplus goods and chattel were to be returned. [28] The first Catholic monarchs had provided chalices and vestments for the parish churches. [29] The bishop and clergy greeted the king who paid a visit to a parish, or spent some time there in transit, with the kiss of peace. [30] The laws of Ladislas I stated that when the king visited a monastery, the monks had to await his departure from the church before exchanging the kiss of peace with him. [31]

Contemporary German sources, as, for instance, annotations in the Quedlinburg Annals, [32] or Wipo's funeral oration over the grave of Emperor Conrad II, depicted the latter as the lord of Europe and of the entire world. [33] One of the biographers of Adalbert of Prague said that just as Rome had for posterity preserved the body of the Prince of the Apostles, so it was Rome that nominated the lord of the world. [34] Therefore, in accordance with the remarks of Berno of Reichenau, the German emperor was the supreme propagator of Christian cause in the world. [35] Peter Damian had expressed similar views in one of his letters to Emperor Henry III (saying, in fact, that the emperor was lord over everybody and everything [36] ), but argued that, in order to have a harmonious understanding in the ruler's council between ecclesiastical and secular interests, the participating advisors needed to cooperate with each other at the meetings of the ruler's council. [37]

## 1. *Royal Legislation and Episcopal Authority*

The anointed and crowned Hungarian monarch was, in a similar manner, chief legislator of his country; his ideal was the heavenly King. He followed in the footsteps of ancient lawgivers and contemporary Christian monarch by striving for the spiritual and physical well-being of his people; "quoniam unaqueque gens propriis regitur legibus." [38]

Legislative power belonged to the monarch, but he had exercised that right with the consent of the Royal Council — reserving for himself the privilege of final decision. He legislated because of his royal authority; or, agreed to an act of legislation because of a request made to him by the Senate. [39] The council had no permanent organization; its members included those who had been invited by the king to attend. [40] Still, once a year, the population itself had formed a party to royal law making. At the annual law-day in Székesfehérvár, the nobles together with the free social element were to assert their grievances and have an influence on legislation. [41] On the other hand, at the (gathering of the) *congregatio generalis* — one instance of its meeting had been recorded in the sources —, the Royal Council played the leading role; the people had an inactive role in it. [42]

The Royal Council (it is from the Laws of Stephen I that we know about the *regalis senatus*; [43] or, about the sessions held by the *concilium regale*, [44] attended by the representatives "de singulis villis," [45] and about the activities of a *tocius senatus* — its function in the field of law making [46] ), in accordance with the Admonitions of King Stephen I, [47] and according to the text of the legislative acts of Coloman the Learned, participated in decision making as a body of advisors, and not as legislators. [48]

The Council continued to exist without permanent memberhisp; but, at the annual law-day (diet) of 1298, held by Andrew III, it had determined that two bishops and a number of specially designated nobles be appointed to the inner circle of the monarch, in order to aid him by their presence, or to advise him in making legal and diplomatic decisions, in making appointments, and distributing gifts. [49]

In the days of Stephen I, the king was the legislator:
"statuimus regni; [50] "volumus, ut;" [51] "decernimus;" [52] the
king "decrevit (decrevimus) legem;" [53] and, "in hoc regali
decreto statutum est;" [54] "secundum decretum regalis
senatus;" [55] and, not infrequently, he agreed with the requests of his advisors, "secundum decretum senatus statuimus," [56] or "consensimus petitioni totius senatus." [57]

The king was Supreme Justice, and defender of the
Church (in his country), [58] who wore a sword to symbolize
his power to punish the wrong. [59] Were he to appear in the
county court (of law), two regional judges joined him, and
he adjudicated controversial legal cases with their aid. [60] Outside of his court he also administered the law at the annual
law-day in Székesfehérvár. [61] The king may exercise his
judicial authority in person, or through his personal official; a noble (*miles*) found guilty of a crime by the county
court of the reeve may appeal his sentence to the king. [62] In
the royal court, the king pronounced sentence in important
cases brought before him, after listening to the arguments
of both parties involved in the case. The record has it that
the royal court and the court of a bishop provide refuge for
anyone fleeing legal persecution. [63]

The head official at the royal court was the Palatine,
*comes palatii*, and Keeper of the Royal Seal, who had to
leave the seal behind when departing from the court.[63a] From
his own court, but without the royal seal, he could issue un-
official writs. The Palatine was, first of all, head official
and judge of all (who were) attached to the royal curia; only
at the court could he hand down judgment in any other case.
On the other hand, anyone may visit with him at his home
to request that he hear the case (presented) in the royal court
(of law). If the individual cited did not appear before him
in court at the appointed time, the individual lost his suit
and paid a fine of five calves. Were the defendant to appear
before the Palatine, but left the court before awaiting sen-
tencing and did not return when a *preco*: royal messenger,
was sent after him, the defendant lost his suit in court and
paid a double fine of compensation. The Palatine could
also cite any county judge who handed down false judgments,
to appear before him and make a reckoning. [64]

The Palatine's permanent deputy was *comes curiae regis*,

who later did become an independent official. [65] The Palatine was also the head tax collector and economic overseer
for the king's court; before whom all county reeves had to
appear on St. Michael's day (Sept. 29), to render a reckoning of their stewardships. [66]

There were three types of courts of law in medieval Hungary: (1) the Royal Court; [67] (2) the county courts,[68] and
(3) the manorial courts. [69] The justices did not, by themselves, impose the sentence, but together with their fellow
judges, who had taken the oath to serve in the courts of law
of the land to the best of their abilities. [70] In court, the accuser had to be of the same social rank as the accused; witnesses bearing testimony in court had to be of the same social stratum as the defendant. [71]

The regional county-fort system of administration had
already existed in the times of Stephen I, but he had to improve it by altering it to serve the needs of his people. [72] Out
of these changes there developed a county court of law system, [73] which was based on the administrative structure
of the county (royal fort district) headed by the reeve, [74] the
deputy reeve, [75] and the appointed judges. [76] The fort-
district county court (of law) handed down legal decisions
concerning the non-noble social stratum, and intervened
in court cases involving the less important judicial cases of
the nobility. [77] Later on, it would hand down decisions involving the nobles, — except when the Palatine visited the
county court, or when the social status of the defendant
(as, for example, clergyman) exempted him from the jurisdiction of the county court. [78]

The *hospites* (or, recently arrived migrants) living in
specially designated communities, could rightfully elect their
own justices every year, who, and twelve elected jurors, acted as judge in the community, — except in criminal cases
which were handled by the judge of the county court of law. [79]

The temporal and spiritual lords handled, by themselves
or through their officials, legal decisions in their (manorial)
courts in instances involving the inhabitants of their respective regions. [80] In matrimonial and other church related
instances the bishops held jurisdiction. [81] (The Széklers
and "Saxons" in Transylvania; [82] in Hungary (proper) the
Cumans, Jews, and "Saxons of Szepes" have courts of law
under their own jurisdiction. [83] )

In the Hungarian courts of law proceeding were, at this time, conducted orally. A court case began with a writ — sending the seal of the court (of law) to invite the defendant to appear in court; the oldest form of a "writ" consisted of sending the seal of the court to the party concerned. [84] At a later date, the accuser: plaintiff, by sending two *pristaldi*, had requested that the defendant appear in court. [85] In the twelfth century, representatives of the *loci credibiles* (as, for instance, canons constituting an episcopal chapter at the bishop's cathedral; or, a chapter of canons), or the court issued sealed writs instructing the accused to appear before it in a particular legal case. [86] The defendant had to make his appearance on a specified date, or send his relative, or a representative, instead. If the defendant failed to appear in court without a reason within a week of the designated date, the court fined him; if the accused did not attend court after being summoned three times, the court condemned him *in absentia*. It could happen, though, that the court had issued seven summons to the accused before pronouncing the final sentence (in the case). [87]

In court, the plaintiff presented his case at first, while the defendant awaited his turn. Both were under oath, and supported their assertions with notarized statements and by witnesses familiar with the case; or, they had to submit to an ordeal. [88] The witness had to be of the same social background as the defendant for whom he bore testimony. A secular person could not testify against a cleric; nor could a slave against a freeman; a Christian had to take along a Jewish witness to bear testimony in court (of law) against a(nother) Jew. [89]

If the plaintiff and the defendant, or both, were Cumans, only their fellow Cumans may testify on their behalf. The same rule applied to the "Saxons." [90]

The witness took his oath in a church — to tell the truth. [91] If he testified in regards to property rights, he took his oath on the property involved (in the case), or, by holding a handful of dirt taken from the property over his head. Eventually, all witnesses took their oaths together in a church, or at a specified location. [92] Jewish witnesses swore by the Book of Moses. [93]

The ordeals consisted of tests by fire, water, or trial by

combat. [94] The first two were usually held at a bishop's see, before the bishop's chapter of canons; however, most of the ordeals were held in front of the cathedral chapter of Várad. Before the ordeal began, the accused had fasted for three days; and, prior to that, his hands were tied together and sealed, lest he may apply preventive medicine for burning pain of the palm of his hands. On the day of the ordeal he made his confession and, accompanied by a priest, went to the place of the trial. [95] There, by answering questions asked by the clergymen, he confirmed his innocence. Then, he took in his hands a piece of burning hot iron (previously blessed by the priest) and carried it to a certain destination. Thereafter, they tied his hands again and sealed them for three more days. If the hands were healed after three days, the court pronounced him not guilty; if not, or if the seal was broken, the court declared him guilty and sentenced him. [96]

Detailed information about ordeals in Hungary may be gained from the Várad Register of recorded court cases dating back to the first half of the thirteenth century. It not only throws some light upon the function of the court(s) in the realm, but upon contemporary political and religious institutions, as well as cultural conditions in the land. The Várad Register is also a treasure house of information on family names and given names; of names of regions, of towns and cities, on the grounds that both plaintiffs and defendants, and their witnesses from every part of the country went to Várad to seek justice. The original Register is lost, but Friar George, bishop of Várad and later governor of Transylvania and Cardinal, had the text(s) published in Kolozsvár, in 1550. [97]

In a court case of trial by combat, both parties had to obtain the king's, or the Palatine's, permission to proceed (meaning that only the monarch or the palatine could authorize such a trial), to be held in their presence. The parties concerned had to appear in person at the trial, or send a hired champion; both parties were allowed to use shield, lance, two swords and a knife for weapons during combat. [98] If the defendant in the case had been accused of treason, or of minting false money, he (or, his companion) could only fight in a shirt against a fully armed and dressed oppo-

nent. The defeated party was declared guilty, — and, for
this reason, strict punishment awaited the champion who
had lost the engagement on purpose. [99]

Thieves and murderers were condemned to lose all of
their property, — out of which the price of value of one third
went to the plaintiff, and two-thirds to the court. Perhaps
this was the reason that the two parties frequently attempted to
seek a negotiated settlement out of court. Death awaited
the condemned thief, robber, murderer and faithless person. In a case like this, the chattel of the party found guilty
were scattered about, and he, and members of his family,
were to be mutilated. The sentence handed down by the
judge(s) was carried out by the sargeant of the court. The
condemned party could appeal the sentence, but if he lost
the appeal, he had to reimburse the court for expenses. [100]

Contemporary Hungarian churchmen looked upon their
first monarch as an Apostle asserting his authority in both
temporal politics and ecclesiastical matters. [101] King Stephen
I had obtained approval from Pope Sylvester II to establish
bishoprics and monasteries, and to name bishops and abbots (*kegyúri jog*). [102] In the early eleventh century, ten Hungarian dioceses were established, headed by the archbishop
of Esztergom; Sebastian was the first Esztergom archbishop,
who was buried at Pannonhalma in the year 1001. [103]

During the First Synod of Esztergom, Seraphim was
archbishop, whose official status was confirmed in the resolutions reached by the Synod of Tarcal; [104] the ordinaries
of Kalocsa and Zagreb were, in the early twelfth century,
bishops. [105] According to the status report of the reign of
Béla III, the ordinary of Bács-Kalocsa was, however, already
an archbishop, who had the bishops of Csanád, Várad,
Transylvania, and Zagreb under his jurisdiction. [106] It is
known from the same source that the archbishop of Esztergom controlled the bishoprics of Eger, Vác, Pécs, Győr,
Veszprém, and Nyitra. [107] In Dalmatia, — at this time under Hungarian rule, — the city republics of Zara and Spalato had their own archbishops. [108]

The Zagreb bishopric was established by King Ladis-
las I, [109] and from the assertion in the king's *vita* that he had
created two bishoprics, one may draw the conclusion that
the other bishopric was the one of (Bihar-)Várad. [110] Sixtus

appears to be the first bishop of Bihar [111] (and of Várad) in the diplomas of Coloman the Learned; [112] the *Chronicon pictum* says on the occasion that Prince Géza had dispatched the bishop of Várad (together with the worthless Vata) to the king. [113] The same source also says that Ladislas had freed the daughter of the bishop of Várad from the hands of a marauding Cuman [114] (though, in a few lines below the chronicler noted that the woman freed by Ladislas was not the daughter of the bishop of Várad). [115]

Therefore, the bishopric of Bihar-Várad had been mentioned on various occasions in royal documents and in the *Chronicon pictum*. According to the latter, King Ladislas had a monastery founded in the honor of the Blessed Mother at Várad, [116] though, as St. Katona correctly argued, the chronicler did not report on the establishment of a bishopric. [117] But to quote from the sermons of the fifteenth century Hungarian Franciscan friar, Pelbárt of Temesvár, local tradition did preserve the notion that an épiscopal community: cathedral chapter, had been founded by the king at Várad. [118]

Coloman the Learned founded the bishopric of Nyitra, [119] the same Coloman who had, in 1106, renounced, in favor of the Roman See, his right of investiture in the realm. [120] The origins of the Nyitra bishopric date back to the ninth century, when Adalrammus of Salzburg had consecrated the first bishop of Nyitra. [121] Adalrammus' successor, Archbishop Liutprand of Salzburg, exercised jurisdiction over *castrum* Nyitra (Nitrava) and, in 850, placed it under the protection of the Blessed Mother of God. [122] A writ attributed to Pope Eugene II, but today held as spurious, made mention of the bishop of Nyitra; [123] and, in early 880, Pope John VIII spoke of the bishop of Nyitra whom "electum episcopum consecravimus sanctae ecclesiae Nitriensis." [124]

One may accept as valid the arguments of St. Katona who wrote that the new bishopric ceased to exist after its first two bishops had died, and it was neither restored, nor terminated by King St. Stephen I, in a sense that its territory may have formed a part of the archdiocese of Esztergom. [125] It may be intimated that King Coloman issued a charter for the bishopric, [126] while a legal brief concerning the possessions of the (arch-)abbey of Pannonhalma recorded the name of Gyárfás (alias Geruasius), bishop of Nyitra, "Nitriensis episcopus." [127] In a (legal) writ dated 1111, and published by L. Fejérpataky, there appears the name of "Willermus grammaticus," a member of the episcopal chapter of Nyitra, [128] the existence of which episcopal chapter is evident from article 22 of the Tarcal Synod. [129] (In 1229, Ugron of Kalocsa created out of his ecclesiastical province the bishopric of Szerém(ség) alongside the Danube with Kő as its see, where a monastery had already existed, named Bánmonostor; [130] and, in 1234, Andrew II created the Bosnia diocese. [131] )

During the reign of Ladislas I, Bács was the seat of the archdiocese of Kalocsa, [132] whose archbishop was next in rank to the primate of Esztergom; it was the archbishop of (Bács-)Kalocsa who, with special dispensation, had crowned Béla III king. [133] The archbishop of Esztergom was the primate of Hungary who, *ex officio* (1) crowned the kings of Hungary; [134] (2) summoned episcopal synods for the kingdom; [135] (3) was the spiritual director of the royal family, [136] and (4) as primate, held under his jurisdiction the royal lands located in the ecclesiastical province of (Bács-)Kalocsa. [137] In Dalmatia, where every city state had its own bishop, there were, according to the status report of the reign of Béla III, twenty dioceses headed by the metropolitan of Spaleto. [138]

In the episcopal cathedrals all clerical orders, from tonsured clerics to ordained clergymen, were represented and they were expected to lead exemplary and regulated lives (that is, to live according to a rule). It ought to be noted that the Hungarian term for "canon" is *kanonok*, while a clerical student was called *diák*, studiosus, though the Hungarian word derives from *diaconus*: deacon. They all dined in common and lived under the same roof. [139] In this regard, the letter of Aurelius Augustinus on communal life; [140] the Rule of Benedict of Nursia; [141] and the guidelines of Chrodegang of Metz in the eighth century had a lasting impact upon the communal manner of clerical living. [142]

In Hungary, the *káptalan*: chapter of canons attached to a bishop's cathedral dates back to the times of Charlemagne and plays an important role in public life. (*Káptalan* = chapter of canons in Hungarian, derived from *capitulum*, that is, *caput*: portion of a chapter of the Rule of St. Benedict read during common meals in a monastic refectory. [143] ) It was at these cathedral chapters that the Frankish monarchs had their legislative acts: *capitularia*, drafted; [144] and, the Hungarian kings had their first legislative enactments prepared or put in a final form more than likely by their bishops' clerics. [145] As it had in fact been duly noted by the acts of the First Synod of Esztergom, the bishops must have had their chapters of canons draft canonical guidelines. [146]

Since the times of Stephen I, members of the *ordo pontificum*: hierarchy, included *seniores*, who were members of the royal legislative council. [147] The chapter of canons at Székesfehérvár (not a bishopric) established by Stephen I, acted as the guardian of the royal Crown and coronation insignia; [148] some of the chapters of canons became *loci credibiles*, acting as public notaries in the realm. [149]

Ladislas I and Coloman the Learned made the juridical innovation that they recognized the local ordinary (in the diocese) as judge having jurisdiction in both the diocesan and the county courts of law, [150] and authorized the bishop to be judged only by his ecclesiastical peers (or, by the king) were he be too lenient with his married and undisciplined clergy. [151] The county reeve was obliged to support the directives of the local ordinary. [152]

It may be characteristic of the synodical decisions that if a married priest — married before his ordination to the priesthood — were elected bishop, his wife had to renounce their married state and refrained from living under the same roof with her husband - now a(n elected) bishop. [153] It was, evidently customary to speak of married priests in spite of the fact that the Second Synod of Esztergom had discouraged the ecclesiastical function of married clergy; evidently, also diocesan bishops were elected to their sees. Of course, the question may be raised, by whom were they elected? - by the lesser clergy, or by the leading lay element of the bishopric? [154]

The diocesan bishop, elected and ordained, had one-fourth of his personal annual income at his personal disposal (discretionary fund); the rest of it went to his clerics; for the maintenance of church buildings; the poor and for the upkeep of visitors. [155] It is of interest to note that if a bishop cared only for his own family and children, — whom he must have made rich while neglecting his ecclesiastical functions —, the monastery he established to serve as the burial place for himself and members of his family, were to be assigned *gratis* to his successor in the see, who had it at his own disposal. [156] In other words, clerical celibacy was taken seriously in case of bishops; nor did public opinion tolerate unlawful heaping of goods (or, of private wealth) by churchmen. Were a bishop to make himself rich in office, or enrich members of his own family, it was his successor who inherited it all, presumably for the benefit of the bishopric. [157]

A Hungarian bishop had to provide with books all of his clerics and parishes; the canons at his cathedral had to transcribe books so that every parish (church and clergy) had its (their) own copies. [158] The bishop maintained two retreat homes at the county-fort, one for men, another for women. [159] The bishop had his own *prestaldus* who collected revenue due to the episcopal household. [160] A guest cleric at the bishop's residence may be requested to work as the bishop's live-in secretary. [161] A bishop in transit may say Mass in a tent. [162] Were a thief to flee to the bishop's cathedral, he avoided hanging, but remained a serf of the Church for the rest of his life. [163]

The king's messenger was not permitted to take away the horse of the person traveling to the bishop's court (of law). [164] The latter meted out punishment in accordance with church canons; for example, it ordered a sinner to fast for three, seven, twelve, or forty days; [165] it ordered physical punishment for a poor person guilty of a crime, and saw to the person's excommunication. [166] Were someone to die in the state of excommunication, the bishop could refuse him a Christian burial. [167]

Jews might reside in episcopal cities only. [168] The bishop was expected to oversee his chapter of canons and to keep under observation all abbots of the monasteries in his diocese. He had the right to visit every monastic community, [169] with the exception of the abbey of Pannonhalma. [170]

The bishop might exercise his jurisdiction in the county court of law through his archdean, *iespris*: archpriest, who knew canon law and the outline of ecclesiastical canons: *breviarium*, by heart. [171] Were someone to observe the archpriest being drunk in public, the individual was to receive three young male calves from the archpriest. [172] The question may, of course, be asked, why? Did the archpriest pay the witness to keep him from talking, or to thank him for reprimanding him? The archpriest lived in the cathedral chapter house, where everyone had to speak in Latin. [173]

Were a student cleric from abroad to join the chapter, [174] he could leave his possessions for his son to inherit only if he had previously made his will, before he had joined the chapter of canons. [175] (It is actually the right to dispose of one's own personal possessions and to make a will that distinguished the canon from the monk, though a canon had to make and keep the vows of celibacy and obedience. [176] )

In matters of education, there had to be a school for young clergymen at the bishop's see, and students had to be accepted for schooling by the bishop or his archpriest; after receiving tonsure, the clerical student was exempt from temporal jurisdiction. [177] If, for example, a cleric in minor orders committed theft for the first time, it was his master at school who beat him with a broom; it was only when he committed theft for a second time that the bishop defrocked him and turned him over to secular justice, where he could be sentenced to death. [178]

If an unordained cleric decided to marry, his sons of that marriage obtained land from the lots of the bishopric. [179] An uneducated person must not be ordained to the priesthood; [180] were someone to educate someone else's slave for the clerical state (the slave may be, upon ordination, emancipated), he had to pay (a fine of) fifty calves to the slave's owner. [181]

Tonsured clerics and ordained clergy may not wear secular clothing. [182] A cleric from abroad seeking acceptance by a Hungarian bishop must have letters of recommendation with him from his former bishop. [183] Deacons and priests must not marry. [184] If a cleric ( = deacon) had married before his ordination, he could, according to the canons of the First Synod of Esztergom, keep his wife. [185] (On this, the earlier synod of Szabolcs had recommended consultation with Rome. [186] ) A priest must not, however, marry for a second time, nor may he marry a widow or a live-in mistress for the first time. [187] If he did, he had to perform penance and return the woman to her family, who could marry her off.

If the mistress was a slave woman, she had to be sold by the priest and the sale price given to the bishop. [188] The priest still suffered temporary suspension from his duties. The insubordinate stubborn priest was to be excommunicated by the ordinary. [189]

Were a parish priest to take money unlawfully from the Church, he repaid it threefold. [190] If he set free a thief who had sought refuge with him, the priest himself became a slave. [191]

## 2. *Administrative Matters and Social Stratification*

During the eleventh century, the Hungarian custom had developed that the heir to the throne could be elected and crowned (junior) king in his father's reign, and exercise direct authority over a portion of the kingdom (that had been) assigned to him. [192]

The royal coronation was held at Székesfehérvár, always performed by the archbishop of Esztergom, — with the exception of the coronation of Béla III in 1173, carried out with special papal permission by the archbishop of Kalocsa. [193] The queen was crowned by the bishop of Veszprém. [194] During the coronation ceremony, the monarch took an oath to the effect that (1) he will honor and keep all commandments of the Church and religion; and (2) govern his people justly. [195] At a later date, the monarch put his promises into writing and issued a Letter of Coronation, *diploma inaugurale*. [196]

In accordance with the laws of Stephen I, royal dignity had its strength in the Catholic faith, [197] and the ruler had ordered his people(s) to lead decent and peaceful lives. [198] He likewise subjected his people(s) to the strict observance of secular laws. [199] The monarch controlled all three branches of government; he was, in one person, the people's judge, [200] the commander of the armed forces, [201] and the executor of the laws of the realm. [202]

The seat of government was the king's court, *curia regis* (or, *curia regalis*), where (1) the headmen of the realm held their meetings with the monarch, taking counsel with him, or, consulted without him; (2) laws were promulgated; (3) taxes collected by the reeves paid, and (4) those cited to appear in front of the king in judicial matters made their appearance.[203] The court was headed by the Palatine, *comes curialis maior* (or, *comes palatinus regalis*; *palatinus comes*), who earlier used to be the judge of the inhabitants of the royal domain - the king's deputy who adjudged personal and legal questions brought by the nobles and freemen (of the domain) before the monarch. [204]

It was the palatine who, upon orders received from the king (1) visited the entire kingdom; held court of law in the districts passing judgment over thieves, robbers and murderers;[205] handed down legal sentences in ecclesiastical courts (of law) also. [206] (2) He led the armed forces into battle during the king's illness or absence. [207] (3) He presided over the annual law-day (field-day held at Székesfehérvár) during the absence of the monarch, and over any important meeting held at the royal court with nobles and freemen. [208] (4) He acted as judge of the nobles, [209] (5) of the Cumans living in the realm, [210] and was guardian of liberties in the realm. [211] According to the concessions made by Stephen III to churchmen, it may be assumed that the position of the palatine was only filled by the consent of the nobles. [212]

The Justiciar of the Realm, *comes curialis* [213] was the palatine's deputy, [214] also known as *comes curialis regis*, [215] or *iudex curiae.* [216] Earlier, the justiciar's authority had been limited to a certain segment of the population in the royal domain, though, eventually, he became the full time judge at the royal court, and was granted title of office of Justiciar of the Kingdom. Directly under him in rank stood the treasurer, *tavernicorum regalium magister*, who (1) administered, as head chamberlain, the royal treasure; [217] (2) supervised all of those who were engaged in levying and collecting royal revenues, as, for example, (a) salt and toll officers; (b) selected stewards and inhabitants of the royal domain; and (c) tax auditor 'counts of the chamber;' at a later date (3) the treasurer exercised judicial authority among the urban population. [218]

The chancellor, *cancellarius aulae regalis*, headed the king's chancery; [219] he was also known as *notarius*. [220] It was his duty (1) to draft and issue official correspondence and documents; [221] (2) to keep the royal seal. [222] The office was always held by a member of the hierarchy. [223] The growth of literacy in the country only enhanced the prestige of the chancellor, [224] whose deputy was the vice-chancellor, [225] usually the archdean (archpriest) of Székesfehérvár. [226]

Other officials included the count of the Queen's court, *comes curialis reginae*, acting as judge of the queen's court; [227] the head buttler, *dapiferorum regalium magister*: [228] the master of royal stables, *magister cubicularium regalium*: [229] head of the king's wine supply, *magister pincernarum regalium*. [230] The king's head messenger, royal hunters, and the royal sword bearers concluded the official roster. [231]

All dignitaries were selected from the ranks of the nobles; they all participated in the meetings of the royal council and could influence decisions made by the monarch. [232] One may recall that because of the lack of good roads and public transportation, it must have been nearly impossible to speak of a fully centralized government. That is why the monarchs were constantly on the road moving about all over the country; and were dispatching officials and itinerant justices to assure administration and to maintain order and (common) law in the land. [233] Royal messengers carried royal directives to all parts of the country and proclaimed them to the regional population. The local administration was in the hands of regional officials. [234]

The main institution of the district government was the royal fort-county system (originally, royal fort districts: *provinci, comitatus*), as it had existed since the days of King St. Stephen. [235] The county's center was the royal fort, — it represented royal authority —, surrounded by lands of the fort: royal domain administered by the royal reeve, *comes parochianus* (or, *comes castri*; *comes provincialis*). [236] If the district had an established geographical designation, the county reeve was known by that designation, as, for example, the reeve of Pozsony - *comes Posoniensis*; or, the reeve of Bihar (*Bihoriensis*). [237] The reeve was the military protector of the district (county), its judge, guardian of its security, and collector of its revenue for the royal fort. [238]

The reeve exercised his authority at the court-in-the-fort: *curia comitis castri*; [239] there, and together with him, the *dux* commanded the county's armed contingent, and the judge of the county court (of law): *comes castri curialis*, carried on with his proper functions. Both of the latter officials could act as deputies of, and for, the reeve: one, in the administration of military affairs, and the other in the field of law and general administration of the county. [240] The *bilochus*, a direct appointee of the monarch, had cooperated with the three county officials and acted as the judge of thieves and murderers in the district. [241] The nobles and free men of the county were exempted from the reeve's jurisdiction, [242] though in matters of taxation, the reeve (and his officials) held them under their jurisdiction. [243]

The territorial subdivisions of the county included (1) the fort itself and its surroundings administered by the *maior* (or, *castellanus*); [244] (2) the hundred and the *ten* ( = one-tenth of the hundred) district headed by the *centurio* and the *decanus* (*decurio*), respectively, who collected taxes and acted as judges in minor court cases in their own particular districts. [245] The affairs of the villages were managed by justices of peace (*villicum maiores*), who were appointees of the county officials. [246] Certain villages, especially those with a large migrant population: *hospites*, had the right to elect their on mayors. [247] Eventually, various self-governing areas had developed within the county, as, for instance, (1) self-administered towns directly under the king's jurisdiction, and exempted by royal writ from the jurisdiction of the county. [248] (2) The settlements of (or, regions settled by) the Cumans; [249] the areas of the Széklers; [250] (3) the localities of German settlers (as, for example, the Saxons of Szepes and in Transylvania); [251] and, finally, the landholdings of various ecclesiastical princes. [252]

The inhabitants of the country were, according to the types of their landholdings, divided into 'estates.' If the landholding(s) dated back to the times of the conquest (the 890's) — as former tribal lands were broken up in the days of King Stephen I —, it would be retained by the previous holder; or, it could be granted anew to another receiver (*szállásbirtok*). [253] Grants could be made by the monarch from his royal domain (or, goods), given for services rendered to the country (*adománybirtok*). [254]

The two types of land (or, office) holdings made no distinction upon their bearers in society. Whether the land- or office-holders had possessed ancient, or recent land (or, office) grants, they were considered as members of the free

social structure (of landholders) in the population. [255] The
free landholders seemed to have had a little more prestige
based upon their office(s); they were known as *seniores,* [256]
*principes,* [257] or *optimates.* [258] In other words, they constituted the country's nobility: *iobagiones* barones (*regi*)
*maiores,* [259] to be distinguished from the free landholding
element of the *milites,* [260] alias *servientes regis,* [261] who had
constituted the social stratum of the lesser (non-nobles),
and yet free landholding group ( = element) of *minores.* [262]

In the system of 'estates,' members of the ecclesiastical
hierarchy enjoyed the usage of landholdings, which obliged
them, in turn, to provide military assistance to the king in
time of war, like any other free man. [263]

The system ( = social structure) included all the officials
of the realm and of the counties, some of whom may have
played roles in the early tribal structure, as, for example,
heads of family clans. On the other hand, a public office
could not be inherited; holding of public offices was based
upon individual merit(s), [264] and, for that reason, it is not
possible to talk, in the age of the Árpáds, of the estates of
churchmen, nobles and free landholders; however, one may
speak of the 'estates' as members of the 'nation.' [265]

There developed, at the same time, another social stratum with various echelons in structure among the free members of the 'nation' and the non-free segment of society: (1)
free men who held no land of their own, but rented use of
the landholdings of others, which they were obliged to cultivate and perform, for the landholders, some services in
return. This segment was connoted with the county structure.
Its members were called fort-serfs: *iobagiones castri,* who
held no lands of their own, but did cultivate the lands that
were under the administration of the fort. They, in return,
owed military service to the fort. [266] Presumably, they cultivated those lots themselves together with their servants,
although, in time of war, the servants had to do the field
work for them. [267] (2) The fort population of *civiles,* or
*castranses,* likewise enjoyed the use of land lots that were
under the administration of the fort, but owed the latter
no military service; [268] they tilled the soil, provided transportation, built roads, constructed and maintained bridges,
and had their share in armaments production and in other

useful crafts. [269] Their responsibilities included provision of lodging for county officials in transit, and payment of taxes (in money, or in kind); they inherited those responsibilities from father to son. [270]

In the county there lived free peasants who were not landholders; and, nobles, too, who had exempted from the reeve's jurisdiction. The free peasants who lived on and cultivated the lands of the nobility, and/or of the free landless agricultural population, had constituted the lower social stratum of the county's social structure. They paid taxes to and for the upkeep of the fort and constituted the non-landholders element. If and when they had, however, fulfilled their obligations, they were free to move about in the entire realm. These free peasants were the descendants of the agricultural *iobagioni, coloni, villani,* or "conditionales," who had lived in the mid-Danuban region at the time of the Hungarian conquest in the late ninth century. [271]

At the lowest social level were the servants: *servi,* who lived on the lands of the free; they were bound to the soil, and were at the mercy of their landlords. They were known as *udwarnoci,* and could be sold with the land, — if and when the landholding changed hands —, and performed tasks that needed some practical training. A sub-group of these servants were domestics who lived in the household(s) of the landholder lord, and were (or, would be) sold any time with, or without, the land. [272]

The town population lived in accordance with its own law. The Germans had, for example their own judges, their elected clergy who were exempted from outside, that is, county supervision. They held exemptions in trade, held free marketing privileges, and paid low taxes. They were, in turn, obliged to provide lodging for the king and queen and the royal retinue in transit; and, to render gifts to the monarch on New Years' day and on other specific occasions. [273]

## NOTES

1. "... ostendit ergo his verbis apostolus manifeste, quoniam omnis potestas, tam apud paganos quam apud Christianos, a Deo ordinata est, sive propitio, sive irato;" cf. Atto of Vercelli, *Expositio in epistolam Pauli ad Romanos,* xiii:1, *MPL*

134, 258c. Ivo of Chartres, *Decretum*, v:378, expressed a similar idea: "duo quippe sunt, ... quibus principaliter mundus his regitur: auctoritas sacra (sacrata) pontificum, et regalis potestas;" cf. *ibid.*, 161, 438a, actually, a quote from a writ of Pope Gelasius I to Emperor Anastasius, - *ibid.*, 59, 42a, and compare with the emperor's letter "Ad episcopos Dardaniae," *ibid.*, 59, 61ff.; Caspar, *Päpste*, II, 47 and 57f. Gratian's *Decretum*, in Ae. Friedberg (ed), *Corpus Iuris Canonici*, 2 vols. (Leipzig, 1879-81; repr. Graz, 1959), I, xv:7:3.

2. For text, cf. Fraknói, I, 403f.; Ganzer, 44; my book, 101; nobody can separate two powers operating in one "realm:" "... libenter accipistis quod lex Christi sacerdotali vos subicit, atque istis tribunalibus subdidit?" Cf. Ivo of Chartres, *Decretum*, v:5 (quote from Gregory of Nazienzen), *MPL*, 161, 323c; no secular power may legislate over religious authority - idem, iv:187, *ibid.*, 161, 307b; D. Baker, *Relations between East and West in the Middle Ages* (Edinburgh, 1973), 77ff.

3. "... ad summam dignitatem pervenisti, vicarius es Christi;" cf. Wipo, *Vita Chounradi*, *MGHSS*, XI, 243,75; on Wipo, see Wattenbach, II, 10ff., and Manitius, III, 378.

4. "Civitas ecclesia; civitatis rex Christus; duo populi duo in ecclesia ordines, clericorum et laicorum; duae vitae, spiritualis et carnalis; duo principatus, sacerdotium et regnum; duplex iurisdictio, divinum ius et humanum. Redde singula singulis et convenient universa;" cf. Stephen of Tournai's *Summa decretorum*, ed. J. F. v. Schulte (Giessen, 1891), xxii:1; O. Gierke, *Political Theories of the Middle Ages*, tr. with an introd. by F. W. Maitland (Cambridge, 1900), 11ff., and 113, note 22.

5. "Quod iustitiae rigor regno conservaret;" cf. Peter Damian, *Opusculum*, lvii:1, *MPL*, 145, 819ff.; compare with his previous assertion: "... qui utriusque dignitatis auctor est, pacis aeternae digna verbis praemia largiatur;" his *Epistolae*, iii:6, *ibid.*, 144, 295b.; Wattenbach, II, 224f.; Manitius, III, 68ff.

6. "... quisquis ergo amissae dignitatis postmodum sibi reverentiam impendit, potius prevaricator quam legum servator existit;" *Ad Gebehardum liber*, c. 43, also, c. 39, *LdL*, I, 303ff.; Wattenbach, II, 52f.; Manitius, III, 27 and 175ff. G. Constable, "The Structure of Medieval Society According to the *Dictatores* of the Twelfth Century," *Law, Church and Society: Essays in Honor of Stephen Kuttner*, ed. K. Pennington (Philadelphia, 1977), 253ff.

7. *Admonitiones*, art. 1, *SSH*, II, 619ff.; *MPL*, 151, 1233ff.; Érszegi, 54ff.; Hóman-Szekfű, I, 234ff.; my book, 110ff.; A. v. Timon, *Ungarische Verfassungs- und Rechtsgeschichte* (Berlin, 1904), 171ff.

8. *Admonitiones*, art. 3-4, and 6.

9. *Ibid.*, art. 2-3, and 5. Gy. Székely, "Koronaküldések és királykreálások a 10-11 századi Európában (Sending of a royal crown and establishing kingship in Europe during the 10th and 11th centuries)," *Századok*, 118 (1984, 905ff.

10. *SSH*, II, 623,2-3, and, II, 621,2-7; Váczy, *Ung. Königtum*, 50ff., and compare with Einhard, *Vita Caroli Magni*, c. 26, *MGHSS*, II, 456.

11. See his *Decretum I*, in *RHM*, II, 325ff.

12. "... nam quis ambigat a sancto patre nostro Stephano, uiro quippe apostolico legem populo nistro datam;" cf. Coloman's *Decretum*, *ibid.*, II, 359; B. Smalley, "Ecclesiastical Attitudes to Novelty, c. 1100-1250," *Church, Society and Politics*, ed. D. Baker (Oxford, 1975), 113ff.

13. *RHM*, II, 349ff.

14. Mansi, *Concilia*, XIX, 631f.; *MPL*, 151, 1257f., and confirmed by the *Chronicon pictum*, c. 86, *SSH*, I, 344,1-6.

15. Esp. art. 2, *RHM*, II, 382ff.

16. Stephen's *Leges*, Preface, *ibid.*, II, 310; his *Admonitiones*, art. 7, *SSH*, II, 625f.

17. Cf. J. McCann, *Saint Benedict* (New York, 1958), 79f., and 194ff., in ref. to Gregory the Great's *Dialogus*, ii:20, *MPL*, 66, 174f., and to art. 2 of the Rule of St. Benedict, *ibid.*, 66, 263ff., influenced by the law code of Justinian the Great - cf. H. J. Chapman, *Saint Benedict and the Sixth Century* (London, 1929), 57ff.; A. Szennay, *Szent Benedeknek, Európa védőszentjének emlékezete* (Memory of St. Benedict, the guardian saint of Europe) (Budapest, 1981), passim, and reviewed by J. Reisinger, "Népek nagy nevelője (The educator of peoples)," *Vigilia*, 47 (1982), 391ff.

18. Cf. *Annales Laurissenses minores*, a. 750, *MGHSS*, I, 116, though the date is certainly wrong; on the background, Einhard, *Vita Caroli Magni*, c. 1, *ibid.*, II, 448. Also Haller, I, 410f.; Seppelt, II, 117ff.

19. Stephen's *Vita maior*, c. 16, *SSH*, II, 392; *MGHSS*, XI, 239,10-14 (c. 18!); *Chronicon pictum*, c. 140, *SSH*, I, 419,24-32.

20. *Admonitiones*, a. 1, *ibid.*, II, 619f.; Ladislas' *Decretum I*, Preface, *RHM*, II, 326; Urban II to Coloman the Learned, *MPL*, 151, 480d.

21. As, e.g., Peter Orseolo in 1046; *Chron. pictum*, cc. 82 and 85.

22. Stephen's *Leges*, ii:17 (c. 51); II Esztergom, aa. 2-3; Otto of Freising, *Gesta*, i:31, *MGHSS*, XX, 368f.

23. Stephen, *Leges*, i:1-13 (cc. 1-12 in Migne); *Admonitiones*, aa. 1-2.

24. Cf. II Esztergom, a. 1.

25. Coloman, *Decretum*, a. 68; I Esztergom, a. 35.

26. Stephen, *Leges*, i:1-2; *Admonitiones*, aa. 1-2; I Esztergom, a. 34.

27. Stephen, *Leges*, i:1; *Admonitiones*, a. 2; Ladislas, *Decretum I*, a. 5.

28. Stephen, *Leges*, ii:2; Coloman, *Decretum*, c. 20.

29. Stephen, *Leges*, ii:1; Ladislas, *Decretum I*, a. 7. Compare with Einhard, *Vita Caroli Magni*, c. 26.

30. Ladislas, *Decretum I*, a. 36.

31. *Ibid.*, a. 37.

32. "... dominum Ottonem, huc usque vocatum regem, non solum Romano, sed et pene totius Europae populo adclamante...;" *Annales Quedlinburgenses, Continuatio*, anno 996, *MGHSS*, III, 73,37-40.

33. "... tu caput est mundi, caput est tibi rector Olympi;" Wipo, *Tetralogus Heinrici regis, ibid.*, III, 249,99.

34. "Roma enim cum caput mundi et urbium domina sit et vocetur, sola reges imperare facit;" *Vita Adalberti*, c. 21, *ibid.*, IV, 590,43-45.

35. Berno of Reichenau (abbas Augiae divitis), ep. 3 to Henry II, rendering thanks to God Who "in modum excelsae pyramidis vestrae dignitatis magnificentiam universis super excellere fecit regnis;" *MPL*, 142, 116ld.

36. "Et cum omnia regna terrarum, quae vestro subiicitur imperio, teste mundo, largissima vestrae pietatis abundantia repleat...;" Peter Damian, *Epistolae*, vii:1, *ibid.*, 144, 435bc.

37. Idem, criticising Gregory VII in his *Disceptatio synodalis*; cf. *LdL*, II, 99.

38. Cf. *Leges*, Preface, *RHM*, II, 310; *MPL*, 151, 1243b-1245a.

39. *Ibid.*, and art. i:6, 14, 15, 20, 22, 23, 26, 28, 29, 30-31, 34-35; ii:2, and 7. Coloman's *Decretum*, Preface, *RHM*, II, 358ff.

40. Stephen's *Admonitiones*, a. 7.

41. Golden Bull of 1222, Preface and art. 1, Marczali, *Enchiridion*, 134a-135a; its 1231 version, Preface and art. 1, *ibid.*, 134b-135b; *RHM*, II, 412ff., and 418.

42. *SSH*, I, 447,1-4; I, 447,19-22.

43. Stephen's *Leges*, i:15, 31, 34 (cc. 14, 29, 32); art. i:14 (c. 16) spoke of "secundum nostri senatus decretum."

44. *Ibid.*, i:20 and 29 (cc. 19 and 27).

45. Summoned by Béla I in 1060; cf. *Chronicon pictum*, c. 94, *SSH*, I, 359,20-22.

46. Stephen's *Leges*, ii:2 (c. 35); Coloman's *Decretum*, Preface, *RHM*, II, 360,5.

47. Cf. *Admonitiones*, aa. 7 and 3-4; *Chronicon pictum*, c. 95.

48. "Placuit regi et omnium concilio...;" Coloman's *Decretum*, a. 1 (*RHM*, II, 361).

49. *Ibid.*, II, 630ff., art. 23; Marczali, *Enchiridion*, 191ff.; Golden Bull of 1222, art. 11.

50. Stephen, *Leges*, Preface.

51. *Ibid.*, aa. i:7, 26, 28, 35 (*RHM*, II, 310ff.; cc. 6, 24, 26, 33 in Migne).

52. *Ibid.*, a. i:27 (c. 25).

53. "... decrevimus regali nostra potentia;" *ibid.*, a. i:6 (c. 5); also, a. ii:7 (c. 41), and Preface.

54. *Ibid.* a. i:30 and 29.

55. *Ibid.*, aa. i:15, 14 (c. 14 and 16 in Migne!), i:20, 31 and 34.

56. *Ibid.*, a. i:34 (c. 32); or, "secundum regalis decretum concilii;" a. i:20 (c. 19).

57. *Ibid.*, a. ii:2 (c. 35).

58. Golden Bull of 1222, aa. 1 and 8; Bull of 1231, aa. 1, 9, 18; Stephen, *Leges*, a. i:13, and ii:9; Ladislas, *Decretum*, *I*, a. 42; *Decretum III*, a. 2; Coloman's *Decretum*, aa. 37 and 46.

59. See, e.g., the *Sachsenspiegel*, ed. C. G. Homeyer (Hannover, 1861), iii:26: "die konig isgemeine richetere over al," and compare with the *Deutschenspiegel*, ed. K. A. Eckhart - A. Hübner, 2nd rev. ed. (Hannover, 1933), "Buch der Könige," ix:4-6, and, to a limited extent, with H. Bracton, *De legibus et consuetudinibus Angliae*, ed. G. G. Woodbine, 2 vols. (London, 1915-22), ii:24, 1: "quod ipse dominus rex, qui ordinariam habet irusdictionem, et dignitatem, et postestatem super omnes, qui in regno suo sunt." Also, Heer, *Geistesgeschichte*, 90ff.

60. Coloman, *Decretum*, aa. 37 and 46.

61. Golden Bull of 1222, a. 1.

62. Stephen, *Leges*, a. ii:9, he had to have a good reason to do so — cf. Ladislas, *Decretum I*, a. 42.

63. Coloman, *Decretum*, a. 64; Bull of 1222, a. 1. Compare with R. Elze, "Die päpstliche Kapelle im 12 und 13 Jahrhundert, "*Zeitschrift der Savigny-Stiftung für Rechtsgeschichte*, kan. Abt., 36 (1950), 145ff., est. 153ff.

63a. *Ibid.*, aa. 1, 8, 30; Bull of 1231, aa. 1, 3, 17; Timon, *Verfassungsgeschichte*, 182ff.

64. Count of the Royal Palace; *Pfalzgraf*; *nadvorni span*; cf. *ibid.*; Ladislas, *Decretum III*, a. 3; Coloman, *Decretum*, a. 36, and 37; Andrew III's legislation of 1291, aa. 9 and 14, in Marczali, *Enchiridion*, 188, or *RHM*, II, 615ff.; Andrew III's legislation of 1298, aa. 7 and 193, *ibid.*, II, 630ff.

65. Golden Bull of 1222, a. 8; Bull of 1231, a. 19.

66. Coloman, *Decretum*, a. 36; Andrew III, of 1291, a. 9 and 79. By comparison, cf. R. Elze, "Das 'Sacrum Palatinum Lateranense' im 10 und 11 Jahrhundert," *Studi Gregoriani*, 4 (1952), 27ff.

67. Stephen, *Leges*, i:14 and 33; Ladislas, *Decretum I*, a. 43; *Decretum II*, a. 3; *Decretum III*, a. 28; Coloman, *Decretum*, aa. 37-38.

68. Stephen, *Leges*, i:2, ii:9; Coloman, *Decretum*, a. 2; Bull of 1222, a. 5;

Bull of 1231, a. 12. Rogerius, *Carmen*, c. 8 (*RHM*, II, 255ff., esp. 260f.); Andrew III of 1291, a. 14; Andrew III of 1298, aa. 31-32.

69. Cf. Béla IV, *Lex Iudaeorum* of 1251, art. 15 and 24, *ibid.*, II, 473ff.; Andrew III of 1291, a. 15, *ibid.*, II, 618.

70. Ladislas, *Decretum III*, aa. 2 and 28; Coloman, *Decretum*, aa. 37-38.

71. Stephen, *Leges*, a. ii:16; Ladislas, *Decretum III*, a. 1.

72. Charlemagne's Gen. Capitulary for the *missi*, anno 802, in *MGHLL*, I, 91ff., no. 33, aa. 1, 3-4, 8. Hóman-Szekfű, I, 211ff.; Váczy, *Erste Epoche*, 30ff.

73. Stephen, *Leges*, ii:2; Ladislas, *Decr. I*, a. 15; Coloman, *Decretum*, a. 37.

74. Stephen, *Leges*, i:2, 8-9, 15, 22, 35; ii:5, 8-10, 16-17; Ladislas, *Decretum I*, a. 8; *Decretum II*, a. 5; *Decretum III*, aa. 15 and 21; Coloman, *Decretum*, a. 2.

75. Andrew III of 1291, art. 5, *RHM*, II, 616.

76. "... quattuor nobiles nominati; quattuor iudices deputati; iudices nobilium;" cf. Andrew III of 1291, aa. 5 and 14, *RHM*, II, 616 and 617.

77. County judges: iudices megales; cf. Coloman, *Decretum*, art. 37.

78. Golden Bull of 1222, a. 5; Bull of 1231, a. 13.

79. Stephen, *Leges*, i:6 and 25; Ladislas, *Decretum I*, art. 17; Golden Bull of 1222, aa. 11, 19 and 26; Bull of 1231, aa. 23, 26 and 32; Andrew III of 1291, aa. 3 and 8.

80. Stephen, *Leges*, i:13, 33-34; secular matter - i:14, 33; Ladislas, *Decretum I*, art 5, 35; secular matter, art. 43; *Decretum II*, art. 3; *III*, art. 28; Coloman, art. 58-61; Bull of 1231, art. 2, 17.

81. Stephen, *Leges*, i:1, 8-13, 19; Ladislas, *Decretum I*, art. 5, 11, 24, 27; infidelity in marriage, art. 13; Coloman, art. 61; I Esztergom, art. 7, 9.

82. Cf. Diploma of Andrew II, anno 1224, *RHM*, II, 430ff.; on Széklers, only much later -, cf. *Iura Siculorum*, art. 6, 7, 9, 10-16, in Marczali, *Enchiridion*, 432ff.

83. Ladislas IV's *Lex Cunaeis data II*, anno 1279, art. 11, *RHM*, II, 559ff.; Béla IV's Jewish Laws, aa. 14, 26, *ibid.*, II, 473ff. Timon, *Verfassungsgeschichte*, 296ff.

84. As, e.g. Ladislas' *Decretum I*, art. 42; *Decretum III*, art. 27.

85. Coloman, *Decretum*, art. 28, 29, 30, 31.

86. Cf. Golden Bull, 1222, art. 31; Bull of 1231, art. 21; "et quia multi in regno laeduntur per falsos prestaldos, citationes, vel testimonia eorum nom valeant, nisi per testimonium dioecesani episcopi, vel capituli; ... in causis vero minorum, vicinorum conventum, vel claustrorum testimoniis." Also, Andrew III's of 1291, art. 5. Horváth *Irodalom kezdetei*, 25.

87. Ladislas, *Decretum I*, art. 42-43; Coloman, *Decretum*, art. 2, 6, 9, 11, 24, 64; Bull of 1222, art. 2; Bull of 1231, art. 4.

88. Ladislas, *Decretum III*, art. 20, 26-27, and *Decr. I*, 29; Coloman, *Decretum*, art. 3, 6, 26, 27, 83, 84; Hóman-Szekfű, I, 310ff.

89. Stephen, *Leges*, i:20, ii:16, 21; Ladislas, *Decr. I*, art. 13, 17; Bull of 1222, art. 9; Coloman, art. 22, 26; Coloman's Jewish Laws, art. 2, 4, 6, *RHM*, II, 371f.

90. See *Lex Cunaeis data*, anno 1279, art. 11, *ibid.*, II, 559ff. Andrew II's *Libertas Saxonum*, anno 1224, art. 8 and 11; Andrew III's 1291, art. 31-32, *ibid.*, II, 615ff.

91. Coloman, art. 26, 27.

92. Coloman, art. 32, 35.

93. Coloman's Jewish Laws, art. 6.

94. Cf. Ladislas, *Decretum I*, a. 29; Coloman, *Decretum*, aa. 22 and 76; on ordeals, "ordines iudiciorum Dei," cf. *MGHLL*, V, 599ff.

95. See, e.g., Gregory of Tours, *Libri miraculorum*, c. 80, in *MGHSS* rerum *Merovingicarum*, I, 542; Hincmar of Rheims, *De divortio Lotharii et Teutbergae*, c. 6, *MPL*, 125, 668f.; Raymond of Agiles, *Historia Francorum qui ceperunt Jerusalem*, c. 18, *ibid.*, 155, 619ff.; E. Meyer, "Der Ursprung der germanischen Gottesurteile," *Historische Vierteljahrschrift*, 20 (1920-21), 289ff. H. Ch. Lea, *The Ordeal*, ed. E. Peters (Philadelphia, 1973), 32ff., and 57ff.

96. Ordeal by hot iron, cf. *MGHLL*, V, 615f.; by hot water, *ibid.*, V, 612ff.; by cold water, *ibid.*, V, 618f., and 689; Ladislas, *Decretum I*, a. 29; Hóman-Szekfű, I, 286.

97. Cf. *Regestrum de Varad*, in *RHM*, II, 640ff., maintained by the episcopal chapter of Várad acting as notary public, *locus credibilis*, from 1208 to 1235. Most of the entries were logged by Master Anianus (Ányos), canon and notary public. It is a rich source for legal, social, cultural and lingusistic studies concerning the period. It has information on ordeals by fire, "iudicium ferrei," conducted in front of the cathedral near the tomb of King (St.) Ladislas I. It has 389 entries of 394 cases; it made mention of some 30 counties (of administration by name), 600 villages (by name), and some 2,500 people appearing as defendants, accusers in legal court matters; also the names of Count Palatines, county reeves, counts, judges, etc., by individual names. The original document did not survive, though many (most) of its loose leaves were collected and published in a book by "Friar George:" György Martinuzzi, a Paulist friar and one time governor (regent) of Transylvania, under the title *Ritus explorandae veritatis* (Colosuarij, 1550); on this edition, see K. Szabó (ed), *Régi magyar könyvtár* (Bibliography of old Hungarian books), 2 vols. (Budapest, 1879-85), II, 10f.; E. Jakubovich-D. Pais (eds), *Ó-magyar olvasókönyv* (Old Hungarian reader) (Pécs, 1929), 81ff.; Still the best edition by J. Karácsonyi-S. Borovszky (eds), *Az időrendbe szedett váradi tüzes-vaspróba-lajstrom* (Budapest, 1903); Pintér, I, 249.; Horváth, *Irodalom kezdetei*, 25.

98. Ladislas, *Decretum III*, art. 28.

99. On this cf. I. Werbőczy, *Tripartitum opus iuris consuetudinarii incliti regni Hungariae*, anno 1517, in S. Kolozsvári-K. Óvári, *Werbőczy István Hármas-könyve* (Budapest, 1892), ii:2. On Werbőczy, see D. Kerecsényi, *Kolostor és humanizmus Mohács után* (Humanismus and the monasteries in Hungary after 1526) (Budapest, 1936), 25; T. Kardos, *A magyarság antik hagyományai* (Ancient Hungarian traditions) (Budapest, 1942), 28f.; E. P. Balázs *et al*, *Werbőczy István* (Lectures on Stephen Werbőczy) (Kolozsvár, 1942), passim; C. Horváth, *Régi irodalom*, 163f.; J. Horváth, *Irodalom megoszlása*, 213ff.

100. Stephen, *Leges*, i:14-15, ii:2-3, 12, 17. Ladislas, *Decretum I*, art. 13; Béla IV's *Lex Judaeis data*, anno 1254, art. 10; *Tripartitum*, i:2, and iii:9. On the role of *praestaldus*, cf. Ladislas, *Decretum III*, art. 13; Bull of 1231, art. 19, 21-22.

101. Hartvic, *Vita* of St. Stephen, c. 9, *SSH*, II, 412ff.; *MGHSS*, XI, 233f. Stephen, *Leges*, i:1-2, 3-13; ii:2. A. S. Czernan, *Die Staatsidee des hl. Stefan* (Klagenfurt, 1953), 9ff.; Gy. Szekfű, "Szent István a magyar történelem századaiban (The image of St. Stephen in the centuries of Hungarian history)," *SIE*, III, 1ff.

102. Hartvic, *Vita*, c. 10.

103. *MGHSS*, XI, 234,40-60.

104. Archbishop from 1095 to 1104; cf. Knauz, I, 68. Seraphim, a former chaplain of Ladislas, was among the *testes* authenticating the charter of Somogyvár abbey, 1091 — cf. Fejér, II, 469 — and was ambassador for Coloman the Learned to the court of Boleslaw of Poland; cf. Knauz, I, 71. Despite the assertion by Endlicher made on grounds of the fifteenth century Thuróczy codex (*RHM*, II, 349),

Seraphim, and not Laurentius was the archbishop at this time. On the other hand, although Péterffy, I, 54, mentioned ten suffragan bishops of Esztergom, and Hefele, V, 291, enumerated the bishops of Eger, Pécs, Veszprém, Vác, Győr and Nyitra, only one of the bishops, Simon of Pécs, was known by name; cf. Gams 376 (perhaps a gloss added to the original - see Pauler, I, 448, n. 320).

105. *RHM*, II, 358.

106. See the status report of the realm under Béla III (the edition is based upon a twelfth century MS, Paris), *RHM*, I, 245f., fourth paragraph.

107. *Ibid.*, third paragraph.

108. *Ibid.*, fifth paragraph.

109. "Zagrabienses episcopatum, ac monasterium Zagrabiense, a s. Ladislao rege sanctissime recordacionis predecessore nostro constructum, qui terram Slauonie ... ab errore idolotarie ad Christi ueritatem conuertens, corone Hungarie subiugauit, qui eciam in eodem banatu episcopatum instituit...;" *ibid.*, II, 409f.; Wenczel, *ÁUO*, XI, 31; Katona, *Historia critica*, II, 484f., though, as Szentpétery, *Regesta*, I, p. 12, anno 1094, noted, the diploma was not a royal document! Compare with the decree of Andrew II, anno 1217, *ibid.*, no. 323; Wenczel, XI, 147ff.

110. "Duos episcopatus ordinavit, et regia largitate locupletavit;" Ladislas *Vita*, c. 5, *SSH*, II, 519,12-13.

111. Szentpétery, *Regesta*, I, no. 43 (anno 1111).

112. Cf. "Constitutio pro clero ecclesiae Arbensis," *RHM*, II, 377f., and 278; in fact, V. Bunyitay, *A váradi püspökség története* (History of the bishopric of Várad), 2 vols. (Nagyvárad, 1882-83), I, 62, and I, 65, n. 5, mentioned a Bishop Nicholas of Várad.

113. To King Salomon; cf. *SSH*, I, 378,17-19; also, I, 379,8-9.

114. *Ibid.*, I, 368,20.

115. *Ibid.*, I, 369,8-9; the reasoning of the editor that she could have been the daughter of Coloman the Learned (*ibid.*, I, 368, n. 3), is without foundation; cf. *ibid.*, I, 379,8-9!

116. "... proposuit constituere monasterium;" *ibid.*, I, 416,8-11.

117. Katona, *Historia pragmatica*, I, 462.

118. "... monasteria episcopalia duo construxit, ... quae regia largitate dotauit...;" cf. *Sermo I de s. Ladislao*, in F. Brisits (ed), *Temesvári Pelbárt műveiből* (Selections from the works of Pelbart of Temesvár), vol. VI of *Irodalmi ritkaságok* (Rare pieces of literature), ed. L. Vajthó (Budapest, 1931), 59ff.; C. Horváth, "Temesvári Pelbárt beszédei (Sermons by P. of Temesvár)," *EPhK* suppl. I (Budapest, 1899), 145ff.; S. V. Kovács (ed), *Temesvári Pelbárt válogatott írásai* (Select writings of Pelbart of Temesvár) (Budapest, 1982), 411ff.

119. "... nec non Posonii et Nitrie;" Coloman, *Decretum*, a. 22, *RHM*, II, 363, and Katona, *Historia pragmatica*, I, 490, rationalized that "ex lege certum est Nitriensem episcopatum hoc tempore nondum extitisse." F. Zagiba, *Die altbayerische Kirchenprovinz und die hll. Slawenlehrer Cyrill und Method* (Salzburg, 1963), 6 (and Pribina's headquarters on Moravian soil, *ibid.*, 11f.), in ref. to *De conversione Bagoariorum et Carantanorum*, *MGHSS*, XI, 1ff.; my essay, "The Unforeseen Far-Reaching Consequences of Charlemagne's mid-Danubian Policy," *Proceedings of the 20th Hungarian Convention, 1980* (Cleveland, OH, 1981), 175ff.

120. See his "Refutatio investiturae episcoporum," in Duchesne, *Liber pontificalis*, II, 373; my article, "The Hungarian Court and Rome during the Reign of Coloman the Learned," *East European Quarterly*, 18 (1984), 129ff., note

77; for a counterargument, cf. U. R. Blumenthal, *The Early Councils of Pope Paschal II, 1100-1110* (Toronto, 1978), 38. Contemporary evidence, taken from *MGHLL*, sectio IV, const. 1, 562, 565 and 566 (Jaffé, *Regesta*, nos. 6092 and 6093), and, for example, from, *Ekkehardi Chronicon*, a. 1106, *MGHSS*, VI, 240,14, indicates that the synod was held.

121. "Archiepiscopum ultra Danubium in sua proprietate loco vocato Nitrava consecravit ecclesiae," .: *MGHSS*, XI, 12,7-8 (archbishop of Salzburg since 821, *ibid.*, XI, 10,20-21; *obiit* in 836, *ibid.*, XI, 12, note 56); Zagiba, 6.

122. In the year 850; cf. *MGHSS*, XI, 12,8-12; my *art. cit.*, in *Proceedings*, 1980 (1981), 175ff.

123. Jaffé, *Regesta*, I, no. 2566; Mansi, *Concilia*, XIV, 412, though spurious - see Palacky, I, 108, note 65.

124. Bishop Vichingys - cf. Jaffé, *Regesta*, I, no. 3319.

125. Katona, *Historia pragmatica*, I, 496f., following Hartvic's *Vita* of King Stephen I (*SSH*, II, 415,29-416,2).

126. "Quod inter annum MC quo Nitriae nondum episcopalem sedem extitisse, Colomanni decretum innuit...;" Katona, *Historia pragmatica*, I, 497; E. Fügedi, "Krichliche Topographie und Siedlungsgeschichte im Mittelalter in der Slowakei," *Studia slavica*, 5 (1959), 363ff.

127. Wenczel, *ÁUO*, VI, 77, no. 36, dated it between 1105 and 1114; Erdélyi, *Pannonhalmi Rendtörténet*, I, 594, no. 4.

128. Fejérpataky, *Kálmán király*, 43.

129. *RHM*, II, 363, a. 22; Hefele, *Conziliengeschichte*, V, 291, mentioned the bishop of Nyitra in conncection with the First Synod of Esztergom, but neither Gams, 376, or Péterffy, I, 54, spoke of him.

130. See Katona, *Historia pragmatica*, I, 770, quoting the letter of Ugrin of Kalocsa, anno 1229; also, his *Historia critica*, V, 544ff., and V, 611ff.

131. *Ibid.*, V, 657ff.; incidentally, Béla (IV) in 1234 told the papal legate that he would not tolerate dissent from churchmen; cf. Szentpétery, *Regesta*, I, no. 604.

132. Fejér, I, 480, though, as Szentpétery, *Regesta*, I, no. 27 (anno 1093), noted, the writ, as it is known today, is a forgery prepared according to an authentic document of 1091.

133. Pope Innocent III to John of Esztergom and to the Esztergom chapter, dated May 15 and May 9, 1209, respectively, *MPL*, 216, 50c and 51c; my article in *Church History* (1980), 380.

134. Innocent III to his legate in Hungary, dated Sept. 15, 1204, *MPL*, 215, 413c.

135. Innocent III to the Esztergom chapter, dated Nov. 22, 1204, *ibid.*, 215, 463bc.

136. Hartvic, *Vita* of Stephen I, c. 11, *SSH*, II, 416; *MGHSS*, XI, 234,40-60; Innocent III to Emery of Hungary, dated Sept. 13, 1204, *MPL*, 215, 412c.

137. *Ibid.*, 215,463d-464ab.

138. *RHM*, I, 246.

139. I Esztergom, a. 4, *ibid.*, II, 351.

140. See St. Augustine's *Regula ad servos Dei*, in *MPL*, 32, 1377ff., or, its original version, ep. 211, *ibid.*, 33, 958ff., written for a community of religious women "praeposita soror mea;" cf. ep. 210. Also, Augustine's sermon 355, "De vita et moribus clericorum," *ibid.*, 32, 37ff.; in his *De doctrina Christiana*, Augustine discussed the idea of clerical education, - *ibid.*, 34, 15ff., esp. 19 and 49f.

141. See *Regula s. Benedicti*, prologue, *ibid.*, 66, 215ff.; G. Schnürer, *Kirche und Kultur im Mittelalter*, 2nd ed.; 3 vols. (Paderborn, 1927-28), I, 210ff. The Rule served as an instrument of reform for the monasteries - cf. H. J. Chapman,

*St. Benedict and the Sixth Century* (London-Toronto, 1929), 194ff.; McCann, *Saint Benedict*, 101ff.

142. See the *Vita canonica*, in Mansi, *Concilia*, XIV, 314ff., or its expanded variant by the Synod of Aachen, 789, *ibid.*, XIV, 147ff. The rule imposed by St. Chrodegang of Metz (ob. 766) was largely borrowed from the Benedictine Rule; cf. Funk-Bihlmeyer, II, 72.

143. McCann, 125ff.; Gregory the Great's Dialogues, ii:36, in *MPL*, 66, 125ff.; A. Gasquet, *Monastic Life in the Middle Ages* (London, 1922), 197ff.

144. *MGHLL*, sectio II: *Capitularia regum Francorum*, 1, 79, 80, 60, 235, etc.; H. Fichtenau, *Beiträge zur Mediävistik*, vol. II: *Urkundenforschung* (Stuttgart, 1977), 18ff.; and my review of this volume in *Austrian History Yearbook*, 17-18 (1981-82), 356ff.; M. Bloch, *Feudal Society*, tr. L. A. Manyon (Chicago, 1961), 109ff.

145. Stephen, *Admonitiones*, 1-3, *SSH*, II, 619ff.; Andrew I's *Constitutio ecclesiastica*, in *MPL*, 151, 1257f., confirmed by the *Chronicon pictum*, c. 76.

146. Cf. I Esztergom, a. 27; Coloman, *Decretum*, prologue.

147. Stephen, *leges*, i:2, *Admonitiones*, a. 3.

148. Cf. J. Deér, *Die hl. Krone Ungarns* (Vienna, 1966), 223f.

149. Golden Bull of 1222, a. 31; Bull of 1231, a. 21; Andrew III of 1291, a. 5; Coloman, *Decretum*, a. 22.

150. Ladislas I, *Decretum I*, a. 41; Coloman, *Decretum*, a. 5-7, referring to Stephen *Leges*, i:2, and *Admonitiones*, a. 3.

151. Ladislas, *Decretum, I*, a. 4; Bloch, 345ff.

152. Stephen, *Leges*, i:1-2; still, "nullus comitum uel militum in ecclesiam praesumat sibi uincicare potestatem, praeter solum episcopum;" cf. Coloman, *Decretum*, a. 65.

153. Ladislas, *Decretum, I*, a. 4, — nor could she inherit anything from him; cf. I Esztergom, aa. 11, 32, 33, and, indirectly, II Esztergom, aa. 9 and 10 (*RHM*, II, 374).

154. Ladislas, *Decretum I*, a. 13; I Esztergom, aa. 1, 23, 31, 53-55; II Esztergom, aa. 8-10.; Bloch, 348, 350 and 351.

155. I Esztergom, a. 12.

156. *Ibid.*, a. 13.

157. *Ibid.*, aa. 14, 25, and 33.

158. *Ibid.*, a. 26.

159. *Ibid.*, a. 49.

160. Ladislas, *Decretum I*, a. 41.

161. I Esztergom, a. 21; still, "nullus clericus, nullus comes quemlibet clericorum suscipiat ad diuinum officium tenendum, nisi per manum parrochiani episcopi;" *ibid.*, a. 68.

162. *Ibid.*, a. 35, not a presbyter, though — cf. Ladislas, *Decretum I*, a. 30.

163. Ladislas, *Decretum III*, a. 4.

164. Coloman, Decretum, a. 2; Andrew III of 1291, a. 2.

165. Stephen, *Leges*, i:10, 14a *and* 14c, 33; I Esztergom, a. 66.

166. *Ibid.*, aa. 7-8; Stephen, *Leges*, i:19 and 34.

167. I Esztergom, a. 9.

168. Coloman, *Decretum*, a. 75.

169. I Esztergom, aa. 6, 19, 27, 37, 57; II Esztergom, aa. 9-11; Coloman, a. 8.

170. Cf. King Stephen's *Privilegium protoabbatiae sancti Martini*, in *MPL*, 151, 1253ff.; *ASS*, Sept. I, 494f.; Szentpétery, *Regesta*, I, no. 2 (based upon an earlier authentic document).

171. Therefore, it may be understandable that "omnes archidiaconi breuiarium canonum habeant;" cf. I Esztergom, a. 62; also, a. 25, with Coloman, aa. 5, 61, and 65.

172. I Esztergom, a. 48.

173. *Ibid.*, a. 5.

174. *Ibid.*, a. 21; Coloman, a. 3.

175. I Esztergom, a. 28.

176. *Ibid.*; Funk-Bihlmeyer, II, 158; W. Holtzmann, "Beiträge zu den Dekretensammlungen des 12 Jahrhunderts," *Zeitschrift für Rechtsgeschichte*, kan. Abt., 16 (1927), 37ff.

177. Cf. Charlemagne's *epistola* (no. 29), in *MGHLL*, I, 78f.; Békefi, *Káptalani iskolák*, 239ff.; and, 66ff.

178. Ladislas, *Decretum II*, a. 11, and compare with Henry II of England, Clarendon Constitution, aa. 3 and 8, in Stubbs, 137ff.

179. I Esztergom, a. 29.

180. *Ibid.*, aa. 6 and 36; Békefi, *Káptalani iskolák*, 297ff.

181. I Esztergom, a. 63, and, indirectly, a. 30.

182. Coloman, a. 70.

183. *Ibid.*, l. 3; I Esztergom, aa. 19 and 21.

184. *Ibid.*, a. 32.

185. *Ibid.*, a. 31.

186. Ladislas, *Decretum I*, a. 3; my book, 108.

187. Coloman, a. 67.

188. Ladislas, *Decretum I*, a. 1.

189. I Esztergom, a. 55; II Esztergom, aa. 10 and 12.

190. Ladislas, *Decretum I*, a. 6.

191. I Esztergom, a. 57.

192. *Chronicon pictum*, c. 91; Bloch, 383ff.

193. Innocent III to John of Esztergom, *MPL*, 216, 50c, and to the Esztergom chapter, *ibid.*, 216, 51c.; my article in *Church History*, 1980, 380.

194. Hartvic, *Vita* of Stephen I, c. 10, *SSH*, II, 415,13-28; *MGHSS*, XI, 234,7-15.

195. *Ibid.*, XI, 234,1-6; *SSH*, II, 415,3-12; Stephen, *Admonitiones*, preface, *ibid.*, II, 619f.; *MPL*, 151, 1235f.

196. See Ladislas IV's Law for the Cumans, anno 1279, preface, *RHM*, II, 554f., and compare with "Instrumentum authenticum coronationis Caroli I regis Hungariae," anno 1310, Marczali, *Enchiridion*, 205ff., or "Diploma Ferdinandi I," anno 1526, *ibid.*, 391f.; Hóman-Szekfű, II, 51ff.; Bloch, 408.

197. Stephen, *Admonitiones*, a. 1, *SSH*, II, 620f.

198. *Ibid.*, a. 2; Stephen, *Leges*, i:5-13 (cc. 4-12).

199. *Ibid.*, i:14-34 (cc. 13-35), *Admonitiones*, a. 5.

200. Stephen, *Leges*, i:14 (cc. 13 and 16), and 17 (c. 15); Ladislas, *Decretum I*, a. 43; *Decretum II*, a. 2. Tarcal, aa. 37 and 46; Bull of 1222, a. 8; of 1231, aa. 9 and 18.

201. Tarcal, a. 40; Otto of Freising, *Gesta*, i:31, *MGHSS*, XX, 368f.; Bull of 1222, a. 7; of 1231, aa. 15-16.

202. Cf. Stephen, *Leges*, preface: "... et quoniam una queque gens propriis utitur legibus, idcirco nos quoque ... decretali meditacione nostre statuimus genti...;" also, aa. i:35 and ii:9 (cc. 33 and 43); Ladislas, *Decretum I*, a. 43; *Decretum III*, a. 1; Tarcal, preface (*RHM*, II, 358ff.).

203. Cf. the report by Bishop Castello of the court of King Matthias Corvinus, anno 1483, Marczali, *Enchiridion*, 277, esp. 279 and 284; St. Katona, *Historia*

*regum Hungariae stirpis mixtae,* 12 vols. (Buda, 1787-92), VII, 310ff., and compare with the Bull of 1222, aa. 11 and 30; of 1231, a. 23; Laws of Andrew III of 1291, a. 9.

204. Ladislas, *Decretum III*, a. 3; Bull of 1222, aa. 1, 8, 30. Timon, 182ff.

205. *Ibid.,* aa. 2 and 8; Tarcal, a. 36; Ladislas IV, Cuman Laws, a. 11; Andrew III of 1291, aa. 9 and 14.

206. Bull of 1231, aa. 1, 3, 17.

207. Bull of 1222, aa. 1 and 3; Hóman-Szekfü, I, 223, and III, 98.

208. Bull of 1222, a. 1.

209. *Ibid.,* a. 8; of 1231, a. 7; Stephen, *Leges,* ii:9.

210. Ladislas IV, Cuman Laws, anno 1279, a. 11.

211. Bull of 1222, a. 31.

212. Duchesne, II, 441f.; *RHM,* II, 383f., confirmed by Andrew III in 1291, a. 9. The letter of Pope Honorius III, in Potthast, *Regesta,* I, no. 6870; Fejér, III-1, 388; Hóman-Szekfü, II, 200ff.; Bull of Lewis the Great, anno 1351, a. 23, in Marczali, *Enchiridion,* 216ff. F. Somogyi - L. F. Somogyi, "The Constitutional Guarantee of 1351: the Decree of Louis the Great," in Vardy, *Louis the Great,* 429ff.

213. Bull of 1222, a. 8.

214. He was, at first, judge of the Queen's court; later, he became Judge for the Realm - cf. *ibid.,* a. 9; of 1231, a. 19; Andrew II of 1291, a. 9.

215. Bull of 1222, a. 30.

216. Andrew III of 1291, a. 9.

217. *Ibid.,* "... thavernicus, qui et camerarius dicitur;" cf. Rogerius, *Carmen,* c. 10, *RHM,* I, 262; *MGHSS,* XXIX, 547ff.

218. *Ibid.* Chancellarius, to intervene in quarrels among the Jewish inhabitants of the realm, see Béla IV's Law for the Jews, a. 8, *RHM,* II, 473ff.; he was referred to as "vice-cancellarius" in Andrew III of 1291, a. 9. Timon, 189f.

219. *Ibid.,* a. 22; Rogerius, *Carmen,* cc. 6 and 11.

220. The charter of Tihany abbey, anno 1055, was signed by Nicholas "qui tunc temporis vicem procurabat notarii in curia regali;" cf. Jakubovich-Pais, 25; or, by comparison, the chronicler Anonymus, "Belae (regis) notarii" (!), in *SSH,* I, 33.

221. Béla IV, Law for the Jews, a. 8.

222. Andrew III of 1291, a. 22.

223. As, e.g. the signature on the Bull of 1222, "... datum per manus Cleti, aule nostre cancellarii, Agriensis ecclesie prepositi;" *RHM,* II, 416f.

224. C. Horváth, 46ff.; J. Horváth, *Kezdetek,* 75ff.

225. Andrew III of 1291, aa. 9 and 22.

226. "... slavo tamen iure Albensis ecclesiae et privilegio, quod Albensis ecclesia nostra in ipsa vice cancellaria habet ... ab antiquo;" *ibid.,* II, 617, art. 9.

227. Bull of 1222, a. 3.

228. Rogerius, *Carmen,* c. 10.

229. Hóman, *Ungarisches Mittelalter,* I, 425.

230. Rogerius, *Carmen,* c. 10.

231. *Comes preconum; comes venatorum; comes ensiferorum regalium;* cf. Hóman-Szekfü, I, 405; Pauler, I, 346f., and 512f. Pauler follows the *Regestrum de Varad,* nos. 255, 290, 331, etc.

232. Stephen, *Leges,* i:15, 20, 29, 31; ii:2; Ladislas, *Decretum I,* preface; Tarcal, preface; Bull of 1222, a. 11, and compare with the writ of Béla IV to Pope Innocent IV (anno 1253), in Fejér, IV-2, 218ff.; A. Kovács, "IV Béla levele a pápához (The writ of Béla IV to the Pope)," *Hungária,* Munich, Dec. 26, 1952, 7.

233. As, e.g., Ladislas, *Decretum III*, aa. 1 and 3.

234. *Ibid.*, a. 1; Tarcal, aa. 11 and 24.

235. Hartvic, c. 8; Stephen, *Leges*, i:1-2, and ii:16. Székely, *Magyarország története*, II, 966ff.

236. *Ibid.*, i:2, 8-9, 15, 22, 35; ii:5, 8-10, 16-17 (cc. 2, 7, 8, 14, 20, 33, 38, 42-43, 50-51, in Migne).

237. *SSH*, I, 346,7-10; *ibid.*, I, 366,6; *ibid.*, I, 394,1-5; *ibid.*, I, 377,2, and 412,10.

238. Stephen, *Leges*, ii:9-10; Ladislas, *Decretum I*, a. 18; *Decretum II*, a. 5 and 14-15; *Decretum III*, aa. 15, 21. Also, Tarcal, a. 25.

239. Bull of 1222, a. 5; of 1231, aa. 12-13 and 34; Rogerius, *Carmen*, c. 8; E. Mályusz, "Entwicklung der ständischen Schichten im mittelalterlichen Ungarn," *Études historique hongroises, 1980*, vol. I (Budapest, 1980), 103ff.

240. Bull of 1222, aa. 16 and 39; of 1231, aa. 25 and 34; Rogerius, cc. 10-11.; Gy. Nováki-Gy. Sándorfi, "Untersuchungen der Struktur und Ursprung der Schanzen der frühen ungarischen Burgen," *Acta archaeologica*, 33 (1981), 133ff.

241. Stephen, *Leges*, i:14; Bull of 1222, a. 5; of 1231, a. 13.

242. Bull of 1222, preface.

243. Stephen, *Leges*, ii:18; Ladislas, *Decretum I*, a. 41; *Decretum III*, a. 13.

244. Stephen, *Leges*, ii:16; Ladislas, *Decretum I*, aa. 1-2; *Decretum III*, aa. 1 and 13; Tarcal, a. 37.; Zs. Miklós, "Árpád-kori földvár Mend-Lányváron (Earthen fort of the Arpadian age at Mend-Lányvár)," *Archeologiai Értesítő*, 108 (1982), 233ff.; I. Berényi, "A kéhidai oklevél: a megyeszervezet 750 éves emléke (The Kéhida document: a 750 year old proof of county structure in Hungary)," *Élet és Tudomány*, 37 (1982), 1445.

245. *Ibid.*, a. 79; Ladislas, *Decr. III*, aa. 1 and 2; on centurio, *ibid.*, aa. 1 and 15; Tarcal, a. 79; on decurio, Decr. III, a. 1.

246. *Ibid.*, aa. 1 and 13; Tarcal, a. 37; Bull of 1222, a. 29; of 1231, a. 24.

247. Ladislas, *Decr. I*, a. 17; Bull of 1222, aa. 11 and 19; Bull of 1231, aa. 23 and 26; Andrew III of 1291, a. 8; E. Fügedi, "Das mittelalterliche Königtum Ungarn als Gastland," in W. Schlesinger (ed), *Die deutsche Ostsiedlung des Mittelalters als Problem der europäischen Geschichte* (Sigmaringen, 1975), 471ff.

248. Cf. Béla IV, *Leges* anno 1267, a. 5, *RHM*, II, 512ff.; Béla IV, town charters, *ibid.*, II, 444ff.; Gy. Györffy, "Zur Frage der Herkunft der ungarischen Dienstleute," *Studia Slavica*, 22 (1976), 40ff., and 311ff.

249. Ladislas IV, *Leges Cumanis datae*, anno 1279, art. 5, 7-8, 13, *RHM*, II, 559ff.

250. Cf. *Diplomata unionis trium nacionum in Transylvania*, annorum 1437 and 1459, Marczali, *Enchiridion*, 266ff.

251. *Ibid.*, and their tax exempt status - *Status regni sub Bela III rege, RHM*, I, 246, c. 6. Also, *Diploma Andreae II regis hospitibus Theutonicis Ultrasilvanis datum*, a. 2, *ibid.*, II, 420ff.

252. Stephen, *Leges*, i:1, 3-7, 33; *Admonitiones*, art. 2-3; Ladislas, *Decr. I*, aa. 17-18, 29; *Decr. III*, a. 15; Tarcal, a. 14; I Esztergom, aa. 1 and 23.

253. Stephen, *Leges*, ii:2 (c. 35); Tarcal, a. 10; Bull of 1222, aa. 10, 16-17; Bull of 1231, a. 26; Rogerius, *Carmen*, c. 5; Andrew III of 1291, a. 6-8.

254. Stephen, *Leges*, i:6; Hartvic, Stephen's *Vita*, cc. 6-8; *Chron. pictum*, cc. 64-66.

255. Stephen's *Leges*, i:7, ii:16 (cc. 6 and 50); Tarcal, aa. 15-16, 39, 41-42; Béla IV, *Lex*, anno 1267; *Lex Cumanis data*, anno 1279, c. 5; Andrew III, anno 1291, c. 8.

256. Stephen's *Leges*, i:21 (*RHM*, II, 316f.); this particular article is missing from Migne reprint, where art. i:20 (c. 19) is followed by art. i:22 (c. 20); also, art. i:23, ii:3-5 (cc. 21, 36-38).

257. Stephen, *Admonitiones*, a. 4 (*SSH*, II, 623,24), though in the Migne version, the wording is different: "confidentia principum, baronum, comitum, militum, nobilium" (*MPL*, 151, 1239c), as if after *militum* a colon should follow, to say that the princes, barons, counts and knights were all (regarded as) *nobiles*: nobility. The first Hungarian usage of *baro* occurred in the Bull of 1231, a. 8; interestingly, the Migne version of the *Admonitiones* is based on a later MS. On the nobles, and the role of the nobility, see also Ladislas, *Decretum I*, a. 42; *Decretum II*, a. 10; *Decretum III*, a. 2; the Bull of 1222, aa. 1 and 31; Rogerius, *Carmen*, cc. 4 and 8.

258. Ladislas *Decretum I*, preface; *Decretum II*, a. 1; *Decretum III*, a. 1.

259. Cf. Bull of 1222, aa. 13 and 30; Gy. Györffy, "Die Entstehung der ungarischen Burgorganisation," *Acta archaeologica*, 28 (1976), 323ff.

260. *SSH*, II, 623,24; Stephen, *Leges*, i:7, 15, 22-23, 25, 27, 35; ii:9-11; Ladislas, *Decretum II*, a. 5; *Decretum III*, . 15; Charter for the abbey of Somogyvár, a. 1091, in Marczali, *Enchiridion*, 102; Tarcal, a. 40.

261. Bull of 1222, aa. 1, 3-4, 5, 7, 10, 15; of 1231, preface, and aa. 10, 12, 18, 22 and 30.

262. Stephen, *Leges*, ii:35, on peace between the *maiores* and *minores* of the population of the land.

263. Stephen, *Leges*, i:1; Tarcal, aa. 1, 16, 18-19; I Esztergom, aa. 12-13; Andrew III of 1291, a. 1; Hóman, *Ungarisches Mittelalter*, I, 222ff.

264. As, e.g., articles 11 and 30 in the Bull of 1222; art. 23 of the Bull of 1231; Andrew III of 1291, a. 9; Ladislas, *Decretum I*, a. 13; *Decretum II*, a. 15; *Decretum III*, a. 15; Tarcal, a. 79.

265. Freedom for all: "libertas tam nobilium ..., quam etiam aliorum," Bull of 1222, preface, to be enjoyed by all, "tam episcopi, quam alii iobagiones ac nobiles regni nostri, universi et singuli, presentes et posteri..." *ibid.*, a. 31. Compare with Béla IV, *Leges*, anno 1267, preface.

266. Bull of 1222, a. 19; of 1231, aa. 15 and 26; Ladislas IV, Law for the Cumans, anno 1279, aa. 6-7: on a *iobagio castri* to become a noble, as, e.g., the King had elevated the Ivánka family to the noble status, anno 1274. Cf. Marczali, *Enchiridion*, 171f.; one is to bear in mind, of course, that until the end of the eleventh century, the Magyar element had formed one classless group — "libertas omnium una eademque fuit conditio;" cf. *ibid.*, 171, and compare with Stephen, *Admonitiones*, a. 4: "quod omnes homines unius sint conditionis et quod nil elevat, nisi humanitas, nil deicit, nisi superbia et invidia." Cf. *SSH*, II, 623,31-32.

267. His Law for the Cumans, aa. 6-7.

268. Tarcal, a. 39; I Esztergom, a. 65; Bull of 1222, aa. 5 and 14; of 1231, a. 13; Law for Cumans, a. 5.

269. Hóman-Szekfű, I, 318ff.; Hóman, *Ungarisches Mittelalter*, I, 395ff.

270. Stephen, *Leges*, i:24; Bull of 1222, a. 19; Andrew III of 1291, aa. 8 and 15.

271. Stephen, *Leges*, i:15, 17, 27, 35; Ladislas, *Decretum I*, aa. 11 and 19; *Decretum II*, aa. 4-5; *Decretum III*, a. 1. On *villanus, rusticus*, see Tarcal, a. 19: "coloni." They appear as *ewri*, in Ladislas, *Decretum II*, a. 15; as *ewnek, wzbeck*, in Ladislas, *Decretum III*, a. 2. *Iobagiones*, in Andrew III of 1298, aa. 70 and 73; cf. Marczali, *Enchiridion*, 196f.

272. Ladislas, *Decretum II*, a. 21; *Decretum III*, a. 3; Béla IV of 1267, c. 2; Ladislas IV of 1279, c. 5; Andrew III of 1291, a. 8.

273. See the town charters and privileges issued and guaranteed anew by Béla IV —*RHM*, II, 444ff., and 482ff.; E. Fügedi, "Die Entwicklung des Stadtwesens in Ungarn," *Alba regia*, 10 (1969), 101ff.

# XII

## Canonization of Ladislas I, Question of Legal Writs, and Status of the Crown at Fin-De-Siècle

His quidem fures et latrones persecutus est
petitionibusque loqui (sic) traxit originem,
ut Romana habet curia et imperii.

Keza, *Gesta Hungarorum*, c. 69

Concerning the canonization of King Ladislas I (1077-95) in the days of Béla III, there are only limited data at the disposal of the historian.[1] The *Vita* of Ladislas most probably written for the occasion,[2] — or, at least the basic narrative of it; the "legenda" as it is known today could easily be a later version,[3] — and the additions made to it state that the canonization did take place: "corpus eius gloriose est canonizatum," in the year 1192.[4]

Thomas of Spaleto, chronicler, mentioned in his opus about the lives of the archbishops of Spaleto that Pope Celestine III had approved of the request by King Béla III and the Hungarian hierarchy for the canonization of Ladislas and had ordered that the canonization take place. Thomas reported that Béla, king of Hungary, had asked the Roman pontiff (here Thomas erroneously wrote Innocent (III) instead of Celestine (III) that he order the (excavation and) elevation of the earthly remains of Ladislas, thereby to enter his name among the saints: "in sanctorum cathalogo decerneret ascribendum."[5]

Celestine III had fulfilled the wish of the monarch and dispatched Cardinal Gregory of Chrescensio as papal legate to conduct proceedings.[6] The legate was accompanied by his chaplain, the learned priest of great eloquence, Bernard, from Perugia in Tuscany. Cardinal Gregory had directed the canonization process in Várad, and, after that, returned to Rome. "In Hungariam profectus legationis suis peregisset

officium, ad propria reversus est." [7] Bernard the priest remained, however, in Hungary in order to become the tutor
of Prince Emery, Béla III's son. When he became king, Emery
I named Bernard archbishop of Spaleto. [8] It is more than
likely that Bernard, the archbishop of Spaleto, was known
to Thomas, the chronicler of Spaleto.

The date of canonization fell on June 27, according to
the entry in the calendar of the Pray codex, a late twelfth
century sacramentary. [9] The 341st letter in the Várad Register recorded that, on that day, Denis ( = Dénes) the crafts-
man, father of Tekus the goldsmith, had opened up the
simple grave of King Ladislas in the Várad cathedral in order
to elevate ( = elevatio) the earthly remains of the deceased —
thereby accomplishing the act of canonization. [10] Because
of his role in the canonization of King Ladislas, Denis the
crafstman received a charter of perpetual nobility from Béla
III. [11]

Still, no Hungarian chronicler recorded the canonization of Ladislas I; and, as noted above, even the remarks
in the *Vita* of Ladislas regarding his canonization seem to
be a later addition. What is more remarkable is that the papal
register made no mention of sending a papal legate to Hungary in this case, nor is there a trace of his report to Rome
about the canonization. On the other hand, the fact that
the calendar in the contemporary Pray codex recorded the
feast of Saint Ladislas; the circumstance that Ladislas
*legendae* frequently appeared in the fifteenth-sixteenth
century breviaries used in Hungary [12] (in fact, the learned
Dom Polycarp Radó had listed in his study on the Divine
Office of St. Ladislas some twenty known MSS of those
breviaries [13] ); that the sixteenth century Érdy codex carried
a sermon for the feast of the saint; [14] furthermore, that the
Ladislas legends provided material (and inspiration) for wall
painters in Hungarian churches, [15] goldsmiths, and craftsmen, [16] can only mean that King Ladislas I had not only
been venerated as a saint in his native country, but, as emphasized by the numerous wall paintings in the churches,
his canonization had indeed taken place. [17]

The writer of the portion of the *Chronicon pictum* who
dealt with the age of Béla III so briefly, — whose statement
has been worked into the *Chronicon* by its mid-fourteenth

century compiler [18] —, said about Béla III that he, by imitating the examples of the Roman curia and the imperial court, had introduced the usage of (legal) writs at his court. [19] The interesting aspect of this report is that he spoke of oral transactions: "petitionibus *loqui* (*sic!*) traxit originem." In other words, no official business could be orally transacted at the court without a previously handed in writ, as explained by (the Italian) Master Rogerius, author of *Carmen miserabile*, who had reported on the early years of the reign of Béla IV (1235-70), depicting in masterful strokes the 1241-42 Mongolian invasion of Hungary. [20]

Although on a different occasion Master Rogerius had said that Béla IV had made such an order "ad instar Romane curie," [21] he said nothing about an imperial custom (= court); therefore, it may be assumed that although the writer of this portion of the *Chronicon pictum* knew Master Rogerius, he had worded his personal opinion and did not relate the assertions of Rogerius regarding Béla IV, to the time of Béla III. [22]

There is an ordinance of the year 1181 by Béla III saying that all business discussed in the king's presence; all decisions made by the king and legal sentences handed down by him; donations made for the Church, — or, for private individuals, — (had to) be placed in writing. [23] This ordinance is the first surviving document of such instance of the reign of Béla III, and it is confirmed by a second ordinance, also dated 1181, that said that gifts or land grants given by the monarch, — or, by private individuals, — to the Church (must) be reconfirmed: "regia auctoritate firmare," presumably in writing. [24]

Although it can be assumed that it was at the Byzantine court that Béla learned about this legal device, which could so easily eliminate any misunderstanding regarding land- or office grants, inheritance, property, etc., there had been in the past, in the legal codes of his predecessors, many instances of dealing with the use of writs in legal matters or court cases, property transactions in the country. For instance, the second article of the Third Code of Laws by Ladislas I emphasized it as useful and necessary to place (judicial) transactions in writing. [25] A good example of a writ issued in the interest of protecting ecclesiastical property is the foundation charter of Somogyvár abbey, dated 1091.[26] Or, the contents of the Synod of Tarcal, article 79 (as drafted by the cleric named Alberic).[27] The first five articles of I Esztergom not only emphasized but furthermore demanded the issuance of judicial writs.[28] King Coloman the Learned's Law for the Jews did determine that commercial transactions and treaties of the Jews be witnessed by seal rings on the grounds that the parties concerned did not, at that time, possess even the rudiments of a legal education.[29]

King Coloman's Jewish Law created, for instance, a decree regarding *notitia*: a need for written reports (or, legal briefs) on a case, or on the use of the judge's seal in inviting someone to appear in court (of law) on a certain day in a given legal case. In view of the fact that it was then only the clerical element that knew how to read and write, and possessed the rudiments of legal training, King Coloman's legislation had only strengthened the position and judicial practices of the hierarchy and the lesser clergy turning those practices into a necessary tool in every day public life and in every commercial transaction.[30]

The law required, for example, that in every financial and trade undertaking between Christians and Jews both parties use sealed writs, thereby introducing, — or, confirming the usage of, — the *cartula sigillata* in the realm.[31] The "cartula" were small sized short writs: *carta*; *cartula*, authenticated by seal-rings; their text(s) dealt with a particular case and carried the names of witnesses, if it (they), served both of the parties concerned, but was (were) drafted by a third party, usually a cleric, perhaps a parish priest.[32] The issue and usage of legal writs must had spread beyond the walls of the monasteries in Hungary by this time;[33] writs were issued at parish offices and even at fairs, — imitating perhaps the example of the Frankish "dusty feet" courts of law at the fairs of Champagne.[34]

There is a document dating back to Géza II and preserved in a transcript in an Admont monastery MS, that contains the remains of such a "cartula." Martin Gut-Keled, royal reeve, had donated, according to this short writ, the enumerated estates and chattel to the abbey of Csatár which abbey had been established by him.[35]

The use of writs and seals in the realm is clearly discernible from various decrees of the law codes of Ladislas and Coloman; [36] and, those kings did not introduce the usage of writs and seals in their country, but only confirmed, through legislation, the established use in the late eleventh and early twelfth century. [37] It ought to be said that, in this regard, the Hungarian kings were not innovators, but the executors of an already established legal practice in their country in that they had assured the judicial practice of writs and sealed legal and commercial transactions, thereby developing further and increasing the social standing and prestige of their people(s) in the then contemporary political structure and mainstream of continental Europe.

It is known about Rogerius that no manuscript of his writings survived, though the first printed edition of his work appeared in Brünn by 1484. [38] His opus is very valuable and, as C. A. Macartney had remarked, the reliability of Rogerius has never been questioned. [39] The author was an Italian cleric, perhaps a native of Torre Maggiore, who for the first time visited Hungary in the company of Johann of Toledo, bishop of Paestum and papal legate, in 1223, and to whom he dedicated his work. [40]

Rogerius' piece is in itself an important thirteenth century historical monograph and source. Rogerius was able to do quality research for his description of the terrible days of the Tartar invasion of the realm and of his own personal experiences during the invasion. Prior to that, the author had visited Hungary on several occasions in the days of Andrew II (1205-35) and Béla IV. He was in the country when the Tartars struck in 1241: at that time, he was a prebendary archdean of the episcopal chapter in Várad. Rogerius was able to escape from his Tartar captors when the latter were already leaving the realm, and he wrote his piece in about 1243. Important it is how he had evaluated the public scene and enumerated all the complaints of the nobles against the king; he also described the answers given by the king's supporters to the charge of the (king's) opposition about the attempts of Béla IV to increase his powers; that is why we have his information about the origins and usage of writs in the realm. [41]

It is also known that Rogerius became the archbishop of Spaleto in 1249, where he died in 1266. [42] Thomas of

Spaleto, the chronicler, received information about him, and from him, or at least relied upon him for data in depicting the Mongolian onslaught of Hungary. And Bernard, mentioned above, also became archbishop of Spaleto, who wrote a book against the heretics. Before Bernard made archbishop, he spent some time tutoring Emery, son and successor of Béla III; Bernard was an able and trusted advisor of Andrew II. [43]  Andrew II had visited him at Spaleto during the fifth crusade, in the year 1217. [44]

Calanus Dalmata, — in Hungarian: Kalán, — bishop of Pécs, ought to be mentioned here; he was the author of a book about Attila the Hun, [45] was, at one time, chancellor of Béla III, [46] and the advisor of Andrew II, who had recommended Calanus for the archiepiscopal see of Esztergom. [47] Calanus was Hungarian governor of Croatia-Dalmatia, [48] but King Emery I (1196-1204) suspended him from that honorable position. The young monarch regarded him as a homosexual who had lived in sin; a heretic; and, as a murderer of his opponents by means of poison. [49] The jurists at the Roman See had a difficult time, indeed, and had to possess patience in proving the charges brought against Calanus as false, and to have him pronounced not guilty by the court of law. Emery I was evidently unable to prove his accusations, or to provide evidence for the charges trumpted up against Calanus. [50]

Prior to his removal from office, Calanus held the trust and served at the pleasure of Béla III. The king had enriched with tremendous privileges the Pécs bishopric (of Calanus). Of the total of royal taxes levied upon the realm, the tax collected in the bishopric was to be retained by the bishop and for the bishopric; the king had renounced his share of tax revenues in the Pécs diocese in favor of the bishop. Likewise, Calanus' (spiritual) subjects were permitted to conduct their own business transactions anywhere in the realm — tax-free.

Calanus as bishop of Pécs was free of any responsibility toward the king, the Count Palatine, Justice of the Royal Court, or the regional county reeve(s). In other words, the bishop was exempted from the jurisdiction of those officials. In judicial and criminal cases, and in court business, his spiritual subjects ( = religious flock) depended entirely upon their bishop's judgment, and the judgment of his officials. This meant that, were the inhabitant of Pécs to be taken to court (of law) in any part of the diocese, they had to adjudge him, or free him, by the testimony of the inhabitants of the diocese. No outsiders could intervene.

One-tenth of tolls collected on the border of the diocese and of the far taxes went to the bishop. In fact, Calanus was entitled to one-tenth of the regional fur tax also. On the other hand, every inhabitant of the diocese, including the upper clergy, had to pay their share of corn, wine, beef and chicken (contributions) — to the bishop. Even the Ismaelites living in the bishopric had to pay. The one-twentieth portion of the tax for the Count Palatine; the one-hundredth portion of taxes for the reeve could not be levied, nor collected in the diocese during the episcopate of Calanus in Pécs.[51]

During the tenure of office by Bishop Calanus, the Count Palatine and the regional reeve(s) were not allowed to make any announcements through their own messengers, in the bishopric without the bishop's permission. According to a spurrious document, no mass diet(s) of the nobles and/or of the realm were to be held in the Pécs diocese — without written approval from Calanus.[52] With the exception of the King and Queen, nobody received free lodging from, or on the estates of, the bishop (Calanus). Were someone to break this rule, he paid a fine of ten gold pieces to the bishop. During the tenure of Calanus, the diocese enjoyed full autonomy in matters of public administration and taxation. The bishop himself was the region's secular administrator, — a function he performed through his own officials. At the same time, he, and, presumably, his clergy and his officials, received the income and benefits derived from the bishopric. Bishop Calanus paid three silver marks a year for the upkeep of the office of the (unemployed) county reeve.[53]

The chroniclers did not mention any of this, — the chroniclers as we have access to them today failed to mention many things, — but it may be assumed that, upon the death of his father, King Béla III, Emery I had strongly disapproved of the almost vice-royal status of the bishop of Pécs, and directed the most incredible charges against Calanus in order to eliminate him from his office and from the public scene.[54]

Why did Béla III spend so much time and attention on
Bishop Calanus? Was the bishop a good administrator? Did
he in the fields of administration and fiscal policy perform
important services for the king's court? Or, did the monarch
display good political judgment in that the Pécs bishopric
was, at that time, a buffer between the realm itself and the
territories of Croatia and Dalmatia under Hungarian administration?

According to tradition, it was already under the reign
of Béla III that the Hungarian Crown was constructed in
the form it is known today, — a crown closed on top in the
form of a cross pieced together out of the remains of the Latin
and of the latter Byzantine diadems; [55] the Crown came
to symbolize the role Béla III had to play in politics and in
diplomacy between the German emperor of the West and
the Byzantine empire in the Southeast. [56] The newly constructed Crown meant that the Hungarian monarch now
would regard himself as a full fledged ruler of his realm who
wore a closed Crown like the two emperors. [57]

Contrary to historical tradition, difficulties arise with
this assumption on the grounds that it is unacceptable by
modern scientific standards. Regardless whether the *Byzantine* crown itself, — according to tradition, a Greek diadem
sent by the Byzantine emperor Michael VII the Ducas to
his sister Synadele, queen of Géza I, — can only be, in its
present form, the product of rather crude, late twelfth century Hungarian craftsmanship: a female fillet made in imitation of a Byzantine example and decorated with ten enamel
plates of Byzantine artistry of the 1070's; they were taken
most probably from the gift sent by Emperor Ducas to Géza
I's wife, but for the monarch, [58] this diadem ( = crown)
could not have been *corona regni*, and it could not have
held a public constitutional position in the realm. [59]

Nor could the "Latin" crown, without the cross on top,
had originally been the "Crown" of the Realm, but, at best,
the remains of some earlier artwork, perhaps the richly decorated cover of a Book of Gospels, or parts thereof, shaped
in two panels forming a cross and built into the fillet, — the
now recognized lower part of the Crown. [60] In other words,
it was out of the crown frame, — produced in Hungary in
the late 1100's and ornamented with enamel plates taken

from an earlier Byzantine art object, — that the Crown of
Béla III had been constructed by means of placing the remains of an earlier artwork shaped in two panels forming
a cross, into it, thereby making it a closed royal crown. [61] It
is possible though that, judged by their style and craftsmanship, the early remains have been fitted into the frame only
in the early thirteenth century, that is, upon the death of
Béla III, but during the reign of his son. [62]

The present day Hungarian Crown is, therefore, not the
product of some continuous historical change; nor did it
develop out of a "Crown of the Realm:" *corona regni.* The
"Latin" crown was not even a crown; [63] nor was the "Greek"
diadem the crown of the realm. [64] Only upon the installa-
tion, shaped in form of a cross, of the two panels of plates
(taken perhaps from the cover of a Book of Gospels and)
placed into the fillet, that the *corona regni* had come into
existence, which was neither the Latin crown, nor a Greek
diadem. [65] Still, tradition must have played a role in creating the Crown; they did not build a new crown, but constructed one out of the remains (enamel plates) of an old
diadem and an artwork, adding some contemporary craftsmanship to it, thereby to give the Crown an authentic look
and archaic status. [66]

In view of the available source material, it can be said
that not even Harvic (most probably) a bishop himself and
the biographer of King Stephen I, mentioned a Crown-of-the-
Realm in his report on the anointment and coronation of
the first Hungarian king. [67] In his words, Stephen was crowned with the diadem of royal worthiness, "diademate regnalis
dignitatis," originating in Rome. [68] It may be, of course,
that Bishop Hartvic obtained the idea of the sending the
crown by the Pope, — by Pope Sylvester II, an actual historical event, [69] — from the letter of Pope Urban II addressed
to King Coloman the Learned, on matters concerning kingship. [70]

King Stephen I's *Vita maior* that provided extracts, copied
verbatim, for the Hartvic report, said nothing about the
crown and the cross sent by Rome and used at the first
Hungarian royal coronation. It only mentioned a papal writ
and blessing (symbolizing approval?): "benedictionibus apostolice litteris allatis." [71] In writing his report Hartvic simply

continued the trend of thought Urban II had held, who had spoken of "et regalis dignitatis iura," [72] the source of which Hartvic had sought to establish in papal power, — in accordance with the then prevalent Gregorian outlook of Lateran politics, [73] by heavily stressing the role of the Roman See in sending a crown to the first Hungarian king. [74]

Hartvic the biographer wished only to emphasize the position held by King Stephen I; [75] he had played down the role of the crown! [76] And yet, according to the ideal of Gregorian renewal in the age of Coloman the Learned, Hartvic attributed a new mystical legislative power to that crown. [77] He said that it was after the anointment and coronation, held with the approval of the Holy See, that the first Hungarian legislation had occurred. [78] Although in this passage he repeated in full the text of the earlier *Vita maior* (of King Stephen), [79] he, by inserting his report on the crown — and cross — received from Rome into the narrative of the *Vita*, presented the first Christian Hungarian legislative activity in an entirely different light. [80] In such a manner Hartvic, the contemporary writer of King Coloman's reign, [81] wanted to point out the essence and importance of the planned, or, already performed, legislation held in the reign of Coloman the Learned. [82]

They did not crown Peter Orseolo, Stephen I's selected successor, but only *made* him king, "regem preficere statuerunt," for very understandable reasons. [83] As the chronicler put it, "Petrus factus est rex;" [84] therefore, as it is evident from a later remark of the chronicler, they had had an easy time deposing Peter. [85] They likewise failed to crown Aba, Peter's successor, but had him anointed; "consecratus est in regem. [86]

Now, it is known about Andrew I that he accepted a (the) royal crown, *regalem coronam est adeptus,* [87] and three bishops had performed his coronation. [88] Although chancellor to the king, the chronicler did not depict the crown. [89] Regardless of the report rendered by Pope Gregory VII that the earlier Hungarian coronation insignia were returned to Rome: *illuc regni direxit insignia, quo principatum dignitatis eius attinere cognovit,* [90] by Emperor Henry III, protector of Peter Orseolo, [91] it is undecided with what crown had the three bishops performed the coronation (of Andrew I) in 1047? The crown could not have been *corona regni.* [92]

Salomon, the five year old son of Andrew I, was crowned junior king during his father's reign, "in regem fecit iniungi et coronari," but the chronicler in this instance said nothing about the crown. [93] And, in spite of the coronation, it was Andrew I's younger brother, Béla I, who inherited the throne in 1060, and the hierarchy had anointed and crowned him with the royal fillet, "regale dyademate." [94] It is not clear from the wording of the chronicler whether there was any difference between the royal crown and the royal fillet. The chronicler thought it unnecessary to mention it. Still, the *corona regis* and *dyadema regale,* even if identical as coronation insignia, could not have been the Crown-of-the Realm. It (they) lacked constitutional status. Placing a (the) *coronam regalem* upon the head of the monarch could only have symbolized the approval, — and, in this sense, transfer, — by the bishops in the realm of authority to the new king. [95] Thus, royal coronations in Hungary following the death of Stephen I mainly symbolized the unbroken continuity of the transfer of jurisdiction from monarch to monarch, after both the nobles, *via* acclamation, and the hierarchy by way of anointing, had consented to the king's acceptance of power. [96] In 1064, they crowned Salomon for a second time, after they had placed him, but without having anointed him, and in the presence of the German emperor, on the Hungarian throne. [97]

Salomon's second coronation took place in 1064, after he made peace with the sons of Béla I, and when Géza (his nephew, Béla I's son), with whom he concluded peace, had crowned him. The chronicler, however, spoke only of the event of the coronation, "est coronatus." [98] In 1074, following the battle of Mogyoród, where the sons of Béla I: Géza and Ladislas, had defeated Salomon (who had been misled: "unreadied," by the wicked Vid, a royal reeve), Ladislas, walking around the battlefield, came upon the slain body of the reeve and burst out saying that Vid had not even been a member of a noble family, but had the false desire to have a noble's status; he was not of royal descent, but had reached out for the royal crown. [99] The crown here mentioned in the complaint of Ladislas, as recorded by the chronicler, appears to be a symbol of royal authority; "quare coronam optabas?" [100]

The term *corona regni* was recorded for the first time in c. 124 of the *Chronicon pictum* while reporting on the unwillingness of Prince Géza to accept the "Crown of the Realm," — *coronam regni suscepit.* [101] In view of the fact that the Holy See did not recognize the royal status of Géza I,[102] the use of the term by the chronicler seems to be unique, indeed.[103] It can be, of course, that the chronicler was not certain about the legal and constitutional meaning of the expression, but relied upon it in order to depict the royal status of Géza I in strong colors at a time when Salomon was still the lawful monarch of the realm.[104] In 1077, therefore, when Géza I died and his younger brother, Ladislas I, took over the government of the kingdom, they ( = the hierarchy and the nobility) elected him — regent.[105] Because he came to power against his will, wrote the chronicler, Ladislas I had crowned himself with the crown: "capite suo coronam posuit." [106]

The question is: what crown? The answer to this question is provided by the *Vita* of Ladislas, whose compiler said that Ladislas was in no hurry to receive either royal anointment, nor the crown from the bishops, and had, for this reason, the coronation insignia: *insignia regis*, carried in front of him when appearing at an official function in public.[107] There must exist a connection between the royal insignia (that had been) carried before Ladislas I and the Crown of the Realm, because Coloman, Ladislas I's successor, whom they had crowned king,[108] — had, records an entry by the Chronicler-of-Obuda in the *Chronicon pictum*, Béla, the son of his brother Álmos, blinded, "ut non sit dignus portare coronam sancti regis. [109]

The emphasis here rested upon the expression *corona sancti regis*: the crown of the saintly king, that is, the crown of the then already canonized King Stephen I; or, the expression used must have been a reference made to King Stephen's crown.[110] Use of the term could imply the far reaching influence of Hartvic upon chronicle composition during the mid-century, or, it could have been a thoughtless remark made by the chronicler who, as it is known, really hated King Coloman.[111] It is for the first instance that a

Hungarian chronicler spoke of the crown of the saintly king, but that crown may have been identical with the crown of the realm used, the chronicler recorded, at Géza I's coronation. In which case, the coronation of King Coloman must have been carried out with the crown of the saintly king. [112]

There is, however, an opposing argument to this hypothesis in that Hartvic, the author of King Stephen I's *Vita*, had, in his time during the reign of Coloman, placed too much emphasis upon the papal origins of the Hungarian crown.[113] It can be that even the chronicler who had hated Coloman so much, had repeated (reflected?) in his unintended remark, the point of view expressed by Hartvic without really understanding or knowing about the constitutional meaning and legal implication of the wording of his report.[114]

Coloman's son and successor, Stephen II, was *crowned king* in 1116.[115] Likewise, they had crowned Béla II the Blind, successor of Stephen II — "coronatur," wrote the Chronicler-of-Obuda.[116] The chronicler used the same expression in reference to Géza II, "coronatus est." [117] With what crown? — the chronicler regarded, probably, the question as unnecessary, or could not answer it. The coronation(s) may have been performed with the crown (diadem) used at the coronations of both Ladislas and Coloman, because the chronicler used, in his scanty wording, the same expression: "coronatur," in recording the successions of Stephen II and Géza II.[118]

The chronicler recorded the same in a caption that formed the title of c. 171 in the *Chronicon*, where chapter titles appear as captions to drawn pictures ( = illuminations) in the MS of the *Chronicon pictum* ( = hence, Picture Chronicle!),[119] writing that "bela tertius coronatur." [120] He repeated the same statement in the body of the text, "Bela coronatus est." [121] It is ironic (but no coincidence) that the chronicler recorded the coronation of the son of Béla III only in a caption, — the title to c. 172. [122] Here the point of view ought to be emphasized anew, by this writer, for one, that by the end of the twelfth century,[123] the Roman See had firmly stressed the right of the archbishop of Esztergom (and primate) to crown and anoint the kings of Hungary. [124]

Besides one or two exceptions, the text material of the

*Chronicon* cannot, really, serve as a source to identify the Hungarian crown. On the other hand, a speech held by Michael Anchialos, a cleric who later became Byzantine Patriarch, — the speech held in the mid-1160's; its text discovered in 1960, [125] — mentioned the crown of the *paion* ruler, that is the king of Hungary, expressing hope that the Hungarian archbishop who had been crowning the Hungarian kings, and the other bishops as well, would soon come under the jurisdiction of the Byzantine *basileus*. [126] The speech by Anchialos stressed the liturgical-ecclesiastical and constitutional importance of the Hungarian crown. Only with this crown could they crown a Hungarian ruler king. [127] Therefore, and for this reason, the Byzantine emperor needed to obtain the crown in order to crown with it [128] the Hungarian anti-kings, — as, for example, a Stephen IV, [129] the rival of King Stephen III, [130] — or even Bela-Alexios ( = the future Béla III) himself. [131] It was the Hungaro-Byzantine war of 1165-66 that served as background of the speech of Anchialos, when Manuel was determined to crush Hungarian resistance and to crown, through constitutional means with the right crown, his protege, Stephen IV, as the lawful king of Hungary. [132] The speech by Anchialos held when Stephen III was the lawful monarch of Hungary also meant that the king, and his predecessors, had been crowned with a (the) "Crown-of-the-Realm."

The Hungarian coronation metropolis was, at this time, Székesfehérvár: *Alba regalis*, [133] "regni sui metropolis," as recorded in 1063 by the *Annales Altahenses maiores*, [134] identical with "regalis sedis civitas" referred to by the author of Stephen I's *Vita maior*. [135] A similar expression occurred in the writ of Pope Alexander III, dated 1179, mentioning "Albensis ecclesia ubi sedes reganalis est." [136] A similar phase was used in the chronicle segment describing events of 1163-64 during the reign of Stephen III, [137] and in the official documents of the time. [138]

The archdean of Székesfehérvár who also was royal chancellor, was the guardian of the crown. [139] The transfer of the archdean recorded in the papal letter of 1179 became necessary because he had previously supported the candidacy of Prince Géza, Béla III's younger brother, to the throne, together with the dowager Queen Euphrozina, against the

rightful claims of Béla III to the royal crown.[140] (Queen
Euphrozina had the basilica built in honor of King St.
Stephen I at Székesfehérvár for the repose of the soul of her
husband, King Géza II; later, she, too, was buried there.[141])

Master Cathaphanus was the archdean and royal chancellor at Székesfehérvár from 1192 to 1198,[142] at a time,
when they crowned Emery for a second time.[143] The writ
of Pope Innocent III of December 21, 1198, also confirmed
the privilege of the archdean of Székesfehérvár to have his
role of *custos*: guardian of the crown, filled by another,
though turstworthy person, who would care for "et diadema
etium regium."[144] It is noteworthy that the papal letter still
spoke of a royal diadem.[145] It could have been an enorreous
slip in the letter addressed by the pontiff to Gotherdus, "prae-
posito Albensi," or, it could have been indirect proof for
the hypothesis that the fusion of the upper part of the crown
with the lower diadem had already occurred in the early
thirteenth century.

One may express the opinion that, from the historical-
cultural point of view, the realm slowly entered, mainly
through the Church and with the aid of the new monastic
orders, the mainstream of western civilization. One ought to,
in this regard, single out the Benedictines of Pannonhalma,
whose monastic community had existed since 1001.[146] A
writ, dated anno 1111, honored with the title *grammaticus*
the Benedictine monk Wilhelm of Mount Zabor community.[147] Béla II the Blind had frequently visited Pannonhalma. His visit in 1137 with a great entourage, is well recorded; then the abbot richly provided for the stay of the
monarch and his retainers.[148] In time, a royal decree regulated the manner of laymen visits to the (a) monastery.[149]

The Third Lateran Synod of 1179 called for educational opportunities to be created at a bishop's cathedral,[150] and
the roster of books, compiled anno 1087 at Pannonhalma,
indicates that the abbey had already by then possessed a
serious book collection, very much in tune with the times.[151]
The 1091 foundation charter of the abbey of Somogyvár
made mention of Peter Arianus of Poitiers, grammarian.[152]
Membership of this abbey had to be French, noted Albericus
Trium Fontium in the mid-thirteenth century.[153]

From a letter of Emperor Isaac Angelos addressed to

Archbishop Job of Esztergom [154] it may seem evident that
the Byzantine ruler conducted, in the name of his empress,
a dogmatic debate with the archbishop on the descent of
the Holy Spirit. [155] Opposing the archbishop who had expressed his views in accordance with the teaching of Rome,
the Emperor publicized the usual Byzantine counterargument by writing that the Holy Spirit descended from God
the Father. The Emperor wrote that nobody in Byzantium
had, as yet, come across the sermon of John Chrysostom
which explained the descent of the Holy Spirit from the
Father *and* the Son. [156] (This latter dogmatic view, *filioque*
( = and the Son), was explained and defended by Paulinus
of Aquileia at the Cividale synod in Friaul in 796; [157] and,
commissioned by Charlemagne, Theodulf of Orleans wrote
a defense prepared for it under the title *De Spiritu Sancto*. [158]
The Aachen synod, 809, discussed and accepted the dogmatic arguments of Theodulf. [159] )

It may bear witness to the loyalty for her religion that
a Lady Margaret had, in 1152, and with the approval of
the nobles, handed over a gold chain weighing seven marks
to the archabbot of Pannonhalma, and furs for the monks
(to keep warm in winter); also, two serf families to the abbey,
together with two furlough of agricultural land, eight oxen,
ten cows, and one hundred sheep, with the request that the
abbot and the monks say a thousand Masses for the souls of
the faithful departed (so that they may rest in peace). She
also prescribed certain services to be performed by the two
serf families for the abbey. Through this gift, she wanted
to express her appreciation to the abbot and her respect for
his monks. [160]

Andrew, a hermit and former archdean of Veszprém,
had, with the king's permission, made a donation to the
abbey of Pilis. [161] (The king was Béla II the Blind.) Lord
Adalbert, ambassador of Géza II to the king of Sicily in about
1150, left all his books for the abbey in case he perished
during his embassy to a foreign land. [162]

In the times of Béla III, a student named Bethlehem
studied in Paris, where he died unexpectedly. The abbot
of St. Genevive reported his death to the king, and, when
his parents found out that he left no debts behind, they
presented the abbey (of St. Genevive) with silver, gold, a
banner, liturgical vestments, and a white horse. [163]

In 1186, Lord Hoda died; before he died, the king paid him a visit. Hoda left some of his lands to the abbey of Pannonhalma with the request that the monks pray for him. He had also freed some of his slaves, because he wished to assure salvation for his soul. [164]

The Canons of Prémontré had entered Hungary in 1179, and they settled down at Garab in Nógrád county and at Jászóvár in Abaúj county. [165] By the thirteenth century, they had about fifty religious houses in the realm inhabited by canons and lay brothers. Hungarian agriculturists and mining engineers owed a good deal to the annual gathering of the Great Chapter of the Order, held at Prémontré. [166] The mines and ironworks at Jászóvár were cultivated and maintained by western methods and aided the economy of the realm, and its relations with the West. [167] The scribes and copyists active in the Premonstratensian religious communities did splendid work in re-writing and producing books and scholarly manuscripts. [168]

Hungary by this time had the three educational and social strata of (1) clerics, including parish priests and assistants; [169] (2) of scholastics, that is, baccalereui and masters, [170] and (3) apprentices, journeymen and master craftsmen among those learning and working in a trade. [171]

The mechanical guild industry included cloth and weapon makers, the non-industrial shippers, agriculturists, hunters, medicine men, and — actors. The *lanificium*: cloth makers guild included among its members taylors, tanners and furriers, also barbers and notaries (because the latter used parchments prepared from animal skin in their official business). [172] The members of the *armatura* guild of weapon makers consisted of carpenters and bricklayers, in addition to the weaponmakers. [173] During the reign of Béla III, the Hungarian realm had become a full fledged member of the European Christian and economic — political mainstream at *fin-de-siècle* of the twelfth century.

NOTES

1. Cf. J. Török, "Szent László liturgikus tisztelete (The liturgy of St. Ladislas)," in Mezey, *Athleta patriae*, 135ff.; Hóman-Szekfű, I, 395, and II, 155f.; Hóman, *Ungarisches Mittelalter*, I, 413; Pauler, I, 362f.

2. Cf. *De sancto Ladislao rege Hungarie*, in *SSH*, II, 515ff.; *RHM*, I, 235ff.;
L. Mezey, "A Szent László legenda legkorábbi irodalmi ábrázolásának kérdéséhez
(On the earliest literary works on the Ladislas legend)," in his *Athleta patriae*,
19ff., esp. 41f.; J. Gerics, "Krónikáink és az I. László legenda szövegkapcsolatai
(Hungarian chronicles and the Ladislas legend)," *Memoria*, I, 113ff., and compare
with Csóka, 527ff.; N. L. Szelesztei, "A Szent László legenda szöveghagyományozódásáról (Ein neuer Fund zur Textüberlieferung der Ladislas Legende)," *MKSz*,
100 (1984), 176ff., with text *ibid.*, 184-96, based upon a fifteenth century codex
of the University of Graz Library (Austria).

3. See E. Bartoniek, in *SSH*, II, 509ff.

4. *Ibid.*, II, 525,11-12.

5. Cf. Thomas of Spaleto, *Historia pontificum Salonitarum atque Spalatensium*, c. xxiv, *MGHSS*, XXIX, 575,15-27; Thomas wrote Innocent (III) instead
of Celestine (III), an error not noticed by J. Horváth, in *Memoria*, I, 158; Török,
*loc. cit.*, 145, n. 22.

6. Idem, *loc. cit.*, 145, n. 23. *MGHSS*, XXIX, 575,20-21.

7. *Ibid.*, XXIX, 575,26-27; or, in *Acta sanctorum*, 66 vols. to October (Ant-
werp, 1643etc.), Iunii V, 315ff., esp. 319; G. Pray, *Dissertatio historico-critica
de sancto Ladislai rege Hungariae* (Posonii, 1774), 5ff., and 10ff.

8. Cf. e.g., B. Gams, *Series episcoporum Ecclesiae Catholicae* (Regensburg,
1873), 420.

9. See Radó, *Libri liturgici*, 38; K. Kniewlad-F. Kühár, *A Pray kódex tartalma,
kora és jelentősége* (Contents, age and importance of the Pray codex), repr. from
*Magyar Könyvszemle* (Budapest, 1939); F. Kühár, "A Pray kódex rendeltetése,
sorsa, szellemtörténeti értéke (Destiny, history and intellectual significance of
the Pray codex)," *Magyar Könyvszemle*, 63 (1939), 213ff.; L. Mezey, "A Pray
kódex keletkezésének problémái (Questions concerning the origins of the Pray
codex)," *ibid.*, 87 (1971), 1ff.

10. Cf. *Regestrum de Varad*, in *RHM*, II, 640ff., par. 341; or, J. Karácsonyi-
S. Borovszky (eds), *Az időrendbe szedett váradi tüzespróba lajstroma* (Ordeals
by fire recorded in the Várad Register and set in chronological order), with a facsimile of the 1550 edition by G. Martinuzzi, *Ritus explorandae veritatis* (Kolozsvár,
1550) (Budapest, 1903), 288. Martinuzzi was at that time governor of Transylvania; cf. Pintér, I, 249f.; J. Horváth, *Irodalmi kezdetek*, 25.

11. L. Balics, *A római katholikus egyház története Magyarországon* (History of
the Roman Catholic Church in Hungary), 2 vols. in 3 (Budapest, 1885-88), II-1, 168.

12. A. Fodor, "László legendák a XV-XVI századi magyarországi breviáriumokban (Ladislas legends in 15th-16th century breviaries in Hungary)," *Athleta patriae*,
57ff. Pelbart of Temesvár, *Sermones Pomerii de Sanctis* (Hagenau, 1500), pars
aestiva, sermons 14-17; on Pelbart, cf. L. Hain, *Repertorium bibliographicum*,
2 vols. in 4 (Stuttgart-Tübingen, 1826-38; repr. Milan, 1948), II-2, 50ff., nos.
12548-60; S. V. Kovács (ed), *Temesvári Pelbárt válogatott írásai* (Selections from
the writings of Pelbart of Temesvár) (Budapest, 1982), 185ff.

13. Cf. *Athleta patriae*, 140ff.

14. E. Madas, "Szent László kiralnak innepéről: az Érdy kódex László napi be-
szédének elemzése (Analysis of the sermon for the Ladislas feast in the Érdy codex),"
*ibid.*, 73ff. On the codex, cf. J. Horváth, *Irodalmi kezdetek, 243ff.*; *I. Daám, A
Szeplőtelen Fogantatás védelme Magyarországon* (In defense of the Immaculate
Conception in Hungary) (Rome, 1955), 80ff.; L. Szegfű, "Szent Gellért prédikációi
(Sermons of Gerard of Csanád, "*Acta historica*, 80 (Szeged, 1985), 19ff.

15. Cf. Zs. Lukács, "A Szent László legenda a középkor magyar falképészeté-

ben (Impact of the Ladislas legend upon medieval wallpaintings in Hungary),"
*Athleta patriae*, 161ff.

16. J. H. Kolba, "Szent László alakja a középkori ötvösművészetben (Ladislas
in the art of medieval goldsmiths)," *ibid.*, 221ff.; Katona, *Historia critica*, IV,
395ff.

17. Gy. Balanyi, "Magyar szentek, szentéletű magyarok (Hungarian saints,
saintly Hungarians)," *Katolikus Szemle*, 15 (Rome, 1963), 100ff.; G. Örterle,
"Heilsprechung," *Lexicon für Theologie und Kirche*, 2nd rev. ed., vol. V (Hanover, 1960), 143. Diether Krywalski, "Das Mittelalter aus heutiger Sicht: Versuch
über die Schwierigkeit, die Vergangenheit zu verstehen," *Stimmen der Zeit*,
204 (1986), 676ff.

18. A. Tornai, "A Képes Krónika forrásaihoz (Sources of the Picture Chronicle)," *Memoria*, I, 203ff.; Horváth, *Kezdetek*, 65ff.

19. *SSH*, I, 462,14-16.

20. M. Rogerii *Carmen miserabile*, c. 6, *ibid.*, II, 556; *RHM*, I, 255ff., c. 6;
Pintér, I, 730f.; Wattenbach, II, 478f.; Macartney, 88; B. Menczer, *A Commentary on Hungarian Literature* (Castrop-Rauxel, 1956), 15. Horváth, *Stílusproblémák*, 239ff. T. Katona (ed), *Tatárjárás emlékezete* (In memory of the
Mongolian invasion (of 1241-42), with introduction by Gy. Györffy (Budapest,
1981).

21. *SSH*, II, 559,7 (c. 11).

22. Cf. L. Erdélyi, *Árpádkor* (Age of the Árpáds) (Budapest, 1922), 165.

23. Szentpétery, *Regesta*, I, no. 130; Forster, 425f.; Fejér, II, 198; Gy. Györffy,
"A magyar krónikák adata a III Béla-kori peticióról (Data in the Hungarian chronicles concerning written requests in the age of Béla III)," *Memoria*, I, 333ff.

24. Szentpétery, *Regesta*, I, no. 131; Wenczel, *ÁUO*, XI, 45.

25. Ladislas' *Decretum III*, a. 2.

26. Marczali, *Enchiridion*, 100; Szentpétery, *Regesta*, I, no. 24.

27. Tarcal, art. 79 (*RHM*, II, 369f.).

28. I. Esztergom, aa. 19, 20, 21, 34 and 69.

29. Coloman's *Lex Iudaeis data*; cf. *RHM*, II, 371f.

30. *Ibid.*, art. 3; the excellent article by B. L. Kumorowitz, "Szent László vásár-törvénye és Kálmán király pecsétes cartulája (St. Ladislas' marketing laws
and the sealed cartula of King Coloman)," *Athleta patriae*, 83ff.

31. *RHM*, II, 371f., aa. 4 and 5; Tarcal, art. 74; S. Kohn, *A zsidók története
Magyarországon*, vol. I: *A legrégibb időktől a mohácsi vészig* (History of the Jews
in Hungary: since the beginnings to 1526) (Budapest, 1884), 72ff.

32. Kumorowitz, *art. cit.*, 87f.

33. I Esztergom, aa. 6, 10, 15, and 20.

34. On this, see J. W. Thompson, *Economic and Social History of the Middle
Ages*, 2 vols. (New York, 1928), I, 269, 443; II, 598. R. C. Cave-H. H. Coulson
(eds), *A Source Book for Medieval Economic History* (Milwaukee, 1936), 120ff.;
R. H. Bautier, *The Economic Development of Medieval Europe* (London, 1971),
107ff.

35. Szentpétery, *Regesta*, I, no. 74; Fejér, II, 88 — though Szentpétery dated
it 1137!

36. Ladislas' *Decretum I*, a. 42; *Decretum III*, aa. 3, 25 and 26; for background,
cf. my book, 97f., and 105ff.

37. Tarcal, aa. 2, 5-6, 14 and 23.

38. Printed as an appendix to M. I. de Thurocz, *Chronica Hungarorum*, —
see E. Mályusz, *A Thuróczy Krónika és forrásai* (The Thuróc Chronicle and its

sources) (Budapest, 1967), 97; J. Fitz, *A magyar nyomdászat, könyvkiadás és könyvkereskedelem története* (History of printing, publishing and book trade in Hungary), vol. I (Budapest, 1959), 149, maintained that its printing in the appendix was sheer coincidence.

39. Macartney, 88; Lhotsky, Quellenkunde, 232f.

40. See Rogerius' *Epistola*, in *SSH*, II, 551f.; E. Mályusz, *Egyházi társadalom a középkori Magyarországon* (Ecclesiastical social structure in medieval Hungary) (Budapest, 1971), 70, and, my review of this book in *Austrian History Yearbook*, 14 (1978), 288ff.

41. E. Mályusz, *Az V. István kori gesta* (Hungarian chronicle compositions in the times of Stephen V, 1270-72) (Budapest, 1971), 13ff.

42. Macartney, 88; Pintér, I, 730f.

43. Spaleto, c. 24.

44. Idem, c. 25.

45. Pintér, I, 731.

46. Szentpétery, *Regesta*, I, no. 133 and 136, — "vero regis cancellarius;" also, L. Szilágyi, in *SSH*, II, 633,38.

47. Cf. A. Potthast (ed), *Regesta pontificum Romanorum*, 2 vols. (Berlin, 1875), I, no. 2550 (dated June 24, 1205).

48. "... et totius Dalmatiae et Croatiae gubernator;" see Katona, *Historia critica*, IV, 422, referring to the diploma for Zagreb by Béla III, in 1193; cf. Smiciklas, II, 264, a title confirmed by the king anew — see Fejér, II, 292 *and* 283; Szentpétery, *Regesta*, I, no. 154 and 155; Katona, *Historia critica*, IV, 419 *and* 410, respectively.

49. See the writ dated June 19, 1205, of Innocent III, in Potthast, *Regesta*, I, no. 2547; Fejér, II, 462; Katona, *Historia critica*, IV, 773; also, the papal letter to Desiderius of Csanád and abbot of Cikádor, to the effect that they ought to defend Bishop Calanus of Pécs against the false charges brought against him. Cf. Potthast, *Regesta*, I, no. 2837 (dated July 7, 1206); Fejér, III-1, 38; J. Koller, *Historia episcopatus Quinqueecclesiarum*, 2 vols. (Posonii, 1784), I, 328; Katona, *Historia critica*, V, 43f.

50. When the accusations did not cease, the pontiff wrote again to the bishop of Csanád and the abbot of Cikádor — see Potthast, *Regesta*, I, no. 3930 (dated March 9, 1210); Fejér, III-1, 98; Katona, *Historia critica*, V, 114f.

51. *Ibid.*, IV, 372f.; Koller, I, 304f.

52. Pauler, II, 591; Szentpétery, *Regesta*, I, no. 151.

53. Calanus "hac suspicione tandem liberatus" now accused the Cistercians and Hospitallers "quod multitudinem emerent vinearum, decimas tamen sibi vel ipsis ecclesiis subtraherent ex eisdem;" Katona, *Historia critica*, V, 169; Rome *admonet* the latter, — an order very much liked by Andrew II, *ibid.*, V, 278; on the papal response, cf. Potthast, *Regesta*, I, no. 4767 (dated June 20, 1213); Fejér, III-1, 141f.

54. Koller, I, 303; Fejér, II, 259, but the text is spurious, cf. Pauler, II, 591.

55. Cf. Gy. Moravcsik, "The Holy Crown of Hungary," *Hungarian Quarterly*, 4 (1938), 656ff.

56. F. Eckhart, "The Holy Crown of Hungary," *ibid.*, 6 (1940), 633ff.; G. Ferdinándy, "Die Thronfolge im Zeitalter der Könige aus dem Arpadienhause," *Ungarische Rundschau*, 2 (1913), 759ff.; F. Dölger, review of P. J. Kelleher, *The Holy Crown of Hungary* (Rome, 1951), in *HJb*, 73 (1954), 262ff.

57. M. v. Bárány-Oberschall, *Die hl. ungarische Krone* (Vienna, 1961), 41ff.; idem, "Problémák a magyar Szentkorona körül (Some questions concerning the Hungarian Crown)", repr. from *Antiquitas Hungarica* (Budapest, 1947.).

58. J. Deér, *Mittelalterliche Frauenkronen in Ost und West*, in *Herrschaftszeichen und Staatssymbolik* series, ed. P. E. Schramm, vol. XIII, part 2 of the *Schriften der MGH* (Stuttgart, 1955), 418ff.

59. J. Deér, *Die hl. Krone Ungarns* (Vienna, 1966), 183ff.; and, the review by J. D. Breckenridge, in *Speculum*, 43 (1968), 138ff.; Timon, 509ff.

60. A. Boeckler, *Die Stephanskrone*, in *Herrschaftszeichen*, vol. XIII-3 of the *Schriften der MGH* (Stuttgart, 1956), 731ff.; Th. v. Bogyay, review of P. J. Kelleher, *The Holy Crown of Hungary* in *Byzantinische Zeitschrift*, 45 (1952), 419ff.

61. Deér, *Hl. Krone*, 185ff.; Gy. Györffy, "Szent István koronája az Árpádkorban (St. Stephen's Crown in the Árpádian age)," *Vigilia*, 49 (1984), 580ff.

62. Cf. Ö. Polner, *A magyar szent Korona felső részének eredetkérdése* (Questions concerning the origins of the upper part of the Hungarian Crown) (Kolozsvár, 1943), 107.

63. Deér, *Hl. Krone*, 91ff.; idem, *art. cit.*, in *Archivum hist. pontificae* (1964), 117ff.; P. Váczy, "Az angyal hozta korona (The Crown Brought by the Angel)," *Életünk*, 19 (1982), 456ff.

64. Deér, *Hl. Krone*, 81ff.

65. *Ibid.*, 202ff.

66. *Ibid.*, 212ff.

67. Hartvic, *Vita* of King Stephen I, c. 10, in *SSH*, II, 414,19-24; *MGHSS*, XI, 233,11-14 (c. 9).

68. *Ibid.*, XI, 234,37; *SSH*, II, 414,18-20.

69. A. Becker, *Papst Urban II*, vol. XIX-1 of *Schriften der MGH* (Stuttgart, 1964), 167.

70. "Reminiscat tunc strenuitas tua religiosi principis Stephani, qui generis sui primus a sancta Romana et Apostolica Ecclesia fidei religionem suscepit, et regularis dignitatis permeruit;" cf. *MPL*, 151, 481b; Jaffé, *Regesta*, no. 5662 (dated June 27, 1096); Macartney, 166.

71. Stephen's *Vita maior*, c. 9, *SSH*, II, 384; *MGHSS*, XI, 233,11-12.

72. *MPL*, 151, 480f.

73. Váczy, *Erste Epoche*, 77f., and 117f.

74. Note the wording of Hartvic in describing the coronation: "benedictionis ergo apostolice litteris cum corona et cruce simul allatis;" *SSH*, II, 414,19-20.

75. *ibid.*, II, 412,9-413,2.

76. "Stephanus ... diademate regalis dignitatis ... coronatur;" *ibid.*, II, 414,22-24; *MGHSS*, XI, 233,13-14.

77. "Post acceptum regalis excellentie signum, ... statutum a se decretum manifestum facit;" *SSH*, II, 415,1-4. One ought to note though that in *MGHSS*, XI, 233,14-234,2, the text reads *imperialis* excellentiae signum (italics mine). Tellenbach, *Libertas*, 15f., and 151.

78. *SSH*, II, 415,1-6.

79. *Ibid.*, II, 384,7-11.

80. *Ibid.*, II, 414,20.

81. *Ibid.*, II, 401,5-8; *MGHSS*, XI, 233,8-9; Pintér, I, 204ff.; Horváth, *Irodalom kezdetei*, 27, 30, and 311.

82. Hartvic, *Vita*, c. 1, *SSH*, II, 402,11-18; Pintér, I, 202f., in ref. to Tarcal.

83. *SSH*, I, 322,20-21.

84. "Postquam autem Petrus factus est rex;" *ibid.*, I, 323,14.

85. *Ibid.*, I, 324f.

86. *Ibid.*, I, 325,18-19.

87. *Ibid.*, I, 343,19.

88. *Ibid.*, I, 343f.

89. Horváth, *Irodalom kezdetei*, 306f., identified the chronicler with Bishop Nicholas chancellor, — see also *SSH*, I, 348, note 3, — who signed the foundation charter of Tihany abbey in 1055; "qui tunc temporis uicem procurabat notarii in curia regali." Cf. E. Jakubovics-D. Pais (eds), *Ó-magyar olvasókönyv* (Old Hungarian reader) (Pécs, 1929), 25.

90. Cf. Caspar, *Register Gregors VII*, ii:13 (dated Oct. 28, 1074), I, 145.

91. Hampe, *Kaisergeschichte*, 20, 33.

92. My book, 70f.

93. *SSH*, I, 332,17-19.

94. "... regali dyademate;" *ibid.*, I, 358,5.

95. "Iniungentibus eum episcopis feliciter est coronatus;" *ibid.*, I, 358,5-6; my book, 78.

96. As, for instance, in the case of Aba (1041-44), elected ("elegerunt Abam et eum super se regem constituerant"), *SSH*, I, 325,4-6, and consecrated king ("Aba vero regali potestate sublimatus consecratus est in regem"), *ibid.*, I, 325,18-19.

97. *Ibid.*, I, 361,15-25. During his reign, Andrew I "filium suum Salomonem infantulum adhuc quinque annorum super totam Hungariam ... in regem fecit iniungi et coronari;" *ibid.*, I, 352,13-19; Váczy, *Erste Epoche*, 75.

98. "Ubi rex Salomon ... assistentibus regni proceribus per manus Geyse ducis honorabiliter est coronatus;" *SSH*, I, 362,21-23.

99. *Chronicon pictum*, c. 122; my book, 87.

100. *SSH*, I, 392,14-23.

101. *Ibid.*, I, 394,12-13. "Die Herrschaft der hl. Krone erstreckt sich im eigenen Sinn auf jenes Gebiet ... durch die Karpathen berenzten Donaubecken;" cf. A. S. Czernan, *Die Staatsidee des Hl. Stefan* (Klagenfurt, 1953), 10.

102. Cf. my book, 84ff., esp. 88, and 185, note 47.

103. Géza took the crown under pressure, "compellentibus Hungaris coronam regni accepit;" *SSH*, I, 394,13.

104. Pope Gregory VII to Salomon, "ad regem Hungarorum;" cf. Caspar, *Register*, ii:13, in full contrast with his letter to Géza I, addressed as "dux Hungarorum;" *ibid.*, ii:71 (dated April 17, 1075).

105. Ladizlaum ... communi consensu ... ad suscipiendum regni gubernaculum concorditer elegerunt;" *SSH*, I, 403f.; "regni gubernacula suscepit;" cf. Ladislas' *Vita*, c. 4, *ibid.*, II, 518,6.

106. "Et quamvis ipsum Hungari in regem absque voluntate sua elegerunt, numquam tamen in capite suo coronam posuit;" *ibid.*, I, 404f.

107. Cf. Ladislas' *Vita*, *ibid.*, II, 518,8-10.

108. "Coronatus est." Cf. *ibid.*, I, 420,25.

109. *Ibid.*, I, 421,1-13.

110. On the canonization of Stephen I, see Bernoldi Constantiensis *Chronicon*, anno 1083, *MGHSS*, V, 438f.; Hartvic, c. 24; Fejér, I, 460; my book, 94 and 97.

111. As proof of the chronicler's hatred toward Coloman — see his personal description of the king, *SSH*, I, 421,13-27.

112. Only one chronicler spoke of the coronation — *ibid.*, I, 420,25; the Chronicler of Óbuda only mentioned his reign, — *ibid.*, I, 420S,23-24. Coloman did attempt to prevent his nephew from gaining the crown of the saintly king — "ut non sit dignus portare coronam sancti regis;" *ibid.*, I, 421,11-12.

113. Hartvic, c. 10, *ibid.*, II, 414,19-24.

114. Cf. Csóka, 406ff.

115. "Stephanum, Colomanni regis filium, in regem coronaverunt;" *SSH*, I, 434,4-6.

116. "Bela Cecus ... Stephano, filio regis Colomanni mortuo ... coronatur;" *ibid.*, I, 446S,5-15.

117. *Ibid.*, I, 453,11, *and*, I, 453S,5-6.

118. *Ibid.*, I, 461,3.

119. See D. Dercsényi (ed), *Képes Krónika: Chronicon pictum* 2 vols. (Budapest, 1964), vol. I: facsimile edition, fol. 61'a, and Dercsényi's introduction, II, 7ff.; review by Gy. Rónay, in *Vigilia*, 30 (1965), 44ff.

120. *SSH*, I, 462,13.

121. *Ibid.*, I, 462,16.

122. "Emericus coronatur;" *ibid.*, I, 463,7, and, Emery's diploma of the year 1198, in Szentpétery, *Regesta*, I, no. 177; Knauz, I, 185.

123. See the letter, dated April 5, 1188, of Clement III, in Jaffé, *Regesta*, II, no. 16193; Knauz, I, 135; and, the writ of Celestine III, dated Dec. 20, 1191, *ibid.*, I, 141; Jaffé, *Regesta*, II, no. 16773.

124. Cf. the letters of Innocent III of May 15, 1209, Potthast, *Regesta*, I. no. 3725; *MPL*, 216, 50; of May 5, 1203, *ibid.*, 215, 56; Potthast, no. 1896; of April 24, 1204, *ibid.*, no. 2196; *MPL*, 215, 340; of Nov. 22, 1204, *ibid.*, 215, 463ff.; Potthast, no.2328; and, decision of Feb. 12, 1212, *ibid.*, no. 4378; *MPL*, 216, 515ff.

125. Cf. R. Browning, "A New Source on Byzantine-Hungaian Relations in the Twelfth Century," *Balkan Studies*, vol. II (Thessalonica, 1961), 173ff.

126. Moravcsik, *Fontes*, 149ff.; idem, *Byzantium*, 68f.; Deér, *Hl. Krone*, 202, note 61.

127. P. Wirth, "Das bislang erste literarische Zeugnis für die Stefanskrone," *Byzantinische Zeitschrift*, 53 (1960), 78ff.

128. *SSH*, I, 461,14-17, whose brother, Ladislas II, also became an anti-king — *ibid.*, I, 461,4-10; on Stephen IV, see also Pauler, I, 305.

129. *SSH*, I, 461,3-8.

130. Cinnamus, i:4, and v:1.

131. *SSH*, I, 462,13.

132. Cinnamus, v:5 and 8; Choniates, *Manuelis Comneni*, iv:1; Dölger, *Regesta*, nos. 1440, 1441, 1452, and 1472-75; A. Theiner (ed), *Vetera monumenta historiam Hungaricam illustrantia*, 2 vols. (Rome, 1859-60), I, 667f.

133. *SSH*, II, 414,13-14.

134. "Wizinburg, quae est regni sui metropolis;" *MGHSS*, XX, 813,50-51, anno 1063; "Weyssenburg," in Mügeln, cc. 54 and 55, *SSH*, II, 201 and 202, and, compare with Chronicle, *ibid.*, I, 462,8.

135. *Ibid.*, II, 385,24.

136. Holtzmann, *loc. cit.* (1926), text 4.

137. Whose body "Strigonii quiescit;" *SSH*, I, 462,9-11; the body of Béla III was laid to rest at Székesfehérvár, "in Albam (sic) ecclesia tumulatur;" *ibid.*, I, 463S,5-6, and I, 463,3-5; also, Keza, c. 69, *ibid.*, I, 183,26-27.

138. Szentpétery, *Regesta*, I, no. 104, dated ca. 1063-64, and no. 108, dated 1165.

139. "... prepositus Albe, curiae regiae concellarius;" *ibid.*, I, no. 155; Timon, 537ff.

140. He was transferred in 1179; for details, see Holtzmann, *loc. cit.*, letters three and four.

141. Szentpétery, *Regesta*, I, no. 155; Knauz, I, 142; Fejér, V-1, 212.

142. Szentpétery, *Regesta*, I, nos. 152, 154 and 155; also, 169. No. 172 (anno 1198) referred to him as the elected bishop of Eger and, *pariter*, chancellor. Nos. 173-77, refer to him as both the bishop of Eger and chancellor.

143. Smiciklas, II, 267; Pauler, II, 8.

144. Potthast, *Regesta*, I, no. 494; Katona, *Historia critica*, IV, 530; Fejér, II, 333.

145. "... cuius curae ornamenta et diadema etiam regium committuntur;" *MPL*, 214, 449; Karácsonyi, *art. cit.* in *Századok*, 35 (1901), 1002ff.

146. Cf. L. Erdélyi (ed), *A pannonhalmi Szent Benedekrend története* (History of the Benedictines of Pannonhalma), 12 vols. (Budapest, 1902-07), I, 589f.; abbreviated version in *MPL*, 151, 1253ff.; however, the writ is an interpolated imitation of the original — cf. Szentpétery, *Regesta*, I, no. 2.

147. "Willermus grammaticus;" cf. L. Fejérpataky (ed), *Kálmán király oklevelei* (Diplomas of King Coloman) (Budapest, 1892), 43. An antiphonale, prepared by a Bavarian monk named Arnold, was used by the clerics in Esztergom in about 1030; cf. Knauz, I, 42; and, there is evidence about another schoolmaster in Esztergom in about 1205. Cf. *ibid.*, I, 180; Fejér, III-1, 26.

148. It was Abbot David who had the church rebuilt, and the king attended the consecration ceremony; cf. Erdélyi, *Rendtörténet*, I, 596, no. 7; Szentpétery, *Regesta*, I, no. 61.

149. Ladislas I, *Decretum I*, art. 36.

150. See Mansi, *Concilia*, XXII, 227f., can. 18; Roger of Hoveden, *Chronica*, anno 1179, R. S. 51-52 (London, 1869), 187; Wright, Map, i:31. Its canons, however, did not come down to posterity; cf. Jedin, *Handbuch*, III-2, 84.

151. Erdélyi, *Rendtörténet*, I, 590, dated it between 1083 and 1095; book list, *ibid.*, I, 590f.; Szentpétery, *Regesta*, I, no. 29, dated it 1093, and so did Katona, *Historia critica*, II, 641. Cs. Csapodi, *A legrégibb magyar könyvtár benső rendje* (Budapest, 1957).

152. Marczali, *Enchiridion*, 102,1-2; Szentpétery, *Regesta*, I, no. 24; Fejér, I, 468; K. Lübeck, "Abtswahl, 1198," *HJb*, 52 (1932), 189ff. Hildegard of Bingen wrote a book on plants in about 1170; cf. *Subtilitatum diversarum naturarum creaturarum libri IX*, in *MPL*, 197, 1118ff., though, as L. Thorndike, *History of Magic and Experimental Science*, 8 vols. (New York, 1923etc.), II, 130, raised the point, the Migne edition lacked a plan arrangement. In 230 entries in the first part of her book, she discussed the natural aspects of honey, milk, salt, vinegar, eggs, sulphur nitrite and medications. In her opinion, the "needless" plants have originated from the sweat of the earth, and the "necessary" and "good" ones from the liquids of the earth; for example, vine, grapes, or trees originated from earthly liquids. H. O. Taylor, *The Medieval Mind*, 2 vols. (New York, 1925), I, 464f.; K. Storck, *Deutsche Literaturgeschichte*, 10th rev. ed., ed. M. Rockenbach (Stuttgart, 1926), 117.

153. "Fundavit abbatiam nobilissimam de Semigis, in qua non solent recipi nisi Franci;" in *MGHSS*, XXIII, 798,51-52 (anno 1077!).

154. Letter had to be written after 1183 on the grounds that royal writs issued by Béla III were signed by Nicholas of Esztergom — cf. Szentpétery, *Regesta*, I, nos. 136, 138. The name of Job of Esztergom appeared for the first time in 1185 — *ibid.*, I, no. 139; Wenczel, *ÁUO*, I, 78; VI, 148.

155. Cf. J. Darrouzes, *Georges et Demetrios Tornikes: Letters et discours* (Paris, 1970), 189ff., and 200f.; Moravcsik, *Fontes*, 249ft.

156. On John Chrysostom, see H. von Campenhausen, *Griechische Kirchenväter*, 3rd ed. (Stuttgart, 1961), 137ff.

157. Funk-Bihlmeyer, I, 182f.; also, *Symbolum fidei* of Pope Leo III, in Mansi, *Concilia*, XIII, 978f.

158. Funk-Bihlmeyer, II, 52; *MGH Poetae Carolini*, I, 437ff.

159. Mansi, *Concilia*, XIV, 17ff.; Jedin, *Handbuch*, III-1, 94f., and 113; on the 'input' of Alcuin, see W. Heil, "Der Adoptianismus Alkuin und Spanien," in W. Braunfels *et al* (eds), *Karl der Grosse: Lebenswerk und Nachleben*, 3 vols. (Düsseldorf, 1965), II, 95ff.

160. Szentpétery, *Regesta*, I, no. 82; Erdélyi, *Rendtörténet*, I, 601; Wenczel, *ÁUO*, I, 62.

161. *Ibid.*, I, 55; Szentpétery, *Regesta*, I, no. 67; Erdélyi, *Rendtörténet*, I, 595, no. 6.

162. *Ibid.*, I, 602; Wenczel, I, 63; Szentpétery, *Regesta*, I, no. 83.

163. See letters of Stephen of Tournai (then) abbot of St. Genovéva, in *MPL*, 211, 334f., and 335f.; second writ also in Fejér, II, 189f.

164. Szentpétery, *Regesta*, I, no. 142; Wenczel, *ÁUO*, VI, 161f.

165. Cf. M. Heimbucher, *Die Orden und Kongregationen der katolischen Kirche*, 2 vols.; 3rd rev. ed. (Paderborn, 1933), I, 438.; G. Schreiber, "Praemonstratenserkultur des 12 Jahrhunderts," *Analecta Praemonstratensia*, 16 (1940), 41ff. K. Elm (ed), *Norbert von Xanten, Adliger, Ordensstifter, Kirchenfürst* (Cologne, 1984).

166. Heimbucher, I, 444; Hóman-Szekfű, I, 389f.

167. A. Oszvald, *A magyarországi premontrei apátságok* (The houses of the Canons of Prémontré in medieval Hungary) (Budapest, 1939), 5ff.; G. Schreiber, "Mönchtum und Wallfahrt," *HJB*, 55 (1935), 160ff.

168. Cf. A. Gábriel, "A Lányi kódex (The Lányi codex)," in his *Emlékkönyv Szt. Norbert halálának 800 éves jubileumára* (Yearbook on the 800 anniversary of St. Norbert's death) (Gödöllő, 1934), 136ff.; idem, "A pozsonyi kódex (The Poson codex)," *MKSz*, 48 (1940), 333ff. Gy. Volf (ed), *Régi magyar kódexek és nyomtatványok* (Old Hungarian codices and prints), 15 vols. (Budapest, 1879-1908), III, 103ff.

169. Mályusz, *Egyházi társadalom*, 120ff., and 140ff.; on background, F. Heer, *Europäische Geistesgeschichte*, 2nd ed. (Stuttgart, 1965), 106ff.

170. Mályusz, *Egyházi társadalom*, 35ff.; Taylor, II, 260ff.

171. Hóman-Szekfű, I, 413ff.; S. R. Packard, *Twelfth Century Europe* (Amherst, Mass., 1973), 45ff., and 59ff.

172. Cf. H. Fichtenau, *Das Urkundenwesen in Österreich vom 8 bis zum frühen 13 Jahrhundert* (Vienna-Graz, 1971), 135ff., esp. 172ff.; idem, *Beiträge zur Mediävistik*, 2 vols. (Stuttgart, 1975-77), II, 100ff.; my reviews of both works in *Austrian History Yearbook*, 9-10 (1973-74), 393f.; *ibid.*, 17-18 (1981-82), 354ff.

173. G. A. J. Hodgett, *A Social, Economic History of Medieval Europe* (London, 1972), 137ff.; H. C. Krueger, "Economic Aspects of Expanding Europe," in M. Clagett *et al* (ed), *Twelfth Century Europe and the Foundations of Modern Society* (Madison, Wisc., 1966), 59ff.; F. Ohly, *Schriften zur mittelalterlichen Bedeutungsforschung* (Darmstadt, 1977), 171ff.

# Appendix I

# Did Rumanians Live in Pannonia and Transylvania during the Twelfth Century?

Anonymus wrote that Tétény, one of the seven leaders of the Hungarian conquest (in the 890's) and the father of Horka, had received news about the good earth of *Ultrasiluania*, where people lived under the rule of 'some Vlach,' named Gelou — "Gelou quidem Blacus." With the approval of Árpád the Conqueror, Tétény decided to occupy the land of the good earth and dispatched Agmand-Apafarkas to survey it for him. Agmand liked the land and reported to his lord that the inhabitants, known as Vlachs and Slovens, were worthless people, whose armaments consisted of bows and arrows, and whose weak ruler would not assert any leadership against the Cumans and Petchenegs, who had harrassed them frequently.

Tétény moved against Gelou and defeated him. Gelou fled from the battle, but Tétény's men killed him near the creek Kapus. Upon his death, his people, on its own, made peace, "sua propria voluntate dextra dantes," with Tétény, and by taking an oath at Esküllő, recognized him as their lord. Tétény now possessed the area in peace, and his descendants retained control over it until the days of King St. Stephen.

The mother of King Stephen, Sarolt, was the younger daughter of Geula (Gyula), the son of Horka. Because Geula refused to become a Christian, Stephen had the uncle arrested and kept under guard at his court.

The importance of the report is not that Anonymus projected a twelfth century view of history into the past (of some 300 years) and recorded Vlach presence in *Ultrasiluania* ( = Transylvania) as if at the time of the Magyar ( = Hungarian) conquest of the mid-Danubian region, but that in the late twelfth century view the Vlachs in Transylvania

were known as a people who had, at the very beginning of
the Hungarian conquest, become, on their own, a subject
people of the conquering Magyars. Anonymus emphasized,
"sicut in annalibus continetur cronicis," that Gelou the Vlach
and his people were weak enemies, easily defeated, and they
had freely, on their own, submitted to their victors after
their defeat. (Cf. Anonymus, *Gesta*, cc. 24-27, *SSH*, I, 65ff.;
in the new edition of Anonymus, *Gesta Hungarorum* (Budapest, 1977), 101ff., cc. 23-27, respectively; Cs. Csapodi,
*Az Anonymus kérdés története* (An appraisal of the
Anonymus question) (Budapest, 1978). Macartney, 74f.,
said that the Tétény 'episode' was an original part of
the *gesta*; Anonymus did refer to his sources, "sunt
antiquiores populi, de quibus hystoriographi ... scrip-
serunt;" *SSH*, I, 36,1-2; Gy. Kristó, "Anonymus magyarországi irott forrásainak kérdéséhez (Remarks on the written
source material available to Anonymus from historic Hungary)," *MKSz*, 88 (1972), 166ff.; J. Horváth, *Stílusproblémák*, 213ff.; on the arrest of Gyula, see the *Chronicon pictum*, c. 65. B. Köpeczi *et al* (ed), *Erdély története* (History
of Transylvania), 3 vols. (Budapest, 1986, I, 235ff., and
575ff. Z. I. Tóth, "Tuhutum és Gelou: hagyomány s történelmi hitelesség Anonymus művében (Tradition and
reliability in the Hungarian Anonymus)," *Századok*, 79-80
(1945-46), 21ff.

Anonymus wrote this, the chronicler quoted so readily
by Nicolae Draganu, Rumanian historian, who, in 1933,
stated 'in accordance with the report of a late twelfth century Hungarian chronicler,' that Rumanians (Vlachs) had
been living in Transylvania already in the days of Árpád
the Conqueror (who died in 907). Now, there are two factors that must have escaped the attention of both Nicolae
Draganu and C. A. Macartney, a British historian of the
Hungarian Middle Ages. The latter spoke, though with good
intentions, of a Hungarian 'problem:' "Anon(ymus) commits
his grand historical *gaffe* of introducing Vlachs, under a
prince of their own, inhabiting Transylvania when the Magyars enter it." (Cf. Macartney, 75) The highly respected
British historian based his assertion on the hypothesis that
there had existed a so-called Gyula-legend whose origins
went back to the tenth century, and Anonymus had merely

interpolated it into his narrative. Aside from the fact that a
"legend" had little or no serious historical value, the hypothesis of Macartney is further weakened by the arguments of
János Horváth, an authority on medieval Hungarian historical literature, who did not know of the existence of such
a "legend." Following the reference to his sources by Anonymus, "ut dicunt nostri ioculatores" (*SSH*, I, 65, 19), Horváth explained that Anonymus must have turned to the historical epic preserved in the songs of *ioculatores* for information, when writing about heroes and historical personages
(cf. his *Stílusproblémák*, 213f., and note 21). Were a chronicler to quote from ioculator songs, he had to rely upon information according to his own personal views and the outlook of his age. The fact that Anonymus used oral data preserved by folksingers (*ioculatores*), and projected it back
in time to events that had taken place some three centuries
earlier, made Macartney's views untenable. Of course, the
Vlachs had been living in Transylvania in the age of
Anonymus — the late twelfth century (cf. Váczy, in *Memoria Hungariae*, I, 13ff.), but, had even a Gyula-legend been
in existence, a report based upon it could only have meant
that those Vlachs in Transylvania had already in the times
of Árpád (late ninth century) submitted to the conquering
Magyars! Anonymus' *gaffe* voided the legal and historical
foundations of the Rumanian claim in the sense that a group
of people who had acknowledged defeat and had, on their
own, surrendered to their victors, did not have, because it
could not have, any historic and legal demands to the territory it had previously held (nor to a social and constitutional
position it had previously maintained in that area). This
particular circumstance has, aside from the rather dubious
existence of a Gyula-legend, escaped the attention of the
learned Professor Macartney.

Draganu made no distinction between *Blacus, Blachii*,
mentioned by Anonymus on the soil of Transylvania, and
the *Blachii* named by Anonymus in Pannonia prior to the
Magyars' conquest in the 890's. "Terram Pannonie habi-
tarent Sclaui, Bulgarii et Blachii ac pastores Romanorum"
(*SSH*, I, 45,11-12). Speaking of Transylvania, Anonymus
mentioned only Vlachs (*Blacs*): *Blachii*; however, in Pannonia, he spoke of them in the company of Slavs, Bul-

garians, and the shepherds of the Romans, — never alone. Anonymus spoke of their principality (*ducatus*) in the north-western corner of Transylvania, the region of Szamos stream and its tributaries, where no major river had Rumanian names, and no Hungarian had borrowed Rumanian place names prior to 1400; cf. I. Kniezsa, *Erdély viznevei* (River names in Transylvania) (Kolozsvár, 1943); G. Schramm, *Eroberer und Eingesessene: geographische Lehnnamen als Zeugen der Geschichte Sudosteuropas im ersten Jahrtausend n. Chr.* (Stuttgart, 1981); L. Szegfű, "Az Ajton monda (The Ajton-legend)," *Acta historica*, 40 (Szeged, 1972), 3ff.

Keza, c. 23, confirmed the assertion of Anonymus by saying that upon the death of Etele ( = Attila), the Slavs lived alone on Pannonian land for about a decade, but were joined by Greek, Teutonic, Messian and *Ulahis* ( = Vlach) newcomers, who had remained in Pannonia after the dis-appearance of the Huns, and who had — and this is impor-tant! — earlier served Attila well; "qui vivente Ethela popu-lari servitio sibi perviebant" (*SSH*, I, 163,17-19). Keza openly stated that, upon the death of Attila, the Slavic element had been predominant in Pannonia amidst the Greek, etc., Vlach newcomers, "advenis remanentibus in eadem" (*ibid.*, I, 46,1). This newcomer element had — this is also impor-tant —, earlier, and together with the Slavic population, served Attila well. Keza's emphasis here is not on the sub-serviance of the peoples of Pannonia to Attila; instead, he stresses the fact that the *Blachii: Ulahii* element had lived under the predominance of the lord of the region in both Pannonia and Transylvania. (The Vlachs in Pannonia left no place names behind, nor names for rivers; therefore, it is not possible to speak of a Pannonian Vlach element that departed eastward, thereby increasing the number of Blachs in Transylvania; cf. *SSH*, I, 157, and 162-63.)

The *Chronicon pictum*, c. 23, confirms the assertions of Keza (regardless of the fact that the wording of the same passage in the *Chronicon Budense*, based upon the fifteenth century Sambucus codex, provides a different word order), in that the chronicler(s) had said that in the days of Attila the Pannonian population had consisted of servile elements, "qui Attyllae serviebant" (*SSH*, I, 269,17-18). The chron-iclers did note earlier that, in the times of Attila, the inhabitants of the Pannonian cities had moved, with their chief's permission, out of Pannonia across the sea (of Adria) to Apulia leaving their belongings and chattel behind. The Vlachs, however, had remained, on their own free will, in Pannonia — "sponte in Pannonia remanentibus." Cf. *ibid.*, I, 218,3-7.

Draganu's argument is further undermined by the comments of Nestor, Russian chronicler who wrote that the Vlachs, who predominated the Slavs in Pannonia, were conquered by the Magyars, who had them expelled (from Pannonia); cf. Cross, *Russian Chronicle*, 62. This is the second factor that had escaped the attention of Draganu, because the appropriate portion of Nestor's Chronicle had existed at the times of Anonymus. Nestor wrote his narrative in about 1110-1112, though his compiler, the writer of the so called Laurentius Chronicle, completed his opus only in the early fourteenth century. (Cf. W. Philip, "Die 'Provest vremennych let'," in his *Aufsätze zum geschichtlichen und politischen Denken im Kiewer Russland* (Breslau, 1940), 24ff., borrowing from earlier sources — cf. R. Buchner, "Die politische Vorstellungswelt Adams von Bremen," *Archiv für Kulturgeschichte*, 45 (1963), 15ff.: "... sind unverarbeitete Abschnitte aus fremden Geschichtswerken aufgenommen worden." Also, M. T. Florinsky, *Russia: History and Interpretation*, 2 vols., rev. ed. (New York, 1953), I, 13f.) There also existed a much earlier text, of about 1039 — cf. A. Pogodin, "Der Bericht der Russischen Chronik über die Gründung des Russischen Staates," *Zeitschrift für Osteuropäische Geschichte*, 5 (1931), 202ff.; W. Scheck, *Geschichte Russlands*, rev. ed. (Munich, 1977), 25f.

Nestor wrote about the Vlakhs (*Vlakhi*) — the term meant "Roman" in old Slavic —, and said that, anno 6396-6406 (that is, 888 to 889 AD) the Magyars (in the text: "Black Ugors" standing for "western" Ugors) had passed by Kiev and the Magyar Hill, *Ugorskaya gora*, and had crossed the Magyar Mountains ( = Carpathians). (Earlier, in an entry under 880-82, Nestor did speak of the Magyars' having passed by Kiev and the Magyar Hill next to Kiev. On the hill, cf. N. Zakrevsky, *Opisanie Kieva* (Moscow, 1868), 191ff.; Györffy, *István király*, 166 and 173, on Black Ugros, the people of Gyula; Köpeczi, *Erdély*, I, 179ff.; Pauler, I, 508f.

All of this could mean that the Slavic element had settled

at first in the region beyond the "Magyar" Mountains. The Vlachs, however, defeated the Slavs, Nestor recorded, and the Magyars had the Vlachs expelled from the region by occupying their lands and settling down among the Slavs, whom they, the Magyars, had made into their servants. The Slavic element had thus become a servile folk to the conquering Magyars, and the area is known since then as the land of the Magyars. Nestor noted that the Magyars had also fought the Byzantines, had raided Thrace and Macedonia as far as south as Thessalonica, and had continued to struggle with the Czechs and the Moravians. Indeed, Anonymus said that it was the Kievan (Russian) princes who had told Álmos, leader of the Magyars and the father of Árpád, that Slavs, Bulgarians and Vlachs, together with the shepherds of the Romans, had inhabited Pannonia. The "Black Ugors" were nomads like the Povlocs, had fought their way through the great mountains ( = of the Carpathians), and had continued to fight with their neighbors, Vlachs and Slavs, in their new country.

The annotations of the Russian chronicler are important because they can be compared with the data of Anonymus and the other chronicles, and confirm the entry of the Magyars into the mid-Danubian region. Nestor had actually stated that (1) It was the Slavs who had found first a home in the mid-Danubian region (after the disappearance of the Huns from the area), but they had been subdued by the Vlachs. (2) The Magyars moving into the region had the Vlachs expelled, and had settled down among the Slavs, but had forced the latter to live under their rule. Nestor made the point that the Magyars did expell the Vlachs, consequently, the Vlachs had, as a result of the Magyar conquest of the mid-Danube region, disappeared from the area.

In connection with the usage by Nestor of the expression "Vlakh," one has to bear in mind that terms such as *Vlasi*, or *Vlakhi* refer to Roman-Italians, as it is, for instance, evident from the Czech term *vlachy*, or *wlochy* in modern Polish.

From the annotations of the *Chronicon pictum*, cc. 14 and 23, as compared with those of Nestor, one may argue that the Pannonian Vlakhs were of late Roman descent, but were not Vlach-Rumanians. "Pannonia extitit ... Sclavis tantummodo, Grecis, Vlachis, Teutonicis advenis, Messia-

nis remanentibus, ... qui vivente Atyla populari servitio sibi
serviebant" (*SSH*, I, 281,3-9). As a matter of fact, Gottfried
of Viterbo, *Pantheon: seu universitatis libri*, xxii:23, argued
that, in the times of Attila, Lombards had inhabited Hungarian soil, "quo tempore Lombardi habitabant in Ungaria"
(*MGHSS*, XII, 140), who had, in the opinion of the compiler of the *Chronicon pictum*, lived as servants in Pannonia,
the pasture of the Romans, during the days of Attila; cf.
*SSH*, I, 269,16-18. (Odo de Deogilo, too, had spoken of Pannonia ( = Hungary) as the pasture of the Romans; cf. *MGHSS*,
XXVI, 62.)

Let it be said in conclusion that, by comparing contemporary records of the Russian and Hungarian chroniclers,
the Vlach element, mentioned by Anonymus as the inhabitants of Pannonia, had been expelled from there by the
conquering Magyars ( = Hungarians); if not totally destroyed,
the Vlachs were so thoroughly subjugated by the Magyars
that the Russian chronicler did not even bother to record
their name or existence anymore. Such a conclusion is further
supported by Anonymus who did say that the spy of Tétény
had reported that the *Blachii* in Transylvania were the most
despised folk among all the peoples known to him; "et habi-
tatores terre illius viliores homines essent tocius mundi, quia
essent Blasii et Sclaui, quia arma non haberent..." Cf. *SSH*,
I, 66,4-6.

In fact, Nestor's assertion that the Vlachs had subjugated the Slavs in Pannonia, but, in turn, the Vlachs had been
totally vanquished by the Magyars, so that the chronicler
took no further notice of their existence, says openly that
the decline of the Vlachs can be regarded as a just punishment, by fate, on account of the false pride that they had
previously shown toward the Slavs. It calls for attention that,
while the Vlachs had subjugated the Slavs in Pannonia
(Nestor), the victorious Magyars had only predominated the
Slavic peoples of their new country.

L. Gáldi, *Le romanisme transdanubien* (Rome, 1937),
16ff., had answered Draganu's arguments, and L. Tamás,
*Rómaiak, románok és oláhok Dácia Trajanában* (Romans,
Rumanians and Vlachs in Dacia Traiana) (Budapest, 1935),
85f., did question, on linguistic, archaeological and historic
grounds, that the Rumanians would be the descendants of

the Dacians. Tamás said that the Balkan origins of the
Rumanians cannot be denied, *ibid.*, 114; had there existed
a Roman-Dacian continuity in Transylvania, or in Pannonia, the names of rivers and towns of the regions would be
of Roman origin, but they are not! Cf. *ibid.*, 120. As A.
Gráf, *Pannonia ókori földrajzára vonatkozó kutatások áttekintő
összefoglalása* (Survey of research activities concerning the
ancient geography of Pannonia) (Budapest, 1936), 120 and
217, had pointed out on archaeological grounds that the
medieval towns in Hungary had had no continuous existence:
their modern names are either Slavic or Magyar in origin —
*ibid.*, 16. E. Tóth, "Dácia római tartomány (Dacia, a Roman
province)," in Köpeczi, *Erdély*, I, 104ff. Dacia remained
a Roman province for 165 years, too brief a period for as-
similation. Not even in Pannonia did 360 years of Roman
rule Romanize the material culture of the population. Town
life in Transylvania did not develop out of the ranks of earlier
peoples, but only out of the *vici* located next to military
camps. The civilian settlement in the legion camp at Apulum
(Gyulafehérvár) had been elevated to the rank of *municipium*,
but its inhabitants had not taken part in its public life. The
Dacians busy with their viticulture lived in the hills, and
had themselves excluded from Romanization. Cf. *ibid.*, I,
92ff., and 561. For a different point of view, see Gy.
Kristó, "Rómaiak és vlachok Nyesztornál és Anonymusnál (The Romans and Vlachs of Anonymus)," *Századok*, 112 (1978), 623ff.; E. Fügedi, "A befogadó: közép-
*kori magyar királyság* (The medieval Hungarian kingdom in the role of 'receiver' of peoples)," *Történelmi Szemle*,
22 (1979), 355ff.

   P. Diaconu, *Les Petchenegues au bas-Danube* (Bucharest,
1970), 34, note 83, stated, fully ignoring the record of
Constantine Porphyrogenitus, *De administrando imperio*,
ed. Gy. Moravcsik *et al*, 2nd ed. (Washington, DC, 1967),
c. xxxvii, that in Vlach countries people were already speaking Rumanian during the tenth century. A. Toynbee, *Constantine Porphyrogenitos and His World* (Oxford, 1973),
457, note 2, has fully discredited the views of Diaconu, while
G. C. Soulis, "The Legacy of Cyrill and Methodius to the
Southern Slavs," *Dumbarkton Oaks Papers* XIX (Washington, DC, 1965), 19ff., explained that as late as the sixteenth

century, the administrative language in the territories of the Rumanian principalities was the Macedonian-Slavonian (dialect), and it remained the official language of the Church in the area until 1679. For an interesting overview, cf. I. Szabó-Torjai, *Erdély szellemi századai* (The intellectual-spiritual growth of Transylvania) (Munich, 1956), 10ff.; and, Zs. Jakó, *Könyv, írás, értelmiség* (Books, writing and the intelligentsia) (Bucharest, 1977).

# Appendix II

## The "Mission" of Gerhoch of Reichersberg to the Hungarian and Russian Courts

In the background of Géza II's military policies in Kiev and in Halich, there is the less well documented ecclesiastical-diplomatic mission of Gerhoch of Reichersberg to the Hungarian and Ruthenian courts during the mid-1140's. (*LdL*, III, 133, anno 1146; there is a different date, *ibid.*, III, 412.) Although the mission did not take place because, to quote Gerhoch, of the rather hostile attitude of the Hungarian ruler (*ibid.*, III, 493,15-24), the fact that it was not a Cardinal of the papal curia, but the provost of Reichersberg who would have been sent as a delegate, might raise some questions. Cf. J. Bach, "Propst Gerhoch I of Reichersberg, ein deutscher Reformator des 12 Jahrhunderts," *Österreichische Vierteljahrschrift für katholische Theologie*, 4 (1865), 19ff., esp. 37. It seems that the provost may have had a fairly clear view of Hungarian church politics because Reichersberg's sphere of influence had reached to the Hungarian border, thus he may have been eligible to represent the interests of Rome at the Hungarian court without being a member of the hierarchy in Rome. Cf. *LdL*, III, 437; Bernhardi, *Lothair*, 495ff., and compare with Freising, *Gesta*, i:33.

Reichersberg came under the jurisdiction of Salzburg, and, at this time, the archbishop maintained close contacts with Géza II; cf. *Vita Conradi*, c. 18f. (*MGHSS*, XI, 73f.). This particular relationship is important because, at this time, Rome and Géza II maintained no contacts at all (Bernhardi, *Lothair*, 528ff.). Gerhoch had personal relations with at least one cleric in Hungary, who had his schooling completed at Reichersberg, and who had been living in the Kalocsa archdiocese. See his comments on Psalm 64,

*MPL*, 193, 1735f.; Classen, *Gerhoch*, 357. This graduate
of Reichersberg had highly praised Gerhoch's commentaries
on the psalms and had a copy of his works requested for the
Kalocsa archbishop — cf. *Thesaurus*, V, 1081; also, the
writ of Gerhoch addressed to Eberhard of Salzburg and (to
an) abbot Gottschalk, perhaps of Heiligenkreuz (it is from
Heiligenkreuz that the first Cistercian monks had entered
Hungary /Cikádor/); *MPL*, 193, 987-90. The Kalocsa archbishop could have been the former abbot of Baumgarten-
burg, a daughter house of Heiligenkreuz, who died in 1156;
cf. *Continuatio Claustroneuburgensis I*, a. 1156, *MGHSS*,
IX, 611.

Why was the provost of Reichersberg regarded, in his
own words, as a "persona non grata" at the court of Géza
II? Was it a remark made in his comments on the 64th Psalm
(Vulgate!) — to the effect that in Hungary, a barbarian and
hardly a Christian country, the bishops had to keep the king
from starting a new and unnecessary military adventure
against Byzantium, — that had caused some rift (*LdL*, III,
463,16ff.; Chalandon, 385ff.; K. J. Heilig, *Ostrom und das
deutsche Reich im 12 Jahrhundert: die Erhebung Österreichs zum Herzogtum und das Bündniss zwischen Byzanz
und das Westreich*, in *MGH Schriften* ser. /1941/, 157ff.),
though it is doubtful that Gerhoch's books would have been
read at the court of Géza II at all? Perhaps, the provost had
made some, entirely innocent remark(s) about the king's
sister at Admont abbey, cf. *ibid.*, 160; Bernhardi, *Konrad
III*, 502, — that could have been misunderstood, or regarded out of context. The argument that the Hungarian monarch did not tolerate the presence of papal delegates in the
realm, is valid; Gerhoch did not dare enter Hungary for fear
of his life — *LdL*, III, 463,16etc.

The Ruthenian mission of Gerhoch may have been connected with Pope Eugene III's diplomatic effort to establish,
at Kiev, a firm foundation for papal diplomacy. Izjaslav,
grand-duke of Kiev, had only recently made the cleric
Clement, a Kievan, Patriarch of Kiev instead of the Metropolitan Michael (a Greek), who returned (or, had been sent
back) to Byzantium. ("Regnum Ruthenorum" in the text
could only mean Halich or Kiev; cf. B. de Baumgarten,
"Chronologie ecclesiastique des terres russes du Xe au XIIIe

siècle," *Orientalia Christiana*, 17 /1930/, 72ff.) In view of the fact that, in 1152, there existed a Hungaro-Kievan alliance vs. Byzantium — see *supra*, chapter seven; Chalandon, 401f., and 403ff., — the Roman See could have decided to intervene and create, for its own diplomatic use, a firm basis for a(n anti-)Byzantine policy in Kiev. Cf. Baumgarten, no. 5 of the documents cited.

It must have been at the same time, during the siege of Halich by Géza II, that the duke of Halich had contact established with Hungarian ecclesiastics. Gerhoch's planned mission may have been connected with such an arrangement; were he to succeed, he could bring Hungary closer to Rome and create closer church ties with Kiev and Halich in an area, or areas, located in the sphere of Byzantine ecclesiastical and diplomatic interests. "Pro ecclesiasticae fidei ac disciplinae seminibus mittendis." On May 26, 1152, Gerhoch was in Salzburg — cf. Th. Ried, *Codex diplomaticus episcopatus Ratisbonensis*, vol. I (Regensburg, 1816), 222, no. 241. He did not cross the Hungarian border.

# Bibliography

Albert of Aachen ( = Aix), *Liber Christianae expeditionis pro ereptione, emundatione et restitutione sanctae Hierosolymitanae, RHC Occ*, IV, 265ff.; *MPL*, 166.

*Acta sanctorum Bollandiana*, 60 vols. to Oct. XI (Paris-Rome, 1864-76) cited as *ASS*

G. Acropolita, *Annales, MPG*, 140

E. Adam, *Baukunst des Mittelalters, II*, vol. 10 of *Ullstein Kunstgeschichte* (Frankfurt/M-Berlin, 1963)

G. Adriányi, "Der Eintritt Ungarns in die christlich-abendländische Volksgemeinschaft," *Ungarn Jahrbuch*, 6 (1974-75), 24ff.

G. Adriányi, "Die ungarischen Synoden," *Annuarium historiae conciliorum*, 8 (1976), 541ff.

Raymond of Agiles, *Historia Francorum qui ceperunt Jerusalem* in *MPL*, 155

K. Albioni, *Memorie per la storia della Dalmazia*, II (Zara, 1809)

Hermann Altahensis, *Geneologia, MGHSS*, XVII, 377f.

M. Angold, *The Byzantine Empire*, 1025-1204 (London, 1984)

Anonymus, *Gesta Hungarorum* (Budapest, 1977)

Anonymus, *Gesta Hungarorum*, in *SSH*, I, 13ff.; *RHM*, I, 1ff.

*Annales Aegidi Brunsvicenses, MGHSS*, XXI

*Annales Augustiani, MGHSS*, III

*Annales Marbacenses, MGHSS*, XVII

*Annales Paderborneneses, MGHSS*, III

*Annales Posonienses, SSH*, I, 125ff.

*Annales Reichersbergenses, MGHSS*, XVII

Anonymi Caietani *Descriptio*, in P. Riant (ed), *Exuviae sacrae Constantinopolitanae*, 2 vols. (Geneva, 1841-43)

Ansberti *Historia de expeditione Friderici Imperatoris, FRASS*, V, 14ff.

*Archivio storico Italiano*, 16 vols. (Florence, 1842-51)

Arnold of Lübeck, *Chronica Slavorum, MGHSS*, XXI

Vitus Arpeckius, *Chronicon Austriacum*, in Pez, *Scriptores*, I

Aurelius Augustinus, *De doctrina Christiana*, *MPL*, 34, 15ff.

Aurelius Augustinus (St. Augustine), *Regula ad servos Dei*, in *MPL*, 32, 1377ff., or, in *epistola* 211, *ibid.*, 33, 958ff.

D. Baker, *Relations between East and West in the Middle Ages* (Edinburgh, 1973)

Gy. Balanyi, "Magyar szentek, szentéletű magyarok (Hungarian saints, saintly Hungarians)," *Katolikus Szemle*, 15 (Rome, 1963), 100ff.

E. P. Balázs *et al*, *Werbőczy István* (Lectures on István Werbőczy) (Kolozsvár, 1942)

M. W. Baldwin, *Alexander III and the Twelfth Century* (Glen Rock, NJ, 1968)

M. W. Baldwin, *Raymond III of Tripolis and the Fall of Jerusalem* (Princeton, 1937)

M. W. Baldwin, "Some Recent Interpretation of Pope Urban's Eastern Policy," *Catholic Historical Review*, 25 (1940), 459ff.

S. Balic, "Der Islam im mittelalterlichen Ungarn," *Südostforschungen*, 23 (1964), 19ff.

L. Balics, *A római katholikus egyház története Magyarországon* 2 vols. in 3 (Budapest, 1885-90)

M. v. Bárány-Oberschall, *Die hl ungarische Krone* (Vienna, 1961)

M. v. Bárány-Oberschall, "Problémák a magyar Szentkorona körül (Some questions concerning the Hungarian Crown)," repr. from *Antiquitas Hungarica* (Budapest, 1947)

F. Barlow, *The English Church, 1066-1154* (London, 1979)

A. Bartha, *Hungarian Society in the 9th and 10th Centuries* (Budapest, 1975)

E. Bartoniek, *Szent István törvényeinek XII századi kézirata, az Admonti kódex*: The Admont codex: the twelfth century MS of King Stephen's Laws (Budapest, 1935)

I. de Batthyány (ed), *Leges ecclesiasticae regni Hungariae et provinciarum adiacentium*, 3 vols., rev. ed. (Claudipoli, 1824), cited as Batthyány, *Leges*

Baudri of Dol, *Historia Jerosolimitana*, bk. I, *RHC Occ*, IV, 12ff.

R. H. Bautier, *The Economic Development of Medieval Europe* (London, 1971)

A. Becker, *Papst Urban II*, vol. XIX-1 of *Schriften der MGH* (Stuttgart, 1964)

R. Békefi, *A czikádori apátság története* (History of Czikádor abbey) (Pécs, 1899)

A. Békefi, *A pilisi apátság története* (History of Pilis abbey) (Pécs, 1891)

I. Bekker (ed), J. Scylitzes-G. Cedrenus, *Historiarum compendium* (Bonn, 1839)

I. Bekker (ed), *Nicetas Choniates: Historia; De imperio Iohannis Comneni Porphyrogeniti* (Bonn, 1839), cited as Choniates, *Iohannis Comneni*

L. Bendeffy, *Fejezetek a magyar mérésügy történetéből* (Chapters from the history of Hungarian weights and measures) (Budapest, 1959)

R. Benson (ed), *Imperial Lives and Letters of the Eleventh Century* (New York-London, 1962)

I. Berényi, "A kéhidai oklevél: a megyeszervezet 750 éves emléke (The document of Kéhida: a 750 year old proof of (Hungarian) country structure)," *Élet és Tudomány*, 37 (1982), 1445

W. Bernhardi, *Konrad III* (Munich, 1883; repr. 1975)

W. Bernhardi, *Lothar von Supplinburg* (Berlin, 1879; repr. 1975)

J. Bernhardt (ed), *Augustinus: Confessiones*, 3rd ed. (Munich, 1966)

*Bernoldi Annales, MGHSS*, V

V. G. Berry, "The Second Crusade," in Baldwin, *Hundred Years*, 463ff.

Bertholdi *Annales*, in *MGHSS*, V

H. Beumann, "Die Historiographie des Mittelalters als Quelle für die Ideengeschichte des Königtums," *HZ*, 180 (1955), 449ff.

F. v. Bezold, "Die 'armen' Leute und die deutsche Literatur des Spätmittelalters," *HZ*, 41 (1879), 1ff.

A. Bielowski (ed), *Monumenta Poloniae historica*, 6 vols. (Lvov-Cracow, 1864-93; repr. Warsaw, 1960-61), cited as *MPH*

Hildegard von Bingen, *Subtilitatum diversarum naturarum creaturarum libri IX,* in *MPL*, 197, 1118ff.

H. Blancas, *Aragonensium regum commentarii* (Caesaraugustae, 1588)

F. Blatt, "Sprachwandel im Latein des Mittelalters," *Historische Vierteljahrschrift*, 28 (1934), 22ff.

M. Bloch, *Feudal Society*, tr. L. A. Manyon (Chicago, 1961)

M. Blöcker, "Zur Haeresie im 11 Jahrhundert," *Zeitschrift für schweizerische Kirchengeschichte*, 73 (1979), 193ff.

B. Blumenkranz, "Jüdische und christliche Konvertiten im jüdischen christlichen Religionsgesprech des Mittelalters," in P. Wilbert (ed), *Judentum und Christentum im Mittelalter* (Berlin, 1966), 264ff.

U. R. Blumenthal, *The Early Councils of Pope Paschal II, 1100-1110* (Toronto, 1978)

U. R. Blumenthal, "Paschal II and the Roman Primacy," *Archivum historiae pontificae*, 16 (1978), 67ff.

I. Bogdán, *Magyarországi hossz- és földmértékek a XVI század végéig* (Hungarian length and surface measures until the end of the 16th century) (Budapest, 1978)

Th. Bogyay, "A 750 éves Aranybulla (The 750 years old Golden Bull)," *Katolikus Szemle*, 24 (Rome, 1972), 289ff.

Th. v. Bogyay et al (eds), *Die hll. Könige* (Graz, 1976)

Th. v. Bogyay, *Grundzüge der Geschichte Ungarns*, 4th ed. (Darmstadt, 1981)

Th. v. Bogyay, "L'iconographie de la 'Porta speciosa' d'Esztergom et ses sources d'inspiration," *Revue des études byzantines*, 8 (1950), 85ff.

Th. v. Bogyay, *Stephanus Rex* (Vienna-Munich, 1975)

Th. v. Bogyay, Review of P. J. Kelleher, *The Holy Crown of Hungary* (Rome, 1951), *Byzantinische Zeitschrift*, 45 (1952), 419ff.

P. Boissonade, *Life and Work in Medieval Europe* (London, 1949)

I. Bolla, *A jogilag egységes jobbágyosztály kialakulása Magyarországon* (The judicial development of the King's Servants as a class in Hungary) (Budapest, 1983)

A. Bonfini, *Rerum Ungaricarum decades quatuor*, ed. J. Fógel et al, 4 vols. (Leipzig-Budapest, 1936-41), vol. I.

Gy. Bónis, "Einflüsse des römischen Rechts in Ungarn," *Ius Romanum medii aevi* (Milan, 1964), 104ff.

Gy. Bónis, *Hűbériség és rendiség a középkori magyar jogban* (Feudalism and feudal order in medieval Hungarian law) (Kolozsvár, 1947)

Gy. Bónis, *A jogtudó értelmiség a Mohács előtti Magyar-országon* (The judicial intelligentsia in Hungary prior to 1526) (Budapest, 1971)

Gy. Bónis, *Középkori jogunk elemei* (Constituent foundations of medieval Hungarian law) (Budapest, 1972)

J. Bödey, "Rilai szent Iván legendájának magyar vonatkozásai (Portions of the legend of St. Ivan of Rila pertinent to Hungarian events)," *Egyetemes Philológiai Közlöny,* 64 (1940), 217ff.

I. Decius Borovius, *Syntagma institutionum iuris imperialis ac Ungarici* (Claudipoli, 1593)

Cs. Borsodi, "800 éves a magyar hivatali írásbeliség (800 years of written Hungarian administrative procedures)," *Századok,* 117 (1983), 450ff.

K. Bosl, "Armut, Arbeit, Emanzipation: zu den Hintergründen der geistigen und literarischen Bewegung vom 11 bis zum 13 Jahrhundert," *Beiträge zur Wirtschafts- und Sozialgeschichte des Mittelalters: Festschrift für H. Helbig* (Cologne, 1976), 128ff.

K. Bosl et al, *Eastern and Western Europe in the Middle Ages* (London, 1970)

Cardinal Boso, *Gesta pontificum,* in Duchesne, *Liber pontificalis,* II, 351ff., or in J. Watterich (ed), *Vitae pontificum Romanorum ab ex saeculo IX usque ad XIII,* 2 vols. (Leipzig, 1872)

A. Brackmann, "Die Ursachen der geistigen und politischen Wandlung Europas im 11 and 12 Jahrhundert," *HZ,* 149 (1934), 229ff.

H. Bracton, *De legibus et consuetudinibus Angliae,* ed. G. G. Woodbine, 2 vols. (London, 1915-22)

C. M. Brand, *Byzantium Confronts the West, 1180-1204* (Cambridge, Mass., 1968)

A. v. Brandt, *Werkzeug des Historikers* (Stuttgart, 1960)

W. Braunfels *et al* (ed), *Karl der Grosse: Lebenswerk und Nachleben,* 3 vols. (Düsseldorf, 1965), vol. II.

H. Bresslau, *Handbuch der Urkundenlehre,* 2 vols., 2nd ed. (Berlin, 1912-31)

L. Bréhier, *Vie et mort de Byzance* (Paris, 1946)

F. Brisits (ed), *Temesvári Pelbárt műveiből* (Selections from the works of Pelbart of Temesvár), vol. VI of *Magyar irodalmi ritkaságok* (Rare pieces of Hungarian literature), ed. L. Vajthó (Budapest, 1931)

G. Brito, *Historia de vita et gestis Philippi Augusti*, in A. Duchesne (ed), *Historiae Francorum coaetanei scriptores*, 5 vols. (Paris, 1636-49), V

Z. N. Brooke, "Lay Investiture and Its Relations to the Conflict of Empire and Papacy," *Proceedings of the British Academy*, 25 (1930), 217ff.

Ch. Brooke, *The Twelfth Century Renaissance* (London, 1969)

R. Browning, "A New Source on Byzantine-Hungarian Relations," *Balkan Studies*, 2 (Thessalonica, 1961), 199ff.

R. Buchner, "Die politische Vorstellungswelt Adams von Bremen," *Archiv für Kulturgeschichte*, 45 (1963), 15ff.

M. Büdinger, *Ein Buch ungarischer Geschichte, 1058-1100* (Leipzig, 1866)

V. Bunyitay, *Szent László király emlékezete* (Essay on King St. Ladislas) (Budapest, 1892)

V. Bunyitay, *A váradi püspökség története* (History of the Várad bishopric), 2 vols. (Nagyvárad, 1882-83)

Burckhardi Urspergensis *Chronicon, MGHSS*, XXIII

Burchard of Worms, *Decretum*, in *MPL*, 140

C. W. Bynum, "Did the Twelfth Century Discover the Individual?" *Journal of Ecclesiastical History*, 31 (1980), 1ff.

*Byzantinische Zeitschrift*, cited as *BZ*

H. v. Campenhausen, *Griechische Kirchenväter*, 3rd ed. (Stuttgart, 1961)

F. Cantor, *Church, Kingship and Lay Investiture in England 1089-1135* (Princeton, 1958)

Gervasius Cantuariensis *Chronica maiora*, 2 vols., R.S. (London, 1879-80), vol. I

A. Cartellieri, "Richard Löwenherz im Heiligen Lande," *HZ*, 101 (1980), 1ff.

E. Caspar (ed), *Das Register Gregors VII, MGH Epp.*, sel. II, 2 vols. (Berlin, 1920-23)

R. C. Cave-H. H. Coulson (eds), *A Source Book for Medieval Economic History* (Milwaukee, 1936)

F. Chalandon, *Jean II Comnène et Manuel I Comnène* (Paris, 1912)

H. J. Chapman, *Saint Benedict and the Sixth Century* (London, 1929)

P. Charanis, "Byzantium, the West, and the Origin of the First Crusade," *Byzantion*, 19 (1949), 17ff.

Ivo of Chartres, *Decretum*, in *MPL*, 161

Ivo of Chartres, *Panormia*, *MPL*, 161

Choniates, *De imperio Iohannis Comneni*

Choniates, *De imperio Isaaci Angeli libri III*, in Bekker,
Choniates, *Historia*; in Dieten, Choniatae *Historia*

*Chronicon Austriacum*, Rauch, II, 221ff.

*Chronicon Budense*: *Budai Krónika*, facsimile, with
introduction by V. Fraknói (Budapest, 1900)

*Chronica s. Petri Erfordensis*, *MGHSS*, XXIII

*Chronicon pictum*, in *SSH*, I, 217ff.; *RHM*, I,

*Chronica regia Coloniensis*, *MGHSS*, XVII, 723ff.

*Chronicon Martini Turonensis*, in Martene-Durand,
V. 917ff.

*Chronicon Venetum libri VIII*, in *Archivo storico Italiano*, vol. VIII; selections only in *MGHSS*, XIV, 5ff.

*Chronicon Venetum continuatio*, *MGHSS*, XIV

Iohannes Cinnamus, *Epitomae rerum ab Iohanne et
Manuele Comnenis gestarum*, ed. A. Meineke (Bonn, 1836),
or, *MPG*, 133.

Bernard of Clairvaux, *De diligendo Deo, MPL*, 182, 973ff.

Bernard of Clairvaux, epistola 256, *MPL*, 182, 464

Bernard of Clairvaux, *Sermones de Cantica*, *MPL*, 183,
785ff.

P. Classen, *Gerhoch von Reichersberg* (Wiesbaden, 1960)

P. Classen, "Res gestae, Universal History, Apocalypse:
Visions of Past and Future," in R. L. Benson *et al* (eds),
*Renaissance and Renewal in the Twelfth Century* (Cambridge,
Mass., 1982), 387ff.

Anna Comnena, *Alexiad*, ed. A. Reifferscheid, 2 vols.
(Leipzig, 1884), or, in *MPG*, 131

G. Constable, "The Abbots and Anti-Abbot of Cluny
during the Papal Schims of 1159," *Revue Bénédictine*, 94
(1984), 370ff.

G. Constable, *Monastic Titles from Their Origins to the
Twelfth Century* (Cambridge, 1964)

G. Constable, "The Second Crusade As Seen by Contemporaries," *Traditio*, 9 (1953), 213ff.

G. Constable, "The Structure of Medieval Society According to the *Dictatores* of the Twelfth Century," in K.
Pennington (ed), *Law, Church and Society: Essays in Honor
of Stephen Kuttner* (Philadelphia, 1977)

Bernald of Constance, *Micrologus de ecclesiasticis observationibus*, in *MPL*, 151, 977ff., or Batthyány, *Leges*, I, 130ff.

*Continuatio Claustroneuburgensis II*, and *III*, *MGHSS*, IX, 615ff.

*Continuatio Zwettlensis II*, *MGHSS*, IX, 541ff.

*De conversione Bagoariorum et Carantanorum*, *MGHSS*, XI, 1ff.

Vincent of Cracow, *Historia Polonica*, in *MPH*, I

F. E. Cranz, "De civitate Dei, xv, 2, and Augustine's Idea of Christian Society)," *Speculum*, 25 (1950), 215ff.

S. H. Cross *et al* (eds), *The Russian Primary Chronicle* (Cambridge, Mass., 1953)

Cs. Csapodi, *A legrégibb magyar könyvtár benső rendje* (Organization of the oldest known library in Hungary) (Budapest, 1957)

Cs. Csapodi, *Az Anonymus kérdés története* (An appraisal of the Anonymus question) (Budapest, 1978)

L. J. Csóka, *A latin nyelvű történeti irodalom kialakulása Magyarországon a XI-XIV században* (Development of Latin language historical literature in Hungary during the 11th through the 14th centuries) (Budapest, 1967)

A. S. Czernan, *Die Staatsidee des hl. Stefan* (Klagenfurt, 1953)

B. Czobor, "A magyar szent korona és a koronázási palást (The Hungarian Crown and the coronation cloak)," in Gy. Forster (ed), *III Béla király emlékezete* (Budapest, 1900), 98ff.

I. Daám, *A Szeplőtelen Fogantatás védelme Magyarországon a Hunyadiak és Jagellók korában* (Defense of the Immaculate Conception in late medieval Hungary) (Rome, 1955)

R. C. Dales, "A Medieval View of Human Dignity," *Journal of the History of Ideas*, 38 (1977), 557ff.

Peter Damian, *Epistolae*, in *MPL*, 144

Peter Damian, *Opusculum*, in *MPL*, 145

Andreas Dandalo, *Chronicon Venetum libri X*, Muratori, *Scriptores*, XII

J. Darrouzès (ed), *Georges et Démétrios Tornikes: lettres et discourses* (Paris, 1970)

H. Decker-Hauff, "A legrégibb magyar-bizánci házassági kapcsolatok kérdéséhez (Essay on the oldest Hungaro-Byzantine marriage contacts)," *Századok*, 81 (1947), 95ff.

J. Deér, "Die Ansprüche der Herrscher des 12 Jahrhunderts auf die apostolische Legation," *Archivum historiae pontificae*, 2 (1964), 153ff.

J. Deér, *Die heilige Krone Ungarns* (Vienna, 1966)

J. Deér, *Mittelalterliche Frauenkronen in Ost und West*, in the *Herrschaftszeichen und Staatssymbolik* series, ed. P. E. Schramm, XIII-2 of *Schriften der MGH* (Stuttgart, 1955)

J. Deér, "Der Weg zur Goldenen Bulle Andreas II von 1222," *Schweizer Beiträge zur allgemeinen Geschichte*, 10 (1952), 104ff.

J. Delaville le Roulx, *Cartulaire genéral de l'Ordre des Hospitaliers de S. Jean de Jérusalem*, vol. I (Paris, 1894), 222ff.

A. Dempf, *Die Hauptform mittelalterlichen Weltanschauung* (Munich-Berlin, 1925)

A. Dempf, *Sacrum imperium*, 4th ed. (Munich-Vienna, 1973)

D. Dercsényi (ed), *Chronicon pictum: Képes Krónika*, 2 vols. (Budapest, 1963), vol. i: facsimile; vol. II: introduction, translation and annotations

D. Dercsényi, *Kolostor és humanizmus Mohács után* (Monastic culture and humanism in Hungary after 1526) (Budapest, 1936)

D. Dercsényi, *Nagy Lajos kora* (The age of Lewis the Great of Hungary) (Budapest, n.d.)

Odo de Deogilo, *De profectione Ludovici VII regis Francorum in orientem*, MGHSS, XXVI, or *MPL*, 185, 1205ff.

*Deutschenspiegel*, ed. K. A. Eckhart-A. Hübner, 2nd ed. (Hanover, 1933)

P. Diaconu, *Les Petchenegues au bas-Danube* (Bucharest, 1970)

I. A. v. Dieten (ed), *Nicetae Choniatae Historia* (Berlin-New York, 1975), cited as Dieten

Iohannes Dlugossius, *Excerpta a fontibus incertis*, in *MPH*, IV

F. Dölger (ed), *Regesten der Kaiserurkunden des oströmischen Reiches*, Reihe A, Abt. I-2 (Munich-Berlin, 1924-65)

F. Dölger, "Ungarn in der byzantinischen Reichspolitik," *Archivum Europae centro-orientalis*, 8 (1942), 5ff.

F. Dölger, Review of P. J. Kelleher, *The Holy Crown of Hungary* (Rome, 1951), in *HJB*, 73 (1974)

M. Doeberl (ed), *Monumenta Germaniae selecta*, vol. III (Munich, 1889)

L. Duchesne (ed), *Liber pontificalis*, 3 vols. (Paris, 1886etc.; repr. Paris, 1955-57)

O. Ducourneau, "De l'institution et des usdes convers dans l'ordre de Citeaux," *Saint Bernard et sons temps*, vol. III (Dijon, 1929), 139ff.

I. Dujcev, "Die Bedeutung der mittelalterlichen slawischen Literatur für die byzantinischen Studien," in *Beitrage zur byzantinischen Geschichte im 9-11 Jahrhundert*, ed. V. Vavrinek (Prague, 1978), 317ff.

F. Duncalf, "The Councils of Piacensa and Clermont," in M. W. Baldwin (ed), *The First Hundred Years*, vol. I of *A History of the Crusades*, ed. K. M. Setton, 4 vols. (Philadelphia, 1955etc.)

Thomas of Ebendorf, *Chronica Austriacum*, in Pez, *Scriptores*, II

F. Eckhart, "The Holy Crown of Hungary," *Hungarian Quarterly*, 6 (1940), 633ff.

H. v. Eicken, *Geschichte und System der mittelalterlichen Weltanschauung*, 4th ed. (Stuttgart-Berlin, 1923)

Einhard, *Vita Caroli Magni*, in *MGHSS*, II

L. Elekes, *A középkori magyar állam megalapításától annak bukásáig* (Beginning and Fall of the medieval Hungarian realm) (Budapest, 1964)

K. Elm (ed), *Norbert von Xanten: Adliger, Ordensstifter, Kirchenfürst* (Cologne, 1984)

I. Elter, "La Hongrie dans la géographie descriptive d'Idrisi (1154)," *Acta historica*, 82 (Szeged, 1985), 53ff.

R. Elze, "Die papstliche Kapelle im 12 und 13 Jahrhundert," *Zeitschrift der Savigny Stiftung für Rechtsgeschichte*, kan. Abt. 36 (1950), 145ff.

R. Elze, "Das 'Sacrum Palatinum Lateranense' im 10 und 11 Jahrhundert." *Studi Gregoriani*, 4 (1952), 27ff.

St. Endlicher (ed), *Rerum Hungaricarum monumenta Arpadiana* 2 vols. (Sangalli, 1849; one vol. repr. Leipzig, 1931), cited as *RHM*

P. Engel, "Honor, vár, ispánság: tanulmányok az Anjou-kori királyság kormányzati rendszeréről (essay on the government of the Anjou kings in Hungary)," *Századok*, 116 (1982), 880ff.

W. Erben, *Die Kaiser- und Königsurkunden des Mittelalters in Deutschland, Frankreich und Italien* (Munich-Berlin, 1907; repr. Munich, 1967)

L. Erdélyi, *Árpádkor* (Age of the Árpáds) (Budapest, 1922)

L. Erdélyi, *Magyar történelem: művelődés és államtörténet* (Hungarian cultural and constitutional history), 2 vols. (Budapest, 1936-38)

L. Erdélyi (ed), *A pannonhalmi Szent Benedekrend története* (History of the Benedictines of Pannonhalma), 12 vols. (Budapest, 1902-07)

C. Erdmann, "Die Aufrufe Gerberts und Sergius IV für das Hl. Land," *Quellen und Forschungen aus italienischen Archiven und Bibliotheken*, 23 (1931-32), 1ff.

C. Erdmann, *Entstehung des Kreuzzuggedankens* (Stuttgart, 1935)

C. Erdmann (ed), *Deutsches Mittelalter: die Briefe Heinrichs IV* (Leipzig, 1937)

G. Érszegi (ed), *Árpád-kori legendák és Intelmek* (Legends and Admonitions of the Arpadian age) (Budapest, 1983)

G. Evans, "Hugh of St. Victor on History and on the Meaning of Things," *Studia monastica*, 25 (1983), 223ff.

D. Farkasfalvy (ed), *Ciszterci lelkiség* (Cistercian spirituality) (Eisenstadt, 1982)

D. Farlatus-I. Coletus (eds), *Illyricum sacra*, 8 vols. (Venice, 1751-1819), cited as Farlatus, *Illyricum sacra*

H. E. Feine, *Kirchliche Rechtsgeschichte*, 5th ed.(Cologne, 1972)

G. Fejér (ed), *Codex diplomaticus Hungariae ecclesiasticus ac civilis*, 44 vols. (Buda, 1829-44), cited as Fejér

Fejérpataky (ed), *Oklevelek II István korából* (Documents of the reign of Stephen II) (Budapest, 1895)

H. Fichtenau, Studien zu Gerhoh von Reichersberg," *MIÖG*, 52 (1938), 1ff.

H. Fichtenau, *Das Urkundenwesen in Österreich vom 8 bis zum frühen 13 Jahrhundert* (Vienna-Graz, 1971)

K. Fisher-Drew (ed), *The Lombard Laws* (Philadelphia, 1953)

J. Fitz, *Hess András, a budai ősnyomdász* (Andrew Hess, the first book printer in Buda) (Budapest, 1932)

J. Fitz, *A magyar nyomdászat, könyvkiadás és könyvkereskedelem története* (The history of printing, publication and book trade in Hungary), 2 vols. (Budapest, 1959-67)

A. Fliché, *Le regne de Philippe Ier, roi de France* (Paris, 1912)

A. Fliché, "Urbain II et la croisade," *Revue de l'historire de l'église de France*, 13 (1927), 289ff.

A. Fodor, "László legendák a XV-XVI századi magyarországi breviárumokban (Ladislas legends in 15th-16th century breviaries in use in Hungary)," *Athleta patriae*, 57ff.

M. F. Font, "II Géza orosz politikája, 1141-52 (The Kievan policy of Géza II between 1141 and 1152)," *Acta historica Szegediensis*, 67 (1980), 33ff.

*Fontes rerum Austricarum*, Abt. I: *Scriptores*, 10 vols. Vienna, 1855etc.), cited as *FRASS*

J. Forey, "The Emergence of the Military Order in the Twelfth Century," *Journal of Ecclesiastical History*, 36 (1985), 175ff.

Gy. Forster (ed), *III Béla magyar király emlékezete* (In memory of Béla III, king of Hungary) (Budapest, 1900)

V. Fraknói (ed), *Chronicon Budense: Budai Krónika* (Bydapest, 1900)

V. Fraknói, *Magyarország és a Szentszék* (Hungary and the Roman See), 3 vols. (Budapest, 1901-03)

Otto of Freising, *Chronicon de duabus civitatibus libri VIII*, MGHSS, XX, 118ff.

Otto of Freising, *Gesta Friderici I Imperatoris libri IV*, MGHSS, XX, 347ff.

Ae. Friedberg (ed), *Corpus Iuris Canonici*, 2 vols. (Leipzig, 1879-81; repr. Graz, 1959), vol. I.

G. Füffer, "Die Anfänge des zweiten Kreuzzuges," *HJB*, 8 (1897), 391ff.

E. Fügedi, "A befogadó: a középkori magyar királyság (The receiver: the medieval Hungarian kingdom)," *Történelmi Szemle*, 22 (1979), 355ff.

E. Fügedi, "Die Entwicklung des Städtewesens in Ungarn," *Alba regia*, 10 (1969), 101ff.

E. Fügedi, "Kirchliche Topographie und Siedlungsgeschichte im Mittelalter der Slowakei," *Studia Slavica*, 5 (1959), 363ff.

E. Fügedi, *Kolduló barátok, polgárok, nemesek* (Mendicant friars, citizens and nobles) (Budapest, 1981)

E. Fügedi, "Das mittelalterliche Ungarn als Gastland," in W. Schlesinger (ed), *Die deutsche Ostsiedlung des Mittelalters als Probleme der europäischen Geschichte* (Sigmaringen, 1975), 471ff.

F. X. v. Funk-K. Bihlmeyer, *Kirchengeschichte*, 2 vols., 8th rev. ed. (Paderborn, 1926-30)

A. Gábriel, "A Lányi kódex (Codex Lányi)," *Emlékkönyv szent Norbert halálának 800 éves jubileumára* (Memorial volume on the 800th anniversary of the death of St. Norbert) (Gödöllő, 1934), 136ff.

A. Gábriel, "A pozsonyi kódex (The Pozsony codex)," *MKSz*, 48 (1940), 333ff.

L. Gáldi, *Le romanisme transdanubien* (Rome, 1937)

M. Gallus, *Chronicon Pdonorum, MGHSS*, IX

B. Gams, *Series episcoporum Ecclesiae Catholicae* (Regensburg, 1873)

K. Ganzer, *Die Entwicklung des auswärtigen Kardinalats im hohen Mittelalter*, vol. 26 of *Bibliothek der Deutschen Historischen Institutes in Rom* (Tübingen, 1963)

A. Gasquet, *Monastic Life in the Middle Ages* (London, 1922)

D. J. Geanakoplos, *Byzantine East and Latin West* (Oxford, 1966) *Ad Geberhardum liber,* in *LdL*, I, 303ff.

B. Gebhardt (ed), *Handbuch der deutschen Geschichte*, 4 vols., 8th rev. ed. (Stuttgart, 1954-60), vol. I.

Sigebert of Gembloux, *Chronicon, MGHSS*, VI

J. Gerics, "Adalékok a Kézai Krónika problémáinak megoldásához (Remarks on solving the Keza question)," *Annales Universitatis de R. Eotvos nominatae*, sectio hist., 1 (1957), 106ff.

J. Gerics, "Judicium Dei a magyar állam XI századi külkapcsolataiban (Judicium Dei in the foreign relations of the Hungarian realm during the eleventh century)," in Mezey, *Athleta patriae*, 111ff.

J. Gerics, "Krónikáink és a Szent László legenda szövegkapcsolata (Similarities between the texts of St. Ladislas' *Vita* and the Hungarian chronicles)," *Memoria Hungariae*, I, 113ff.

J. Gerics, *Legkorábbi gesta szerkesztéseinknek keletke-*

*zésrendjének problémái* (Questions concerning the chronology of editing of the Hungarian gesta) (Budapest, 1981)

J. Gerics, "Ständewesen in Ungarn am Ende des 13 Jahrhunderts," in R. Vierhaus (ed), *Herrschaftsverträge, Wahlkapitulationen, Fundamentalgesetze* (Göttingen, 1977), 129ff.

J. Gerics, "Über das Rechtsleben Ungarns um die Wende des 13-14 Jahrhunderts,"

J. Gerics, "Textbezüge zwischen den ungarischen Chroniken under Sankt Ladislas Legende," *Acta historica*, 19 (1973), 273ff.

*Gesta Henrici et Ricardi regum Angliae, MGHSS,* XXVII

O. Gierke, *Political Theories of the Middle Ages,* with intro. by F. W. Maitland (Cambridge, 1800)

W. Giese, "Zur Bautätigkeit von Bischofen und Äbten des 10 bis 12 Jahrhunderts," *Deutsches Archiv,* 38 (1982), 388ff.

W. v. Giesebrecht, *Geschichte der deutschen Kaiserzeit,* rev. ed. ed. W. Schild, 6 vols. (Meersburg, 1929-30)

W. Goetz, "Zur Persönlichkeit Gregors VII," *Römische Quartalschrift,* 73 (1978), 193ff.

A. Gráf, *Pannonia ókori földrajzára vonatkozó kutatások áttekintő összefoglalása* (Survey of research activities concerning the ancient geography of Pannonia) (Budapest, 1936)

A. Gransden, *Historical Writing in England, 550 to 1307* (Ithaca, 1974)

Gratian's *Decretum,* ed. E. Friedberg, vol. I (Leipzig, 1879)

J. A. Green, *The Government of England Under Henry I* (Cambridge, 1986)

Gregory the Great, *Dialogus,* in *MPL,* 66

L. Grill, "Die Kreuzzugsepistel St. Bernhards Ad pregerinantes Jerusalem." *Studien und Mitteilungen des Benediktinerordens,* 67 (1956), 237ff.

C. Grot, *From the History of Ugria and the Slavs in the Twelfth Century* (in Russian) (Warsaw, 1889)

H. Grotefend, *Zeitrechnung des deutschen Mittelalters und der Neuzeit,* 2 vols. (Hanover, 1891-92)

H. Grundmann, "Geschichtsschreiber im Mittelalter," *Deutsche Philologie im Aufriss,* 26 (1952-59), 1273ff.

A. Gieysztor, "The Genesis of the Crusades: the Encyclica

of Sergius IV," *Medievalia et humanistica*, 5 (1948), 3ff., and 6 (1950), 3ff.

M. Gyóni, "A legkorábbi magyar-bizánci házassági kapcsolatok kérdéséhez (On the earliest Hungaro-Byzantine marriage contacts)," *Századok*, 81 (1947), 212ff.

M. Gyóni, *Magyarország és a magyarság a bizánci források tükrében: Ungarn und das Ungartum im Spiegel der byzantinischen Quellen* (Budapest, 1938)

M. Gyóni, "Niketas Akominatos lakodalmi költeménye (The wedding poetry of Nicetas Choniates)," *Egyetemes Philológiai Közlöny*, 47 (1923), 79ff.

Gy. Györffy, "Abfassungszeit und Glaubwürdigkeit der Gesta Hungarorum des Anonymen Notars," *Acta antiqua*, 20 (1972), 209ff.

Gy. Györffy, "Die Entstehung der ungarischen Burgorganisation," *Acta archaeologica Hungarica*, 28 (1976), 323ff.

Gy. Györffy, *István király és műve* (King Stephen I and his work) (Budapest, 1977)

Gy. Györffy, *Krónikáink és a magyar őstörténet* (Early Hungarian history in the Hungarian chronicles) (Budapest, 1948)

Gy. Györffy, "A magyar krónikák adata a III Béla-kori petícióról (Data in the Hungarian chronicles concerning written requests in the times of Béla III)," *Memoria Hungariae*, I, 333ff.

Gy. Györffy, "Les débuts de l'evolution urbaine en Hongrie," *Cahiers de civilization mediévale*, 12 (1969), 127ff., and 253ff.

Gy. Györffy, "Szent István koronája az Árpád-korban (The Crown of Saint Stephen in the Árpádian age)," *Vigilia*, 49 (1984), 580ff.

Gy. Györffy, "Zur Frage der Herkunft der ungarischen Dienstleute," *Studia Slavica*, 22 (1976), 40ff.

J. Győry, *Gesta regum — gesta nobilium* (Budapest, 1948)

H. Hagenmeyer, *Anonymi Gesta Francorum* (Heidelberg, 1890); *RHC Occ*, III, 119ff.

H. Hagenmeyer (ed), *Ekkehard von Aura* (Leipzig, 1884)

H. Hagenmeyer (ed), Fulcher von Chartres, *Gesta Francorum Iherusalem peregrinantium* (Heidelberg, 1913), 130ff.

G. Hahn, *Die abendländische Kirche im Mittelalter* (Freiburg i. Br., 1942)

L. Hain, *Repertorium bibliographicum*, 2 vols. in 4 (Stuttgart-Tübingen, 1826-38; repr. Milan, 1948)

J. Hannenheim, *Ungarn unter Béla II und Geisa II in seinen Beziehungen zu Deutschland* (Hermannstadt, 1884) *HJB* = *Historisches Jahrbuch*, cited as *HJB*

J. Haller, *Das Papsttum: Idee und Wirklichkeit*, rev. ed., 5 vols. (Stuttgart, 1952-59)

K. Hampe, *Deutsche Kaisergeschichte in der Zeit der Salier und Staufer*, 12th rev. ed., ed. F. Baethgen (Heidelberg, 1968)

K. Hampe, *Das Hochmittelalter*, 5th rev. ed. (Cologne-Graz, 1963)

H. Hantsch, *Geschichte Österreichs*, 2 vols., 5th rev. ed. (Vienna, 1969), vol. I.

C. H. Hapgood, *Maps of the Ancient Sea Kings*, rev. ed. (New York, 1979)

A. Hauck, *Kirchengeschichte Deutschlands*, 6 vols., 9th ed. (Berlin, 1956-58)

T. Havet (ed), *Lettres de Gerbert, 983-997* (Paris, 1889)

F. Heer, *Europäische Geistesgeschichte*, 2nd ed. (Stuttgart, 1965)

F. Heer, *Die Tragödie des Heiligen Reiches* (Vienna-Munich, 1952)

C. J. c. Hefele, *Conziliengeschichte*, 6 vols., 2nd rev. ed. (Freiburg i. Br., 1873-90)

W. Heil, "Der Adoptianismus Alkuin und Spanien," in W. Braunsfels (ed), *Karl der Grosse: Lebenswerk und Nachleben*, 3 vols. Düsseldorf, 1965), II, 95ff.

K. Heilig, "Ostrom und das Deutsche Reich um die Mitte des 12 Jahrhunderts," in his *Kaisertum und Herzogsgewalt im Zeitalter Friedrichs I* (Leipzig, 1944), 159ff.

M. Heimbucher, *Die Orden und Kongregationen der katholischen Kirche*, 2 vols., 3rd ed. (Paderborn, 1933)

F. Helbig, "Fidelis Dei et regis: zur Bedeutungsentwicklung von Glauben und Treue im hohen Mittelalter," *Archiv für Kulturgeschichte*, 33 (1951), 275ff.

S. Hellmann, *Das Mittelalter bis zum Ausgange der Kreuzzüge*, rev. ed. (Stuttgart, 1924), 228ff.

E. Hermann, *A katolikus egyház története Magyarországon 1914-ig* (A history of the Catholic Church in Hungary until 1914) (Munich, 1973)

320                                        Bibliography

F. Hervay, "Nyolcszáz éves a pilisi apátság (The abbey of Pilis is 800 years old)," *Vigilia*, 49 (1984), 830ff.

R. Hiestand, "Zum Leben und zur Laufbahn Wilhelms von Tyrus," *Deutsches Archiv*, 34 (1978), 345ff.

Hincmar of Rheims, *Capitula*, Mansi, Concilia, XV

Hincmar of Rheims, *De divortio Lotharii et Teutbergae*, *MPL*, 125.

*Historia ducum Veneticorum, MGHSS*, XIV, 72ff.

G. A. Hodgett, *A Social Economic History of Medieval Europe* (London, 1972)

A. Hodinka (ed), *Az orosz évkönyvek magyar vonatkozásai* (Data concerning Hungary in the Russian Annals) (Budapest, 1916)

P. Hofmeister, *Mitra und Stab der wirklichen Preläten ohne bischöflichen Charakter* (Stuttgart, 1928)

H. Hoffman, "Kirche und Sklaverei im frühen Mittelalter," *Deutsches Archiv*, 42 (1986), 1ff.

K. Holl, "Die Entstehung der vier Fastenzeiten in der griechischen Kirche," *Gesammelte Abhandlungen zur Kirchengeschichte*, vol. II (Tübingen, 1928), 155ff.

W. Holtzmann, "Alexander III und Ungarn," *Ungarische Jahrbücher*, 6 (1926), 397ff.

W. Holtzmann, "Beiträge zu den Dekretensammlungen des 12 Jahrhunderts," *Zeitschrift für Rechtsgeschichte*, kan. Abt., 16 (1927), 37ff.

W. Holtzmann, "Studien zur Orientenpolitik des Reformpapsttums und zur Entstehung des ersten Kreuzzüges," *Historische Vierteljahrschrift*, 22 (1924-25), 167ff.

W. Holtzmann, "XII századi pápai levelek kánoni gyűjteményéből (Twelfth century papal letters taken from canonical collections), *Századok*, 92 (1959), 414f.

W. Holtzmann, "Unterhandlungen Urbans II mit Kaiser Alexius II," *BZ*, 28 (1928), 38ff.

J. Holub, "Le role de l'age la droit hongroise du moyen age," *Revue historique de droit francaise et étranger*, 1 (1922), 78ff.

J. Holub, "Quod omnes tangit," *Revue historique de droit francaise et étranger*, 4 (1951), 97ff.

J. Holub, "A vásárolt fekvő jószág jogi természete régi jogunkban (Legal characters of purchased real estate in ancient Hungarian law)," in S. Domanovszky (ed), *Károlyi Árpád Emlékkönyv* (Budapest, 1933), 246ff.

B. Hóman, *Geschichte des ungarisches Mittelalters*, 2 vols. (Berlin, 1940-43)

B. Hóman, *Magyar pénztörténet* (Hungarian monetary history) (Budapest, 1916)

B. Hóman, *A Szent László-kori Gesta Hungarorum és XII-XIII századi leszármazói* (The eleventh century Gesta Hungarorum and its continuators in the 12th and 13th centuries) (Budapest, 1925)

B. Hóman, *Történetírás és forráskritika* (Historiography) (Budapest, 1938)

B. Hóman-Gy. Szekfű, *Magyar történet* (Hungarian history), 5 vols., 6th ed. (Budapest, 1939)

H. Homeyer, *Attila der Hunnenkönig von seinem Zeitgenossen dargestellt* (Berlin, 1951)

C. Horváth, *A régi magyar irodalom története* (History of early Hungarian literature) (Budapest, 1899)

I. Horváth, "Klastrompuszta - a pálos rend bölcsője ('Monastic Manor:' the cradle of the Hungarian Paulist Order)," *Vigilia*, 39 (1974), 611ff.

J. Horváth, *Árpád-kori latinnyelvű irodalmunk stílusproblémái* (Stylistic questions concerning the Lating language literature of the Arpadian age) (Budapest, 1954)

J. Horváth, "Die ungarischen Chronisten aus der Angiovienzeit," *Acta linguistica*, 21 (1971), 321ff.

J. Horváth, "Ein weiteres Fragment der Esztergom Porta speciosa," *Acta archaeologiae Academiae scientiarum Hungariae*, 32 (1980), 345ff.

J. Horváth, *Magyar irodalmi műveltség kezdetei* (Origins of Hungarian literary culture), 2nd ed. (Budapest, 1944)

A. Huber, "Über die älteste ungarische Verfassung," *MIÖG*, 6 (1885), 385ff.

A. Huber, "Studien über die Geschichte Ungarns im Zeitalter der Árpáden," *Archiv für österreichische Geschichte*, 65 (1884), 156ff.

R. Ignácz, "Szent László (Ladislas the Saint)," *Vigilia*, 48 (1983), 687ff.

Ilosvay codex, *Fol. lat.* 4023 of the Hungarian National Museum Széchenyi Library, Budapest

Ivo of Chartres, *Decretum*, in *MPL*, vol. 161; *Pannormia*, in *MPL*, vol. 161

K. Jacob, *Quellenkunde der deutschen Geschichte im Mittelalter*, 2 vols. (Berlin, 1943-49)

H. H. Jacobs, "Studien über Gerhoch von Reichersberg: zur Geistesgeschichte des 12 Jahrhunderts," *Zeitschrift für Kirchengeschichte*, 50 (1931), 315ff.

Ph. Jaffé (ed), *Bibliotheca rerum Germanicarum*, 6 vols. (Berlin, 1862etc.; repr. Darmstadt, 1964), cited as Jaffé, *Bibliotheca*

Ph. Jaffé (ed) *Regesta pontificum Romanorum*, 2 vols. (Leipzig, 1885), cited as Jaffé, *Regesta*

H. Jedin (ed), *Handbuch der Kirchengeschichte*, vol. III-1: *Die mittelalterliche Kirche vom kirchlichen Frühmittelalter zur Gregorianischen Reform* (Freiburg-Vienna, 1973)

K. Jordan, *Investiturstreit und frühe Staufenzeit* (Munich, 1973)

L. Juhász (ed), *P. magister: Gesta Hungarorum* (Budapest, 1932)

I. Kapitánffy, "Magyar-bizánci kapcsolatok Szent László és Kálmán uralkodása idejében (Hungaro-Byzantine relations during the reigns of St. Ladislas and Coloman)," *Acta Universitatis Szegediensis*, 75 (1983), 19ff.

I. Karácson, *A XI és XII századbeli magyarországi zsinatok és azoknak a külföldi zsinatokhoz való viszonya* (Hungarian synods of the 11th-12th centuries and their relations with synods held abroad) (Győr, 1888)

J. Karácsonyi, *Magyar nemzetségek a XVI század közepéig* (Hungarian noble families to the mid-16th century) (Budapest, 1901)

F. Kampers, "Rex et sacerdos," *HJB*, 45 (1925), 495ff.

J. Karácsonyi-S. Borovsky (eds), *Az időrendbe szedett váradi tüzespróba lajstroma* (Ordeals by fire recorded in the Várad Register and set in chronological order), with a facsimile of the 1550 edition by G. Martinuzzi, *Ritus explorandae veritatis* (Kolozsvár, 1550), (Budapest, 1903)

T. Kardos, *A magyarság antik hagyományai* (Ancient Hungarian traditions) (Budapest, 1942)

G. Karsai, "Névtelenség, névrejtés és szerzőnév középkori krónikáinkban (Anonimity and authorship of medieval Hungarian chronicles)," *Századok*, 97 (1963), 666ff.

St. Katona, *Historia critica regum Hungariae stirpis Arpadianae*, 7 vols. (Pest-Buda, 1779-81)

St. Katona, *Historia pragmatica Hungariae*, 3 vols. (Buda, 1782etc.)

St. Katona, *Historia regum Hungariae stirpis mixtae*, 12 vols. (Buda, 1787-92)

T. Katona (ed), *Tatárjárás emlékezete* (In memory of the Mongolian invasion (of 1241-42), with introduction by Gy. Györffy (Budapest, 1981)

B. R. Kemp, "Monastic Possession of Parish Churches in England in the Twelfth Century," *Journal of Ecclesiastical History, 31* )1980(, 195ff.

F. Kempf, *Die Register Innozenz' III: eine palaeographisch-diplomatische Untersuchung* (Rome, 1945)

R. Kerbl, *Byzantinische Prinzessinnen in Ungarn swischen 1050 und 1200, und ihr Einfluss auf das Árpád Königreich* (Vienna, 1979)

Simon de Keza, *Gesta Hungarorum*, in *SSH*, I, 129ff.; *RHM*, I, 83ff., cited as Keza

W. Kienast, *Deutschland und Frankreich in der Kaiserzeit*, 3 vols. (Stuttgart, 1974-75)

I. R. Kiss, "III Endre királyunk 1298-évi törvénye (The 1298 Law of Andrew III of Hungary)," *Fejérpataky László Emlékkönyv* (Budapest, 1917), 262ff.

T. Klaniczay, "A középkori magyar szent-kultusz kutatásnak problémái (Questions concerning veneration of the saints in medieval Hungary)," *Történelmi Szemle*, 24 (1981), 273ff.

T. Klaniczay, *A magyar irodalom története 1600-ig* (History of Hungarian literature to 1600) (Budapest, 1964)

F. Knauz (ed), *Monumenta ecclesiae Strigoniensis*, 2 vols. (Strigonii, 1873-74)

K. Kniewlad-F. Kühár, *A Pray kódex miserendje* (Order of the Mass in the Pray codex), repr. from *Theológia* (Budapest, 1939)

K. Kniewald-F. Kühár, *A Pray kódex sanctoráléja* (The sanctoral cycle of the Pray codex), repr. from *MKSz* (Budapest, 1939)

I. Kniezsa, *Erdély víznevei* (River names in Transylvania) (Kolozsvár, 1943)

I. Kniezsa, "Ungarns Völkerschaften im XI Jahrhundert," *Archivum Europae centro-orientalis*, 4 (1938), 241ff.

G. M. v. Knonau, *Jahrbücher des deutschen Reiches unter Heinrich IV und Heinrich V*, vol. VI (Berlin, 1907; repr. 1965)

D. Knowles, *The Religious Orders in England* (Cambridge, 1950)

G. Koch, *Auf dem Wege zum Sacrum imperium* (Vienna-Graz, 1972)

B. Köpeczi *et al* (*eds*), *Erdély története* (History of Transylvania), 3 vols. (Budapest, 1986), vol. I.

R. Köstler, "Der Anteil des Christentums an den Ordalien," *Zeitschrift der Savigny Stiftung für Rechtesgeschichte*, kan. Abt., 2 (1912), 208ff.

S. Kohn, *A zsidók története Magyarországon*, vol. I: *A legrégibb időktől a mohácsi vészig* (History of the Jews in Hungary, from early times to 1526) (Budapest, 1884)

J. H. Kolba, "Szent László alakja a középkori ötvösművészetben (Ladislas in the art of medieval goldsmiths)," *Athleta patriae*, 221ff.

F. A. Kollar, *De originibus et usu perpetuo potestatis legislatoriae circa sacra Apostolicorum regum Ungariae* (Vienna, 1764)

J. Koller, *Historia episcopatuus Quinqueecclesiarum*, vol. I-III and VII (Pest, 1782-84 and 1812)

S. Kolozsvári - K. Óvári, *Werbőczy István Hármaskönyve* (The 'Tripartitum opus iuris' by Stephen Werbőczy) (Budapest, 1892)

Z. J. Kosztolnyik, *Five Eleventh Century Hungarian Kings; Their Policies and Their Relations with Rome*, vol. 79 of *East European Monographs* (New York, 1981)

Z. J. Kosztolnyik, "The Church and Béla III of Hungary (1172-1196): the Role of Archbishop Lukács of Esztergom," *Church History*, 49 (1980), 375ff.

Z. J. Kosztolnyik, "The Church and the Hungarian Court Under Coloman the Learned," *East European Quarterly*, 18 (1984), 129ff.

Z. J. Kosztolnyik, "Did Géza II of Hungary Send Delegates to the 'Synod' of Pavia, 1160?" *Annuarium historiae conciliorum*, 16 (Augsburg, 1984), 40ff.

Z. J. Kosztolnyik, Review of Th. v. Bogyay, *Stephanus Rex* (Vienna-Munich, 1975), *Austrian History Yearbook*, 14 (1978), 290ff.

Z. J. Kosztolnyik, Review of H. Fichtenau, *Beiträge zur Mediävistik: ausgewählte Aufsätze*, vol. II: *Urkundenforschung* (Stuttgart, 1977), in *Austrian History Yearbook*, 17-18 (1981-82), 354ff.

Z. J. Kosztolnyik, Review of Gy. Györffy, *István király és műve* (King Stephen and his work) (Budapest, 1977), in *Austrian History Yearbook*, 17-18 (1981-82), 356ff.

Z. J. Kosztolnyik, Review of L. Mezey, *Athleta patriae*: *tanulmányok Szent László történetéhez* (Budapest, 1980), in *Catholic Historical Review*, 68 (1982), 130f.

S. V. Kovács (ed), *Temesvári Pelbárt válogatott írásai* (Selected writings of Pelbart of Temesvar) (Budapest, 1982)

A. V. Krey, "Urban II's Crusade: Success of Failure?" *American Historical Review*, 53 (1948), 235ff.

A. C. Krey, "William of Tyre," *Speculum*, 16 (1941), 149ff.

Gy. Kristó, "Anjou-kori krónikáink (Hungarian chronicles of the fourteenth century)," *Századok*, 101 (1967), 457ff.

Gy. Kristó, *A feudális széttagolás Magyarországon* (Feudal divisions in Hungary) (Budapest, 1979)

Gy. Kristó, "Kézai Simon s a XIII századvégi köznemesi ideológia néhány vonása (Simon de Keza and his attitude toward the outlook of the lesser nobility in the late 13th century)," *ITK*, 76 (1972), 1ff.

Gy. Kristo, "Kralj Koloman, Kralj Stjepan I Hrvatska," *Historijski sbornik*, 33-34 (Zagreb, 1980-81), 263f.

Gy. Kristó, "Legitimitás és idoneitás: adalékok Árpád-házi eszmetörténetünkhöz (Legitimacy and aptness: some data on the concept of Arpadian kingship)," *Századok*, 108 (1974), 585ff., and 606ff.

Gy. Kristó, "Kiev a magyar krónikákban (Kiev in the Hungarian chronicles)," *Tiszatáj*, 36 (1982), 61ff.

Gy. Kristó, *Korai levéltári és elbeszélő forrásaink kapcsolatához* (The relationship between early Hungarian narrative sources and archival material), vol. XXI of *Acta historica Szegediensis* (Szeged, 1966)

Gy. Kristó, "Rómaiak és vlachok Nyesztornál és Anonymusnál (The Romans and the Vlachs in Nestor and in Anonymus)," *Századok*, 112 (1978), 623ff.

Gy. Kristó, "Szempontok Anonymus gestájának megítéléséhez (Some comments on the values of Anonymus' gesta)," *Acta Szegediensis*, 66 (1979), 45ff.

Gy. Kristó, "A XI-XIII századi epikáink és az Árpád-kori írásos hagyomány (The 11th-13th century Hungarian epics and written historical tradition of the Arpadian age)," *Ethnographia*, 83 (1972), 57ff.

Gy. Kristó, "Anonymus magyarországi írott forrásainak kérdéséhez (Remarks on the written sources available to Anonymus from historic Hungary)," *MKSz*, 88 (1972), 166ff.

Gy. Kristó, *Magyarország története 895-1301* (Hungarian history 895-1301) (Budapest, 1986)

Gy. Kristó-F. Makk (eds), *III Béla emlékezete* (Béla III Memorial volume) (Budapest, 1981)

Gy. Kristó-F. Makk, "Krónikáink keletkezéstörténetéhez (Essay on the formation of Hungarian chronicles)," *Történelmi Szemle*, 15 (1972), 198ff.

H. C. Krueger, "Economic Aspects of Expanding Europe," in M. Clagett (ed), *Twelfth Century Europe and the Foundations of Modern Society* (Madison, Wisc., 1966), 59ff.

D. Krywalski, "Das Mittelalter aus heutiger Sicht: Versuch über die Schwierigkeit, die Vergangenheit zu verstehen," *Stimmen der Zeit*, 204 (1986), 676ff.

F. Kühár, *Mária tiszteletünk XI s XII századi emlékei a liturgiában* (Remembrances of Mary, Mother of God, in 11th-12th century liturgy in Hungary) (Budapest, 1939)

F. Kühár, "A Pray kódex rendeltetése, sorsa, szellemtörténeti értéke (The purpose, history and intellectual meaning of the Pray codex)," *MKSz*, 63 (1939), 213ff.

A. Kubinyi, "Burgstadt, Vorburgstadt und Stadtburg: zur Morphologie des mittelalterlichen Buda," *Acta arhaeologica Academiae Scientiarum Hungaricae*, 33 (1981), 161ff.

B. Kumorovitz, "Szent László vásár-törvénye és Kálmán király pecsétes kartulája (The merchant laws of King Ladislas and the sealed briefs in Coloman's reign)," in Mezey, *Athleta patriae*, 83ff.

Á. Kuncz, "Anjou-kori történetíróink kérdéséhez (Remarks on the chroniclers of the Angevin age)," *ITK*, 68 (1965), 358ff.

D. Kurze, "Haeresie und Minderheit im Mittelalter," *HZ*, 229 (1979), 529ff.

S. Kuttner, "Liber canonicus: a Note on the Dictatus papae, c. 17," *Studi Gregoriani*, 2 (1947), 387ff.

S. Kyriakidis, *Eustazio di Thessalonica, la espugnazione di Thessalonica* (Palermo, 1961)

G. Labuda, "Bazoar Anonymus Gallus krónikájában ('Bazoar' in the chronicle of the anonymous Gallus)," *Századok*, 104 (1970), 173ff.

G. LeBras, *Histoire du droit et des institutions de l'église en occident*, vol. III (Paris, 1958)

B. M. Lacroix, "The Notion of History in Early Medieval Histories," *Medieval Studies*, 10 (1948), 219ff.

De s. *Ladislao rege Hungariae*, *SSH*, II, 515ff.

Ladislas I, *Decreta I, II* and *III*, in *RHM*, vol. II.

B. Ladner, *Die Papstbildnisse des Altertums und des Mittelalters* (Vatican City, 1941)

K. Langosch (ed), *Die Briefe Kaiser Henrichs IV* (Munster-Cologne, 1954)

Manegold of Lautenbach, *Ad Gebehardum liber, MGH LdL*, I, 303ff.

H. Ch. Lea, *The ordeal*, ed. E. Peters (Philadelphia, 1973)

P. Lehmann, "Die Vielgestalt des 12 Jahrhunderts," *HZ*, 178 (1954), 225ff.

B. Leib, *Rome, Kiev et Byzance a la fin du XIe siècle* (Paris, 1924)

H. Leisegang, "Der Ursprung der Lehre Augustins von der Civitas Dei," *Archiv für Kulturgeschichte*, 16 (1925), 127ff.

L. J. Lékai, "Zirc 800 éve (The 800th anniversary of Zirc abbey)," *Ciszterci lelkiség*, ed. D. Farkasfalvy (Eisenstadt, 1982), 7ff.

L. J. Lekai, *The White Monks* (Okauchee, Wisc., 1953)

J. F. Lemarignier, *Le government royal aux premiers temps Capétiens, 987-1108* (Paris, 1965)

K. Lechner, *Die Babenberger* (Vienna-Graz, 1976)

J. Lelewel, *Géographie du moyen age*, 4 vols. (Brussels, 1852-57; repr. Amsterdam, 1966), vol. I.

C. S. Lewis, "Imagination and Thought in the Middle Ages," in his *Studies in Medieval and Renaissance Literature*, ed. W. Hooper (Cambridge, 1966)

A. Lhotsky, *Aus dem Nachlass* (Vienna, 1976), 284ff.

A. Lhotsky, "Die Historiographie Ottos von Freising," in his *Europäisches Mittelalter* (Vienna, 1970), 49ff.

A. Lhotsky, "Otto von Freising, seine Weltanschauung," in his *Europäisches Mittelalter* (Vienna, 1970), 64ff.

A. Lhotsky, *Quellenkunde zur mittelalterlichen Geschichte Österreichs* (Graz-Cologne, 1963)

A. Linder, "The Knowledge of John of Salisbury in the Middle Ages," *Studi medievali*, 18 (1977), 315ff.

Richard of London, *Itinerarium peregrinorum, MGHSS*, XVII

Arnold of Lübeck, *Chronica Slavorum, MGHSS*, XXI

K. Lübeck, "Abtswahl, 1198," *HJB*, 52 (1932), 189ff.

A. Luchaire, *Louis VI le Gros, annales de sa vie et de son regne* (Paris, 1890)

B. Lyon, *A Constitutional and Legal History of Medieval England* (New York-London, 1960)

J. McCann, *Saint Benedict* (New York, 1958)

C. A. Macartney, *The Medieval Hungarian Historians* (Cambridge, 1953)

R. McKitterich, *The Frankish Church and the Carolingian Reforms* 789-95 (London, 1977)

M. Maccarone, "Die Cathedra Petri im Hochmittelalter: vom Symbol des päpstlichen Amtes zum Kultobjekt," *Römische Quartalschrift*, 76 (1981), 137ff., and 573ff.

E. Madas, "Laszlo kiralnak inneperől' az Érdy kódex László-napi beszédének elemzése (Analysis of the sermon for the feast of King Ladislas in the Érdy codex)," *Athleta patriae*, 73ff.

E. Madas, "Az Érdy-kódexről (Comments on the Érdy codex)," *Vigilia*, 50 (1985), 635ff.

F. W. Maitland, *The Constitutional History of England* (Cambridge, 1911)

B. Majláth, "A 'kalandos' társulatok (The *kalendae* confraternities)" Századok, 19 (1885), 563ff.

F. Makk, "III Béla és Bizánc (Béla III and Byzantium)," *Századok*, 116 (1982), 33ff.

F. Makk, "Contributions a l'histoire des relations hungaro-byzantines au XIIe siècle," *Acta antiqua*, 29 (1981), 445ff.

F. Makk, "A XII századi főúri csoportharcok értékeléséhez (Importance of group struggle among the nobility of the 12th century)," *Acta Szegediensis*, 71 (1981), 29ff.

F. Makk, "Megjegyzések III István történetéhez (Comments on the reign of Stephen III)," *Acta Szegediensis*, 66 (1979), 29ff.

F. Makk, "Megjegyzések II Béla történetéhez (Comments on the reign of Béla II)," *Acta Szegediensis*, 40 (1972), 31ff.

F. Makk, "Megjegyzések a II Géza kori magyar-bizánci konfrontáció Kronológiájához (Some remarks aboaut the time-sequence of the Hungaro-Byzantine conflict during the reign of Géza II)," *Acta Szegediensis*, 67 (1980), 21ff.

F. Makk, "Byzantium and the struggles for the throne in Hungary in the twelfth century," *Acta classica*, 17-18 (Debrecen, 1981-82), 49ff.

F. Makk, *Magyarország a 12 században* (Hungary in the twelfth century) (Budapest, 1986)

F. Makk, "Megjegyzések Kálmán külpolitikájához (Remarks on the foreign policy of Coloman)," *Acta historica Szegediensis*, 67 (1980), 21ff.

F. Makk, "Megjegyzések II István történetéhez (Comments on the reign of Stephen II)," *Memoria Hungariae*, I, 251ff.

F. Maksay, "Das Agrarsiedlungsystem des mittelalterlichen Ungarns," *Acta historica*, 24 (1978), 83ff.

F. Maksay, "Umwandlung der ungarischen Siedlungs- und Agrarstruktur 11-14 Jahrhundert," *Zeitschrift für Agrargeschichte und Agrarsoziologie*, 23 (1975), 154ff.

E. M. Makowski, "The Conjual Debt and Medieval Canon Law," *Journal of Medieval History*, 3 (1977), 99ff.

William of Malmesbury, *De gestis regum Anglorum*, ed. W. Stubbs, R.S. 2 vols. (London, 1887-89)

E. Mályusz, "Die Eigenkirche in Ungarn," *Studien zur Geschichte Osteuropas: Gedenkschrift für H. F. Schmid*, 3 (1966), 76ff.

E. Mályusz, *A Thuróczy Krónika és forrásai* (The Thuróczy Chronicle and its sources) (Budapest, 1967)

E. Mályusz, "Geschichte des Bürgertums in Ungarn," *Vierteljahrschrift für Wirtschafts- und Sozialgeschichte*, 20 (1928), 357ff.

E. Mályusz, *Az V István kori gesta* (Hungarian chronicle of the reign of Stephen V) (Budapest, 1971)

E. Mályusz, *Egyházi társadalom a középkori Magyarországon* (Ecclesiastical social structure in medieval Hungary) (Budapest, 1971)

E. Mályusz, "Entwicklung der ständischen Schichten im mittelalterlichen Ungarn," *Études historique hongroises*, *1980*, vol. I (Budapest, 1980), 103ff.

William of Malmesbury, *De gestis regum Anglorum*, R. S., 2 vols. (London, 1887-89)

M. Manitius, *Geschichte der lateinischen Literatur des Mittelalters,* 3 vols. (Munich, 1911-31)

J. D. Mansi (ed), *Sacrorum conciliorum nova et amplissima collectio*, 31 vols. (Florence-Venice, 1759-98)

Walter Map, *De nugis curialium*, ed. M. R. James (Ocford, 1914)

H. Marczali (ed), *Enchiridion fontium historiae Hungarorum* (Budapest, 1901)

H. Marczali, *Ungarns Geschichtsquellen im Zeitalter der Árpáden* (Berlin, 1882)

Roberti s. Mariani Autissiodorensis *Chronicon*, MGHSS, XXVI

E. Martene-U. Durand (eds), *Thesaurus novus anecdotorum*, 5 vols. (repr. New York, 1968)

E. Martene-U. Durand (eds), *Veterum scriptorum et monumentorum collectio*, 9 vols. (repr. New York, 1968), cited as Martene-Durand

Martinus Gallus, *Chronicon Polonorum*, MGHSS, IX

G. Martinuzzi (ed), *Ritus explorandae veritatis* (Colosuarij, 1550)

P. Mass, "Die Musen des Kaisers Alexios I," *BZ*, 22 (1913), 348ff.

E. Mayer, "Der Ursprung der germanischen Gottesurteile," *Historische Vierteljahrschrift*, 20 (1920-21), 289ff.

H. E. Mayer, *Geschichte der Kreuzzüge*, 3rd ed. (Stuttgart, 1973)

A. v. Meiller (ed), *Regesta arhciepiscoporum Salisburgensium* (Vienna, 1866)

A. Meineke (ed), *Iohannes Cinnamus: Epithomae rerum ab Ioanne et Alexio Comnenis gestarum* (Bonn, 1836), cited as Cinnamus

B. Menczer, *A Commentary on Hungarian Literature* (Castrop-Rauxel, 1956)

S. Mester, "De initiis canonici iuris culturae in Hungaria," *Studi Gregoriani*, 2 (1954), 659ff.

E. Meyer, "Der Ursprung der germanischen Gottesurteile," *Historische Vierteljahrschrift*, 20 (1920-21), 289ff.

L. Mezey, *Athleta patriae: tanulmányok Szent László történetéhez* (Studies in the history of St. Ladislas) (Budapest, 1980)

L. Mezey, *Deákság és Európa* (Medieval Latinity and /the concept of/ Europe) (Budapest, 1979)

L. Mezey, "A Pray kódex keletkezésének problémái (Questions concerning the origins of the Pray codex)," *MKSz*, 87 (1971), 1ff.

L. Mezey, "Ungarn und Europa im 12 Jahrhundert: Kirche und Kultur zwischen Ost und West," *Vorträge und Forschungen*, 12 (1968), 255ff.

Matthias Miechovius, *Chronica Polonorum*, in P. Pistorius (ed), *Poloniae historiae corpus*, 3 vols. (Basel, 1582), II

J. P. Migne (ed), *Patrologiae cursus completus, series latina*, 221 vols. (Paris, 1844-55), cited as *MPL*

J. P. Migne (ed), *Patrologiae cursus completus, series graeca*, 166 vols. (Paris, 1857-66), cited as *MPG*

Zs. Miklós, "Árpád-kori földvár Mend-Lányváron (Earthen fortifications of the Árpádian age at Mend-Leányvár)," *Archeológiai Értesítő*, 108 (1982), 233ff.

C. Mirbt (ed), *Die Publizistik im Zeitalter Gregors VII* (Leipzig, 1894)

H. Mitteis, *Der Staat des hohen Mittelalters*, 8th rev. ed. (Weimar, 1968)

Gerlaucus Milovicensis *Chronicon Bohemiae*, MGHSS, XVII

E. Molnár, *A magyar társadalom története az őskortól az Árpád-korig* (Hungarian social formation from early times to the age of the Árpáds), 2nd ed. (Budapest, 1949)

Robert the Monk, *Historia Iherosolimitana*, RHC Occ, III

MGH Libelli de lite, ed. E. Dümmler, 3 vols. (Hanover, 1891-97) cited as *MGH LdL*

*Monumenta spectantia historiam Slavorum meridionalium*, 48 vols. (Zagreb, 1868-1918)

Gy. Moravcsik, *Byzantinoturcica*, vol. I: *Die byzantinischen Quellen der Türkvölker* (Budapest, 1942)

Gy. Moravcsik, "Die byzantinische Kultur und mittelalterliches Ungarn," *SB der Deutschen Akademie der Wissenschaften zu Berlin*, phil.-Gesch., *1955* (Berlin, 1956), No. 4.

Gy. Moravcsik, "III Béla és a bizánci birodalom Manuel halála után (Relations between Bela III and Byzantium after Manuel)," *Századok*, 67 (1933), 513ff.

Gy. Moravcsik, "The Holy Crown of Hungary," *Hungarian Quarterly*, 4 (1938), 656ff.

Gy. Moravcsik, *Hungary and Byzantium* (Amsterdam-Budapest, 1970)

Gy. Moravcsik (ed), *Fontes byzantini historiae Hungaricae aevo ducum et regum ex stirpis Arpad descendentium* (Budapest, 1984)

Gy. Moravcsik, "Les relations entre la Hongrie et Byzance a l'époque des croisades," *Studia byzantina* (Budapest, 1967), 315f.

Gy. Moravcsik, "A magyar szent Korona az archaeológiai és történeti kutatások megvilágításában (The Hungarian Holy Crown in the light of archaeological and historical research)," *SIE*, III, 426ff.

Gy. Moravcsik, "A magyar szókincs görög elemei (Byzantine elements in the Hungarian vocabulary)," *Emlékkönyv Melich János 70 születésnapjára* (Memorial volume to J. Melich' 70th birthday) (Budapest, 1942), 264ff.

Gy. Moravcsik, "Pour une alliance byzantino-hongroise (seconde moitié du XII siècle,," *Byzantion*, 8 (1933), 555ff.

D. C. Munro, "A Crusader," *Speculum*, 7 (1932), 321ff.

D. C. Munro, "Did Emperor Alexios I Ask for Aid at the Council of Piacenza?" *American Historical Review*, 27 (1922), 731ff.

D. C. Munro, "The Speech of Pope Urban II at Clermont," *American Historical Review*, 11 (1906), 231ff.

P. Munz, *Frederick Barbarossa* (Ithaca, 1969)

L. A. Muratori (ed), *Scriptores rerum Italicarum*, 28 vols. (Milan, 1723-51)

H. A. Myers, "The Concept of Kingship in the 'Book of Emperors' (Kaiserchronik)," *Traditio*, 27 (1971), 205ff.

*Narratio de electione Lotharii*, *MGHSS*, XX, 511.

A. Négyessy, "The Magna Carta, 1215, and the Bulla Aurea, 1222," *The New Hungarian Quarterly*, 5 (New York, 1965), 135ff.

C. Neumann, *Griechische Geschichtsschreiber und Geschichtsquellen im zwölften Jahrhundert* (Leipzig, 1888)

P. Németh, "Előzetes jelentés a szabolcsi árpádkori megyeszékhely kutatásának első három esztendejéről (Preliminary report on the first three years of excavations at the county seat of Szabolcs of the age of the Árpáds)," *Archaeológiai Értesítő*, 100 (1973), 167ff.

W. Neuss, *Das Problem des Mittelalters* (Kolmar im Elsass, n.d.)

Guibert of Nogent, *Historia quae dicitur Gesta Dei per Francos RHC Occ*, IV, 137ff.; *MPL*, 166, 705ff.

Gy. Nováki-Gy. Sándorfi, "Untersuchungen der Struktur und Ursprung der Schanzen der frühen ungarischen Burgen,"

*Acta archaeologica Academiae Scientiarum Hungaricae*, 33 (1981), 133ff.

*Novellae constitutiones* of Emperor Manuel, in *MPG*, 133

D. Obolensky, *The Byzantine Commonwealth* (London, 1971)

W. Ohnsorge, "Kaiser Konrad III: zur Geschichte des staufischen Staatsgedankens," *MIÖG*, 46 (1932), 343ff.

G. Örterle, "Heilsprechung," *Lexikon für Theologie und Kirche*, rev. ed., vol. V (Hanover, 1960), 143

G. Ostrogorsky, *Geschichte des byzantinischen Staates*, 2nd ed. (Munich, 1952)

A. Oszvald, *A magyarországi középkori premontrei apátságok* (The communities of the Canons of Prémontré in medieval Hungary) (Budapest, 1939)

E. F. Otto, "Otto von Freising und Friedrich Barbarossa," *Historische Vierteljahrschrift*, 31 (1938), 27ff.

S. R. Packard, *Twelfth Century Europe* (Amherst, Mass., 1973)

F. Palacky, *Geschichte vom Böhmen*, vol. I (repr. Prague, 1844)

F. Palacky, *Würdigung der alten böhmischen Geschichtsschreiber*, rev. ed. (Prague, 1869)

Matthew of Paris, *Chronica maiora*, R.S., 7 vols. (London, 1872-1883), vol. VI

R. Parisiensis *Imagines historiarum*, *MGHSS*, XXVI

E. Pásztor, "Sulla origini della vita comune del clero in Ungheria," *La vita comune del clero nei secoli XI-XII*: atti di settimana di studio, Mandola, 1959, vol. II (Milan, 1962), 71ff.

E. Patzelt, *Österreich bis zum Ausgang der Babenbergerzeit* (Vienna, 1946)

Gy. Pauler, *A magyar nemzet története az árpádházi királyok alatt* (History of the Hungarian nation under the Arpads), 2 vols. 2nd ed. (Budapest, 1899; repr. Budapest, 1984)

K. Pennington (ed), *Law, Church and Society*: Essays in Honor of St. Kuttner (Philadelphia, 1977)

G. H. Pertz (ed), *Monumenta Germaniae historica, Scriptores*, 32 vols. (Hanover, 1854etc.), cited as *MGHSS*

C. Péterffy (ed), *Sacra concilia ecclesiae Romanae Catholicae in regno Hungariae celebrata*, 2 vols. (Vienna, 1742-43)

H. C. Peyer, "Gastfreundschaft und harmonielle Gast-
lichkeit im Mittelalter," *HZ*, 235 (1982), 265ff.

H. Pez (ed), *Scriptores rerum Austricarum*, 3 vols. (Regensburg, 1721-45), cited as Pez, *Scriptores*

W. Philip, "Die 'Provest vremennych let'," in his *Aufsätze zum geschichtlichen und politischen Denken im Kiewer
Russland* (Breslau, 1940), 24ff.

J. Pintér, *Magyar irodalomtörténet* (Synthesis of Hungarian literature), 8 vols. (Budapest, 1930-41), vol. I.

Iohannes de Piscina, *De transferatione Friderici I*,
*MGHSS*, XXIX

V. Pfaff, "Das kirchliche Eherecht am Ende des 12 Jahrhunderts," *Zeitschrift der Savigny Stiftung für Rechtsgeschichte*, kan. Abt., 63 (1977), 557ff.

A. Pogodin, "Der Bericht der Russischen Chronik über
die Gründung des Kiewischen Staates," *Zeitschrift für Osteuropäische Geschichte*, 5 (1931), 202ff.

Ö. Polner, *A magyar szent korona felső részének eredet-
kérdéséhez* (Questions concerning the origins of the upper
part of the Hungarian Crown) (Kolozsvár, 1943)

A. Potthast, *Bibliotheca historica medii aevi*, 2 vols. rev.
ed. (Berlin, 1896)

Cosmas of Prague, *Chronica Bohemorum libri III*,
*MGHSS*, IX

W. Pöchl, *Geschichte des Kirchenrechts*, vol. II (Vienna,
1955)

G. Pray, *Annales regum Hungariae*, 5 vols. (Vienna,
1764-70)

G. Pray, *Dissertatio historico critica de s. Ladislao rege
Hungariae* (Posonii, 1774)

H. Prutz, *Kulturgeschichte der Kreuzzüge* (Berlin, 1883;
repr. Hildesheim, 1964)

P. Radó, *Index codicum manu scriptorum liturgicorum
bibliothecarum regni Hungariae* (Budapest, 1941)

P. Radó, *Libri liturgici manu scripti bibliothecarum
Hungariae* (Budapest, 1947)

P. Ransanus, *Epithoma rerum Hungararum*, the last book
of his *Annales temporum omnium*, ed. P. Kulcsár (Budapest, 1977)

Ratherius of Verona, *Praeloquiorum libri VI*, *MPL*, 136,
172f.

A. Rauch (ed), *Rerum Austricarum Scriptores*, 3 vols. (Vienna, 1793-94), cited as Rauch

Raymond of Agiles, *Historia Francorum qui ceperunt Jerusalem*, in *MPL*, 155.

*Recueil des historiens des croisades*, 16 vols. (Paris, 1841-1906): *Historiens occidentaux*, 5 vols. (Paris, 1844-95), cited as *RHC Occ.*

Regino of Prüm, *Chronicon*, *MGHSS*, I, 536ff.

*Regula s. Benedicti*, *MPL*, 66, 215ff.

B. Hirsch-Reich, "Joachim von Fiore und das Judentum," *Judentum im Mittelalter*, ed. P. Wilpert (Berlin, 1966), 228ff.

J. Reisinger, "Népek nagy nevelője (Great educator of nations: Benedict of Nursia)," *Vigilia*, 47 (1982), 391ff.

E. Reiszig, *A jeruzsálemi Szent János lovagrend Magyarországon* (The Knights of St. John in Hungary), 2 vols. (Budapest, 1925-28), vol. I.

Gerhoch of Reichersberg, *De aedificatione Dei*, *MPL*, 194, 1187ff.

Gerhoch of Reichersberg, *De investigatione antichristi*, *LdL*, III, 305ff.

Gerhoch of Reichersberg, *Opusculum de aedificatione Dei*, *MPL*, 194, 1228ff.

Gerhoch of Reichersberg, *De ordine donorum Sancti Spiritus*, *MGH LdL*, III, 273ff.

Gerhoch of Reichersberg, *De quarta vigilia noctis*, *MGH LdL*, III, 503ff.

Magnus Prfesbyter of Reichersberg, *Chronica*, *MGHSS*, XVII

Hincmar of Rheims, *De divortio Lotharii et Teutbergae*, in *MPL*, 125

P. Riant (ed), *Exuviae sacrae Constantinopolitanae*, 2 vols. (Geneva, 1841-43), cited as Riant, *Exuviae*

S. Riezler, "Der Kreuzzug Kaiser Friedrichs I," *Forschungen zur deutschen Geschichte*, 10 (1870), 1ff.

J. P. Ripoche, "La Hongrie entre Byzance et Rome: probleme de choice réligieux," *Ungarn Jahrbuch*, 6 (1974-75), 9ff.

M. Ritter, "Studien über die Entwicklung der Geschichtwissenschaft: die christlich-mittelalterliche Geschichtschreibung," *HZ*, 107 (1911), 237ff.

Gy. Rónay, Review of D. Dercsényi (ed), *Chronicon*

*pictum*: *Képes Krónika*, 2 vols. (Budapest, 1963), in *Vigilia*, 30 (1965), 44ff.

M. Rule (ed), Eadmer, *Historia novorum in Anglia*, R.S. (London, 1884)

J. B. Russel, *Witchcraft in the Middle Ages* (Ithaca, NY, 1972)

*Sachsenspiegel*, ed. C. G. Homeyer (Hanover, 1861)

John of Salisbury, *Policraticus*, ed. C. C. J. Webb, 2 vols. (Oxford, 1909)

G. O. Sayles, *The Medieval Foundations of England* (London, 1948)

W. Scheck, *Geschichte Russlands*, rev. ed. (Munich, 1977)

Th. Schieder (ed), *Handbuch der europäischen Geschichte*, vol. I (Stuttgart, 1976)

B. Schimmelpfennig, "Ex fornicatione nati: Studies on the Position of Priests' Sons from the Twelfth to the Fourteenth Centuries," *Studies in Medieval and Renaissance History*, 12 (1979), 1ff.

W. F. Schirmer, "Die kulturelle Rolle des englischen Hofes im 12 Jahrhundert," in J. Bumke (ed), *Literarisches Mäzenatentum,* vol. 598 of *Wege der Forschung* (Darmstadt, 1982), 232ff.

F. J. Schmale, "Zu den Konzilien Paschals II," *Annarium historiae conciliorum*, 10 (1978), 279ff.

G. Schnürer, *Kirche und Kultur im Mittelalter*, 3 vols., 2nd ed. (Paderborn, 1927-28)

G. Schramm, *Eroberer und Eingesessene*; *geographische Lehnnamen als Zeugen der Geschichte Südosteuropas im ersten Jahrtausend n. Chr.* (Stuttgart, 1981)

G. Schreiber, "Praemonstratenserkultur des 12 Jahrhunderts," *Analecta Praemonstratensia*, 16 (1940), 41ff.

J. G. Schwandtner (ed), *Scriptores rerum Hungaricarum*, 3 vols. (Vienna, 1746-48), cited as Schwandtner

E. Schwartz, "750 Jahre Stift St. Gotthard in Ungarn," *Cisterzienser Chronik*, 45 (1933), 97ff.

Isidore of Seville, *Sententiarum, MPL,* 83

Sigebert of Gembloux, *Chronicon*, in *MGHSS,* VI

G. J. Simons, *The Witchcraft World* (New York, 1974)

H. Simonsfeld, *Jahrbücher des deutschen Reiches unter Friedrich I* (1152-58) (Munich, 1908; rep. Berlin, 1967)

B. Smalley, "Ecclesiastical Attitudes to Novelty, c. 1100-

1250," *Church, Society and Politics*, ed. D. Baker (Oxford, 1975), 113ff.

B. Smalley, *Historians in the Middle Ages* (New York, 1975)

T. Smiciklas (ed), *Codex diplomaticus regni Croatiae, Dalmatiae et Slavoniae*, 14 vols. (Zagreb, 1904-16)

F. v. Sisic (ed), *Enchiridion fontium historiae Croaticae*, vol. *I-1* (Zagreb, 1916)

F. Somogyi, *Küldetés: a magyarság története* (Destiny: a History of the Hungarians), 3rd repr. of 2nd rev. ed. (Cleveland, Ohio, 1978)

F. Somogyi and L. Somogyi, *Faith and Fate: Hungarian Cultural History* (Cleveland, Ohio, 1976)

F. Somogyi - L. F. Somogyi, "The Medieval University of Pécs," in S. B. Vardi *et al* (eds), *Louis the Great, King of Hungary and Poland* (New York, 1986), 221ff.

F. Somogyi - L. F. Somogyi, "The Constitutional Guarantee of 1351: The Decree of Louis the Great," in Vardi, *Louis the Great*, 429ff.

Z. Soltész, "Milyen tervekkel és felszereléssel jöhetett Budára Hess András? (What were the plans and equipment of Andrew Hess arriving at Buda?)," *MKSz*, 90 (1974), 1ff.

G. C. Soulis, "The Legacy of Cyrill and Methodius to the Southern Slavs," *Dumbarkton Oaks Papers*, XIX (Washington, DC), 19ff.

R. W. Southern, *St. Anselm and His Biographer* (Cambridge, 1963)

R. W. Southern, *Life of St. Anselm of Canterbury* (Oxford, 1962)

R. W. Southern, *Medieval Humanism* (New York-Evanston, 1970)

Thomas of Spaleto, *Historia Salonitarum*, in Schwandtner, III, 532ff.

J. Spörl, "Wandel des Welt- und Geschichtsbildes im 12 Jahrhundert, *Unser Geschichtsbild*, 2 (1955), 99ff.

R. Sprandel, *Ivo von Chartres und seine Stellung in der Kirchengeschichte* (Stuttgart, 1962)

G. Stadtmüller, "Die ungarische Grossmacht des Mittelalters," *HJB*, 70 (1951), 151ff.

W. v. d. Steinen, *Der Kosmos des Mittelalters*, 2nd ed. (Bern-Munich, 1967)

J. Streisand (ed), *Deutsche Geschichte*, vol. I (Berlin, 1967), 230ff.

H. Strzewitzek, *Die Sippenbeziehungen der Freisinger Bischöfe im Mittelalter* (Munich, 1938)

St. Stephen I, *Leges*, in *RHM*, II, 310ff., or *MPL*, 151, 1243ff.

St. of Tournai, *Summa decretorum*, ed. J. F. v. Schulte (Giessen, 1891)

W. Stubbs (ed), *Select Charters of English Constitutional History*, 8th ed. (Oxford, 1895)

J. Stülz, "Propst Gerhoch of Reichersberg," *Denkschriften der kaiserlichen Akademie der Wissenschaften*, phil.-hist. Kl., 1 (Vienna, 1850), 113ff.

Suger of St. Denis, *Vita Ludovici VI*, *MGHSS*, XXVI *Supplementum ad historiam ducum Venetorum*, *MGHSS*, XVII

H. Svrita ( = J. Zurita), *Indices rerum ab Aragoniae regibus gestarum ab initiis regni ad annum MCDX* (Caesaraugustae, 1578)

H. Sybel, *Geschichte des ersten Kreuzzüges*, 2nd ed. (Leipzig, 1881)

F. v. Sybel, "Über den zweiten Kreuzzug," *Zeitschrift füe Geschichtswissenschaften*, 4 (1845), 197ff.

K. Szabó (ed), *Régi magyar könyvtár* (Bibliography of early Hungarian books), 2 vols. (Budapest, 1879-85)

Gy. Székely, "Koronaküldések és királykreálások a 10-11 századi Európában (Sending og a royal crown and establishing kingship in Europe during the 10th-11th centuries)," *Századok*, 118 (1984), 905ff.

Gy. Székely et al (eds), *Magyarország története; előzmények és magyar történet 1242-ig* (History of Hungary: Origins and Hungarian History to 1242), 2 vols. (Budapest, 1984)

L. Székely, *Az 1171-évi bakonybéli összeírás és I András győri püspöksége* (The 1171 Bakonybél census and the episcopate of Andrew I, bishop of Győr) (Győr, 1914)

L. Szegfű, 'Az Ajton monda (The Ajton legend)," *Acta historica*, 40 (Szeged, 1972), 3ff.

L. Szegfű, "I László alakja a középkori forrásokban (Ladislas I in the Medieval Chronicles)," *A Juhász Gyula Tanárképző Főiskola közleményei* (Szeged, 1978), 37ff.

L. Szegfű, "Szent Gellért prédikációi (Sermons of Gerard of Csanád)," *Acta historica*, 80 (Szeged, 1985), 19ff.

J. Szekfű, *Ungarn: eine Geschichtsstudie* (Stuttgart, 1918)

N. L. Szelesztei, "A Szent László legenda szöveghagyományozódásáról (Ein neuer Fund zur Textüberlieferung der Ladislas Legende)," *MKSz*, 100 (1984), 176ff.

A. Szennay, *Szent Benedeknek, Európa védőszentjének emlékezete* (To the memory of St. Benedict, the guardian saint of Europe) (Budapest, 1981)

*Szent István Emlékkönyv* (Memorial volumes to the 900th anniversary of the death of King St. Stephen), ed. J. Card. Serédi, 3 vols. (Budapest, 1938), cited as *SIE*

A. Szentirmai, "Die Anfänge des Rechts der Pfarrei in Ungarn," *Österreichisches Archiv für Kirchenrecht*, 10 (1959), 30ff.

A. Szentirmai, "Der Einfluss des byzantinischen Kirchenrechts auf die Gesetzgebung Ungarns," *Jahrbuch der Österreichischen Byzantinischen Gesellschaft*, 10 (1961), 76ff.

A. Szentirmai, "Das Recht des Erzdechanten in Ungarn während des Mittelalters," *Zeitschrift der Savigny Stiftung für Rechtsgeschichte*, kan. Abt., 43 (1957), 132ff.

A. Szentirmai, "Der Ursprung des Archidiakonats in Ungarn," *Österreichisches Archiv für Kirchenrecht*, 7 (1956), 231ff.

E. Szentpétery (ed), *Regesta regum stirpis Arpadianae critico-ciplomatica*, 2 vols. (Budapest, 1923-61)

E. Szentpétery (ed) *Scriptores rerum Hungaricarum*, 2 vols. (Budapest, 1937-38), cited as *SSH*

L. Szilágyi, "III Endre 1298 évi törvénye,"

L. Szilágyi, "Írásbeli supplicatiók a középkori magyar adminisztrációban (Written requests, their use, in the medieval Hungarian administration)," *Levéltári Közlemények*, 10 (1932), 157ff., - and in *MIÖG* Erg. Band VI, 220ff.

J. Szűcs, "Kézai problémák (Questions concerning Keza's gesta)," *Memoria Hungariae*, I, 187ff.

J. Szűcs, "Társadalomszemlélet, politikai teória és történetszemlélet Kézai Simon Gesta Hungarorumában (Social outlook, political ideology and specific views of history in Keza's gesta)," *Századok*, 107 (1973), 569ff., and 823ff.

L. Tamás, *Rómaiak, románok és oláhok Dacia Trajanában* (Roman, Rumanians and Vlachs in Dacia Traiana) (Budapest, 1935)

B. Tárkány-Szűcs, *Magyar jogi népszokások* (Hungarian legal folk-customs) (Budapest, 1981)

A. v. Tasnádi-Nagy, "Der Geist der ungarischen Verfassung," *Ungarische Jahrbücher*, 22 (1942), 1ff.

A. Tarnai, "A Képes Krónika forrásaihoz (Sources of
the Chronicon pictum)," *Memoria Hungariae*, I, 203ff.

H. O. Taylor, *The Medieval Mind*, 2 vols. 4th rev. ed.
(London, 1925)

G. Tellenbach, *Libertas: Kirche und Weltordnung im
Zeitalter des Investiturstreites* (Stuttgart, 1936)

Pelbart of Temesvár, *Rosarium aureum theologiae ad
Sententiarum libri IV* (Venice, 1589)

Pelbart of Temesvár, *Sermones Pomerii de Sanctis*
(Hagenau, 1500)

L. Thallóczy, "III Béla és a magyar birodalom ?The realm
of Béla III)," in Forster, *III Béla*, 157ff.

L. Thallóczy, "III Béla és a magyar birodalom (The realm
Hungarian realm of King Béla III), in the *Magyar Könyvtár* series, ed. A. Radó (Budapest, 1906), 12ff.

A. Theiner (ed), *Vetera monumenta historiam Hungariae
sacram illustrantia*, 2 vols. (Rome, 1859-60), vol. I

L. Thorndike, *History of Magic and Experimental Science*,
8 vols. (New York, 1923etc.), vol. II

Thuróczy codex, *Clme* 407 of the Hungarian National
Museum Széchenyi Library, Budapest

A. Timon, *Ungarische Verfassungs- und Rechtsgeschichte*,
2nd ed., ed. F. Schiller (Berlin, 1904)

J. Török, "Szent László liturgikus tisztelete (The liturgy
of St. Ladislas)," Mezey, *Athleta patriae*, 135ff.

I. Torma, "Mittelalterliche Ackerfeld-Spuren im Wald
von Tamási, Komitat Tolna," *Acta archaeologica Academiae
Scientiarum Hungaricae*, 33 (1981), 245ff.

Gregory of Tours, *Libri miraculorum*, in *MGH SS rerum
Merovingicarum*, vol. I

S. Tóth, "Megjegyzések Toynbee magyar őstörténeti
koncepciójához (Comments on Toynbee's Idea of Hungarian
Origins)," *Acta historica Szegediensis*, 71 (1981), 13ff.

Z. Tóth, *A Hartvik legenda kritikájához* (Essay on the
Hartvic-legend) (Budapest, 1942)

Z. I. Tóth, "Tuhutum és Gelou: hagyomány s történelmi
hitelesség Anonymus művében (Tradition and reliability
in the work of the Hungarian Anonymus)," *Századok*, 79-80
(1945-46), 21ff.

A. Toynbee, *Constantine Porphyrogenitus and His World* (Oxford, 1973)

Stephen of Tournai, *Summa Decretorum*, ed. J. F. v. Schulte (Giessen, 1891)

William of Tyre, *Historia transmarinis gestarum*, *RHC Occ,* I

Ekkehardi Uraugensis *Chronica universale*, *MGHSS*, VI

P. v. Váczy, *Die erste Epoche des ungarischen Königtums* (Pécs, 1935)

P. v. Váczy, *A középkor története* (Medieval history), vol. II of *Egyetemes történet* (Universal history), ed. B. Hóman, 4 vols. (Budapest, 1935-37)

P. Váczy, "Az angyal hozta korona (The Crown brought by the Angel)," *Életünk*, 19 (1982), 456ff.

P. Váczy, "Anonymus és kora (Anonymus and his age)," *Memoria Hungariae*, I, 13ff.

L. Varga, "Imre Karácson," *Vigilia*, 48 (1983), 874ff.

A. A. Vasiliev, *History of the Byzantine Empire* (Madiscon, Wisc., 1952)

Atto of Vercelli, *Expositio in epistolam Pauli ad Romanos*, in *MPL*, 134

*Vita Conradi archiepiscopi Salzburgensis*, *MGHSS*, XI

*Vita Godfredi*, *MGHSS*, XII, 513ff.

*Vita s. Ladislai regis Hungariae*, *ASS*, Iunii V, 315ff.

*Vita Norberti*, *MGHSS*, XII, 678ff.

Gottfried of Viterbo, *Pantheon, seu universitatis libri*, in *MGHSS*, XII

C. Vogel, "La reforme liturgique suos Pépin le Bref," in Erna Patzelt, *Die karolingische Renaissance*, 2nd ed. (Graz, 1965), 178ff.

E. Voigt, "Zum Charakter der 'staufischen' Städtepolitik," in *Volksmassen: Gestalten der Geschichte: Festschrift Stern* (Berlin, 1962), 19ff.

Gy. Volf (ed), *Régi magyar kódexek és nyomtatványok* (Old Hungarian codices and prints), 15 vols. (Budapest, 1879-1908), vol. III.

H. Vollrath, "Konrad III und Byzanz," *Archiv für Kulturgeschichte* 59 (1977), 321ff.

E. Waldapfel, "Nemesi birtokjogunk kialakulása a középkorban (Formation of property rights of the medieval nobility)," *Századok*, 65 (1931), 131ff.

W. Wattenbach, *Deutschlands Geschichtsquellen im Mittelalter* 2 vols., 6th ed. (Berlin, 1893-94)

C. C. J. Webb (ed), Iohannes Saresberiensis *Policraticus*, 2 vols. (Oxford, 1909)

C. C. J. Webb, *John of Salisbury* (London, 1932)

S. Weinfurter, "Norbert von Xanten - Ordensstifter und 'Eigenkirchenherr'," *Archiv für Kulturgeschichte*, 59 (1977), 66ff.

G. Wenczel (ed), *Árpádkori Új Okmánytár* (New document collection of the Arpadian age), 12 vols. (Pest, 1860-74), cited as Wenczel, *ÁUO*

I. Werbőczy, *Tripartitum opu iuris consuetudinarii incliti regni Hungariae*, anno 1517, in S. Kolozsvári-K. Óvári (eds), *Werbőczy István Hármaskönyve* (Budapest, 1892)

M. Wertner, *Az Árpádok családi története* (Family history of the Árpáds) (Nagybecskerek, 1892)

R. Wiegand, "Zur mittelalterlichen kirchlichen Ehegerichtsbarkeit: rechtsvergleichende Untersuchungen," *Zeitschrift der Savigny Stiftung für Rechtsgeschichte*, kan. Abt., 67 (1981), 213ff.

W. Williams, *St. Bernhard of Clairvaux* (London, 1935)

N. Wilson-J. Darrouzes, "Restes du cartulaire de Jiéra-Xérochoraphion," *Revue des études* byzantines, 26 (1968).

Canon of Wishegrad, *Continuatio Cosmae Praguensis Chronica, MGHSS*, IX

P. Wirth, "Das bislang erste literarische Zeugnis für die Stefanskrone," *Byzantinische Zeitschrift*, 53 (1960), 78ff.

C. Wojatsek, "F. Palacky and the Intellectual Leaders of Hungarian Society," *Catholic Hungarians' Sunday*, Youngstown, Ohio, Jan. 15, 22 and 29, 1984

F. Zagiba, *Die altbayerische Kirchenprovinz und die hll. Slawenlehrer Cyrill und Method* (Salzburg, 1963)

M. Zalán, "A Pray kódex forrásaihoz (Sources of the Pray codex)," *MKSz*, 1 (1926), 246ff.

N. Zakrevsky, *Opisanie Kieva* (Moscow, 1868)

L. Závodszky (ed), *A Szent István, Szent László és Kálmán korabeli törvények és zsinati határozatok* (Sourcebook of the legal enactments and synodical acts of the reigns of St. Stephen, St. Ladislas and Coloman) (Budapest, 1904)

H. U. Ziegler, "Der Bamberger Erzpriester Gotebold, Hauptkraft in der Beurkundungsstelle Bischof Eberhards

II (1146-70), Hermanns II (1170-77) und Verfasser von Urkunden Friedrich Barbarossas," *Mitteilungen des Institutes für österreichische Geschichtsforschung*, 92 (1984), 35ff.

A. Zimmermann, *Methoden in Wissenschaft und Kunst des Mittelalters* (Berlin, 1970)

E. Zöllner, *Geschichte Österreichs*, 4th rev. ed. (Munich, 1970)

Iohannes Zonaras, *Epitomae historiarum*, ed. Th.Büttner-Wobst (Bonn, 1897), - or, in *MPG*, 135.

Iohannes Zonaras, *Epithomae historiarum*, ed. Th. Büttner-Wobst (Bonn, 1897)

# Index

probably a royal fillet: *dyadema regale*, 277; its use to symbolize continuity; Ladislas I had placed himself the /a/ crown upon his head, 278; coronation capital: Székesfehérvár, 280; the archdean of Székesfehérvár the guardian of the Crown, 280-81; the crown and Béla III, 274-75; legislative power of the Crown, 276, 287 n78-82, 288 n106-10

crusade, the first crusade, 25, 37 n62-65, and King Coloman, 24-25; Pope Urban II's expectations from it, 25-26, 38 n72; crusading armies entering Hungary, 26-27, 38 n77; Peter the Hermit, Count Emerich, 27-28; second crusade, during which the emperor had exploited his status as a crusader, 131; third crusade, 210, 214-16

*Decretum I* of Ladislas I: acts of the Synod of Szabolcs, 1092, 7-11, 13 n7, 15 n68-113, the acts of which were *autochton*, 7; *Decretum II* of Ladislas I, 1078, 1, 2-3; *Decretum III* of Ladislas I, 1084, 4-7

education, the Third Lateran Synod on education, 281, 290 n150-51; need for educated clergymen, 59-60; bishop(s) to provide books for his /their/ clergy, 246 and learning in Hungary, mid-twelfth century, 281-83, 151, 152, 290 n147

Esztergom, *Archbishop* of, the primate of Hungary, who crowns the kings of Hungary, 279, 244; his official main functions, 244; *Synod I* of, 58-62, held *ca* 1100 and 1104, 58, 71 n4, more lenient in its decrees than Szabolcs, 58, with royal authority in church affairs still intact, 58-59; recognized the priest's first marriage, 59, but did not tolerate married bishops, 59; placed abbeys, monasteries under the bishop's control, 59; stressed the need for strict clerical discipline and proper behavior in public /and in private/, 59, 72 n20-23; emphasized the need for an educated clergy, 59-60, and ordered that, in order to function, a clergyman had to have the bishop's written permission, or, if in transit, the bishop's recommendation, 60; emancipated slaves may be ordained to the priesthood, 60; the bishop to keep an eye on his clerics, 60; church property protected by law, 60-61, its abuse by a cleric is punishable, 61; bishoprics and parishes to have annual budgets, 61, 72 n35; 73 n36; abbots may not wear episcopal insignia, nor may they do parish work, 61; nor may a clergyman perform work unworthy of

of it, 173, 171-76; Coloman the Learned to renounce it, 63-64; Ladislas I firmly in control of it, 11 and 17 n115; Coloman and Urban II on investiture, 42, 41-46; the Concordat of Worms, 1122, 45-46

*iobagiones*, temporal lords, 7; *iobagiones regi maiores*, 252, 265 n257; *iobagiones /regi servantes/ minores*, 251, 265 n260-62; high churchmen enjoyed a social status, 252

Job of Esztergom, archbishop, his controversy with Emperor Isaac Angelos over the doctrine of the Descent of the Holy Spirit, 281-82, 290 n154-59

Jews, Coloman the Learned's Jewish Laws, 65, 76 n105-07; Jews in Hungary to reside in a bishop's city only, 246; Jews and Ismaelites in business, 48-49; major business transaction between a Jew and a Christian to be confirmed in writing, 49, 55 n69-71

Keza, Simon de, Hungarian chronicler, 23, 24, 107 n10; 295

king, in Hungary the monarch had to be "most Christian," worthy of office, defender of the Church and the faith, 235-36, 255 n20-27; legislator, 237-42, aided by his Royal Council: body of advisors, 237, with no permanent membership before the late thirteenth century, 237; chief justice, 238, 248; as chief justice, he may hold in person, or through a representative, 238; in one person, the monarch is (a) Chief Justice; (b) Commander in Chief of the armed force(s); and (c) Chief Executor of the country's laws, 248; the king's head /principal/ official is the Palatine, 238, the latter being also chief tax collector and economic overseer, 238, whose deputy was the Count of the Queen's Court, later /more/ independent, 238-39; the king's courts of law were of various types, 239, where the accuser had to be of the same rank as the accused, 239; in the king's administration, the county-fort system had existed very early: the eleventh century, and had developed into a county court of law, 239; in the king's administrative and legal system, the *hospites* may elect their own justices annually, who, together with 21 jurors act as judges for (or, among) them, 239; secular and spiritual lords could hold courts of law, 239; in church related cases, only the bishops, 239; court proceedings in a king's court of law,